In this book an attempt has been made to cover the essential requirements of the A-Level Geology syllabuses of England, Wales and Northern Ireland and the H-Grade Scottish syllabus. The recommendations contained in the **Core Syllabus for A-Level Geology** prepared by the Inter-Board Committee of GCE Examining Boards and in the **Normal and Further Level Geological Sciences Syllabi** produced by the Association of Teachers of Geology, the Geological Society of London and the Institution of Geologists Ltd have also been taken into account. Besides being suitable for upper school courses the book should prove useful to first year students in universities and colleges.

The text is concise yet wide ranging. Fundamental syllabus topics such as minerals, rocks, surface and internal processes, geophysics, structural geology, fossils, stratigraphy and resources have all been considered in detail. In addition, some consideration has been given to less ubiquitous subjects such as phase chemistry, minerals under the microscope, grain size analysis of sediments and the use of isopachytes. The historical development of geology has also been mentioned. The text is enhanced by the liberal use of diagrams, photographs, tables and keys.

Lastly, the author would like to thank the many people and organizations who kindly supplied photographs.

Andrew McLeish

Preface

The author and publisher would like to thank the following for permission to reproduce copyright material:

Director, Institute of Geological Sciences (NERC copyright reserved): page 12 (top and bottom); page 13 (top and bottom); page 14 (top, middle and bottom); page 26; page 54; page 170; page 200; page 205; page 223 (top)
Professor E.K. Walton: page 17; page 55 (top); page 101 (bottom left, top right, bottom right); page 107 (top); page 108 (top left); page 109 (top, bottom); page 110 (top)
Dr C.H. Donaldson: page 55 (middle and bottom)
Wyoming Travel Commission: page 57 (bottom); page 76 (bottom left and right); page 150 (bottom right)
Istituto Italiano di Cultura: page 61 (top); page 296 (top)
Idaho Office of Tourism: page 61 (bottom)
Camera Press: page 62 (Photo by Astor Magnusson); page 116 (top) (Photo by Mike Milner); page 116 (bottom) (Photo by Fritz Schimke)
US Dept of Agriculture – Forest Service: page 64
Australian News and Information Service: page 69; page 98 (bottom) (Photo by Patrick McArdell); page 126 (bottom) (Photo by W. Pedersen); page 280 (top) (Photo by Michael Jensen)
Aerofilms: page 71 (left); page 79; page 80; page 85 (top and bottom); page 87; page 97; page 154; page 157 (top)
Geoffrey N. Wright: page 71 (right); page 75 (top and bottom); page 93
US National Park Service (Photo by Fred E. Mang Jr): page 76 (top)
National Publicity Studios, New Zealand: page 77; page 294
Dr J.A. Henry: page 83 (left and right)
Greenland Geological Survey (Photo by Jakob Lautrup): page 88; page 89 (top)
Yukon Government Photo: page 89 (bottom)
Swiss National Tourist Office: page 90 (top and bottom)
Norwegian National Tourist Office: page 92 (top)
Arizona Office of Tourism: page 97; page 98 (middle); page 223 (bottom)
California Office of Tourism: page 98 (top)
Dr M.R.W. Johnson: page 143 (bottom right); page 150 (top right); page 157 (bottom right); page 159 (top and bottom)
British Museum (Natural History) Crown Copyright Reserved: page 194; page 218
RTZ Services Ltd: page 279
CRA Services Ltd: page 280 (bottom)
National Coal Board: page 284 (top, bottom left and bottom right)
Shell Photographic Service: page 286
Marathon (UK) Ltd: page 287; page 288 (left)
Society for Cultural Relations with the USSR: page 288 (right); page 300
ICI Mond Division: page 296 (bottom); page 297
De Beers Consolidated Mines: page 298 (top and bottom)
English China Clays Group: page 299

Any photograph not acknowledged above is the author's copyright

The cover photograph was kindly supplied by Britoil p.l.c. and the birefringence chart was supplied by Professor W.S. MacKenzie, University of Manchester.

(Acknowledgments continued on page 308)

Acknowledgments

· Andrew McLeish ·

GEOLOGICAL SCIENCE

First published in 1986 by Blackie and Son Ltd
ISBN 0-216-91198-2

Second edition published by Thomas Nelson and Sons Ltd 1992

Reprinted in 2002 by:
Nelson Thornes Ltd
Delta Place
27 Bath Road
CHELTENHAM
GL53 7TH
United Kingdom

02 03 04 05 / 14 13 12 11 10 9 8

A catalogue record for this book is available from the British Library

ISBN 0-17-448221-3

Printed and bound in China by L.Rex Printing Co., Ltd.

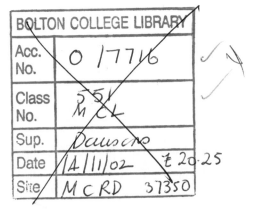

Contents

PLANET EARTH

Geology

Geology is the science which deals with the study of the Earth. As such, it is concerned with the study of the materials which make up the Earth; the form and structure of the Earth; the processes which take place inside and on the surface of the Earth; and the changes which have affected the Earth and its life forms through its long history. Geology is a very broad-based science. It is related to other Earth sciences such as geophysics, oceanography and meteorology and it overlaps a great deal with chemistry, physics, biology and geography. Mathematics, engineering, metallurgy, surveying, astronomy and economics also contribute to geological studies. In addition, some acquaintance with history will help you to understand how geology and other sciences have developed through time.

Geology can be divided into a large number of smaller subject areas such as **mineralogy** (the study of minerals), **petrology** (the study of rocks), **palaeontology** (the study of fossils), **stratigraphy** (the study of Earth history), **physical geology** (the study of Earth processes) and **structural geology** (the study of rock deformation). Fieldwork and geological mapping are very important parts of geology. Indeed, a great deal of geological knowledge has been gained by careful field observation. When studying the geology of an area, field observations, laboratory work and information from other sources are combined to give an interpretation of the area's geological structure and history. Such interpretations are liable to change as more information becomes available. Experiments also play an important part in some aspects of geology. For example, apparatus capable of producing high pressures and temperatures can imitate conditions under which rocks form within the Earth; long tanks with water flowing through them can show how sand is deposited in a river; and rocks can be squeezed to find out how they deform. Geology, too, is becoming more mathematical and computers allow the rapid analysis of large quantities of data.

Geology is a very useful science because it helps us to find coal, oil, gas, metals and building materials. It shows us, too, that such limited resources must be carefully handled. Geology also allows us to find sources of underground water and geothermal power. In engineering, geology helps with problems encountered in tunnelling and in building dams, bridges and harbours. Geology can also play a part in the prevention of coastal erosion, landslides and the silting up of harbours. Finally, geology may help in the prediction of earthquakes and volcanic eruptions.

The solar system

The **solar system** consists of the Sun (a star) and its nine orbiting planets. From the Sun outwards the planets are Mercury, Venus, Earth, Mars, Jupiter, Saturn, Uranus, Neptune and Pluto. Some details of the solar system are given in table 1.1. The four inner planets are much denser than the five outer planets. The rocky inner planets (the terrestrial or Earth-like planets) consist largely of iron-rich silicates. Silicates are common rock-forming substances consisting mostly of metals, silicon and oxygen. The outer planets consist largely of hydrogen and helium though they probably have rocky cores. Between Mars and Jupiter there is a band of about 40 000 asteroids whose compositions closely resemble those of the inner planets. With the exception of Pluto the outer planets are much larger than the inner planets. The orbits of Pluto and Neptune overlap so Pluto may have originated as a moon of Neptune. The Sun is extremely large but, like the outer planets, it has a very low density. About 70 percent of the Sun is hydrogen.

The planets follow nearly circular orbits round the Sun. They move in the direction of the Sun's rotation. The planets lie very nearly in the same plane (the plane of the ecliptic). Also, all the large satellites except the Moon and Triton (a moon of Neptune) have nearly circular orbits in the equatorial planes of their planets. All the

Unit 1

planets except Venus spin in the same direction. The four large outer planets (Jupiter, Saturn, Uranus and Neptune) rotate very rapidly while the Sun and the inner planets rotate slowly. This means that most of the kinetic or movement energy of the solar system lies in the outer planets.

Origin of the solar system

The solar system is thought to have formed about 4600 million years ago. There are two main theories to account for its origin. To explain the fact that most of the kinetic energy of the solar system is located in the outer planets Jeans and Jeffreys suggested that another star passed close to the Sun and drew off a stream of material. This material condensed to form planets set in orbit by the passing star (figure 1.1). The passing star theory is now thought to be unlikely because the chances of another star approaching the Sun are very small and because high temperature material drawn from the Sun or from the other star would disperse rather than condense.

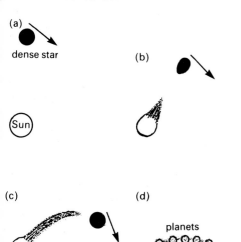

1.1 Passing star theory of the origin of the solar system.
(a) to (c) A passing star pulls material from the Sun.
(d) The solar material condenses to form the planets. The pull of the passing star sets the planets in orbit.

Alternatively, the solar system may have formed from a cloud or nebula of gas and dust (figure 1.2). As the nebula rotated it flattened into a disc with a high concentration of material

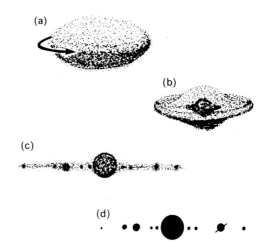

1.2 Nebular theory of the origin of the solar system.
(a) and (b) The spinning cloud of dust and gas flattens into a disc.
(c) and (d) The Sun and planets condense.

at its centre. In the cold outer areas of the disc substances such as methane and ammonia condensed while hydrogen and helium remained as gases. In this region the planets which formed were gas giants (Jupiter, Saturn, Uranus and Neptune) with small rocky cores surrounded by water, methane, ammonia, hydrogen and helium. Nearer the centre of the nebula the temperatures were much higher (about 300°C in the area in which the Earth formed). Volatile materials could not condense so the planets formed from dust grains. The gas in this area was probably swept outwards as the newly forming Sun shed some of its own gas. The shedding of gas by the Sun allowed it to lose some of its spin energy so it slowed to rotate only about once every 25 days. The planets formed by the accumulation of particles which initially bumped into each other and grew to sizes large enough to exert forces of gravitational attraction on each other. Continued aggregation produced asteroid-sized bodies most of which accumulated further to form the planets.

The Earth's surface

Only 29 percent of the Earth's surface is land. Study of heights and depths above and below sea level (table 1.2) might be expected to show that most of the land and sea floor lies just

NAME OF BODY	DISTANCE FROM SUN (million km)	DIAMETER (km)	DENSITY (g cm⁻³)	MASS RELATIVE TO EARTH	PERIOD OF ROTATION	PERIOD OF REVOLUTION ROUND SUN	SURFACE TEMPERATURE (°C)	MAIN GASES OF ATMOSPHERE	NUMBER OF SATELLITES	OTHER DETAILS
SUN	—	1 392 000	1.41	332 946	25.38 days	—	6000	—	Surrounded by 9 planets	32 000 light years from centre of galaxy. Takes 225 million years to revolve round centre of galaxy. Holds 99% of mass of solar system. Composition: hydrogen 71%; helium 27%; other elements 2%. Temperature at centre 14 million °C. Energy comes from transformation of hydrogen to helium. Sun loses mass at the rate of 4 million tonnes a second. Sun-spots appear in cycles of 11 years. Spots have associated magnetic fields
MERCURY	57.9	4880	5.5	0.055	58.6 days	88 days	Day 350 Night −170	Atmosphere almost non-existent. Main gas is helium which has escaped from the Sun	—	Surface cratered like that of Moon. Other surface features include plains, ridges and scarps. Weak magnetic field. Dense core about 3600 km in diameter
VENUS	108.2	12 104	5.25	0.815	243 days	224.7 days	460	Very dense cloudy atmosphere. 96% carbon dioxide with nitrogen and water vapour. Clouds of sulphuric acid	—	Surface cannot be seen but radar imagery has shown that about two-thirds of Venus is relatively flat. There are also huge plateaux, mountains, volcanoes and rift valleys. Impact craters are fairly numerous. Russian spacecraft found a rocky surface
EARTH	149.56	12 756 (equatorial diameter)	5.52	1 Mass of Earth is 5.976 × 10²⁴ kg	23.93 hours	365.26 days	22	Nitrogen 78% Oxygen 21% Argon 1% With water vapour (0—4%) and carbon dioxide (0.03%)	1	
MOON	Distance from Earth 384 400 km	3 475.6	3.34	0.012	27.32 days	Period of revolution round Earth 27.32 days	120 in sunlight −153 in darkness	—	—	Surface features smooth maria and rough terrae formed by impact cratering and volcanic activity. Surface layer (regolith) of loose broken material usually less than 50 m thick. Largest impact crater about 1000 km in diameter. Most large craters and mare basins excavated before 3600 million years ago. Lavas filled mare basins by about 3200 million years ago. Major volcanism ceased by 3000 million

Table1.1   The Solar System

	Distance	Diameter	Mass	Density	Rotation period (hours/days)	Orbital period	Temperature (°C)	Atmosphere	Number of moons	Notes
(MARS)								Nitrogen 2.7% Argon 1.6% Oxygen 0.15% Atmosphere thin	small with irregular shape (Phobos 22 km long; Deimos 12 km long)	volcanoes, water-cut valleys, lava flows, sand dunes, wind-blown dust and wind-eroded rocks. Wind speeds of up to 400 km h^{-1} cause dust storms. Polar ice caps consist of water ice with a layer of solid carbon dioxide. No magnetic field. Surface material iron 16%, silicon 15—30%, calcium 3—8%, aluminium 2—7%. Between Mars and Jupiter are more than 40 000 asteroids. Ceres, the largest asteroid, has a diameter of 1003 km. Total mass of asteroids equal to about 0.02% mass of Earth. Asteroids are not formed from broken-up planets
JUPITER	778.34	142 200 (equatorial diameter)	317.89	1.33	9.8 hours	11.86 years	−150	Hydrogen Helium Methane Ammonia	14	Pale orange in colour. Small rocky core surrounded by liquid hydrogen and helium. Thick cloudy atmosphere. Clouds are ice, solid ammonia and solid ammonium hydrogen sulphide. Rising gas gives white and yellow zones while descending gas gives red-brown belts. The Great Red Spot may be a high pressure area. Jupiter has a strong magnetic field and it is surrounded by a single dust ring. Of the four large moons Io has active sulphurous volcanoes; Europa looks like a cracked white snooker ball; Ganymede is cratered and grooved; and Callisto is cratered.
SATURN	1427	119 300 (equatorial diameter)	95.17	0.69	10.2 hours	29.46 years	−180	Hydrogen Helium Methane Ammonia	17	Yellowish in colour with a deep cloudy atmosphere. Clouds are solid ammonia. Surrounded by numerous distinct rings. The rings consist of ice blocks up to about 1 m in diameter. The moons consist of rock (35%) and ice (65%). Titan, the largest moon, has an atmosphere of methane, nitrogen and argon. Minor planet (Chiron) between Saturn and Uranus
URANUS	2869.6	51 800	14.6	1.7	23 hours	84.01 years	−210	Hydrogen Helium Methane	5	Discovered in 1781. No visible surface markings. Faint banding may indicate presence of atmosphere. Surrounded by nine faint rings
NEPTUNE	4496.7	49 500	17.2	1.77	22 hours	164.8 years	−220	Hydrogen Helium Methane	2	Discovered in 1846. Blue-green in colour. Deep, clear atmosphere
PLUTO	5900	2284	0.002	1.7	6.39 days	247.7 years	−230	Methane	1	Discovered in 1930. Appears bright. Has a rocky core surrounded by ice. The surface is ice and frozen methane.

HEIGHT OR DEPTH (m)	LAND SURFACE AREA ($km^2 \times 10^6$)	SEA FLOOR AREA ($km^2 \times 10^6$)
To 1000	106.6	18.2
1000–3000	33.8	39.7
3000–5000	8.0	189.9
More than 5000	0.5	85.5
	Average height of land 875 m	Average depth of sea 3554 m

Table 1.2 Areas of land surface and sea floor at various heights and depths

above or just below sea level. However, the distribution of percentage areas of heights and depths has two peaks (figure 1.3). This shows that much of the sea floor is 4–5 km deep while much of the land is 0–1 km high. (The average depth of the oceans is about 3550 m and the average height of the land is about 875 m.) This step-like separation between the ocean floor and the continents is indicative of a fundamental difference between them.

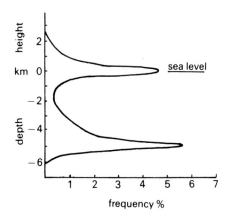

1.3 Areas of heights and depths over the Earth's surface. The two distinct levels correspond to the ocean basins and to the continents.

A line of underwater mountains called **oceanic ridges** forms a continuous system running through all the oceans. The ridge system is about 60 000 km long and about 1000 km wide. The system runs down the middle of the Atlantic and round into the Indian Ocean. Here, it divides into a ridge which runs up into the Red Sea and a ridge which passes south of

Australia into the Pacific. In the Pacific the main ridge system runs up into the Gulf of California. The ridge usually rises 1–3 km above the ocean floor. Each ridge is split by a central rift valley. In the north Atlantic this rift valley is 30 km wide and 1500 m deep. The ridge is symmetrical about the rift valley with the topography on one side of the ridge being the mirror image of the topography on the other side. The oceanic ridges are the youngest parts of the sea floor and they show marked volcanic and earthquake activity. Most of the ridges are submerged but occasionally, they rise above sea level to form islands such as Ascension and St. Helena. Iceland is the largest island sitting astride an oceanic ridge. The ridge systems are frequently offset by major fracture zones running at high angles to the ridges. The fracture zones may be 100 km wide and 2000 km long and they may offset ridges by several hundred kilometres.

On each side of the oceanic ridges the ocean floor falls to the flat **abyssal plains** which generally lie at depths of 3–6 km. The abyssal plain may be interrupted by underwater mountains called **guyots** and **seamounts**. Guyots are sunken islands with tops carved flat by wave action before the islands sank. Seamounts are conical submarine volcanic mountains which rise 1–4 km above the sea floor. Small seamounts are sometimes called sea knolls. Seamounts projecting above sea level form islands such as the Canary and Madeira Islands.

The slope over the abyssal plain is only about 1 m km^{-1}. Towards the continents at an average depth of about 4 km the slope gradually steepens up to about 10 m km^{-1} to form the **continental rise**. The continental rise may be up to 600 km wide. Moving upwards, the ocean floor steepens further to about 70 m km^{-1} to form the **continental slope** (20–100 km wide). At an average depth of about 130 m the slope flattens again to 1.7 m km^{-1} to form the **continental shelf** (average width 75 km). The edge of the shelf varies in depth from 40–500 m. The continental shelf and slope are sometimes jointly called the **continental terrace**. The continental terrace may be cut by V-shaped **submarine canyons** which may have delta-like **submarine fans** at their mouths.

Oceanic trenches occur mostly round the Pacific. They are usually about 100 km wide and their depths exceed 6000 m. The greatest depth of about 11 000 m is found in the Marianas Trench of the west Pacific. Trenches may be found close to continents. For example,

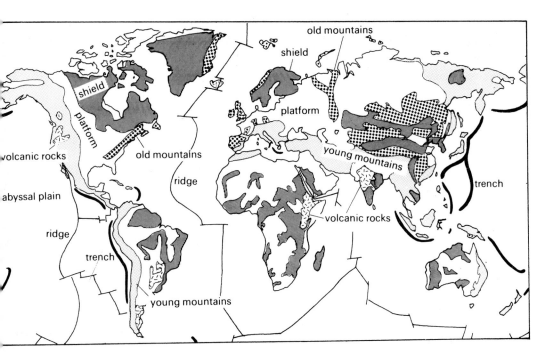

1.4 *Major features of the Earth's surface.*

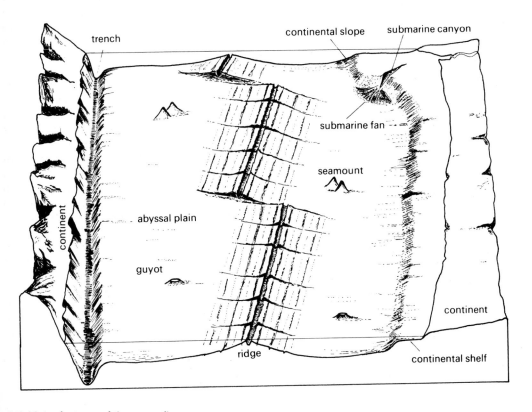

1.5 *Major features of the ocean floor.*

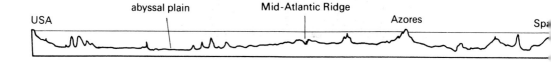

1.6 Profile of the floor of the Atlantic Ocean from USA to Spain.

the Peru-Chile Trench lies close to the west coast of South America. Where there is no continent the landward side of a trench is marked by an **island arc** such as those of the Pacific Aleutian, Marianas, Kermadec and Tonga Islands.

While the great majority of oceanic islands are of volcanic origin the Seychelles in the Indian Ocean consist of continental rock types. For this reason, the Seychelles are sometimes described as being a **microcontinent**. The submarine Rockall Bank to the north-west of Britain also seems to be of continental origin.

While the ocean floor consists of relatively young rocks the continents are much more variable in age. The oldest continental rocks are about 3900 million years old. The structure of the continents may be described in terms of mountain belts of different ages. Very old mountain belts (older than about 600 million years) have been worn down to form relatively flat,

geologically stable areas called **cratons**. The Canadian and Baltic Shields are examples of cratons. In many places such as the Great Plains of North America, the Steppes of USSR and the north African deserts the ancient cratons are covered by relatively undeformed rocks. Such areas are called **platforms**. Mountain building between about 600 and 300 million years ago brought areas such as the Scottish Highlands, the Appalachians and the Ural Mountains into being. Like the cratons these areas are geologically stable. Mountains formed in the last 300 million years lie in two bands. The first runs round the Pacific from the Andes and Rockies, through Kamchatka and Japan to New Zealand. The second young mountain chain runs from the Alps to the Himalayas. The geological activity of these young mountains is shown by their frequent earthquake and volcanic activity and by the fact that, in places, they are still rising.

MINERALS

Atoms, elements and compounds

All substances consist of very small particles called **atoms**. Atoms are made up of still smaller particles called **protons, neutrons and electrons**. Each proton has a single positive charge; a neutron has no charge and electrons each have a single negative charge. Since atoms are electrically neutral the number of protons in an atom equals the number of electrons. A proton and a neutron both have about 2000 times the mass of an electron. The protons and neutrons together make up a central mass called the **nucleus** of the atom. The electrons move in orbits around the nucleus.

Atoms differ from each other in the number of particles which they contain. **Elements** are substances consisting of atoms which all have the same number of protons. The simplest element is hydrogen; its atoms consist of one proton and one electron. Helium has two protons, two neutrons and two electrons in its atoms. Oxygen atoms have eight protons, eight neutrons and eight electrons. The number of protons in an atom is called the **atomic number** so each element has a different atomic number. Hydrogen has an atomic number of one; helium has an atomic number of two and oxygen has an atomic number of eight.

Among the atoms of an element there may be variation in the number of neutrons present. Carbon, for example, has atoms which contain six protons and six electrons. Most of these atoms also contain six neutrons but some carbon atoms have seven or eight neutrons. The atoms of an element which differ in the number of neutrons are called **isotopes**. The number of protons and neutrons in an atom is its **mass number** so isotopes have the same atomic numbers but different mass numbers.

To represent an element or an atom of the element a symbol is used. The symbol may be a letter or letters taken from the name of the element, e.g. the symbol for carbon is C; for calcium the symbol is Ca but for copper the symbol is Cu from the Latin 'cuprum'. The mass number of the atom may be written near the top of the symbol with the atomic number underneath, e.g. carbon could be represented in this way: $^{12}_{6}$C. Since the atomic numbers of the atoms of an element are all the same the lower number may be omitted so the isotopes of carbon can be written as ^{12}C, ^{13}C and ^{14}C and read as 'carbon 12', 'carbon 13' and 'carbon 14'.

When elements combine they form new substances called **compounds**. The **valency** of an element is a measure of its ability to combine with other elements. Hydrogen has a valency of one and the valency of another element is given by the number of hydrogen atoms which one of its atoms will combine with or replace, e.g. one atom of chlorine (symbol Cl) combines with one atom of hydrogen to give hydrogen chloride (formula HCl) so the valency of chlorine is one; one atom of oxygen joins with two atoms of hydrogen to give water (formula H_2O) so the valency of oxygen is two.

Atoms may join in two main ways. There may be exchange of electrons so the atom which loses them becomes positively charged and the atom which gains them becomes negatively charged. Such charged particles are called **ions**. When sodium (symbol Na) joins with chlorine, the sodium atom loses an electron to become Na^+ and the chlorine atom gains the electron to become Cl^-. Sodium chloride can then be written Na^+Cl^-. Magnesium (Mg) loses two electrons to form ions so when joining with chlorine two atoms of chlorine are needed to take up the electrons. The formula of magnesium chloride is then $Mg^{2+}Cl_2^-$ and the valency of magnesium is two. Atomic joining involving electron exchange is called **electrovalent bonding**.

Another way in which atoms combine is by sharing electrons. When carbon joins with hydrogen four hydrogen atoms share their single electrons with four electrons from the carbon and the compound formed, methane, has the formula CH_4. This type of atomic joining is **covalent bonding**.

Unit 2

Chemistry of minerals

Minerals are natural elements and compounds which usually form crystals. The arrangement of atoms within a crystal can be found by shining a beam of X-rays through it. X-rays have such a short wavelength that they appear to bounce off layers of atoms inside the crystal. The reflected (or more properly 'diffracted') X-rays then form a pattern on a photographic plate which can be interpreted to find the way in which the atoms are arranged (figure 2.1). It has been found that the atoms in crystals are arranged in three-dimensional frameworks called **lattices**. Most minerals are made up of ions and the way in which the ions are packed together depends partly on the sizes of the ions. The sizes of some ions are given in table 2.1. The ionic radii are given in picometres (pm); a picometre is 10^{-12} metre, or a metre divided by a million million.

NAME OF ION	SYMBOL AND CHARGE	RADIUS (picometres: x 10^{-12} m)
Sodium	Na^+	97
Potassium	K^+	133
Magnesium	Mg^{2+}	66
Calcium	Ca^{2+}	99
Iron	Fe^{2+}	74
Aluminium	Al^{3+}	51
Silicon	Si^{4+}	42
Oxygen	O^{2-}	140
Hydroxide	OH^-	140
Chlorine	Cl^-	181

Table 2.1   Radii of some common ions.

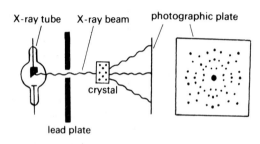

2.1 When X-rays are shone through a crystal the diffracted beams form a pattern on a photographic plate. From the pattern the atomic structure of the crystal can be worked out.

One of the simplest crystal structures is that of sodium chloride (Na^+Cl^-). Here, the sodium and chlorine ions are situated as if they were at the corners of cubes. You will see from figure 2.2 that each sodium ion is surrounded by six chlorine ions and that each chlorine ion is surrounded by six sodium ions.

Graphite consists of sheets of hexagonally-arranged carbon atoms linked by covalent bonds. Within the layers each carbon atom is strongly bonded to three adjacent atoms but bonds between the widely-spaced layers are very weak. Diamond also consists of carbon but here the atoms are arranged in a strong framework made up of tetrahedra with each atom surrounded by four others. (A tetrahedron is a pyramid shape with four faces which are all equilateral triangles.) Graphite and diamond clearly show the relationship between atomic structure and physical properties. Graphite splits very easily parallel to its internal atomic layers while diamond is extremely hard and it does not split easily.

Substances which have the same chemical composition but different atomic structures are said to be **polymorphs**. Graphite and diamond are polymorphs of carbon. Polymorphism is

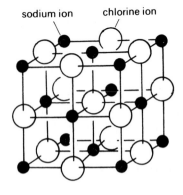

2.2 The atomic structure of sodium chloride (halite).

·ry common among minerals. It also happens
·at substances with different compositions
·ve the same type of atomic structure and
·ystal form. Such substances are said to be
·ostructural or isomorphous. Isomorphism
·sults from the replacement of one ion by
·nother in the crystal lattice.

Minerals are often found whose composition
·ould seem to have resulted from the mixing
· other minerals, e.g. Mg_2SiO_4 is the mineral
·rsterite and Fe_2SiO_4 is the mineral fayalite.
·livine has a composition between these two
·· it is written $(MgFe)_2SiO_4$ to signify that both
·agnesium and iron are present in unspecified
·oportions. This intermediate composition of
·livine results from ionic substitutions between
·g^{2+} and Fe^{2+} in the mineral lattice. Olivine used
· be thought of simply as a mixture of forsterite
·d fayalite and because of this such 'mixtures'
·ere called **solid solutions** or **mixed crystals**. Do
·ot confuse isomorphism with solid solution.
·any isomorphous substances will form solid
·olutions but other isomorphous substances do
·ot form solid solutions. Also, solid solution can
·ke place between substances which are not
·omorphous.

The alums are hydrated double sulphates of
·ono- and trivalent metals. Grow a crystal of
· coloured alum such as chrome alum,

$$K_2SO_4.Cr_2(SO_4)_3.24H_2O,$$

·en transfer it to a saturated solution of potash
·um,

$$K_2SO_4.Al_2(SO_4)_3.24H_2O.$$

·hat happens? The colourless potash alum
·ontinues to grow on the purple, octahedral
·hrome alum crystal. Can you explain why this
·appens? (Note that the ionic radii of aluminium
·d chromium are 51 and 63 picometres,
·spectively.)

The coloured Tutton salts also provide excellent
·xamples of isomorphism. They are double salts
·onsisting of ammonium sulphate with a sulphate
·f cobalt, nickel, copper, iron or manganese. A
·ypical formula is

$$CuSO_4.(NH_4)_2 SO_4. H_2O.$$

·utton salts form crystals of squashed matchbox
·hape and, like the alums, one salt will continue
· grow on crystals of another.

Identifying minerals

·Most minerals can be identified by means of
· few simple tests. Here are some of the ways
·n which minerals differ from each other.

Colour

Some minerals such as galena (silvery), azurite
(blue), malachite (green) and sulphur (yellow)
have distinctive colours which are very helpful
in identification. Some minerals, though, are
very variable in colour, e.g. quartz can be
transparent (rock crystal), purple (amethyst),
white (milky quartz), pink (rose quartz), brown
(cairngorm) or black (morion). Also, fluorite can
be colourless, yellow, blue, green, purple or
white while corundum can be yellow, brown,
green, grey, red (ruby) or blue (sapphire). The
variation in colour is caused by impurities in
the mineral. In the case of corundum (Al_2O_3)
the presence of some chromium produces ruby
while the presence of some iron and titanium
gives sapphire.

Lustre

The **lustre** of a mineral is the appearance of
its surface under reflected light. Lustre is described by reference to well-known materials,
e.g. if a mineral looks like metal it is said to
have a metallic lustre while if it looks like glass
it is said to have a vitreous lustre. Other terms
used to describe lustre include pearly, silky,
adamantine (like diamond), greasy, waxy, resinous and earthy. Lustre may vary from face to
face on a crystal and the lustre of a single crystal
may differ from that of an aggregate of the same
mineral, e.g. crystals of gypsum have a vitreous
or pearly lustre whereas fibrous aggregates
have a lustre like satin or silk.

Streak

The **streak** of a mineral is its colour when
powdered. A mineral powder often has a different colour from the mineral crystals, e.g.
pyrite forms brassy-yellow crystals but when
powdered it is greeny black. The streak is
obtained by rubbing the mineral on a piece of
white unglazed porcelain called a **streak plate**.
White and coloured glassy minerals usually give
a white streak which does not help in identification. Streak is of most use in identifying opaque
ore minerals such as the iron oxides: magnetite
(black streak), haematite (red-brown streak) and
limonite (yellow-brown streak).

Crystal form

When minerals form good crystals the crystal shape helps in identification, e.g. pyrite is often found as cubes with lined faces. Usually, though, the shapes of individual crystals cannot be seen.

Minerals may form distinctive aggregates (figure 2.3) some of which are described as follows:

fibrous the crystals are like threads;

acicular consisting of needle-like crystals;

mamillated the surface of the mineral mass consists of rounded lumps;

botryoidal the aggregate resembles a bunch of grapes;

massive the mineral aggregate has no definite form.

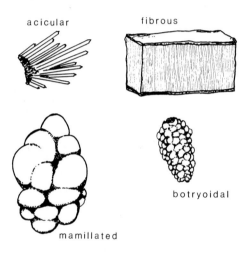

acicular   fibrous

botryoidal

mamillated

2.3 Forms of crystal aggregates.

Cleavage and fracture

Crystals may break along internal planes of weakness called **cleavage planes** which may or may not be parallel to crystal faces. You should take care not to confuse crystal faces with the more commonly seen cleavage planes. Where cleavage planes run in one direction the crystal tends to break into sheets. Where there are two cleavage planes the crystal tends to break into elongate fragments and where there are three or more cleavages the crystal tends to break into roughly equidimensional fragments (figure 2.4). The different cleavage directions which may exist within a crystal are not always equally well developed.

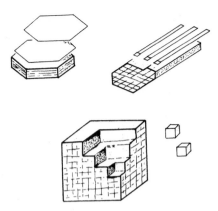

2.4 Cleavage. Minerals with one cleavage tend to break into sheets. Minerals with two cleavages tend to break into elongate fragments. Minerals with three or more cleavages tend to break into equidimensional fragments.

Some minerals have no internal planes of weakness so they break or **fracture** in any direction along irregular surfaces, e.g. quartz has no cleavage but it breaks like glass along curving, shell-like surfaces. Fracture of this type, **conchoidal** fracture, is best seen in the form of silica called **flint**. Where the fracture surfaces

Monoclinic crystal of gypsum. There is one cleavage parallel to the largest crystal face.

Cubic crystals of galena. There are three cleavages parallel to the cube faces.

e flat, or nearly so, the fracture is described
s being **even** while breakage along a rough
urface is **uneven** fracture.

ardness

he variation in hardness (H) among minerals
a useful guide to identification. Hardnesses
e given on **Mohs' scale of hardness** (table 2.2)
which talc, the softest mineral, has hardness
and diamond, the hardest mineral, has hard-
ess 10. On this scale the differences in hardness
etween adjacent minerals are not necessarily
qual.
A good idea of the hardness of a mineral can
e found by testing with things such as your
ngernail which will scratch minerals of hard-
ess 1 and 2; a 'copper' coin such as a penny
hich will scratch minerals up to hardness 3;
good knife blade which will scratch minerals
p to hardness 6; and a file which will scratch
inerals up to hardness 7. When testing for
rdness remember that a soft material will rub
f on a hard material leaving a mark which
ay look like a scratch. Also, hard minerals may
e brittle. Do not confuse ease of breaking with
rdness.

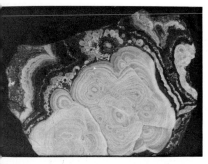

alachite often occurs in mamillated or
tryoidal forms showing concentric
anding.

rigonal crystal of quartz. There is no cleav-
ge but the crystal shows irregular fractures.

HARDNESS (H)	MINERAL	
1	Talc	
2	Gypsum	
		← Fingernail
3	Calcite	
		← Penny
4	Fluorite	
5	Apatite	
6	Orthoclase	
		← Good knife blade
7	Quartz	
		← File
8	Topaz	
9	Corundum	
10	Diamond	

Table 2.2   Mohs' scale of hardness

Density

The **density** of a substance is its mass in kilo-
grams or grams divided by its volume in cubic
metres or cubic centimetres. If a material with
a volume of 4 cm³ had a mass of 12 g then
its density would be 3×10^3 kg m⁻³ or 3 g cm⁻³.
The **relative density** (specific gravity) of
a substance is the number of times it is as heavy
as an equal volume of water. Unlike density,
relative density (*d*) has no units. Since water
has a density of 1 g cm⁻³ the numerical values
of the density and relative density are the same.
When finding densities pure specimens of minerals must be used. Can you see why? The
specimen can be weighed then its volume can
be found by seeing how much water it displaces.
Another way of finding density or relative density is to weigh the specimen in air then in water.
When in water the specimen is lighter by an
amount equal to the weight of water displaced
so the weight difference divided into the weight
in air gives the relative density:

$$\text{relative density (symbol } d) = \frac{\text{weight of specimen in air}}{\text{weight in air} - \text{weight in water}}$$

Minerals which do not look metallic tend to have relative densities between about 2.5 and 3.0 though baryte with a relative density of 4.5 feels distinctly heavy in the hand. Metallic looking minerals tend to have high relative densities, e.g. the relative density of galena (lead sulphide) is 7.5; pyrite (iron sulphide) has a relative density of 5.0 while gold has a relative density of 19.

This garnet crystal has cubic symmetry. There is no cleavage.

Mica shows perfect cleavage in one direction.

Asbestos showing fibrous crystals.

Twinning

Crystals may grow in such a way that they look as if they have stuck together or as if they have grown through each other (figure 2.5). Such crystals are said to be **twinned**. The recognition of twinning is probably of most use in identifying feldspar since feldspar crystals may consist of many narrow layers which give parts of the crystal a faintly striped appearance.

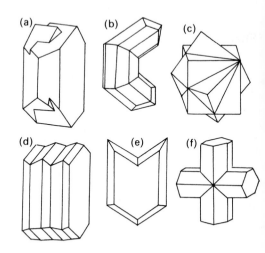

2.5 Twinned crystals: (a) orthoclase feldspar; (b) rutile; (c) fluorite; (d) plagioclase feldspar; (e) gypsum; (f) staurolite.

Flame tests

Moisten the end of a piece of platinum wire then dip the wire into some powdered copper sulphate. Now hold the copper sulphate in the edge of a bunsen flame. What do you see? Repeat the process with a variety of salts making sure the wire is clean every time. This test cannot identify a mineral but it can help in identification by telling you the metal it contains. The colours obtained for different metals include:

sodium–yellow;
calcium–red;
copper–blue or green;
potassium–lilac;
barium–yellow-green.

When testing for potassium the flame may have to be viewed through a piece of blue glass because the lilac colour may be obscured by other stronger colours.

MINERALS

Acid test

Some minerals react with dilute hydrochloric acid. Calcite (calcium carbonate) fizzes in acid and gives off carbon dioxide while dolomite (calcium and magnesium carbonate) will only react with the hot acid. Sulphides such as galena (lead sulphide) give off hydrogen sulphide (rotten eggs smell) with dilute hydrochloric acid. Haematite (iron oxide) slowly dissolves in concentrated hydrochloric acid.

Effects of heat

Heat some powdered malachite (copper carbonate) in a test-tube. What happens? The malachite has been decomposed by the heat so that carbon dioxide has been given off and black copper oxide has been left. If you mix some carbon with the oxide and heat further you should get some copper metal on the inside of the test-tube. Calcite also gives off carbon dioxide on strong heating but it does not change colour. When sulphides are heated they may change colour and give off a smell like burning sulphur.

Structure of silicate minerals

Silicates are minerals in which metals such as magnesium, iron, calcium, sodium, potassium and aluminium are combined with silicon and oxygen. Silicates are the most abundant rock-forming minerals. Along with quartz (silicon dioxide) they make up all common rocks apart from materials such as limestones and salt deposits.

In silicates the silicon and oxygen form tetrahedra with each small silicon ion surrounded by four oxygen ions (figure 2.6). Different silicates have their tetrahedra arranged in different ways. In the simplest case the SiO_4

(a)

(b)

2.6 (a) SiO_4 tetrahedron. The small silicon ion is surrounded by four large oxygen ions.
(b) The symbol sometimes used to represent the SiO_4 tetrahedron.

tetrahedra are separate from each other. **Olivine** (figure 2.7) and **garnet** have structures of this type. Minerals possessing a structure of separate SiO_4 tetrahedra are very compact so they have high densities (olivine d 3.2–4.4; garnet d 3.6–4.3), they are hard (olivine H 6½; garnet H 6–7½) and they have no distinct cleavage.

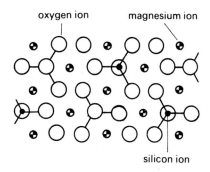

oxygen ion   magnesium ion

silicon ion

2.7 The atomic structure of magnesium olivine (forsterite). Magnesium ions lie between the separate SiO_4 tetrahedra.

In the **pyroxenes** the SiO_4 tetrahedra form chains with each tetrahedron sharing an oxygen ion with the tetrahedra on each side (figure 2.8). The chains are held together by metallic ions. Since the silicon-oxygen bonds within the chains are stronger than the bonds holding separate chains, pyroxenes tend to split parallel to the chains in two directions which are nearly at right angles to each other (figure 2.8).

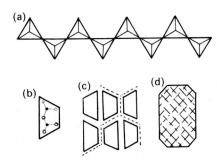

2.8 (a) Chain of SiO_4 tetrahedra in pyroxene.
(b) View along an SiO_4 chain.
(c) Showing how the cleavages run between the chains.
(d) Cleavage in a pyroxene crystal cut at right angles to its length.

Pyroxenes have relatively high densities (d 3.2-3.9) and they are relatively hard (H 5-6) because their ions are quite densely packed.

The **amphiboles** have their SiO_4 tetrahedra in double chains (figure 2.9). The large hexagonal holes in the chains are occupied by hydroxide ions (OH^-) and the double chains are held together by ions such as those of calcium and magnesium. The double chains are not strongly held together so amphiboles have two pronounced cleavages at about 60° to each other (figure 2.9). The cleavages do not break the silicon-oxygen bonds of the chains. Amphiboles tend to form long or fibrous crystals and they are relatively hard (5-6) and dense (d 2.9-3.6).

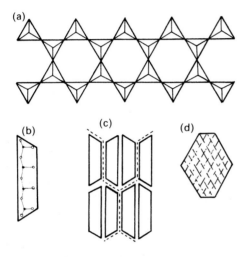

2.9 (a) Double chain of SiO_4 tetrahedra in amphibole.
(b) View along the double chain.
(c) Showing how the cleavages run between the double chains.
(d) Cleavage in an amphibole crystal cut at right angles to its length.

Minerals such as **talc, mica** and **clay** have their SiO_4 tetrahedra in sheets (figure 2.10). The sheets form double layers with the tips of the tetrahedra pointing inwards. The inward pointing tetrahedra are not exactly opposite each other. The spaces within the sheets are occupied by hydroxide ions while in talc, magnesium ions inside each double layer hold it firmly together. In talc there are no ions between the double layers so the double layers are weakly

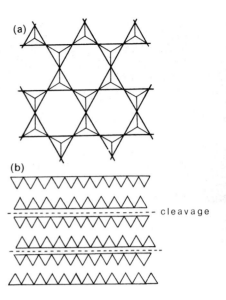

2.10 (a) Sheet of SiO_4 tetrahedra in minerals such as talc and mica.
(b) The cleavage runs between the double layers.

held against each other. The double layers can slide past each other very easily so talc is very soft (H 1) with a perfect cleavage parallel to the layers.

Mica is similar to talc but a quarter of the silicon ions are replaced by aluminium ions. To balance the charges an ion such as potassium (K^+) is introduced between the double sheets. Because of this the double sheets are more firmly held together than in talc and they will not slide over each other. However, the bonds between the double sheets are still weak so mica has a very good cleavage parallel to the sheets.

The simplest clay mineral is **kaolinite**. It consists of single sheets of SiO_4 tetrahedra with the tips of the tetrahedra all pointing in the same direction. Hydroxide ions lie in the spaces in the sheets and also provide a roof to the layer. Aluminium ions under the roof of hydroxide ions hold the layer together. Other clays such as **montmorillonite** are made up of double layers as in talc and mica (figure 2.10).

In the framework silicates every corner of each SiO_4 tetrahedron is shared with adjacent tetrahedra (figure 2.11). The framework of **quartz**, SiO_2, is not too compact so the relative density of quartz is only 2.65. The structure is a strong one, however, so quartz has a hardness of 7 and it lacks cleavage.

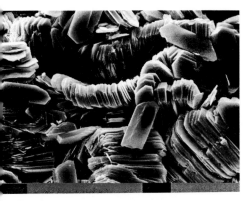

Kaolinite seen under a scanning electron microscope. The crystals are triclinic but they look hexagonal. Note the perfect cleavage.

In the **alkali feldspars** aluminium ions replace quarter of the silicon ions so the tetrahedra have the general formula $AlSi_3O_8$. In orthoclase, $KAlSi_3O_8$, the charge is balanced by the inclusion of a potassium ion (K^+). The plagioclase feldspars form an isomorphous series with the end members being **albite**, $NaAlSi_3O_8$, and **anorthite**, $CaAl_2Si_2O_8$. In albite, an alkali feldspar, a quarter of the silicons are replaced by aluminium. In anorthite, half of the silicons are replaced and the resulting double negative charge is balanced by the inclusion of Ca^{2+}. Solid solution between albite and anorthite is complete. Like quartz, the framework of feldspars is not too tightly packed so feldspars do not have high densities (d 2.55-2.76). The rigid framework does, however, make them quite hard (H 6-6½). Cleavage is quite well developed as a result of weaknesses introduced by ionic substitutions.

2.11 Arrangement of SiO_4 tetrahedra in a framework silicate such as quartz and feldspar.

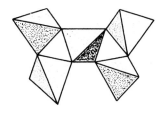

Phase chemistry

Substances which differ physically from each other are described as being different **phases**, e.g. hydrogen oxide may exist as the phases ice, water or water vapour. Also, graphite and diamond are separate solid phases of carbon. Solutions such as salt in water are single phases. A **system** is made up of phases, e.g. ice in water is a two phase system. A **phase diagram** is a graph which shows the stability relationships of phases under conditions of changing temperature, pressure and concentration, e.g. you know that water boils at 100°C at atmospheric pressure, but what would happen to the boiling point of the water if we slowly increased or decreased the pressure? We could find the boiling point of water at various pressures and we could plot a graph showing how the boiling point varies with pressure. The line on the graph would separate liquid and gas phases. A line like this is called a **phase boundary** and it gives the pressure and temperature at which one phase changes to another (figure 2.12). Examples where all the phases are solid are given by carbon (graphite and diamond) and by the three phases of the aluminium silicate, Al_2SiO_5 (figure 2.13). Adding sodium chloride to water depresses its freezing point. However, the freezing point cannot be lowered indefinitely and a solution of 29 percent sodium chloride has the minimum freezing point of −21°C. The solution giving the lowest possible freezing point is called a **eutectic mixture** and the minimum freezing point is the **eutectic point**. What

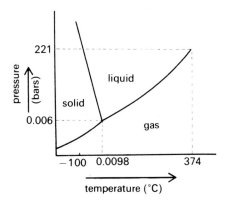

2.12 Phase diagram of water showing the conditions of temperature and pressure under which it is solid, liquid or gas.

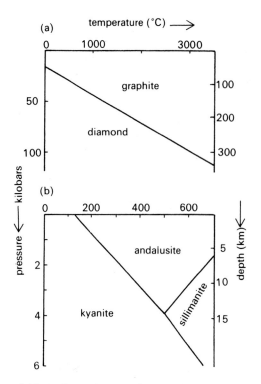

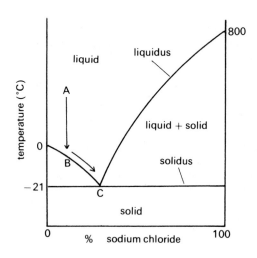

2.14 *Phase diagram of the system water-sodium chloride. A mixture starts to freeze when it cools to the temperature of the liquidus. Freezing is completed at the solidus temperature.*

2.13 *(a) Phase diagram of carbon. Graphite forms at low pressure, diamond forms at high pressure.*
(b) Phase diagram of aluminium silicate. Kyanite is the high pressure form, sillimanite exists at high temperatures while andalusite exists at low temperatures and pressures.

The behaviour of a solution of sodium chloride and water is similar to that shown when molten mineral mixtures such as that of anorthite ($CaAl_2Si_2O_8$) and diopside ($CaMgSi_2O_6$) are allowed to cool (figure 2.15). Liquid of composition A (anorthite 80 percent; diopside 20 percent) cools to meet the liquidus at B. Anorthite

happens during freezing or crystallization can be seen by cooling a 10 percent solution of sodium chloride from point A on figure 2.14. The solution cools from A to reach point B at −4°C. Here, ice separates from the solution so the proportion of sodium chloride in the remaining solution rises above 10 percent. The increased sodium chloride concentration depresses the freezing point below −4°C so the liquid cools from B to C as ice is continuously removed. The path followed lies on a curve called a **liquidus**. At any point on the liquidus ice and sodium chloride solution coexist. When the solution cools to C the salt and ice crystallize together before the solid mass can be cooled any further. The line below which only solid exists is the **solidus**; it lies at −21°C. The solid which results from the crystallization of liquid A has the same composition as the initial liquid; that is, it is 90 percent ice and 10 percent sodium chloride.

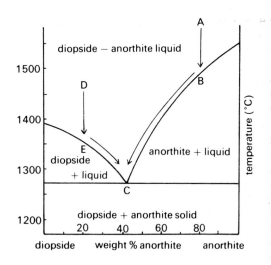

2.15 *Phase diagram of the diopside-anorthite system. Diopside is a pyroxene, anorthite is a feldspar.*

MINERALS

en begins to crystallize causing the percent-
ge of diopside in the melt to rise. This lowers
e freezing point of the remaining liquid which
en cools along BC as anorthite continues to
ystallize. At C, the eutectic point, anorthite
nd diopside crystallize together at about
275°C. At the eutectic point the liquid has
e composition: diopside 58 percent and anor-
ite 42 percent so when the liquid crystallizes,
3 percent of the crystals are diopside and 42
ercent are anorthite. However, a good deal of
e anorthite has already crystallized before the
quid reaches C so the solid which results from
e crystallization of liquid A consists of 80
ercent anorthite crystals and 20 percent diop-
de crystals. A liquid of composition D cools
meet the liquidus at E. Diopside then begins
crystallize leaving the remaining melt
nriched in anorthite. This lowers the freezing
oint of the remaining liquid which then cools
wards C as more diopside crystallizes. At C,
northite crystallizes along with diopside.
The diopside–anorthite system has minerals
fixed compositions. Where solid solution
xists the crystallization of melts follows a dif-
rent pattern. In the albite-anorthite system
gure 2.16) the melting points of the various
bite-anorthite mixtures are shown by the soli-
us curving between the melting points of albite
120°C) and anorthite (1550°C). The liquidus
howing the temperatures at which melts of
rious compositions begin to crystallize lies
ove the solidus but meets it at both ends.
melt such as A cools to meet the liquidus
B. At this temperature, solid of composition
begins to crystallize. C is much richer in
northite than the liquid with which it is in
ntact and as cooling proceeds the liquid,
eing depleted in anorthite, moves towards D.
he solid reacts with the liquid, constantly
hanges its composition and moves towards
where crystallization is completed. The last
quid to crystallize (composition D) is much
cher in albite than the original melt. However,
ecause the solid and liquid continuously react
ith each other the composition of the solid
hich finally crystallizes has the same compo-
tion as the original liquid. The fayalite-
orsterite system is similar to that of the pla-
ioclase feldspars. Forsterite is the high tem-
erature end member so crystals initially formed
re enriched in forsterite while the remaining
quid is depleted in forsterite.

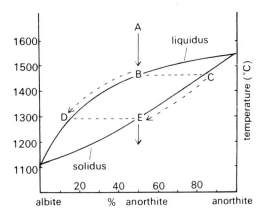

2.16 *Phase diagram of the albite-anorthite system. Both minerals are feldspars.*

Crystallography—the study of crystals

Most minerals occur as **crystals**. Crystals have
regular shapes which arise from the regular
arrangement of the atoms making up the crystal
lattice. Get 91 equal sized marbles and put 36
of them into a square on the bench. Make sure
the marbles are touching each other and hold
them in position with a narrow Plasticine strip
stuck to the bench. Now pour the other
marbles onto the square until all the marbles
have settled into place. What shape have you
built? Why does it have regular faces?

The study of crystals depends more on the
study of the angles between crystal faces than
it does on the shapes of the faces themselves.
The angle between two faces or the **interfacial
angle** is the angle between lines drawn at right
angles to the faces. Figure 2.17 shows sections
through crystals which look completely differ-

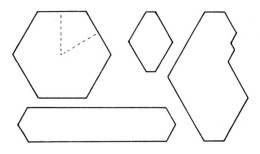

2.17 *Sections through crystals of the same mineral. The shapes of the crystals vary but the
interfacial angles are constant.*

ent. While corresponding faces in the two crystals have different relative sizes the interfacial angles are always 60°. Despite the different appearances of the crystal faces we can say that these crystals are of the same type because the interfacial angles are equal. The relationship which states that crystals of the same substance, even though they are misshapen or distorted, have the same interfacial angles between corresponding faces is called the **Law of Constancy of Interfacial Angles**. In science, a law is a rule which always seems to be true. An instrument called a **goniometer** is used to measure interfacial angles. The simplest type, the contact goniometer, is really just a protractor with a swinging arm (figure 2.18). The optical goniometer uses a beam of light reflected from the crystal faces. The crystal is turned from one reflecting position to the next and the angle of rotation noted.

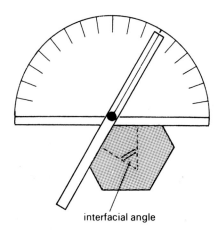

interfacial angle

2.18 A contact goniometer for measuring interfacial angles.

Besides using interfacial angles we can describe crystals in terms of the types and arrangements of the faces present. A set of faces which are all alike is called a **form**. Figure 2.19 shows a crystal made up of a combination of two forms — the faces marked *x* could all belong to a cube and the faces marked *y* could all belong to an octahedron. A **zone** is a set of faces which are all parallel to a direction called the **zone axis**. When faces in a zone lie next to each other the edge along which they meet gives the direction of the zone axis.

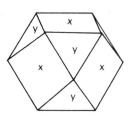

2.19 A crystal made up of two forms–the cube (x) and the octahedron (y).

An important property of crystals is their symmetry. A **plane of symmetry** divides a crystal so that the two parts are mirror images of each other. Different crystal types have different numbers of symmetry planes. A cube has nine planes of symmetry; a matchbox shape has three; a squashed matchbox has only one while some crystal shapes have no planes of symmetry. An **axis of symmetry** is a line about which a crystal can be rotated so it looks the same before it has been turned through a complete circle. If the crystal looks the same every time it has been turned through 180° then the symmetry axis is called a **diad**. How many diads does a matchbox have? If a crystal looks the same three times during a rotation the symmetry axis is a **triad**. How many triad axes does a Toblerone box have? A **tetrad** axis makes a crystal look the same four times and a **hexad** makes a crystal look the same six times during a rotation. How many tetrad axes are there on a cube and on a tea packet? Many pens and pencils have six-sided shapes. How many hexads would be present in such a pen or pencil. The third element of symmetry is the **centre of symmetry**. A crystal has a centre of symmetry if it has pairs of similar, parallel faces on opposite sides of the centre of the crystal.

Crystal types may be grouped into seven **systems** by the symmetry elements which they possess. Each system, within its total group of symmetry elements, has one group which is unique and which can be used to characterize the crystal system. Figures 2.20–2.27 and table 2.3 give details of the crystal systems and their symmetry elements. You will see that the possession of four triad axes is characteristic of the cubic system. If you cut the corners off a cube you get an eight-sided shape called an octahedron. Using your models of crystal shapes can you find the symmetry elements of an octahedron? Are they the same as those of

MINERALS

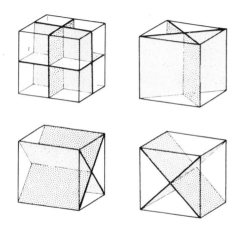

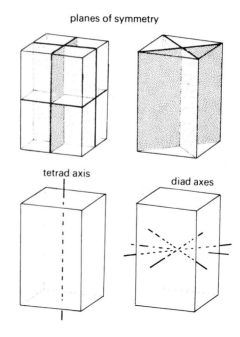

2.20 *The nine planes of symmetry in a cube.*

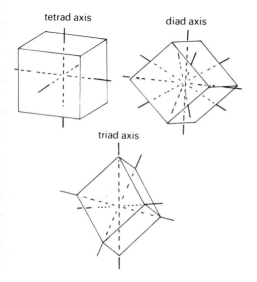

2.22 *Symmetry elements of a tetragonal crystal. There are five planes of symmetry, four diads and one tetrad.*

tetrad axis

diad axis

triad axis

2.21 *The directions of the axes of symmetry in a cube. There are six diads, four triads and three tetrads.*

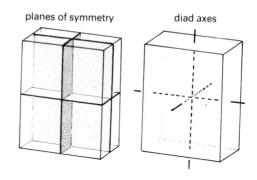

planes of symmetry   diad axes

2.23 *Symmetry elements of an orthorhombic crystal. There are three planes of symmetry and three diads.*

a cube? Since an octahedron has four triad axes it is placed in the cubic system. The cubic system, then, includes many crystal shapes in addition to the cube (figure 2.28). How are all these shapes related? Similarly, any crystal system may contain a wide variety of shapes. All shapes in one system, though, possess the symmetry elements characteristic of the system.

Crystal faces can be named according to their positions on the crystal. **Prism** faces are on the sides of the crystal and they run parallel to the length of the crystal. A **basal pinacoid** is a pair of faces at right angles to the length of the crystal, e.g. in a tea packet the four long sides would form a square prism while the top and bottom of the packet would be a basal pinacoid. A **pyramid** consists of faces at the end of a crystal which meet at a point or which would meet at a point if they were extended, e.g. an octahedron is a double pyramid. A **dome** looks

MINERALS

like the roof on a house in the game Monopoly. That is, a dome is made up of two sloping faces at the end of a crystal. The faces meet along a line or they would meet in this way if they were extended (figure 2.29).

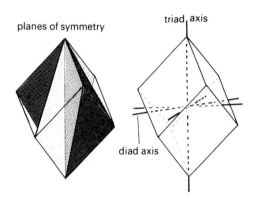

2.24 Symmetry elements of a trigonal crystal. There are three vertical planes of symmetry, three diads and one triad.

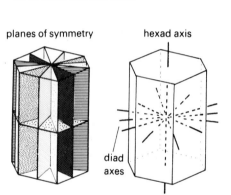

2.25 Symmetry elements of a hexagonal crystal. There are seven planes of symmetry, six diads and one hexad.

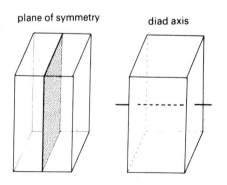

2.26 A monoclinic crystal has one plane of symmetry and one diad.

2.27 A triclinic crystal has no planes or axes of symmetry. Like other crystals it does have a centre of symmetry.

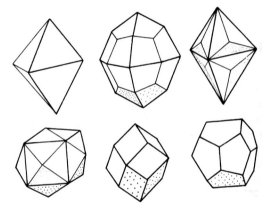

2.28 Some crystals of the cubic system.

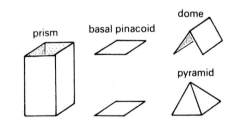

2.29 Types of crystal face.

MINERALS

CRYSTAL SYSTEM	CHARACTERISTIC SYMMETRY ELEMENTS	OTHER SYMMETRY ELEMENTS
Cubic	4 triads	9 planes of symmetry, 6 diads, 3 tetrads, a centre of symmetry
Tetragonal	1 tetrad	5 planes of symmetry, 4 diads, a centre of symmetry
Orthorhombic	3 diads	3 planes of symmetry, a centre of symmetry
Trigonal	1 triad	3 planes of symmetry (all vertical), 3 diads, a centre of symmetry
Hexagonal	1 hexad	7 planes of symmetry (6 vertical, 1 horizontal), 6 diads, a centre of symmetry
Monoclinic	1 diad	1 plane of symmetry, a centre of symmetry, (the diad is at 90° to the plane of symmetry)
Triclinic	No axes	A centre of symmetry

Table 2.3   Symmetry elements of the seven crystal systems

Minerals and the microscope

The microscope which is used to study rocks and minerals is called a **polarizing** or **petrological microscope**. (Petrology is the study of rocks). It differs from an ordinary microscope in using polarized light and in having a graduated, rotating stage. Before rocks can be viewed under the polarizing microscope they have to be cut and ground to a standard thickness of 30 micrometres (μm). The thin rock slices are stuck to a microscope slide with Canada balsam or synthetic resin.

Polarized light

If you shake a rope which is fixed at one end you can make waves pass along the rope. If you shake the rope up and down, from side to side or diagonally the waves still pass along. This is similar to the way in which light travels. The light waves can be imagined as travelling in a series of planes vertically, horizontally and all angles in between (figure 2.30). If a tied rope were passed through a set of railings then shaken at various angles only the vertical waves would pass through. Polaroid has a structure quite like a set of railings so if light is shone at it only the waves on one plane can pass

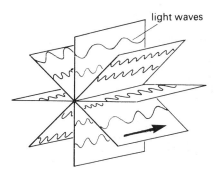

2.30 Light waves can be thought of as travelling along a series of planes at various angles.

through (figure 2.31). The light which passes through is said to be **plane polarized**. What would happen if a second sheet of polaroid was placed in the light with its barred structure at right angles to the first? The light waves passing through the first sheet cannot pass through the second sheet. Why is this so? In figure 2.32 how does the plane polarized light from the first polaroid sheet strike the second sheet?

Take two pieces of polaroid and place one on the other so no light gets through. Now put a piece of cellophane or mica between the polaroid sheets. What do you see? The material has become strongly coloured. The petrological

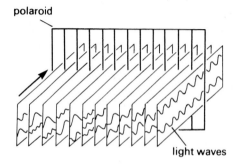

2.31 *Plane polarized light. After passing through a sheet of polaroid the light waves lie in one plane.*

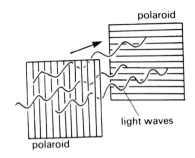

2.32 *A second sheet of polaroid with its barred structure at right angles to the first stops light from passing through.*

microscope uses two sheets of polaroid in this way to produce colours in many minerals which would otherwise be virtually colourless. One piece of polaroid, the **polarizer**, is situated between the light source and the rock slide on the stage while the other sheet, the **analyser**, is in the barrel of the microscope below the eyepiece. The polarizer is permanently in position but the analyser may be moved in or out. With the analyser out the minerals on the stage are viewed under **plane polarized light**. With the analyser in position the minerals are viewed under **crossed polarized light** or under **crossed polars**. (Sometimes, this is referred to as **crossed nicols** because, before polaroid was invented, light was polarized using a prism invented by William Nicol in 1828). The eyepiece of the microscope has two **cross-wires** running east-west and north-south so they are parallel to the planes of polarization of the polarizer and

analyser. The polarizer may polarize light in the east-west or north-south plane depending on the make of microscope. Usually, though, the polarizer polarizes light in the east-west plane and the analyser polarizes light in the north-south plane.

Now let us look at some of the mineral properties which can be examined under the petrological microscope using plane polarized light.

Refractive index and relief

What happens when you shine a light beam on to a prism? When light crosses at an angle from one transparent substance into another its velocity and direction change. In figure 2.33 the incident beam makes an angle *i* (the angle of incidence) with a line (the normal) at right angles to the surface of the glass. On entering the glass the light beam slows down and it is bent over making an angle *r* (the angle of refraction) with the normal. The ratio of the velocity of the incident beam in a vacuum to the velocity of the refracted beam is called the **refractive index** (RI) of the medium which the beam enters. Since this velocity ratio is equal to the ratio of the sines of the angles of incidence and refraction the refractive index is given as:

$$\text{refractive index (RI)} = \frac{\sin i}{\sin r}$$

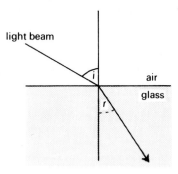

2.33 *When light passes into a substance such as glass the light slows down and changes direction. The ratio of the sines of the angles of incidence and refraction is the refractive index of the substance.*

Where a light beam in a vacuum enters a medium in which the velocity of light does not change then the medium has a refractive index

MINERALS

f 1.0. In this case an angled beam would not
e bent. The more the light is bent the greater
the refractive index of the material.

It is difficult to see a piece of glass in water
ecause the refractive indices of the glass and
ater are similar. It is, however, easy to see
diamond in water because it has a markedly
ifferent refractive index from the water so it
tands out very well. Since rock slices are
nounted in Canada balsam (RI=1.54), minerals
ith a similar refractive index to the balsam
nerge with it and are difficult to see. Such
ninerals are said to have **low relief**. Minerals
vhose refractive indices are very different from
nat of the Canada balsam are easy to see and
ney are said to have **high relief**. If a mineral
as a refractive index above that of Canada
alsam it is said to have **positive relief** while
its refractive index is below that of the balsam
has **negative relief**. The **Becke test** is used
o find if a mineral has positive or negative relief.
ocus on a mineral grain at the edge of the
lide and reduce the light as much as possible.

line called the Becke line appears at the
oundary of the mineral and balsam. When the
nicroscope is racked up the Becke line moves
nto the material which has the higher refractive
ndex. The relative refractive indices of adjacent
ninerals can also be found by this method.

Colour and pleochroism

Minerals which are pale in hand specimen are
olourless in thin section while minerals which
re dark in hand specimen usually appear in
nades of green or brown. **Pleochroic** minerals
hange colour in plane polarized light as the
nicroscope stage is turned, e.g. biotite changes
om dark brown when the grain is parallel to
ne plane of the polarized light to pale yellow
vhen the grain is at right angles to the plane
f polarization. If you have biotite in a slide you
an easily check the vibration direction of the
olarizer.

Crystal form and cleavage

Minerals seen under the microscope are two-
imensional slices of three-dimensional grains.
ecause of this the true shape of a grain may
e difficult to discern. Cut a cuboid of Plasticine
n various directions. What do you find? Sim-
arly, other regular solids can be cut to produce

a variety of sectional shapes. Sections of grains
with no fixed shape may have very irregular
forms.

Some crystal sections seen under the microscope are distinctive enough to be helpful in
mineral identification, e.g. in sections cut at
right angles to the length of the crystal pyroxenes are eight-sided and amphiboles are six-
sided (figure 2.34).

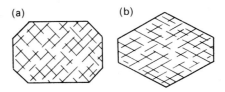

2.34 *Sections of pyroxene and amphibole cut at
right angles to the lengths of the crystals.*

Like crystal shape, the observation of cleavage depends on the orientation of the mineral
grain. Where one cleavage is present the cleavage does not show up if the mineral grain has
been cut parallel to the cleavage and in some
orientations only one of two cleavages may be
seen. Within any one type of mineral the angles
between cleavages are constant so knowing the
angles may be useful in identification. The angle
between two cleavages can be measured when
the cleavages are at right angles to the plane
of the slide. To measure the angle, turn the stage
of the microscope until the trace of one cleavage is parallel to one of the cross-wires. Take
the reading on the scale of the stage and turn
the stage again until the second cleavage trace
is parallel to the same cross-wire. Note the
second reading on the scale and subtract to
find the angle between the cleavages.

Now let us look at some mineral properties
which can be seen under crossed polars.

Polarization colours and extinction

Isotropic materials have the same properties in
all directions. Cubic minerals are isotropic and,
like glass, they appear black under crossed
polars. Non-cubic minerals are **anisotropic**
because they have different properties in different directions. Anisotropic minerals allow
light through under crossed polars but, since

they can sometimes appear to be black, a mineral which looks black does not have to be cubic.

When an anisotropic mineral is placed in a ray of plane polarized light it breaks the ray up into two plane-polarized rays vibrating at right angles to each other. Since the two rays travel through the mineral in different directions at different speeds the mineral has a different refractive index for each ray. The faster ray gives a lower refractive index than the slower ray. The property of having two refractive indices is called **double refraction** or **birefringence**. Lay a cleavage rhomb of clear calcite (Iceland spar) on a dot on a piece of paper. What did you see? What happens when you turn the piece of Iceland spar? The birefringence or strength of the double refraction is the numerical difference between the minimum and maximum refractive indices, e.g. quartz has refractive indices of 1.544 and 1.553 so its birefringence is 0.009 while calcite has refractive indices of 1.486 and 1.658 so its birefringence is very high at 0.172.

The fact that anisotropic minerals break light up into two beams leads to the production of **polarization colours**. When the two beams from the mineral arrive at the upper polar or analyser they are acted on in such a way that some colours are removed from the white light leaving only certain colours to pass through.

Since the colours produced depend partly on the thickness of the mineral section, all rock sections are ground to a standard thickness of 30 μm. You can see how thickness affect colour if you build up different thicknesses of Sellotape on a slide and examine it under crossed polars. Examination of a mineral such as quartz cut in the shape of a wedge shows colour bands in a pattern called **Newton's scale** (see back cover) which looks like a series of repeated rainbows. Each rainbow is called an **order**. The **first order** colours are seen at the thin end of the wedge. They are strongly developed but they do not form a complete rainbow since grey and white come before yellow. The **second order** colours are also strongly developed and they form a complete rainbow from violet to red. **Third order** colours again form a rainbow but they are somewhat pale. The higher order colours developed at the thick end of the wedge are very pale bands of pink, green and pearly white.

The interference colours also depend on the birefringence of the mineral. The greater the birefringence the higher the position of the colour on Newton's scale. Quartz with a birefringence of 0.009 shows low order white while calcite with a birefringence of 0.172 shows pearly high-order colours. Figure 2.35 shows a quartz crystal cut with one section parallel to the long axis of the crystal and with the other section at right angles to the long axis. The section parallel to the long axis shows the maximum double refraction for quartz since the ray which vibrates parallel to the long axis gives

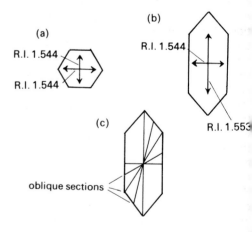

Double refraction shown by a cleavage rhomb of clear calcite (Iceland spar).

2.35 Quartz crystal cut (a) at right angles to its length and (b) parallel to its length. Such sections have minimum and maximum birefringence, respectively. Sections cut at intermediate angles (c) have intermediate values of briefringence.

MINERALS

a refractive index of 1.553 while the ray which vibrates at right angles to the long axis gives a refractive index of 1.544. This produces a birefringence of 0.009 which gives this section the colour of first order white. The section at right angles to the long axis behaves as an isotropic mineral because both rays give the same refractive index of 1.544. Since this section has a birefringence of zero it appears black under crossed polars. Oblique sections between these two extremes have intermediate values of birefringence giving colours which become progressively brighter as the section approaches the long axis. This means that in a rock section containing randomly oriented quartz grains, the grains show a variety of colours from that which corresponds to the maximum birefringence down Newton's scale through a series of greys to black.

Arguments similar to those given for quartz apply to other anisotropic minerals. You should realize that the grains of any minerals in a rock may show a range of colour from that corresponding to its maximum birefringence through all the colours lower down Newton's scale. It should also be noted that the colours change as the microscope stage is rotated and that four times in every rotation each mineral grain goes black. When the grain goes black it is said to be in **extinction**. Extinction occurs when the vibration directions of the mineral are parallel to the vibration planes of the polars. The **angle of extinction** is the angle between the positions of extinction and some prominent crystal direction which is often the cleavage, e.g. mica has an extinction angle of zero on the cleavage because it is in extinction when its cleavage is parallel to the cross-wires. Such extinction is described as being **parallel** or **straight**. A mineral with **oblique** or **inclined extinction** goes to extinction when some prominent crystal direction is not parallel to the cross-wires. To find the angle of extinction rotate the stage until the mineral grain goes black then note the reading on the graduated microscope stage. Rotate the stage until the cleavage or other crystal direction is parallel to the nearest cross-wire then note the stage reading again. Subtraction gives the angle of extinction. You will find that grains of a mineral on a slide may show various extinction angles up to a maximum; this highest possible value is the one required. Since you are measuring extinction angles to the nearest cross-wire the highest

value you will ever obtain will be 45°

Twinning

Within a twinned crystal the adjacent twins reach extinction at different positions as the microscope stage is rotated. In pyroxene and amphibole the crystal occasionally appears as light and dark halves. Such twinning is described as **simple**. Since amphibole is pleochroic its twinning can also be detected in plane polarized light. Twinning is often seen in feldspars. The common types of twinning in feldspars are **lamellar twinning** which takes the form of parallel stripes and **cross-hatched twinning** which gives the grains a tartan appearance (figure 2.36).

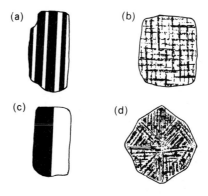

2.36 *Twinning in crossed polarized light: (a) lamellar twinning, e.g. plagioclase feldspar; (b) cross-hatched twinning, e.g. microcline feldspar; (c) simple twinning, e.g. feldspars, pyroxene, amphibole; (d) repeated twinning in leucite.*

Zoning

Can you recall what happens when plagioclase crystallizes from a melt (figure 2.16). The first formed plagioclase is relatively rich in calcium. The solid plagioclase then reacts continuously with the remaining liquid to become gradually more sodic. If cooling is fairly rapid the plagioclase may not react fully with the liquid so a crystal forms with a calcic interior and a sodic exterior. Such crystals are said to be **zoned** and under crossed polars the variation in composition shows up as concentric grey bands. In coloured minerals zoning may be seen in plane polarized light as bands of varying colour.

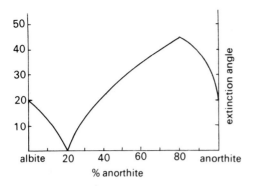

2.37 *Graph showing how the extinction angle of plagioclase feldspar varies with composition.*

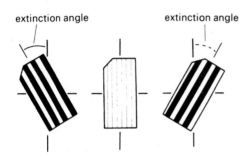

2.38 *Finding the extinction angle of plagioclase feldspar. Rotate the crystal to each side of a cross-wire till the twin lamellae go into extinction. Average the two readings.*

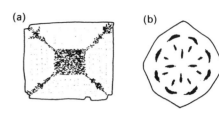

2.39 *Inclusions in (a) andalusite (chiastolite) and (b) leucite.*

Opaque minerals under the microscope

While most minerals are transparent when ground to a thickness of 30 μm a few remain opaque. Opaque minerals have to be examined under light shone down on to the thin section. Under reflected light graphite (carbon) and magnetite (Fe_3O_4) are shiny black while pyrite (FeS_2) and chalcopyrite ($CuFeS_2$) are brassy yellow.

Mineral properties

Mineral properties are summarized in tables 2.4-2.6. In addition, Key 2.1 will help you to identify minerals under the microscope.

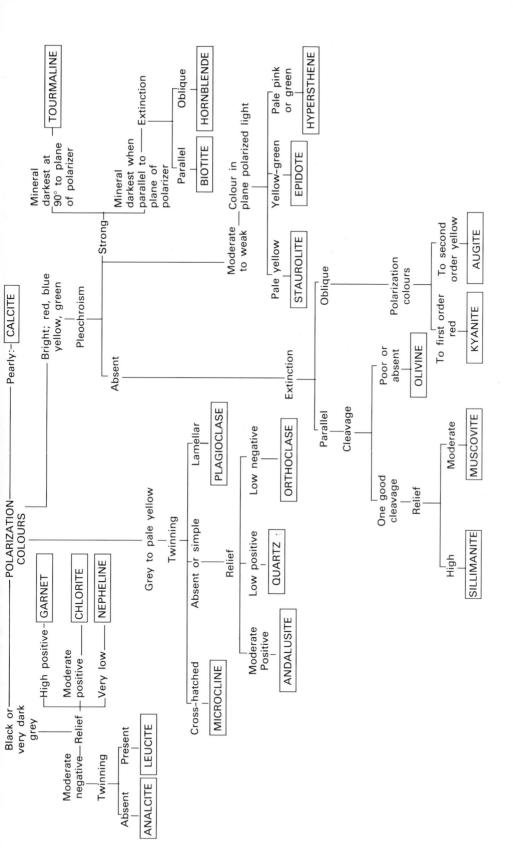

Key 2.1   Identification of some common minerals under the microscope

MINERAL TYPE	NAME	CRYSTAL SYSTEM	RELATIVE DENSITY (specific gravity)	LUSTRE	CLEAVAGE
	COMPOSITION	HARDNESS	COLOUR	STREAK	FRACTURE
ELEMENTS	GRAPHITE	Hexagonal	2.0	Metallic	One perfect
	C (carbon)	1½	Grey-black	Shiny black	—
	SULPHUR	Orthorhombic	2.0	Resinous	Poor
	S (sulphur)	2	Yellow	Yellow or white	Uneven
	COPPER	Cubic	8.9	Metallic	—
	Cu (copper)	3	Red-brown	Shiny red-brown	Hackly (fracture surface jagged and rough)
	GOLD	Cubic	19.3	Metallic	—
	Au (gold)	3	Yellow	Yellow	Hackly
OXIDES AND HYDROXIDES	QUARTZ	Trigonal	2.7	Vitreous	—
	SiO$_2$ (silicon dioxide)	7	Variable; usually white or colourless	White	Conchoidal
	HAEMATITE	Trigonal	5	Metallic or dull	—
	Fe$_2$O$_3$ (iron oxide)	6	Black or red-brown	Red-brown	Uneven
	MAGNETITE	Cubic	5.2	Metallic	Poor
	Fe$_3$O$_4$ (iron oxide)	6	Black	Black	Uneven
	GOETHITE	Orthorhombic	4.3	Adamantine, silky or dull	One good
	Fe O.OH (hydrated iron oxide)	5	Black to yellow-brown	Yellow-brown	Uneven

Table 2.4   Mineral properties

DISTINGUISHING FEATURES	USES
OCCURRENCE	OTHER DETAILS

DISTINGUISHING FEATURES / OCCURRENCE	USES / OTHER DETAILS
Greasy feel. Writes on paper. May feel cold because it is a good conductor of heat Usually as scaly masses in metamorphic rocks	Heat resistant so used in foundry moulds and crucibles. Also used in electrodes, pencils, paints and as a lubricant
Melts easily. Burns with a blue flame giving off poisonous sulphur dioxide. (Should only be burned in a fume cupboard) Dissolves in solvents such as xylol As encrusting masses in volcanoes. In salt domes associated with gypsum	For making sulphuric acid, matches, insecticides and for vulcanizing rubber
Can be hammered into sheets. May be stained green. When dissolved in nitric acid gives a blue colour when ammonium hydroxide added As lumps, sheets and branching forms in veins and filling gas bubbles of lavas	In electric cables, water pipes, coins and in the alloys brass and bronze
Extremely dense. Can be cut with a knife. Softer than other brassy-looking minerals As irregular masses in quartz veins. As lumps (nuggets) and flakes in gravel deposits	In currency, jewellery, medicine, dentistry, electronics
Hardness and fracture distinctive. Forms six-sided crystals terminated by pyramids. Prism faces often marked with horizontal lines Major constituent of many rocks. After feldspar, quartz is the most abundant mineral at the Earth's surface	Quartz sand is used in building, moulding and glass making. Also used as an abrasive, in making ceramics and in electronics. Quartz occurs in a wide variety of colours. ROCK CRYSTAL is clear; MILKY QUARTZ is white; AMETHYST is purple; ROSE QUARTZ is pink; CAIRNGORM is pale brown; SMOKY QUARTZ is dark brown; CITRINE is yellow. CHALCEDONY is made up of microscopic quartz grains. It is slightly softer (H 6½) than quartz and it often has a waxy lustre. There are many varieties of chalcedony; JASPER is opaque and usually red; AGATE is made up of concentric bands of differing colour while in ONYX the coloured bands are parallel to each other. FLINT is a grey or black form of chalcedony which occurs as nodules in chalk. Since it breaks with a conchoidal fracture to give sharp-edged fragments, flint was much used by early man to make tools and weapons. CHERT is brown or black chalcedony occurring as nodules and layers in limestones and shales. Chert has an even fracture. OPAL is hydrous silica ($SiO_2.nH_2O$) which is usually milky or pearly white. Precious opal shows a wide range of colour because it consists of small spheres of silica which break light up into different colours as it passes through.
Distinctive cherry red streak. Dissolves slowly in concentrated hydrochloric acid. Becomes magnetic on heating. Often forms rounded masses called kidney iron ore. The rounded lumps have an internal radiating structure. The shiny crystalline form of haematite is called specular iron ore A major constituent of ancient sedimentary banded ironstones. Found in veins and as a weathering product of iron-containing minerals. Often gives a red colour to sedimentary rocks.	The main ore of iron. Also used as a pigment and as a polishing agent
Strongly magnetic. Black streak. Dissolves in hydrocholoric acid. Crystals often octahedral Often found in igneous and metamorphic rocks. Also in veins and in economically usable sands	An ore of iron
Yellow-brown streak. Soluble in hydrochloric acid. Usually forms lumpy or sausage-shaped masses with internal radiating crystals An oxidation product of iron-bearing minerals. Precipitates from water as bog iron ore	An ore of iron. The pigment in yellow ochre

| MINERAL TYPE | NAME | CRYSTAL SYSTEM | RELATIVE DENSITY (specific gravity) | LUSTRE | CLEAVAGE |
	COMPOSITION	HARDNESS	COLOUR	STREAK	FRACTURE
OXIDES AND HYDROXIDES	LIMONITE	Non-crystalline	2.7–4.3	Earthy	—
	$FeO.OHnH_2O$ (hydrated iron oxide)	4–5½	Yellow to brown	Yellow-brown	Irregular
	CASSITERITE	Tetragonal	7	Adamantine	Indistinct
	SnO_2 (tin oxide)	6–7	Brown or black	White to pale brown	Uneven or subconchoidal
HALIDES	HALITE	Cubic	2.2	Vitreous	Three perfect sets parallel to cube faces
	Na Cl (sodium chloride)	2–2½	Usually colourless to white	White	Conchoidal
	FLUORITE (fluorspar)	Cubic	3.2	Vitreous	Four perfect cleavages cutting corners of cube
	CaF_2 (calcium fluoride)	4	Variable; colourless yellow, blue, purple, pink, green	White	Conchoidal to uneven
CARBONATES	CALCITE	Trigonal	2.7	Vitreous	Three perfect cleavages causing it to break into squashed cube shapes
	$CaCO_3$ (calcium carbonate)	3	Usually colourless or white	White	Conchoidal; but rarely seen
	DOLOMITE	Trigonal	2.86	Vitreous or pearly	As for calcite
	$CaMg(CO_3)_2$ (calcium magnesium carbonate)	3½–4	Honey colour, colourless or white	White	Conchoidal or uneven
	ARAGONITE	Orthorhombic	2.95	Vitreous	Poor
	$CaCO_3$ (calcium carbonate)	3½–4	Colourless, white or grey	White	Subconchoidal
	MALACHITE	Monoclinic	4	Dull, silky or fibrous	One good cleavage. Not always seen since mineral usually massive
	$Cu_2CO_3(OH)_2$ (hydrated copper carbonate)	3½–4	Bright green	Pale green	Subconchoidal

Table 2.4 Mineral properties (contd.)

DISTINGUISHING FEATURES	USES
OCCURRENCE	OTHER DETAILS

Similar to goethite but non-crystalline	An ore of iron
Oxidation product of iron-bearing minerals. Major constituent of some sedimentary iron ores. Also found as bog iron ore	
Hardness and high density are distinctive. Often forms twinned crystals shaped like bent knees. When added to zinc and dilute hydrochloric acid becomes coated with tin metal	The ore of tin
Found in granites and in veins around granites. Also in sediments derived from granites	
	Other oxides and hydroxides. CORUNDUM Al_2O_3 is a very hard mineral (H9) used as the abrasive, emery. Gem varieties are ruby and sapphire. BAUXITE, the ore of aluminium consists of hydrated aluminium oxides such as GIBBSITE, $Al(OH)_3$, and DIASPORE, $AlO(OH)$, Bauxite remains after rocks have suffered considerable weathering under tropical conditions. RUTILE, TiO_2, and ILMENITE, $FeTiO_3$, are sources of titanium while CHROMITE, $FeCr_2O_4$ provides chromium, PYROLUSITE MnO_2 is an important ore of manganese while URANINITE or PITCHBLENDE, UO_2 is an important ore of uranium.
Salty taste. Colours a flame yellow. Very soluble in water. Crystal faces often hollowed in a stepped fashion	Numerous industrial and domestic uses, e.g. used in making hydrochloric acid, sodium hydroxide, soap and glass. Also used to de-ice roads
Found in sedimentary rocks formed by the evaporation of sea water	
Often forms good cubic crystals. May show twinning in which corners of one cube protrude from faces of another cube	Used in making steel, hydrofluoric acid, ceramics and fluorocarbons such as Freon and Teflon
Often found in veins with lead and silver ores	BLUE JOHN is a miners' term for Derbyshire fluorite. It gets its name from a corruption of the French 'bleu jaune' ('blue yellow'). Blue John is often banded; it is much used in making ornaments
Reacts vigorously with cold dilute hydrochloric acid. Can be distinguished from quartz by its hardness and cleavage. Often found as six-sided crystals ending in pyramids	Very numerous, e.g., limestone is used in making cement and as a flux in steel making. Also used in construction, agriculture and in making glass, ceramics and paper
	NAIL-HEAD SPAR consists of calcite crystals with blunt pyramidal ends while DOG-TOOTH SPAR has sharp-ended crystals. ICELAND SPAR is pure, transparent calcite
Very common. The main mineral of many limestones, chalk and marble. Also occurs in mineral veins, shells, stalactites and stalagmites	Magnesite, $MgCo_3$, is like calcite but reacts only slightly with cold hydrochloric acid. It is also harder ($H3\frac{1}{2}$-$4\frac{1}{2}$) than calcite.
Reacts with hot, dilute hydrochloric acid. (Powder reacts with cold acid.) Often found as rhombohedral (squashed cube shape) crystals with curved faces. Slightly harder and denser than calcite	Used in building and for making furnace linings
Found mostly in limestones. Sometimes formed by the alteration of calcite	Siderite, $FeCO_3$ is like dolomite but it is denser (relative density 3.96). It is often brown or dark brown in colour
Reacts with dilute hydrochloric acid. Goes lilac or pink when boiled in cobalt nitrate solution. Often twinned in such a way that it looks hexagonal	Corals, pearls and shells used for jewellery and ornaments
Corals, pearls and many shells consist of aragonite. May precipitate from sea water and from hot springs. Aragonite readily changes to calcite	
Colour distinctive. Goes black on heating. Reacts with dilute hydrochloric acid. Usually forms lumpy masses showing radiating fibrous structure and concentric banding	An ore of copper. Also used for making ornaments
Found in near-surface oxidized zone of copper deposits	

MINERAL TYPE	NAME	CRYSTAL SYSTEM	RELATIVE DENSITY (specific gravity)	LUSTRE	CLEAVAGE
	COMPOSITION	HARDNESS	COLOUR	STREAK	FRACTURE
	AZURITE $Cu_3(CO_3)_2(OH)_2$ (hydrated copper carbonate)	Monoclinic $3\frac{1}{2}$–4	3.8 Deep blue	Vitreous Light blue	One good Conchoidal
SULPHATES	GYPSUM $CaSO_4 . 2H_2O$ (hydrated calcium sulphate)	Monoclinic 2	2.3 Colourless or white	Vitreous or pearly. Fibrous forms silky White	One perfect. Gives flexible, non-elastic sheets Conchoidal
SULPHATES	BARYTE (barytes, barite) $BaSO_4$ (barium sulphate)	Orthorhombic $2\frac{1}{2}$–$3\frac{1}{2}$	4.5 Variable; usually white	Vitreous or pearly White	Two good cleavages at 78° with third cleavage at 90° to these Uneven
PHOSPHATE	APATITE $Ca_5(PO_4)_3F$ (calcium fluorophosphate	Hexagonal 5	3.2 Variable; usually pale green	Vitreous White	Poor Conchoidal to uneven
SULPHIDES	PYRITE (iron pyrites) FeS_2 (iron sulphide)	Cubic 6–$6\frac{1}{2}$	5.0 Brassy yellow	Metallic Greenish black	None Uneven
SULPHIDES	CHALCOPYRITE $CuFeS_2$ (copper iron sulphide)	Tetragonal $3\frac{1}{2}$–4	4.2 Brassy yellow	Metallic Greenish black	None Uneven
SULPHIDES	GALENA PbS (lead sulphide)	Cubic $2\frac{1}{2}$	7.5 Lead-grey	Metallic Grey	Three perfect cleavages parallel to cube faces Subconchoidal
SULPHIDES	SPHALERITE ZnS (zinc sulphide)	Cubic $3\frac{1}{2}$–4	4.1 Variable; usually brown or black	Resinous to adamantine White or brown	Six good cleavages at 60° to each other Conchoidal
SILICATES FELDSPARS					

34

Table 2.4 Mineral properties (contd.)

DISTINGUISHING FEATURES	USES
OCCURRENCE	OTHER DETAILS
Colour distinctive. Goes black on heating. Reacts with dilute hydrochloric acid.	An ore of copper
Found in oxidized zone of copper deposits	
Can be scratched by a fingernail. May form distinctive swallow-tail twins (figure 2.5). Dissolves in hot hydrochloric acid giving a white precipitate if barium chloride solution added.	Numerous, e.g. making plaster and as a filler for paper and paint. Also used as fertilizer. Added to cement to slow its setting rate
Usually found in sedimentary rocks formed by the evaporation of sea water.	SELENITE is transparent gypsum. ALABASTER is white, fine-grained gypsum. SATIN SPAR is fibrous gypsum with a silky lustre. ANHYDRITE, $CaSO_4$, is similar to gypsum but it is orthorhombic and it has three cleavages. It is also harder (H $3—3^1/2$) and denser (relative density 2.9—3.0)
Unusually high density for a white mineral. (Feels heavy in the hand). Colours a flame yellowish green	Used to make white pigment for paint and as a filler in paper. Also used to give weight to muds used in drilling oil and gas wells
Usually found in veins	
Often forms elongate hexagonal crystals. Soluble in hydrochloric acid; if sulphuric acid is added calcium sulphate precipitates	Mostly used as a phosphate fertilizer
Occurs in many igneous rocks. Also found in sedimentary phosphate deposits	
Pale brassy yellow colour is distinctive. May have a brown tarnish. Harder than chalcopyrite. Cube faces often striated	Not an ore of iron. Used to make sulphuric acid
The most common sulphide mineral. Found in veins and in a wide variety of rocks	Pyrite is also called fool's gold. MARCASITE is a very pale yellow, or silver, orthorhombic form of iron sulphide
Distinguished from pyrite by being softer and by having a blue, purple and reddish tarnish. The colour is usually deeper yellow than that of pyrite. Sulphur precipitates when dissolved in nitric acid	The most important copper ore
Mostly found in mineral veins	
Lead grey or silvery colour distinctive. Gives off hydrogen sulphide with hydrochloric acid. High density, hardness and cleavage also useful in identification. Often forms good cubic crystals	The main ore of lead
Mostly found in mineral veins	
One of the few common sulphides which does not have a metallic lustre. Gives hydrogen sulphide with hydrochloric acid. Variable colour may make it difficult to recognize. Crystals tetrahedral in shape	The most important ore of zinc
Mostly found in mineral veins	
	The aluminosilicate feldspars can be divided into the potassium and PLAGIOCLASE (sodium-calcium) feldspars. Potassium feldspar is ORTHOCLASE, sodium feldspar is ALBITE and calcium feldspar is ANORTHITE. Albite and anorthite are end members of the isomorphous plagioclase series. The ALKALI FELDSPARS lie between albite and orthoclase. At low temperature, ionic substitution between albite and orthoclase is limited because the potassium ion is much bigger than the sodium ion

	NAME	CRYSTAL SYSTEM	RELATIVE DENSITY (specific gravity)	LUSTRE	CLEAVAGE
MINERAL TYPE	COMPOSITION	HARDNESS	COLOUR	STREAK	FRACTURE
SILICATES — FELDSPARS	ORTHOCLASE	Monoclinic	2.6	Vitreous to pearly	Two good cleavages at 90°
	$KAlSi_3O_8$ (potassium aluminium silicate)	6–6½	Pink, white or grey	White	Conchoidal
SILICATES — FELDSPARS	PLAGIOCLASE	Triclinic	2.6–2.8	Vitreous to pearly	Two good cleavages almost at 90°
	$NaAlSi_3O_8$ to $CaAl_2Si_2O_8$ (sodium calcium aluminium silicate)	6–6½	Usually white or grey	White	Conchoidal to uneven
SILICATES — FELDSPATHOIDS	LEUCITE	Tetragonal but looks cubic	2.5	Vitreous to dull	Poor
	$KAlSi_2O_6$ (potassium aluminium silicate)	5½–6	White to grey	Colourless	Conchoidal
SILICATES — FELDSPATHOIDS	NEPHELINE	Hexagonal	2.6	Vitreous to greasy	Poor
	$NaAlSiO_4$ (sodium aluminium silicate)	5½–6	White, pink or grey	Colourless	Subconchoidal
SILICATES — ZEOLITE	ANALCITE (analcime)	Cubic	2.26	Vitreous	Poor
	$NaAlSi_2O_6.H_2O$ (hydrated sodium aluminium silicate)	5½	White, pink or grey	White	Subconchoidal
SILICATES — OLIVINE	OLIVINE	Orthorhombic	3.2–4.4 Increases with iron content	Vitreous	Poor
	$(MgFe)_2SiO_4$ (magnesium iron silicate)	6½–7	Green, yellow or brown	Colourless	Conchoidal
SILICATES — PYROXENES	HYPERSTHENE	Orthorhombic	3.6	Vitreous	Two good cleavages nearly at 90°
	$(MgFe)SiO_3$ (magnesium iron silicate)	5½	Variable; usually brown or green	White	Uneven
SILICATES — PYROXENES	AUGITE	Monoclinic	3.4	Vitreous	Two good cleavages nearly at 90°
	$(CaMgFeAl)_2(SiAl)_2O_6$ (calcium magnesium iron aluminium silicate)	6	Black or greenish black	White	Uneven to conchoidal

Table 2.4 Mineral properties (contd.)

DISTINGUISHING FEATURES	USES
OCCURRENCE	OTHER DETAILS

Often forms box-like crystals. Simple twinning common Orthoclase and microcline are found in igneous rocks such as granite, in many metamorphic rocks and in some sedimentary rocks. Sanidine occurs in lavas	Feldspar is used for making glass and ceramics. Some is used as an abrasive SANIDINE is the high temperature form of potassium feldspar while MICROCLINE (triclinic) is the low temperature form. Microcline differs from orthoclase and sanidine in having two twin directions nearly at right angles (cross-hatched twinning). PERTHITE consists of thin streaks of albite in a crystal of orthoclase. The two alkali feldspars mix completely at high temperature but, on cooling, unmixing and separation occur
Often shows twinning in the form of repeated thin layers. (Appears as fine parallel lines on the better cleavage surfaces.) A very common mineral. Found in many igneous and metamorphic rocks. Also found in some sedimentary rocks	The plagioclase feldspars show continuous variation between albite, $NaAlSi_3O_8$, and anorthite, $CaAl_2Si_2O_8$. Plagioclases are divided into six minerals according to the percentages of albite (Ab) and anorthite (An): ALBITE Ab_{90-100} An_{0-10}; OLIGOCLASE Ab_{70-90} An_{10-30}; ANDESINE Ab_{50-70} An_{30-50}; LABRADORITE Ab_{30-50} An_{50-70}; BYTOWNITE Ab_{10-30} An_{70-90}; and ANORTHITE Ab_{0-10} An_{90-100}. Usually, the anorthite percentage alone is used to give the composition of a plagioclase
Crystals look nearly round. Crystal faces may be striped. Similar to analcite Found in lavas rich in potassium but low in silica	Used as a potash fertilizer Leucite is cubic above 625°C. The crystal shape is formed at high temperature and its outer form is retained as the crystal cools
Forms stumpy, hexagonal crystals. Greasy lustre distinctive. Turns to jelly in strong hydrochloric acid Mostly found in silica-poor, sodium-rich igneous rocks	Used instead of feldspar in making glass and ceramics
Gives off water when heated. Crystal shape like that of leucite but analcite often found lining cavities in lavas (leucite is not found in this way) Gelatinizes in hydrochloric acid In igneous rocks low in silica	Zeolites have very open lattices so they can be used as 'molecular sieves' to separate gas mixtures. Synthetic zeolites are used to purify water by removing positive ions.
May look like green glass. Not often found with quartz Common in igneous rocks poor in silica. Also found in some meteorites	Used in making refractory bricks and in foundry sand. PERIDOT is gem quality olivine
	The pyroxene group can be divided into the orthorhombic orthopyroxenes and the monoclinic clinopyroxenes. The most common orthopyroxene is hypersthene and the common clinopyroxene is augite
The cleavage is distinctive. May show a bronze, almost metallic lustre caused by reflection of light from minute plates of ore mineral inside the crystal In igneous rocks low in silica and in some metamorphic rocks. Also found in some meteorites	
Cleavage and stumpy crystals with eight-sided sections distinctive. Two faces on ends of crystals. May show twinning Common in most dark coloured igneous rocks. Sometimes found in metamorphic rocks	SPODUMENE (lithium pyroxene) is a source of lithium. JADEITE (green jade) is used in jewellery

| MINERAL TYPE | NAME | CRYSTAL SYSTEM | RELATIVE DENSITY (specific gravity) | LUSTRE | CLEAVAGE |
	COMPOSITION	HARDNESS	COLOUR	STREAK	FRACTURE
SILICATES — AMPHIBOLE	HORNBLENDE	Monoclinic	3–3.5	Vitreous	Two good cleavages at 60°
	$Ca_2(MgFeAl)_5$ $(SiAl)_8O_{22}(OH)_2$ (hydrated calcium magnesium iron aluminium silicate)	5–6	Black often with a greenish tinge	White	Subconchoidal to uneven
SILICATES — MICAS	MUSCOVITE	Monoclinic but looks hexagonal	2.8–2.9	Vitreous to pearly	One perfect
	$KAl_2(AlSi_3)O_{10}(OH)_2$ (hydrated potassium aluminium silicate)	2½–3	Colourless, white or silvery	White	—
	BIOTITE	Monoclinic	2.7–3.3	Vitreous to pearly	One perfect
	$K(FeMg)_3(AlSi_3)O_{10}$ $(OH)_2$ (hydrated potassium iron magnesium aluminium silicate)	2½–3	Black or dark brown	White	—
SILICATES	TALC	Monoclinic	2.6–2.8	Pearly	One perfect
	$Mg_3Si_4O_{10}(OH)_2$ (hydrated magnesium silicate)	1	White	White	—
	KAOLINITE (china-clay)	Triclinic but looks hexagonal	2.65	Dull	One perfect
	$Al_2Si_2O_5(OH)_4$ (hydrated aluminium silicate)	2–2½	White	White	—
	GARNET	Cubic	3.6–4.2	Vitreous to resinous	—
	$Fe_3Al_2Si_3O_{12}$ (representative formula)	6–7½	Variable; usually red or brown	White	Subconchoidal to uneven
	SERPENTINE	Monoclinic but looks hexagonal	2.6	Greasy or silky	One cleavage not always seen
	$Mg_3Si_2O_5(OH)_4$ (hydrated magnesium silicate)	2½–3½	Variable; often green	White	Conchoidal to splintery

Table 2.4 Mineral properties (contd.)

DISTINGUISHING FEATURES	USES
OCCURRENCE	OTHER DETAILS
Cleavage and six-sided crystal sections distinctive. Three faces on ends of crystals	Some types of asbestos are fibrous amphiboles. NEPHRITE is a green and white form of jade
Common in a wide variety of metamorphic rocks. Also found in some igneous rocks	The amphiboles are a group of complex silicates which chemically resemble pyroxenes. However, amphiboles always contain hydroxide, OH . Hornblende is by far the most common amphibole
	The micas are hydrated silicates. The main types are white mica or muscovite and black mica or biotite
Pale colour and cleavage are distinctive. Splits into very thin, transparent, elastic sheets	Mica is used as a heat and electrical insulator. It is also used in paints, as backing for roofing felt and as a filler for rubber. Mica also has decorative use in wallpaper and building materials
Found in a wide variety of rocks. SERICITE is fine-grained white mica often found as an alteration product of feldspar	
Colour and cleavage distinctive. Splits into thin elastic sheets	
Found in a wide variety of rocks	
Hardness, colour and slippery feel are distinctive. Cleavage flakes are flexible but not elastic	Used as a lubricant and as a heat and electrical insulator. It is also used as talcum powder, French chalk and as a filler for paint and paper
Found in some metamorphic rocks	SOAPSTONE or STEATITE is a massive, impure form of talc
	Among the clay minerals, kaolinite and montmorillonite are hydrated aluminium silicates. Illite is a hydrated potassium aluminium silicate. Only kaolinite is described here
Often found as earthy masses. Greasy feel. May have a clayey smell	Used in making ceramics and as a filler in paper, paint and rubber
Formed as an alteration product of feldspar	
Often forms near-round crystals with 12 or 24 sides. Hardness and lack of cleavage also distinctive	Used as an abrasive and as a semi-precious gemstone
Found mostly in metamorphic rocks	The garnets are silicates of various metals including magnesium, iron, calcium and aluminium. The commonest garnets are red PYROPE, brown ALMANDINE and green GROSSULAR
Colour may be mottled. Usually breaks irregularly. Usually found as massive forms with no visible crystals or cleavage. Feels smooth or greasy. Cleavage flakes flexible but not elastic	CHRYSOTILE (a type of asbestos) is a fibrous serpentine. Also used as an ornamental stone
Formed by the alteration of igneous rocks which are low in silica	

MINERAL TYPE	NAME	CRYSTAL SYSTEM	RELATIVE DENSITY (specific gravity)	LUSTRE	CLEAVAGE
	COMPOSITION	HARDNESS	COLOUR	STREAK	FRACTURE
SILICATES	CHLORITE	Monoclinic but looks hexagonal	2.6–3.3	Pearly	One perfect
	$(MgFeAl)_6 Si_4 O_{10} (OH)_8$ (hydrated magnesium iron aluminium silicate)	2–3	Green, yellow or brown	Colourless to pale green	Earthy
	TOURMALINE	Trigonal	3–3.25	Vitreous	Poor
	$Na(MgFe)_3 Al_6 B_3 Si_6 O_{27}(OH)_4$ (complex hydrated silicate of sodium, magnesium, iron, aluminium and boron)	7	Variable; usually black	Colourless	Subconchoidal to uneven
	ANDALUSITE	Orthorhombic	3.1	Vitreous	Two cleavages at 90°
	Al_2SiO_5 (aluminium silicate)	6½–7½	Pink, red or grey	White	Subconchoidal to uneven
	SILLIMANITE	Orthorhombic	3.25	Vitreous	One perfect
	Al_2SiO_5 (aluminium silicate)	6½-7½	White to grey-green	White	Uneven
	KYANITE	Triclinic	3.6	Vitreous to pearly	Three cleavages parallel to crystal faces. One cleavage is indistinct
	Al_2SiO_5 (aluminium silicate)	5½-7	Blue, white or grey	White	—
	STAUROLITE	Monoclinic but looks orthorhombic	3.8	Vitreous to resinous	One good
	$(FeMg)Al_4Si_2O_{11} (OH)$ (hydrated iron magnesium aluminium silicate)	7½	Shades of brown	White	Subconhoidal
	EPIDOTE	Monoclinic	3.4	Vitreous	One good
	$Ca_2Fe Al_2Si_3O_{12}(OH)$ (hydrated calcium iron aluminium silicate)	6	Yellow-green to blackish green	White	Uneven

Table 2.4 Mineral properties (contd.)

DISTINGUISHING FEATURES	USES
OCCURRENCE	OTHER DETAILS

Often forms flaky masses. Cleavage flakes flexible but not elastic

Found in some metamorphic rocks. In igneous rocks as an alteration product of iron and magnesium minerals. Also found in fine-grained sedimentary rocks

---

Colour may vary within one crystal. Colour of a crystal may change when viewed from a different direction. Forms long crystals with triangular cross-sections. Crystals have longitudinal striations

Used mostly as a gemstone

Mainly in coarse-grained igneous rocks such as granite and granite pegmatite

SCHORL is black tourmaline

Crystals often long with nearly square cross-sections. Cleavages parallel to long faces of crystal. Surface may be altered to white mica. May be an internal cross of black inclusions

In metamorphic rocks derived from fine-grained sedimentary rocks

---

Long, needle-like crystals distinctive

In some metamorphic rocks

H.5½ on long crystal faces; H.7 on ends of crystals. Crystals long and flat. Patchy blue colour

In some metamorphic rocks

Often forms distinctive cross-shaped twins (Fig. 2.5). Crystals stubby

In some metamorphic rocks

Distinctive yellow-green colour. Crystal faces often grooved parallel to the length of the crystal

In some metamorphic rocks

MINERAL	QUARTZ	MAGNETITE	CALCITE	DOLOMITE	ORTHOCLASE	PLAGIOCLASE
COLOUR IN PLANE POLARIZED LIGHT	Colourless		Colourless		Colourless	Colourless
REFRACTIVE INDEX	1.544–1.553		1.486–1.658		1.518–1.526	1.527 (albite)–1.590 (anorthite)
RELIEF	Low; positive		Variable; high positive to low negative		Low; negative	Low negative to low positive
CLEAVAGE	—		Obvious; as two lines meeting at angles up to 75°		Not obvious; may be seen as two cleavages at 90° or as one cleavage trace	Not obvious; may be seen as two cleavages nearly at right angles or as one cleavage trace
PLEOCHROISM	—		—		—	—
BIREFRINGENCE	0.009		0.172		0.008	0.007–0.013
POLARIZATION COLOURS (UP TO)	First order white		High order pearly white		First order white	First order yellow
EXTINCTION	Parallel		Parallel or symmetrical to cleavage		0–12°	Up to 45° on the twinning
TWINNING	—		Common; seen as parallel lines or as lines meeting obliquely		Simple twinning may be seen in orthoclase and sanidine. Cross-hatched twinning in microcline	Lamellar twinning characteristic
ALTERATION	—		Sometimes replaced by quartz		Often shows cloudy alteration to clay mineral	Often shows cloudy alteration to clay mineral

Table 2.5 Optical properties of some common minerals

Usually has very distinctive twinning giving the grains a finely striped appearance. Grains may be zoned with calcic centres and sodic margins. Cloudy alteration often present. Albite has low negative relief — the other plagioclasses have low positive relief

Other details

The extinction angle measured by reference to the narrow twin bands varies according to the composition of the plagioclase (figure 2.37). In a thin section a number of grains must be identified to find the maximum value which is required to identify the plagioclase. The extinction angles are measured to each side of a cross-wire and each pair of readings is averaged (figure 2.38). Unfortunately, plagioclases of differing compositions may have the same extinction angles. Albite can be distinguished by the fact that its refractive index is below that of balsam. An_{80-100} is not very common so grains with extinction angles between 20 and 45° would usually have compositions in the range An_{40-80}

Can be distinguished from quartz by its low refractive index and by the twinning, cleavage and cloudy alteration which may be present. Microcline is easily identified by its cross-hatched twinning (figure 2.36). May show streaky perthitic intergrowths with albite

Very similar to calcite but the refractive indices (1.500–1.679) and birefringence (0.179) are slightly higher

Polarization colours pearly pink, green and grey. On rotation, most grains show extremes of relief from appearing to have rough surfaces, sharp boundaries and obvious cleavage to having smooth surfaces and indistinct boundaries. This change of relief in which grains seem to appear and disappear is called twinkling

In thin section often appears as squares or hexagons as these shapes are formed by slicing through octahedra. Appears steel grey under reflected light

Usually grey under crossed polars. Often has wavy extinction and it shows no twinning or alteration. May look like feldspar

DISTINGUISHING FEATURES

43

MINERAL	LEUCITE	NEPHELINE	ANALCITE	OLIVINE	HYPERSTHENE	AUGITE	HORNBLENDE
COLOUR IN PLANE-POLARIZED LIGHT	Colourless	Colourless	Colourless	Usually colourless	Colourless, pale green or pink	Colourless, pale green or pale brown	Green to brown
REFRACTIVE INDEX	1.508–1.511	1.526–1.546	1.487	1.635–1.878	1.673–1.731	1.688–1.737	1.615–1.730
RELIEF	Moderate; negative	Very low; usually positive	Moderate; negative	High; positive	High; positive	High; positive	High; positive
CLEAVAGE	Not usually seen	Not always seen; may be irregular	May be seen as two lines at 90°	Poor or none	Two nearly at 90°	Two nearly at 90°	Two at 60°
PLEOCHROISM	—	—	—	—	Pink to green	None or weak	Strong; usually from pale to dark green. Darkest when mineral parallel to plane of polarizer
BIREFRINGENCE	0.001	0.004	0.002	0.035–0.052	0.016	0.018–0.033	0.014–0.026
POLARIZATION COLOURS (UP TO)	First order dark grey	First order dark grey	First order very dark grey	Third order green	First order red	Second order yellow	Second order blue but colours may be dimmed by strong colour of the mineral
EXTINCTION	Always dark; may be wavy	Parallel	Always dark	Parallel	Parallel	45°	13–30°
TWINNING	Common in lines at 90° and 45° to each other	—	None or rare	Not often seen	—	May show simple or multiple twinning	Usually simple but may be multiple
ALTERATION	—	Often altered to white mica and other minerals	—	Often partly altered to serpentine and opaque iron oxide along irregular cracks	May be altered to fibrous amphibole or to serpentine	May show alteration to amphibole or chlorite	May show alteration to chlorite

Table 2.5 Optical properties of some common minerals (contd.)

Pleochroism, cleavage and six-sided basal sections are distinctive (figure 2.34)

May show hour-glass or concentric zoning. Twinning may have a herringbone appearance. Crystals may be eight-sided. May have aligned opaque inclusions or thin parallel layers of hypersthene

The pleochroism, parallel extinction, low birefringence and cleavage are distinctive. Often has opaque inclusions in sets of parallel planes. May have fine parallel layers of augite in the middle of the crystal. Crystals may have eight sides

Often occurs as well-formed crystals looking like rectangles with points on each end. Alteration along cracks is distinctive

Often found filling spaces between other grains. Distinguished from leucite by its lack of twinning

Often appears in hexagonal or nearly square shapes. Often shows alteration to an aggregate of white mica flakes

Twinning characteristic (figure 2.36). Crystal shapes nearly round and eight sides may be seen. Radial or concentric inclusions may be present. May resemble microcline but microcline has brighter polarization colours and lower relief. Similar to analcite but analcite has no twinning

DISTINGUISHING FEATURES

45

MINERAL	MUSCOVITE	BIOTITE	TALC	SERPENTINE	CHLORITE	GARNET	TOURMALINE	ANDALUSITE	SILLIMANITE	KYANITE	STAUROLITE	EPIDOTE
COLOUR IN PLANE – POLARIZED LIGHT	Colourless	Brown, yellow or green			Colourless to green	Colourless to pale pink	Yellow-brown, green, blue or colourless	Colourless to pale pink	Colourless	Colourless to pale blue	Pale yellow	Yellow-green
REFRACTIVE INDEX	1.552–1.616	1.565–1.695			1.570–1.670	1.714–1.887	1.610–1.675	1.633–1.653	1.654–1.683	1.712–1.734	1.739–1.761	1.715–1.797
RELIEF	Moderate; positive	Moderate; positive			Moderate; positive	High; positive	High; positive	Moderate; positive	High; positive	High; positive	High; positive	Very high; positive
CLEAVAGE	One obvious cleavage	One obvious cleavage			One good cleavage	–	–	Two good cleavages	One good cleavage	Two good cleavages nearly at 90°	Indistinct in one direction	One good cleavage
PLEOCHROISM	–	Strong; from yellow to brown. Darkest when mineral grain parallel to plane of polarizer			Moderate; from colourless to green	–	Strong; from pale to dark brown. Darkest when mineral grain at 90° to plane of polarizer	Weak; from pale pink to colourless	–	May show weak pleochroism from colourless to pale blue	Distinct; colourless to yellow-brown	May be distinct; pale yellow to yellow-green
BIREFRINGENCE	0.036–0.049	0.04–0.08			0.00–0.01	None or very weak	0.021–0.035	0.01	0.02	0.012–0.016	0.014	0.015–0.049
POLARIZATION COLOURS (UP TO)	Third order green	May be fourth order but usually up to second order red. Polarization colours may be dimmed by strong colour of mineral			First order dark grey, but brown and inky blue common	Black under crossed polars	Second order red. Polarization colours often dimmed by strong colour of mineral	First order yellow	Second order blue	First order red	First order red	Third order green
EXTINCTION	Parallel	Parallel			Usually parallel	Always dark	Parallel	Parallel	Parallel	Up to 30°	Parallel	Parallel
TWINNING	–	–			–	May show twinning in triangular sectors	–	–	–	Common	Not often seen	Sometimes seen
ALTERATION	–	May show alteration to chlorite			–	May show alteration to chlorite	May show alteration to mica	May show alteration to white mica	–	–	–	–

Table 2.5 Optical properties of some common minerals (contd.)

The pale yellow colour in plane polarized light is distinctive. Polarization colours often uneven. Sections showing first order grey have a peculiar blue or yellow-green tinge

Colour, pleochroism and high relief are distinctive. Crystals often have near-diamond or six-sided shapes. Grains may look spongy with numerous quartz inclusions. May show zoning

Crystals are usually wide, elongate rectangles. Cleavage often appears as black lines. High relief and extinction angle also useful in identification

Often shows cross fractures. Occurs as needle-like or fibrous crystals which may be bent. Crystals nearly square or diamond shaped in cross-section

Pleochroism, square cleavage in cross-section and low birefringence are distinctive. Basal sections may show a cross of black inclusions

Crystals often well formed with triangular basal sections. Strong pleochroism and lack of cleavage distinctive. Often has fractures at right angles to the length of the crystal. May show zoning

Crystals show irregular fractures. Mineral surface appears rough under plane polarized light. Crystals may look nearly round with six or eight sides. May hold numerous inclusions

Often occurs as an alteration product of pyroxene, amphibole and biotite. May form radiating masses. The grey but sometimes peculiar polarization colours are distinctive. Green colour, parallel extinction, weak pleochroism and good cleavage also helpful in identification

Usually seen with iron oxide as an alteration product of olivine, pyroxene or hornblende. Serpentine is usually pale green or colourless. Polarization colours are first order greys.

Very like muscovite. Talc tends to be associated with minerals (e.g. dolomite) rich in magnesium

Pleochroism, colour and cleavage distinctive. Near extinction has a mottled or crinkly appearance like the surface of orange peel. Often has black pleochroic spots. May show zoning

Occurs as elongate flakes with obvious cleavage. Bright polarization colours. At extinction may have irregular wavy colours like those of watered silk

DISTINGUISHING FEATURES

COLOUR IN PLANE-POLARIZED LIGHT		RELIEF	CLEAVAGE	PLEOCHROISM
OPAQUE	BROWN	HIGH POSITIVE	NONE OR POOR	STRONG
Chalcopyrite	Augite	Augite	Analcite	Biotite
Chromite	Biotite	Calcite	Garnet	Hornblende
Graphite	Garnet	Epidote	Leucite	Tourmaline
Haematite	Hornblende	Garnet	Nepheline	
Ilmenite	Tourmaline	Hornblende	Olivine	MODERATE
Limonite		Hypersthene	Quartz	
Magnetite		Kyanite	Staurolite	Chlorite
Pyrite	YELLOW	Olivine	Tourmaline	Epidote
	Biotite	Sillimanite		Hypersthene
	Epidote	Staurolite		Staurolite
COLOURLESS	Staurolite	Tourmaline	IN ONE DIRECTION	
Analcite	Tourmaline		Biotite	WEAK
Andalusite			Chlorite	
Augite		MODERATE	Epidote	Andalusite
Calcite	GREEN	POSITIVE	Muscovite	Augite
Chlorite	Augite		Sillimanite	Kyanite
Garnet	Biotite	Andalusite	Staurolite	
Hypersthene	Chlorite	Biotite		
Kyanite	Epidote	Calcite		
Leucite	Hornblende	Chlorite	IN MORE THAN	
Microcline	Hypersthene	Muscovite	ONE DIRECTION	
Muscovite	Tourmaline		Analcite	
Nepheline			Andalusite	
Olivine		LOW POSITIVE	Augite	
Orthoclase	BLUE		Calcite	
Plagioclase		Calcite	Hornblende	
Quartz	Chlorite	Nepheline	Hypersthene	
Sanidine	Kyanite	Plagioclase	Kyanite	
Sillimanite	Tourmaline	Quartz	Orthoclase	
			Plagioclase	
		LOW NEGATIVE		
PALE PINK		Calcite		
Andalusite		Nepheline		
Garnet		Orthoclase		
Hypersthene		Plagioclase		
		MODERATE		
		NEGATIVE		
		Analcite		
		Leucite		

Table 2.6 Summary of the optical properties of minerals

POLARIZATION COLOURS	EXTINCTION	TWINNING	MINERALS WHICH MAY SHOW ZONING	FORMS IN WHICH MINERALS MAY OCCUR
ALWAYS DARK (Birefringence zero) Analcite Garnet FIRST ORDER (Birefringence up to 0.018) Analcite Andalusite Chlorite Garnet Hypersthene Kyanite Leucite Nepheline Orthoclase Plagioclase Quartz Staurolite SECOND ORDER (Birefringence 0.018–0.037) Augite Hornblende Sillimanite Tourmaline THIRD ORDER (Birefringence 0.037–0.055) Epidote Muscovite Olivine FOURTH ORDER AND ABOVE (Birefringence above 0.055) Biotite Calcite	PARALLEL Andalusite Biotite Calcite Chlorite Epidote Hypersthene Muscovite Nepheline Olivine Quartz Sillimanite Staurolite Tourmaline OBLIQUE Augite Hornblende Kyanite Orthoclase Plagioclase	SIMPLE Augite Hornblende Kyanite Orthoclase LAMELLAR Calcite Plagioclase CROSS-HATCHED Leucite Microcline IN SECTORS Garnet	Augite Biotite Garnet Plagioclase Staurolite Tourmaline
			MINERALS WHICH MAY HAVE WELL-FORMED CRYSTALS	NEARLY ROUND Garnet Leucite FIBRES OR NEEDLES Sillimanite Tourmaline NEARLY RECTANGULAR Andalusite Biotite Chlorite Epidote Kyanite Muscovite Nepheline Orthoclase Plagioclase Staurolite Tourmaline
			Andalusite Augite Epidote Garnet Hornblende Leucite Nepheline Olivine Orthoclase Plagioclase Staurolite Tourmaline	

IGNEOUS ROCKS

A **rock** is a natural material which consists of one or more minerals. Rocks are commonly thought of as always being hard but the term can also be used to include soft or unconsolidated materials such as clay, sand and gravel. Rocks are of three types: **igneous rocks** form from molten material coming from inside the Earth; **metamorphic rocks** form through the alteration of pre-existing rocks by heat and pressure; and **sedimentary rocks** form by the accumulation of material formed by surface processes. **Petrology** is the study of rocks.

Igneous rocks

Igneous rocks form by the crystallization of molten material called **magma** which comes from inside the Earth. Since igneous rocks form from liquids their crystals can grow freely in any direction so their crystals usually show random orientation. Magma is not just molten rock. In addition to the materials which will eventually form rock, magma contains a large number of **volatiles**. Volatiles are substances which vaporize easily. They include water, carbon dioxide, hydrogen sulphide, hydrogen chloride, nitrogen, hydrogen fluoride, sulphur, sulphur dioxide, chlorine and fluorine. Water is, by far, the major volatile and it may constitute as much as 8 percent of a magma.

Igneous rocks are classified according to the mineral grain size, the minerals present and the chemistry of the rock.

Grain size

Coarse-grained igneous rocks have average grain diameters greater than 5 mm; **medium-grained** igneous rocks have average grain diameters between 1 and 5 mm, and **fine-grained** rocks have average grain diameters less than 1 mm. Glassy igneous rocks have no crystals.

Minerals present

Any igneous rock may contain a large number of different minerals but only a few minerals are used in classification. These **essential minerals** include quartz, feldspar, feldspathoid, olivine, augite, hornblende, and biotite. **Accessory minerals** are the additional minerals in an igneous rock which are not used in classification.

Compostion

It is customary to present the chemical compositions of rocks in terms of their constituent oxides despite the fact that these oxides do not necessarily exist in the rock as oxides; for this reason a quartz-free rock may have a SiO_2 content of 50 percent because the silicon and oxygen are contained in minerals such as feldspar, pyroxene and olivine.

Oxides such as sulphur dioxide give acids when they are added to water; for this reason, such oxides are described as being **acidic**. On the other hand, oxides such as calcium oxide give alkali when added to water. Such oxides are **basic**. At one time SiO_2 was classified as an acidic oxide so rocks which were rich in SiO_2 (more than 66 percent) were called **acidic igneous rocks** while **basic igneous rocks** have much less SiO_2 (44–52 percent). **Intermediate** rocks have 52–66 percent SiO_2 while **ultrabasic** or **ultramafic igneous rocks** have less than 44 percent SiO_2.

Also, igneous rocks rich in oxides such as those of sodium and potassium are described as **alkaline**. Alkaline rocks have feldspars which are dominantly potassic or sodic. They generally have more sodium and potassium than is needed to form feldspars so feldspathoids, sodic pyroxenes and sodic amphiboles may be present. If the calcium level is also high the rock may be described as **calc-alkaline**. Calc-alkaline rocks have feldspars which are calcium rich and the pyroxene and amphibole may be calcic.

		ACIDIC ROCK GRANITE	INTERMEDIATE ROCK SYENITE	BASIC ROCK GABBRO	ULTRABASIC ROCK PERIDOTITE
OXIDE (PERCENTAGE COMPOSITION)	SiO_2	70	63	48	43.5
	Al_2O_3	15	17	15	4
	Fe_2O_3	1	2.5	3	2.5
	FeO	2	2	8	10
	MgO	1	2	10	34
	CaO	2.5	4	10	3.5
	Na_2O	4	4.5	2	0.5
	K_2O	3	4.5	1	0.3
	TiO_2	0.5	1	2.5	1
	H_2O	1	0.5	0.5	0.7
MINERALS (PERCENTAGE VOLUME)	Quartz	30	5	—	—
	Potassium feldspar	45	55	—	—
	Plagioclase	15	25	60	—
	Biotite	10	—	—	—
	Hornblende	—	15	—	—
	Pyroxene	—	—	30	15
	Olivine	—	—	10	85

Table 3.1   Chemical compositions and mineralogy of representative igneous rocks

There is often a close relationship between the chemistry of a rock and the minerals it contains, e.g. acidic rocks always contain quartz, intermediate rocks often consist largely of feldspar while basic and ultrabasic rocks are often rich in ferromagnesian (iron-magnesium) minerals such as pyroxene and olivine. Table 3.1 shows rock compositions along with the minerals present. How are differences in oxides such as SiO_2, MgO and K_2O reflected in the mineralogy of the rocks?

Colour index

The **colour index** of an igneous rock is indicative of the amount of dark, ferromagnesian minerals which are present. Rocks with less than 30 percent of dark mineral are pale in colour and they are described as **leucocratic**. Those with 30-60 percent of dark mineral tend to be grey in colour and they are described as **mesocratic** or **mesotype** while igneous rocks with more than 60 percent of dark mineral are dark in colour and they are **melanocratic**.

Textures of igneous rocks

The **texture** of a rock is a description of the relationships between the grains. Textural features include grain size, degree of crystallinity, grain shapes, grain orientations and the ways in which grains come into contact with each other (figure 3.1).

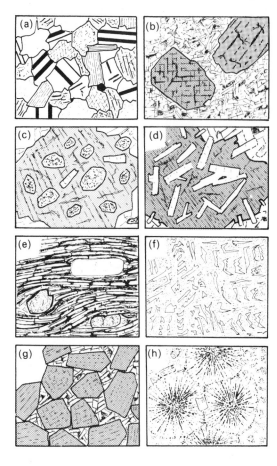

3.1 *Textures of igneous rocks: (a) granular; (b) porphyritic; (c) poikilitic; (d) ophitic (augite encloses plagioclase crystals); (e) flow structure; (f) graphic; (g) interstitial; (h) spherulitic.*

We have already seen that igneous rocks may be described as coarse-, medium- or fine-grained. Sometimes, a rock contains large crystals called **phenocrysts** set in a matrix of finer grains. Such rocks are described as being **porphyritic**. Igneous rocks which consist of mineral grains are **holocrystalline** (wholly crystalline) while glassy non-crystalline rocks are described as **hyaline**. **Euhedral** mineral grains show well-developed crystal forms, **subhedral** grains show imperfect crystal forms while **anhedral** grains show no recognizable crystal shapes. The grains in an igneous rock usually show random orientation. It may happen,

though, that crystals are lined up by flow of the magma during cooling giving a preferred orientation called **flow structure**.

Where the mineral grains grow to form a mosaic of similar-sized grains the texture is described as **granular**. Where large crystals of one mineral enclose smaller grains of other minerals the texture is **poikilitic**. In the similar **ophitic** texture large augite crystals enclose plagioclase crystals. Where a mineral fills the spaces left between early-formed crystals the texture is described as **interstitial**. Intergrowths of quartz and alkali feldspar may look like some forms of writing. For this reason such a texture is described as **graphic**. On a smaller scale the intergrowth gives **micrographic** or **granophyric** texture.

Glassy igneous rocks form crystals very slowly by a solid-state process called **devitrification** so that there are no glassy igneous rocks older than about 60 million years. It often happens that the crystals form in round masses consisting of radiating aggregates of very small crystals giving a **spherulitic** texture.

Naming igneous rocks

Table 3.2 shows how igneous rocks may be classified using grain size and the minerals which are present. In naming rocks use can also be made of important non-essential minerals, e.g. the essential minerals of gabbro are plagioclase feldspar and pyroxene. If quartz is present the gabbro may be described as quartz gabbro and if olivine is present it can be described as olivine gabbro.

Descriptions of igneous rocks

Granite, microgranite and rhyolite

These rocks consist essentially of quartz (20–40 percent) and alkali feldspar (orthoclase, perthite, microcline and albite) though sodic plagioclase such as oligoclase may be present. Mica is usually present and hornblende may be present. Accessory minerals include apatite, tourmaline and magnetite.

Granite is a coarse-grained rock which is usually pink or grey. The texture is usually granular but it may be porphyritic with pheno-

Table 3.2 Classification of igneous rocks

GRAIN SIZE (diameter)	ACIDIC		INTERMEDIATE		BASIC	ULTRABASIC
COARSE >5 mm	Granite	Granodiorite	Syenite	Diorite	Gabbro	Peridotite
MEDIUM 1–5 mm	Microgranite	Microgranodiorite	Microsyenite	Microdiorite	Dolerite	
FINE <1 mm	Rhyolite	Dacite	Trachyte	Andesite	Basalt	
GLASSY	Obsidian				Tachylyte	
MAIN MINERALS (approximate %)	Quartz 30 Orthoclase 45 Plagioclase 15 Mica + Hornblende 10	Quartz 20 Orthoclase 20 Plagioclase 50 Biotite + Hornblende 10	Orthoclase 55 Plagioclase 25 Quartz 5 Hornblende + Biotite + Pyroxene 15	Plagioclase 70 Hornblende + Biotite + Pyroxene 30	Plagioclase 60 Pyroxene 40	Pyroxene 50 Olivine 50

OTHER PROPERTIES

—— Decrease in Si, Na, K ——→

—— Increase in Ca, Mg, Fe ——→

Sodic plagioclase ———————————→ Calcic plagioclase

———— Colour becoming darker ————→

2.6 g cm^{-3} —— Increase in density ——→ 3.3 g cm^{-3}

Granite showing phenocrysts of orthoclase feldspar in a matrix of quartz, feldspar and biotite crystals.

crysts of alkali feldspar. Granites may contain **geodes** or **drusy cavities**. These are cavities lined by well-formed crystals of the granite minerals. **Pegmatite** is an igneous rock of extremely coarse grain. The average grain diameter is greater than 3 cm but some grains may be many metres long. **Granite pegmatite** is the commonest type of pegmatite. It consists of quartz, feldspar and mica (usually muscovite) with large crystals of accessory minerals such as beryl, tourmaline, topaz and apatite. Granite pegmatites provide a source of rare metals such as lithium, zirconium and beryllium.

Microgranite is medium-grained. When porphyritic it is known as **quartz porphyry**. Phenocrysts are commonly quartz, alkali feldspar, biotite and hornblende. The colour of the rock is variable from pink to pale grey. **Granophyre** is a microgranite with a granophyric texture.

Rhyolite is fine-grained or glassy. It is often porphyritic with phenocrysts of feldspar, quartz, biotite and hornblende. Rhyolites often show **flow banding** with layers of differing colours and with aligned phenocrysts. Spherulites of quartz and feldspar may be present and rhyolite may show curving cracks (**perlitic structure**) under the microscope. Rhyolite is usually pale in colour being generally grey or pale shades of red, yellow and green. **Pumice** is a frothy-looking glassy rock which is often of rhyolitic composition. Gas bubbles called **vesicles** give pumice its frothy appearance.

Felsite is a general term used to describe fine-grained, perhaps porphyritic, acidic igneous rocks. Felsite may crystallize directly from magma or it may be formed by the alteration of rhyolite, microgranite or glass.

Pitchstone is a glassy rock which is often dark green or black in colour. It has a dull lustre like pitch or resin and it may break with a conchoidal or flat fracture. Early stages in de vitrification may be marked by the presence of poorly-formed **crystallites** or **microlites**. (Crystallites show no birefringence while microlite do show polarization colours.) The crystallite and microlites may be skeletal crystals or they may have feathery, tree-like, spherical or rod like forms. Pitchstones may have numerous phenocrysts of quartz, alkali feldspar, biotite hornblende or pyroxene. Pitchstone may show perlitic cracks and flow structure. **Obsidian** also glassy. It is usually black with a conchoidal fracture and vitreous lustre. Phenocrysts are no common but spherulites, crystallites and micro lites may be common. Flow banding may be present.

Granodiorite, microgranodiorite and dacite

These rocks consist essentially of quartz (more than 10 percent and often 20–40 percent calc-alkali feldspar (calcic oligoclase or and sine) and alkali feldspar such as orthoclase. The alkali feldspar makes up less than one third the total feldspar. The most common ferromag nesian minerals are biotite and hornblend Apatite and magnetite are also common. Gr nodiorite, microgranodiorite and dacite tend be darker in colour than their granitic equiva ents. Dacite is usually porphyritic with pheno crysts of quartz, plagioclase (sometimes zoned biotite, hornblende and pyroxene.

Syenite, microsyenite and trachyte

These rocks consist essentially of alkali feldspar (orthoclase, perthite, microcline and albite) with some plagioclase such as oligoclase or and sine. The plagioclase makes up less than 4 percent of the total feldspar. Hornblende, py oxene or biotite are usually present. Quartz nepheline may be present.

Syenite is coarse-grained. It is usually red pink but it may be grey. **Microsyenite** is mediur grained. It may be pink or grey. Most micr syenites have phenocrysts of orthoclase. Suc a porphyritic microsyenite is sometimes calle **porphyry**. (The term 'porphyry' is best avoided **Trachyte** is fine-grained and usually grey b it may be yellowish or pink. It is usually po phyritic with phenocrysts of feldspar, horn blende, biotite or pyroxene. Flow structure (tra ytic texture) is often present and the oundmass may be partly glassy.

orite, microdiorite and andesite

ese rocks consist of plagioclase (oligoclase d andesine) usually making up 60-70 percent the rock. Hornblende is common and biotite pyroxene may also be present along with all quantities of quartz and orthoclase. **Diorite** is coarse-grained. It is usually speckled ack and white. **Microdiorite** is usually grey. s often porphyritic with phenocrysts of feldar, hornblende, biotite or pyroxene. **Andesite** usually grey, brown or black. It is often porphyc with phenocrysts of plagioclase (often ned), hornblende, mica or pyroxene. The oundmass may be partly glassy and it may ve gas bubbles (vesicles) or **amygdales**. Amygles are vesicles filled by later, secondary nerals such as agate or calcite.

abbro, dolerite and basalt

ese rocks consist of plagioclase (labradorite) aking up about 50-60 percent of the rock th augite being the dominant ferromagnesian neral. Olivine, orthopyroxene, hornblende, ptite or quartz may be present. **Gabbro** is coarse-grained. It is usually mottled ey and black. Gabbro often shows ophitic xture. **Dolerite** is a medium-grained rock ich is usually black in colour. **Basalt** is fine-grained and black in colour. enocrysts of plagioclase, augite and olivine common. Basalt may be vesicular or amygloidal with a partly glassy groundmass. The ean floors consist of a type of basalt called pleiite while the basalt of volcanic islands is en of a type called **alkali basalt**. When basalt xtruded on to the sea floor it may be altered the introduction of sodium and water to come **spilite**. Spilite consists largely of chlor- and albite. **Tachylyte** is basaltic glass. It is usually brown black in colour and it is often rich in very all particles of magnetite. It may be vesicular.

ridotite

ridotite consists of olivine and pyroxene. It coarse-grained, dark green to black in colour d it has a noticeably high density (3.2 g cm⁻³).

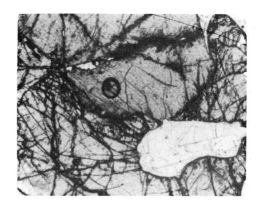

Gabbro (plane polarized light) showing pyroxene with cleavage (top), much-fractured olivine (bottom and sides and plagioclase (low relief mineral bottom right). The round feature on the augite is an air bubble. Field of view 6 mm across.

Porphyritic basalt (crossed polars) showing phenocrysts of plagioclase (some zoned) in a matrix of plagioclase, pyroxene and opaque minerals. Field of view 6 mm across.

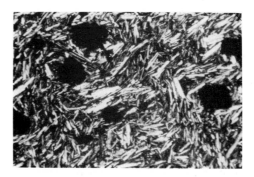

Trachyte (crossed polars) showing feldspar (elongate crystals) with amphibole and opaque minerals. The large dark patches are vesicles. The feldspars show flow structure (trachytic texture). Field of view 4 mm across.

Igneous intrusions

When magmas solidify before they reach the Earth's surface they form bodies of igneous rock called **intrusions**.

Batholiths are enormous intrusions (often of granite or granodiorite) which have no observable bases. They are several kilometres thick and, in some cases, they taper out downwards. They are found in mountain belts and they are elongated parallel to the mountain ranges (figure 3.2). The granites of south-west England are part of a single batholith. A **stock** is a small batholith. The granites of south-west Scotland are stocks. Another major intrusion is the basin-shaped **lopolith**. A lopolith at Lake Superior, USA, has a diameter of about 250 km and a thickness of about 15 km. A **laccolith** is shaped like the head of a toadstool. The magma which supplies a laccolith probably comes through sideways running feeder pipes from a nearby stock. There are no laccoliths in Britain.

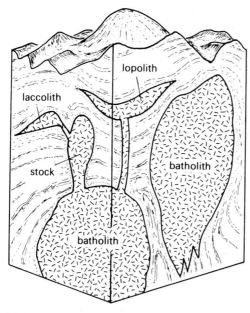

3.2 Igneous intrusions.

The igneous rocks found in large intrusions are described as **plutonic**. These rocks are coarse-grained because they have cooled slowly in large intrusions which may have been deeply buried. Large intrusions are sometimes called **plutons**.

A **sheet** is a tabular intrusion, i.e. the intrusion has a shape which resembles a sheet of hard board. A **dyke** is a vertical or near-vertical sheet which cuts discordantly across the intruded rocks. A **sill** is a sheet which lies parallel to the layering of the intruded rocks (figure 3.3). **Ring-dykes** have the form of hollow, near cylinders whose diameters usually measure few kilometres. **Cone-sheets** also have near circular outcrops but they taper downwards.

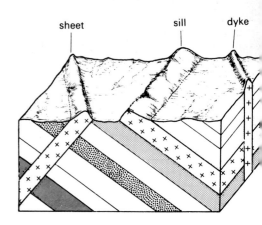

3.3 Igneous intrusions.

A **volcanic plug** or **neck** is a cylindrical intrusion representing the conduit which fed material to the volcano.

When an intrusion is formed the space for the magma might be created by fracturing and pulling apart of the intruded rock so leaving room for the magma to enter. Possibly, the magma can exert enough force simply to push the rocks aside to make room for itself. Possibly too, the intruded rock might be eaten away by breaking off and sinking into the magma.

In the case of sills and laccoliths it appears that the pressure of the magma has been sufficient to raise the overlying rocks. It would seem, though, that dyke and cone sheet intrusion requires the intruded rocks to be in a state of tension. On entering a crack the pressure of the magma may act like a wedge to open the fracture and allow the magma to work its way along. Dykes are often found in groups called **dyke swarms** in which the dykes may be parallel to each other or they may radiate away from a centre. The dyke patterns reflect the distribution of tensional forces in the intruded

IGNEOUS ROCKS

Salisbury Crags, Edinburgh. A dolerite still intruded into sedimentary rocks which dip to the left. Arthur's Seat in the background is the eroded remains of an ancient volcano.

oar's Tusk, Wyoming. An eroded olcanic plug

ocks. Radial swarms come from volcanic cen- es or from stocks and the dykes occupy actures produced by the main body of magma ushing up and cracking the overlying rocks. arallel swarms indicate tension on a larger cale. Oceanic ridges are probably underlain y dykes stacked against each other like books n a shelf. The dykes run parallel to the ridge idicating that the ridge is being pulled apart. ne degree of extension suffered by an area an be found by adding the thicknesses of the arallel dykes. In part of Arran in the Firth of lyde the extension from the total thickness of ore than 500 dykes amounts to about 1600 . The Troodos Massif of Cyprus represents piece of ocean floor which was pushed up form land. The very numerous dykes indicate an extension of 130 km which occurred when the Troodos rocks were part of an ocean ridge.

Cone sheets occupy fractures produced by the upward push of magma in a chamber under the centre of the sheets (figure 3.4). A ring dyke occupies a fracture which encloses an area of volcanic **cauldron subsidence** (figure 3.5). Ring fractures are probably caused by the upward push of underlying magma. Following up-doming, stretching and fracture the block enclosed by the fault sinks and magma rises up the fracture to feed volcanoes at the surface. Some volcanic pipes contain rocks such as basalt. Others are filled by fragmented rock material thought to have been broken and rounded by the upward flow of seething, turbulent gas.

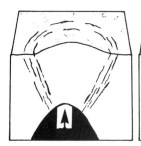

3.4 Formation of a cone sheet. The cone sheet occupies a fracture formed by the rising magma.

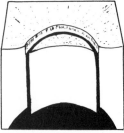

3.5 Cauldron subsidence. The rising magma forms a ring-shaped fracture. The rocks enclosed by the fracture sink and a ring dyke occupies the fracture.

Because of their very large sizes batholiths create a considerable space problem. It is probable that they rise as **diapirs** pushing the surrounding rocks aside (figure 3.6). A diapir consists of low density material which rises like

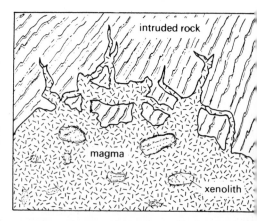

3.7 Stoping. Rising magma may eat its way through overlying rocks.

a blob of oil through water. It has been suggested that a rising batholith will 'eat' its way through the overlying rock by a process called **stoping** (figure 3.7). The intruded rock is detached and it sinks as **xenoliths** into the magma. Xenoliths ('strange stones') are fragments of pre-existing rocks found in an igneous rock. The xenoliths may be 'digested' and incorporated into the magma by a process called **assimilation**. It is probable that stoping is only a minor process in batholith emplacement.

A small xenolith seen here in a granite gravestone.

Formation and crystallization of magma

Basaltic magma is thought to form at depths of between 50 and 250 km. Between these depths the Earth is thought to consist of peridotite which is about 5 percent molten and the

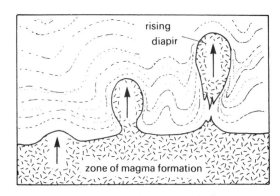

3.6 Batholiths are probably intruded as diapirs which push the surrounding rocks to one side.

saltic magma is thought to be the result of s partial fusion. By virtue of its low density e magma then rises through fractures in the erlying layers.

Granite is characteristically of continental gin. Granitic magmas are thought to form hen the heat generated by mountain building ocesses partly melts the rocks at the base the continent. While granite and granodiorite e the common plutonic rocks of the conti- nts, andesite is the common volcanic rock. desite is thought to be produced by partial elting of oceanic crust pushed under devel- ing mountain ranges.

The melting-point of a rock is affected by essure and by the presence of water. At the rth's surface, wet and dry granite both melt about 900°C. At the pressure equivalent to depth of burial of 20 km the melting-point wet granite is about 650°C while the elting-point of dry granite is about 1000°C. e melting-point of dry peridotite similarly creases with pressure from about 1200°C at e Earth's surface to about 1500°C at a depth 100 km. The melting-point of peridotite with ery small proportion of water falls from about :00°C at the surface to about 1000°C at depth of 100 km. Wet granitic magmas obably form at relatively shallow depths out 20 km) and at relatively low temperatures out 650°C). With a wet melt the freezing int rises with fall in pressure so a wet melt 650°C would probably solidify at a depth about 10 km. On the other hand, dry granitic elts can reach the surface to produce rhyolitic vas. Basaltic magmas are relatively dry so they en appear at the surface to form lavas.

n its simplest sense a magma can be thought as a group of minerals melted and mixed gether. As the magma cools the minerals with e highest freezing points will crystallize first. rther cooling will allow other minerals to ystallize until the magma solidifies. When a gh-temperature mineral forms it does not cessarily retain its identity. Instead, it reacts th the surrounding liquid so its composition anges, e.g. olivine may be the first ferromag- sian mineral to crystallize from a magma. As e temperature falls the olivine may react with e remaining liquid to form pyroxene. As the mperature falls further the pyroxene may react th the liquid to form hornblende which may en react to form biotite. A sequence such olivine → pyroxene → hornblende → biotite called a **discontinuous reaction series** because

these minerals have different structures and compositions. On the other hand, the plagio- clases form a **continuous reaction series** because the first formed calcium-rich plagio- clase reacts with the remaining liquid to give a progressively more sodic form.

Rapid cooling may not allow complete reac- tion between the early crystals and the remain- ing liquid. One effect of this non-equilibrium type of crystallization is that plagioclase crystals may be calcium-rich in the centre and sodium- rich at the edge. Such plagioclase crystals show zoning. Another effect is that two magmas of the same composition cooled at different rates may have different minerals. The rapidly cooled magma may produce a rock containing high- temperature members of a reaction series which have not been removed by reaction, e.g. granite cools slowly and it has hornblende and biotite as its ferromagnesian minerals. Rhyolite is of the same composition as granite but it cools rapidly and it may contain pyroxene or iron-rich olivine.

Early formed crystals often sink to form layers at the base of a magma chamber. Because of this the early crystals lose contact with the remaining liquid so they do not react with it. In a basaltic magma, if the first-formed minerals sink the remaining magma becomes enriched in oxides such as SiO_2, K_2O, Na_2O and H_2O. This happens because early formed minerals such as olivine, calcic plagioclase, pyroxene, magnetite, chromite and ilmenite are poor or lacking in these oxides. Rocks formed by the sinking of minerals are called **cumulates**. Cumu- lus crystals may also be deposited from con- vection currents in the magma chamber. Crys- tallization of the liquid which remains after the removal of the early cumulate fraction would give a rock more siliceous than the original magma.

The processes by which a magma separates into liquids which differ in composition from the original magma are described as **magmatic differentiation**. Magmatic differentiation leads to the formation of different kinds of igneous rock from a single parent magma. The main differentiating process is **fractional crystalliza- tion**. In fractional crystallization crystals and liquid are separated by gravity settling of early- formed crystals, by **filter pressing** in which the liquid is squeezed out of a slush-like mass of partly crystallized magma, or by crystals being carried away and deposited by convection cur- rents in the magma chamber.

A good example of the effects of gravity settling is given by the Palisades Sill of New Jersey, USA. This dolerite sill (about 300 m thick) has fine-grained **chilled margins** top and bottom where the magma has cooled rapidly on coming into contact with the intruded rock. The chilled margins consist of pyroxene and plagioclase. Above the lower chilled margin is a layer rich in olivine. Olivine then disappears and the bulk of the dolerite consists of pyroxene and plagioclase (figure 3.8). Going up through the sill the pyroxene changes from being Mg rich to being Fe rich and the plagioclase changes from being Ca rich to being Na rich. How would you account for these changes?

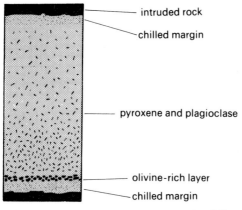

intruded rock

chilled margin

pyroxene and plagioclase

olivine-rich layer

chilled margin

3.8 Vertical section through the Palisades Sill, New Jersey, USA.

If fractionation continues to a late stage in crystallization a small quantity of low-temperature melt remains which is enriched in silica and water. Such end liquids crystallize as **pegmatites**. Pegmatites attain very coarse grain sizes because volatiles such as water aid crystal growth. Pegmatites are most often derived from acidic magmas because they contain much more water than basic magmas. Pegmatites contain minerals rich in elements such as lithium, zirconium, beryllium and tin which have been unable to enter the crystal structures of the minerals forming the main body of the rock.

You can get some idea of what happens during crystallization if you melt some salol or acetamide on a slide then watch it under a microscope. What happens? You can also study crystallization behaviour by using sodium thio-

sulphate (commonly called 'hypo'). Put crysta to a depth of about 5 cm in a boiling tub Place the tube in a water-bath at 90°C ar record the temperature every minute. When th crystals have completely melted remove th boiling tube from the water and continue record the temperature. When the liquid h cooled to about 30°C add a crystal of sodiu thiosulphate. What happens? How does th temperature change? Draw a graph showir how temperature changes with time. Can yc interpret the graph? When a magma crystallize it does not go solid all at once. Instead, nume ous crystals begin to form at scattere nucleation centres. Studies of the crystallizatic of rock melts have shown that the melts hav to be cooled below their freezing points befo crystallization begins. Such melts are said be **supercooled**. Also, rapid cooling allows f a greater degree of supercooling. With slo cooling, little supercooling is achieved and on a few crystal nuclei form. Crystal growth fro few nuclei allows the formation of large crysta so the rock becomes coarse-grained. Rap cooling leads to crystal growth from numerot nuclei so the rock which forms is fine-graine If cooling is extremely rapid the melt becom very viscous, few nuclei form and the roc solidifies as glass (figure 3.9).

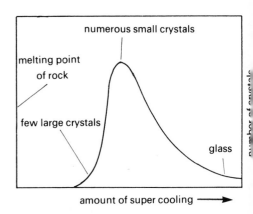

3.9 Relationship between crystal formation and supercooling in a magma.

Extrusive igneous rocks

Magma comes to the surface of the Earth a **lava** through **volcanoes** (figure 3.10). In a centr

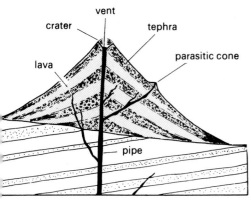

10 Section through a volcano.

vent type of eruption the magma rises through a cylindrical **pipe** and it leaves the volcano through an opening called a **vent**. Eruptions of this type may build large cones. In a **fissure** eruption the lava comes from a vertical crack and any cones which form tend to be small.

Volcanoes give off lavas, airborne fragments and gases. The main lavas are basalt, andesite and the less common trachyte and rhyolite. Sometimes very rapid cooling leads to glass formation. Rhyolite glass (obsidian) is much more common than basalt glass (tachylyte). The gas in magma tends to escape as the magma rises and pressure on it falls. When the gas does not escape fully the lava remains full of

Crater of Mount Etna, Sicily.

mall extinct volcanic nes, Craters of the oon National Monument, Idaho.

bubbles or vesicles. Basalt lavas are more often vesicular than other types especially in the upper parts of the lava flow. Lava rich in mineral-filled vesicles (amygdales) is described as being **amygdaloidal**.

At the time of the eruption, basalt lava is at a temperature of about 1100°C. Hot basalt lava flows very freely but as it cools it becomes more viscous and it solidifies with a ropy-looking surface as **pahoehoe lava** or with a rubbly surface as **aa** lava. **Pillow lava** looks like a pile of closely-packed pillows each about 1 m in diameter. Pillows result from lava extrusion under water. As the basalt flows its skin is cooled by the water but the hard skin frequently bursts and a blob of lava leaks out like toothpaste from a tube to be cooled and hardened into a pillow (figure 3.11).

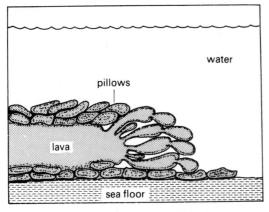

3.11 Formation of pillow lava. The cooling effect of the water causes the lava to solidify in a series of blobs.

Andesite lava is much more viscous than basalt lava so it tends to form thicker flows and it does not give pahoehoe lava. Instead, andesite flows have rough, blocky surfaces. (Rubbly intermediate or acidic lavas are sometimes called **block lavas**.) Andesites, too, usually have many more phenocrysts than basalts.

Rhyolites are extremely viscous and they tend to form short lava flows and **lava domes**. Rhyolite domes form above vents as lava added from underneath pushes up the outer cooled layers. Rhyolites very often show flow banding.

Solid airborne fragments from a volcano are called **pyroclasts**. Pyroclastic material usually comes from eruptions in which a gas-rich viscous magma suddenly separates into liquid and gas. The gas bubbles grow explosively giving a mixture of fragments and gas which is shot from the volcano. If the gas separates deep in the volcano the volcanic pipe acts like a gun barrel and the glass, mineral and rock fragments are shot high into the air. The fragments fall back to form a pyroclastic fall deposit often called **tephra**. Tephra consists of **ashes** (less than 4 mm in diameter); **lapilli** (4–32 mm in diameter); and **blocks** and **bombs** (more than 32 mm in diameter). Blocks are fragments which are solid before ejection. Bombs are lumps of molten or partly molten lava which in flight may acquire shapes something like lemons. **Bread-crust bombs** look like crusty loaves. On consolidation, ashes and lapilli form **tuffs** while blocks and bombs form **agglomerate**. **Scoria** consists of variously sized fragments of cinder-like, vesicular basic lava. **Pumice** is again highly vesicular but it is usually derived from acidic lava.

Partial destruction of Heimaey, Iceland, by ash and lava, 1973.

IGNEOUS ROCKS

When gas is suddenly released from magma close to the volcanic vent the material spills out sideways as a **pyroclastic flow** which rolls down the side of the volcano as a hot gaseous cloud similar to the base surge of a nuclear explosion. A **nuée ardente** is a moving cloud which is able to flow because the contained fragments are buoyed up by hot, turbulent gas. Nuées deposit material with a wide range of grain sizes. Large blocks may be carried in the base of the cloud while small particles are carried at the top of the cloud. One reason for the relative scarcity of rhyolite is that it is easily frothed up to make pumice which is then broken and blasted from the volcano in huge explosive clouds. The fragments are deposited as **ignimbrite**. Nuées ardentes do not travel far from their volcanoes but **ignimbrite clouds** can travel for many kilometres because the pumice particles give off gas which sustains the flowing cloud. Ignimbrite clouds have never been seen but they must be very violent. It is thought that an eruption in Alaska in 1912 produced a cloud which travelled 20 km and deposited more than 0 km³ of ignimbrite.

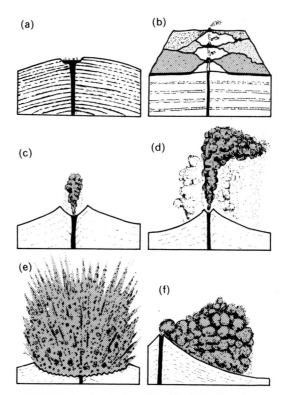

3.12 Types of volcanic eruption: (a) Hawaiian;
      (b) fissure; (c) Strombolian; (d) Vulcanian;
      (e) Krakatoan; (f) Peléan.

Types of eruption

The way in which a volcano erupts depends on the viscosity of the magma. In general, the higher the silica content the more viscous the magma. Basic lavas have a low viscosity so they run freely from fissures or from low cones of central vent type. Acidic lavas are highly viscous and since they do not flow readily away from the vent they tend to build steep cones. Acidic lavas also tend to clog up the vents often causing explosions as gas pressure builds up in the volcano. The varying degrees of explosive behaviour allow eruptive styles to be classified. A volcano may, however, show more than one type of behaviour (figure 3.12).

In **Hawaiian** eruptions the basalt lava has a very low viscosity so gas is easily released. The lack of high gas pressures means that explosive activity is slight producing lava fountains which give only small amounts of tephra. Hawaiian type eruptions may build huge, gently sloping **shield volcanoes**. Mauna Loa, Hawaii, is the world's largest volcano. Its diameter on the sea floor is 480 km and its height from the sea floor is 9.75 km. **Strombolian** eruptions produce

basaltic lava which is more viscous than that from Hawaiian type volcanoes. Gas is released every few minutes in small explosions. **Vulcanian** eruptions are markedly explosive producing large clouds of tephra and gas above the volcano. **Vesuvian** eruptions are more explosive still with huge clouds spreading tephra over large areas. **Plinian** eruptions are extremely violent Vesuvian eruptions. Huge quantities of tephra are produced and large parts of the volcanic cone are blown away. This style of eruption is named after Pliny the Younger's description of the eruption of Vesuvius which devastated Pompeii in AD 79. Pompeii was buried by about 3 m of tephra which killed about 2000 of its 20 000 inhabitants. Bodies buried by the ash decayed leaving cavities which when filled with plaster produced detailed casts of the corpses. Pompeii, south-west of Vesuvius, suffered badly from the tephra fall because it was down-wind of the volcano. Herculaneum to the west of Vesuvius was buried to a depth of 20 m by ignimbrite.

Of all eruptions, **Krakatoan** are the most violent. Here, the volcanic cone is almost entirely blown away by enormous explosions. Krakatoa itself lies between Java and Sumatra It erupted in 1883 with an explosion that was heard nearly 5000 km away. About 18 km³ of material were ejected into an explosive plume which reached a height of about 80 km. Huge waves drowned about 36 000 people on neighbouring islands.

Peléan eruptions produce pyroclastic flows from the sides of volcanoes whose vents are choked with extremely viscous lava. Mont Pelée is on the island of Martinique in the Caribbean. In 1902 it gave off a nuée ardente which rolled over the nearby port of St. Pierre killing about 30 000 people in two or three minutes.

The eruptions of Mount St. Helens, northwest USA, which took place in 1980 have been very well documented. The main eruption o 18 May began when the north side of th mountain slid away to form an avalanche fluic ized by steam. The avalanche of broken rock an ice flowed down valleys at speeds of up t 250 km h⁻¹ forming a deposit 21 km long 1–2 km wide and up to 150 m deep. As th avalanche began to move it released the press ure on the magma inside the volcano. Explosiv gas release produced a debris-laden steam cloud which surged north at speeds of up t 400 km h⁻¹ devastating an area of about 55 km². The ash cloud produced by the eruptio quickly reached a height of over 20 km. Th ash was carried east by the wind; on 19 Ma a slight amount of ash fell on Denver 160 km from the volcano and by 21 May the as cloud had crossed the USA.

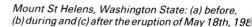

Mount St Helens, Washington State: (a) before, (b) during and (c) after the eruption of May 18th, 198

(a)

(b)

(c)

IGNEOUS ROCKS

Fissure eruptions occur when lava runs from long fractures in the Earth's surface. At ocean ridges the ocean floor is moving apart and basalts come to the sea floor through cracks running parallel to the ridges. On land, fissure eruptions are marked by a string of small cones. Fissure eruptions in Iceland, where the Mid-Atlantic Ridge rises above sea level, produce large volumes of very fluid lava. Such eruptions are sometimes called **flood eruptions**. In 1783 at Laki, Iceland, basalt ran from a fissure 30 km long. Over a period of six months 12 km³ of lava covered an area of about 600 km². **Flood basalts** or **plateau basalts** are also found in continental areas. They cover large areas in places such as western USA and India. In Britain, flood basalts form the Clyde Plateau round Glasgow and the Antrim Plateau of Northern Ireland. The Hawaiian Islands are formed by volcanoes intermediate between central vent and fissure type because the lava comes from craters on fissure zones.

Calderas

A **caldera** is a giant crater. Calderas up to a diameter of about 1.5 km may form by the blowing away of volcanic cones. Larger calderas form by the collapse of a cone into a partly emptied magma chamber. To begin with, the ground surface may be pushed up by the intrusion of acidic magma. The magma escapes as ignimbrite through cracks in the arched foot of the magma chamber. The roof then sinks by cauldron subsidence into the partly vacated chamber (figure 3.13). The world's largest caldera is the Lake Toba Caldera of Sumatra. It measures 50 by 20 km. The best known caldera is Crater Lake in Oregon, USA. It has diameter of about 10 km.

Predicting eruptions

Trying to say when a volcano will erupt depends on the collection and assessment of detailed information. Evidence may come from studying the history of a volcano to find if it erupts at regular intervals. This approach does not allow exact predictions to be made but it may allow an apparently extinct volcano to be identified as potentially dangerous. Monitoring earthquake activity provides very useful information. Eruptions are often preceded by swarms of

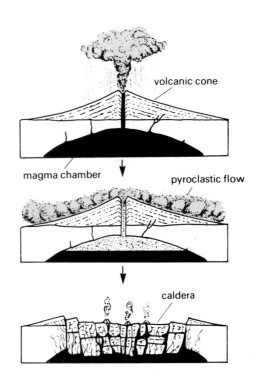

3.13 A caldera is formed by the sinking of a volcano into its underlying magma chamber.

small, shallow earthquakes. In the two months before the major eruption of Mount St. Helens on 18 May 1980, thousands of earthquakes occurred about 2 km below the north flank of the mountain. The earthquakes indicated that magma was being injected into this part of the volcano. Visual observations and accurate surveying of a volcano may also help to predict eruptions. Aerial photographs can be turned into very accurate maps, laser beams allow distances to be measured very accurately and instruments called tiltmeters detect tilting of the ground surface. On Mount St. Helens a bulge was seen to form on the north side of the mountain on 27 March 1980. By 12 April the bulge was 2 km in diameter and it had swollen up by 100 m. In early May the bulge was swelling at the rate of 1.5 m a day. On Kilauea, Hawaii, tiltmeters have detected swelling on the side of the mountain for two years before eruptions. Other, less useful, information comes from: infra-red aerial photography to find if any hot areas are developing; changes in the magnetic and electrical fields round a volcano; and changes in the composition and volume of escaping gases, liquids and solids.

Hydrothermal alteration and pneumatolysis

The water and other volatiles left towards the end of magma crystallization may react with the newly formed igneous rock or with the surrounding country rock, e.g. **hydrothermal fluids** (hot, watery solutions) affected parts of the granite of south-west England. The orthoclase was altered to kaolinite while the quartz and mica remained unchanged. In **pneumatolysis** the alteration is caused by volatiles (perhaps gaseous) other than water, e.g. in **tourmalinization** boron-rich volatiles react with earlier minerals to produce tourmaline. **Greisen** is a granite altered to quartz, white mica and topaz. The mica may be rich in fluorine or lithium. Ore minerals may be deposited by both hydrothermal and pneumatolytic action.

SURFACE PROCESSES

The surface of the Earth is made up of features such as hills, valleys and plains. Features such as these are called **landforms**. **Landscapes** are made up of landforms, e.g. a coastal landscape might include landforms such as cliffs and beaches. **Geomorphology** is the study of the origin and change of landforms and landscapes Landforms may result from internal processes, e.g. volcanic mountains, or from surface processes, e.g. deltas. Surface processes include **weathering** and **erosion**. Weathering is the breakdown of exposed rocks and erosion is the removal of rock and mineral fragments by water, wind and ice. Weathering and erosion operate together to lower the surface of the land and their combined effects are known as **denudation**.

Weathering

Rock breakdown may take place by physical, chemical and biological processes. In **physical** or **mechanical** weathering the rock is broken into fragments without being chemically changed. This may take place in various ways.

Rocks such as granite which are formed at depth suffer pressure release when they are exposed at the Earth's surface. The release of pressure allows the rock to expand and this causes the rock to split by large-scale **exfoliation** or flaking away along cracks or **sheet joints** which lie roughly parallel to the ground surface. Large-scale exfoliation may give rise to bare, rounded hills sometimes called **exfoliation domes**.

The effects of the expansion and contraction of rock caused by daily temperature changes are not completely known. Laboratory experiments have shown that fresh rock is unaffected by repeated heating and cooling over the type of daily temperature changes found at the Earth's surface. (The maximum daily ranges of about 50°C occur in hot deserts.) However, if the rock has been weakened by chemical processes or if the rock is cooled with water then it may break by splitting or by small-scale exfoliation.

Water freezing in cracks in rocks, by virtue of the fact that it expands by about 10 percent, exerts an enormous pressure which can break the rock apart by a process called **frost shattering** or **frost riving**. Frost shattering is especially effective where daily temperatures rise above and fall below freezing point. Growth of salt crystals in rock can also lead to disintegration. This process is sometimes called **salt weathering**.

Chemical weathering processes all take place in solution and they result in the formation of solutions and new minerals by various chemical reactions.

Minerals may be directly dissolved by water. Mineral solubilities, which are generally very slight, depend on factors such as the temperature, pH (a measure of acidity or alkalinity) and oxygen content of the water. Increase in temperature causes a general increase in mineral solubilities. Quartz dissolves over a wide pH range but is most soluble in alkaline water. (Acidic water can dissolve about 0.12 g SiO_2 per litre whereas slightly alkaline water can dissolve about 0.6 gl^{-1}.) Sulphide minerals are relatively insoluble but in the presence of oxygen, sulphides may be converted to soluble sulphates.

When minerals combine with oxygen they are said to have been **oxidized**. Iron-containing silicates such as olivine, amphibole, pyroxene and biotite may be altered by oxidation to give iron oxides such as haematite and limonite. This causes a red-brown weathering crust to develop on iron-containing rocks.

Carbonation is the reaction of minerals with the carbonic acid produced by the solution of carbon dioxide in water. Carbonation causes limestones to be rapidly dissolved in the manner shown by the following equation:

$$H_2CO_3 + CaCO_3 \rightarrow Ca^{2+} + 2HCO_3^-$$

carbonic acid   calcite   calcium ion   hydrogen carbonate ions

In **hydration** water molecules enter the mineral lattice. Since it is held in weak chemical combination the water can be easily driven off. An example of hydration is the reversible change between anhydrite and gypsum:

$$CaSO_4 \;+\; 2H_2O \;\rightleftharpoons\; CaSO_4.2H_2O$$
$$\text{anhydrite} \qquad\qquad\qquad \text{gypsum}$$

Since hydration is accompanied by volume increase the growth of hydrated minerals in rocks can exert pressures which may cause the rocks to break up.

The most important weathering reaction is **hydrolysis** in which minerals break down by reacting with water. Under acidic conditions clay minerals may be produced by the hydrolysis of feldspar:

$$2KAlSi_3O_8 + 2H^+ + H_2O \rightarrow$$
$$\text{orthoclase}$$
$$2K^+ + Al_2Si_2O_5(OH)_4 + 4SiO_2$$
$$\text{kaolinite}$$

Generally, the acid present is carbonic acid so potassium carbonate is a common product of the reaction.

Organisms contribute to rock breakdown by both physical and chemical means. Roots can exert considerable pressures and they can prise rocks apart by growing into previously formed cracks. You may have seen similar effects where tree roots lift and crack pavements and roads. In general, chemical weathering is speeded up by organisms and their products, e.g. lichens slowly dissolve the rock which they encrust and bacteria can aid the solution of silica. Respiration of soil organisms causes the carbon dioxide level of soil air to rise to levels about one hundred times those of the atmosphere. The carbon dioxide can then be dissolved to produce carbonic acid. Organic compounds help considerably in dissolving iron. Water in swampy areas may have much more dissolved iron than the water of other areas.

Resistance of minerals to weathering

Many rocks are formed under high temperatures and pressures and the minerals which they contain are stable under the conditions of rock formation. Under the new conditions present at the Earth's surface these minerals are unstable so they tend to react to form stable weathering products.

In general, silicate minerals with high proportions of silicon are more stable than minerals rich in metal ions, e.g. olivine (Mg_2SiO_4) is less stable than pyroxene ($MgSiO_3$) and anorthite ($CaAl_2Si_2O_8$) is less stable than albite ($NaAlSi_3O_8$). This means that minerals formed at high temperatures are less resistant to weathering than minerals formed at low temperatures. Minerals can be arranged in order of their resistance to chemical weathering as follows:

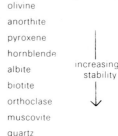

olivine
anorthite
pyroxene
hornblende
albite   increasing stability
biotite
orthoclase
muscovite
quartz

How does this sequence compare with the crystallization sequence of minerals in igneous rocks?

Chemical weathering effectively separates the elements of weathered minerals into various products. Quartz is very resistant so it accumulates as a residue. The silicon in silicates along with aluminium and some potassium ends up in clay minerals. Iron is oxidized to insoluble $Fe(OH)_3$. Calcium, magnesium, sodium and some potassium are removed in solution.

Resistance of rocks to weathering

The resistance of rocks to weathering depends on numerous factors. In general, igneous and metamorphic rocks are more resistant than sedimentary rocks because crystalline rocks are not porous so water cannot penetrate them. Also, rocks composed of quartz are more resistant than rocks made of silicates. Since limestones are composed of carbonate minerals they have little resistance to chemical weathering because they are readily attacked by carbonic acid. Well-bedded and fractured rocks tend to weather faster than massive, unfractured rocks. In addition, coarse-grained rocks are generally less resistant than fine-grained rocks. Overall, the most resistant rock is metaquartzite followed, in order, by granite, basalt, sandstone, siltstone and limestone. Where igneous rocks

SURFACE PROCESSES

The Devil's Marbles, Northern Territory, Australia are huge granite boulders produced by spheroidal weathering.

...ich as basalt and dolerite are cracked or ...inted into blocks, the blocks are often attacked ...y chemical weathering in such a way that shells ...decomposed rock flake off in a chemically ...aused form of exfoliation known as **spheroidal ...onion weathering**.

...actors which influence weathering

...sually, all types of weathering operate together ...o break down rocks. Climatic differences, ...nough, dictate the dominant weathering pro...esses. Since the rates of chemical reaction ...ouble for every increase of 10°C and since ...hemical weathering requires water, it follows ...at humid, tropical areas will show the effects ...f chemical weathering most strongly. In tem...erate regions the end-product of feldspar ...ecomposition is clay but in the wet tropics ...lays are broken down further. Their silica is ...arried away in solution to leave insoluble, ...ydrated aluminium oxides along with hydrated ...on oxides to form a soil called **laterite**. Laterites ...ave had all their soluble constituents washed ...own to lower levels by a process called ...eaching.

In tropical deserts physical processes domi...ate. Any water which is present tends to be ...rawn to the rock surface. Here, it evaporates ...nd leaves its dissolved salts whose growing ...rystals cause the rock to disintegrate. Sheet ...oints allow steep slopes and cliff faces to

persist. Salt weathering also helps to maintain cliffs because it undercuts them by causing cavities to form at their bases.

In temperate areas physical and chemical weathering operate together so that, in general, neither is dominant. Precipitation is, however, very variable from place to place so in dry areas physical processes may dominate while in wet areas chemical processes may be the major factors in rock breakdown. In temperate regions, chemical processes reach only a few metres below the surface whereas in the humid tropics such weathering may penetrate over 100 m. In winter, frost shattering is the dominant process. Indeed, you may have seen its effects in causing damage to roads.

Under Arctic conditions and on cold mountain tops the low temperatures mean that the dominant weathering processes are physical. Frost shattering is the most important process accompanied by subsidiary salt weathering and hydration.

Mass movement

The downward movement of material under gravity is called **mass movement** or **mass wastage**. Water is often involved in mass movement since it provides the moving material with extra weight and lubrication. The processes by which movement takes place are creep, flow, slide and fall.

Creep is the exceedingly slow movement of **regolith**. Regolith is the layer of broken and weathered rock above the unweathered **bedrock**. The main creep movements are caused by wetting and drying or by freezing and thawing. Expansion of the regolith by wetting or freezing pushes particles out at right angles to the slope. On drying or thawing the regolith shrinks but because of the effects of gravity the particles tend to move vertically downwards instead of back to their original positions. In this way the particles move progressively downwards (figure 4.1). In easily deformed materials such as clays, creep can take place by a continuous process quite like the flow of a very viscous liquid. The rate at which creep takes place decreases rapidly from the regolith surface down to the bedrock. In one reported case the surface rate was 5 cm per year, at a depth of 10 cm the creep rate was 3.8 cm a year while at a depth of 60 cm the rate had decreased to zero. Surface rates vary a great deal depending on slope, type of material in transit and degree of saturation. Rates are usually less than about 10 cm per year but rates as high as 45 cm a year have been recorded.

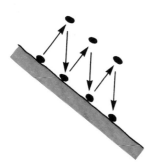

4.1 Creep of particles down a slope. Wetting or freezing of the soil pushes the particles out at right angles to the slope. Drying or thawing then allows the particles to move vertically downwards.

Creep causes numerous visible effects such as the piling up of soil on the uphill sides of walls and hedges and the cracking of hillside roads and pavements. Since the surface soil layers creep faster than the underlying layers, fences, poles, walls and gravestones are tilted with their tops pointing downhill. Trees on hillsides often have bent trunks because after being tilted they then grow vertically upwards. On steep slopes, small step-like features called **terracettes** form in a roughly horizontal direc-

tion. Creep also causes steeply inclined beds to bend downslope just below the surface (figure 4.2).

4.2 Some effects of soil creep.

Soil creep causes fences to tilt and trees to grow with bent trunks.

Flow may begin when the regolith is saturated with water. In tundra regions a thawed layer may form in summer above permanently frozen layers beneath. The soggy surface layer behaves something like thick porridge and it may flow downhill in lobe-like masses by a process called **solifluction** (soil flow) at a rate of a few centimetres a day. On slopes steeper than about 30° saturated regolith may run downhill as **earthflows** along narrow tracks at speeds of up to about $15ms^{-1}$. Earthflows do not travel very far once they reach the valley floor because their water rapidly drains away so the debris particles are no longer buoyed up. In semi-arid mountainous regions heavy rain picks up large quantities of weathered fragments. The resultant slurries run along valley floors as **mudflows**. Mudflows may run for many kilometres before

SURFACE PROCESSES

ater loss causes the mud to thicken and stop
owing.

Landslides result from sudden movement
ong surfaces of weakness. Regolith tends to
de, especially when saturated, on planes
rallel to the slope surface. The failure surfaces
ay lie on soil horizons, bedrock surfaces or
rmafrost boundaries. Sometimes, after the
golith begins to slide the material disinte-
ates and begins to flow because the debris
rticles are buoyed up by water. A slide of
s type devastated part of Aberfan, Wales, in
66 when a saturated tip of coal waste flowed
o the town and killed 150 people. Such
wslides as they are called may move at speeds
up to 44ms⁻¹. Large-scale landslides usually
cur where beds dip roughly parallel to the
ope. Failure may take place because the slope
undercut and becomes unstable or sliding
ay take place on weak or impermeable layers
ch as shale which act as lubricants for the
cks above. Limestones are often involved in
des of this type because they may dissolve
vay to leave a plane of weakness between the
cks above and below. A large-scale landslide
used the Vaiont Reservoir disaster in northern
ly in 1963. In less than a minute, a landslide
early 2 km long, 1.5 km wide and 150 m thick
d into the reservoir. The water spilling out
the reservoir caused floods which killed 3000
ople. In relatively weak rocks such as clay
shale slip may occur along deep planes which

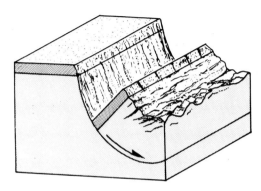

*4.3 A rotational slide. In weak rocks, slip may
occur on curved planes.*

are often curved upwards (figure 4.3). Such
landslides are called **rotational slides** or **slumps**.

Rockfalls from steep slopes are produced by
weakness in the rock, by heavy rainfall and by
frost action. Rainfall causes the build up of
water pressure in cracks between weathered
blocks while the expansion of water on freezing
prises blocks apart so they fall when the thaw
sets in. Extreme drying of regolith causes it to
lose cohesion so it may crack and fall. Erosive
undercutting of slopes also causes rockfalls.
Scree or **talus** slopes at angles of about 35°
form as a result of the accumulation of fallen
material.

rockfall from a chalk cliff near Dover in Kent.

Scree slope at Great Gable in the Lake District

Ground water

There are thought to be about 1500 million km³ of water at or near the Earth's surface. Of this, about 97.3 percent is in the oceans, 2.7 percent is on land and about 0.0001 per cent is in the atmosphere. Table 4.1 shows how much water is found in places such as lakes and rivers and how much occurs as ice.

LOCATION OF WATER	VOLUME PRESENT (km³)
Oceans	1 370 000 000
Atmosphere	13 000
In rocks	60 000 000
Glacier ice	29 000 000
Rivers	1700
Swamps	3600
In soils	65 000
Lakes and reservoirs	125 000

Table 4.1 Distribution of water at or near the Earth's surface

The circulation of water between the sea, the land and the atmosphere is called the **water** or **hydrological cycle**. The volumes of water which are exchanged each year are shown in figure 4.4.

Rain water may collect in lakes and rivers o it may enter or infiltrate the soil and percolate downwards into the regolith and rocks. The por spaces of the surface regolith may be occupie by air with a thin water film on the grains. A some distance below the surface the por spaces may be completely filled with water. The surface which separates the saturated and unsaturated zones is called the **water table** and the water beneath this surface is called **groun water**. Ground water which comes from pre cipitation is called **meteoric water**. **Connate water** is trapped in sedimentary rocks during their formation and is buried with them. Con nate water is usually deep below the surface It tends to be salty and rich in dissolved min erals. A small quantity of water may be derive from deep within the Earth by igneous pro cesses. Such water is described as being **juvenile**.

The quantity of water held in a rock or i the regolith depends on the amount of por space between the grains. This is given in term of **porosity** which is defined as follows:

$$\text{porosity} = \frac{\text{volume of pore space}}{\text{total volume of rock}} \times 100\%$$

Porosity does not depend on grain size bu it does depend on factors such as grain shap and on how the grains are packed togethe

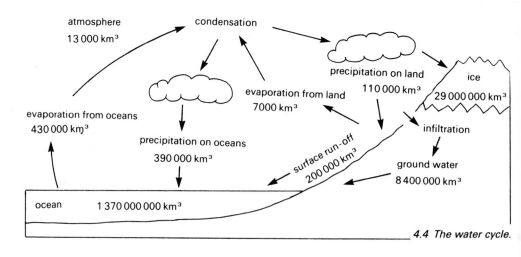

4.4 The water cycle.

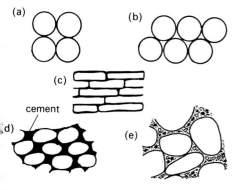

5 Factors affecting porosity. In (a) the porosity is nearly 50%; in (b) it is just over 25%; in (c) and (d) it is 0%. In (e) porosity is reduced by the presence of small grains between the larger grains.

figure 4.5 (a) the grains are all spheres packed one on top of the other. In a material like this the porosity is nearly 50 percent. Where spherical grains are packed more closely with each grain sitting in the depression formed by the four grains underneath the porosity is just over 25 percent. Porosity also depends on the amount of cement and smaller grains between the larger grains. Since igneous and metamorphic rocks are made up of interlocking grains they are virtually non-porous. Sedimentary rocks and loose surface materials may have high porosities. The porosities of some common materials are given in table 4.2

Permeability is a measure of the ease with which a fluid can pass through a rock. **Per-**

MATERIAL	APPROXIMATE POROSITY (%)
Limestone	10
Sandstone	18
Shale	18
Clay	45
Sand	35
Gravel	25
Granite	1
Basalt	1

Table 4.2 Porosities of geological materials

meable rocks allow liquids and air to pass through fairly easily while **impermeable** rocks do not allow fluids to pass through. Materials with the largest pore spaces have the greatest permeabilities so rocks of equal porosity do not necessarily have equal permeabilities, e.g. shale and sandstone may both have porosities of about 20 percent but sandstone is much more permeable because its larger pore spaces offer less resistance to fluid movement. Gravel is very permeable because it has very large pore spaces.

It should be noted that the formation of cavities and fractures (joints and faults) in rocks may render them more porous and more permeable. Limestones may become very permeable because water enlarges cavities by solution as it passes through. Also, igneous rocks may be made permeable by the presence of joints.

Springs and wells

While the water table follows the surface topography it has a more subdued form. Lakes, marshes and rivers occur where the land surface is below the water table (figure 4.6). **Springs** or lines of **seepage** occur where the water table meets the ground surface. This often happens where the water table has been deflected to the surface by the presence of an impermeable rock such as a shale or an igneous rock. Some of the geological conditions giving rise to springs are shown in figure 4.7. Since the water flows from such springs under the action of gravity they are sometimes called **gravity springs**.

An **aquifer** is a porous and permeable rock or body of surface material from which water flows relatively easily. An **unconfined aquifer** is not covered by impermeable rock; a **confined aquifer** is sandwiched between impermeable beds called **aquicludes**. **Perched aquifers** are bodies of permeable rock which hold water

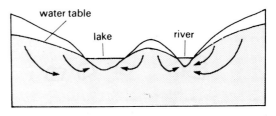

4.6 The relationship of the water table to the ground surface. The arrows indicate the directions of ground water flow.

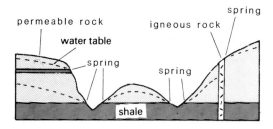

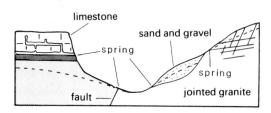

*4.7 Some positions at which springs appear. The
shale and igneous rock are impermeable.*

the water to the surface. In a non-flowing
artesian well the water in the well rises above
the aquifer but it does not come all the way
to the surface. Where the aquifer is folded into
a large, wide downfold an **artesian basin** is
formed. A well-known artesian basin covers
about 1.5 million km² of eastern Australia. The
sandstone aquifer picks up water in its outcrop
along the Eastern Highlands and the water
migrates beneath the arid region west of the
mountains where it is tapped by the wells up
to 1.5 km deep.

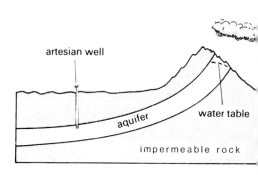

*4.8 An artesian well. Water pressure in the
aquifer pushes the water to the surface.*

above the regional water table. The most common aquifers are sandstones, limestones, sands
and gravels. **Wells** are holes dug or drilled to
the water table or into an aquifer for the purpose
of extracting water. The water surface in the
well is at the same level as the water table and
extraction of water lowers the water table.
Normally, water has to be drawn or pumped
from a well but in an **artesian well** the water
from an aquifer is under enough pressure to
make it flow out at the surface. **Hydrostatic
pressure** is the water pressure at any point in
a body of water at rest. Hydrostatic pressure
increases with depth. The **hydrostatic** or
hydraulic head is the height of a vertical column
of water (of unit cross-section) whose weight
equals the hydrostatic pressure at its base. If
areas of high and low hydrostatic pressure are
connected, water flows from the area of high
pressure towards the area of low pressure. The
hydraulic gradient is the difference in hydrostatic pressure between two points divided by
the distance between them. The slope of a water
table would be its hydraulic gradient. For artesian conditions an inclined or downfolded confined aquifer is exposed up-dip in a raised area
where it can take in rain water (figure 4.8). The
difference in level between the water table and
the point where the well strikes the aquifer
produces a hydrostatic pressure which forces

London lies in a basin underlain by Chalk
forming an aquifer downfolded between the
Chiltern Hills and the North Downs. Formerly
the water in the Chalk was tapped by flowing
artesian wells. Indeed, the fountains of Trafalgar
Square were originally supplied by artesian
water. Now, over-extraction has lowered the
water table so much that water can only be
obtained by pumping. It used to be, too, that
where the aquifer came to the surface water
flowed from artesian springs into the Thames.
At present, flow is the other way so parts of
the Chalk aquifer have been contaminated by
salty tidal water.

Some **oases** are springs of artesian water
which occur where an aquifer reaches the
surface because of folding or faulting (figure
4.9). Most of the aquifers of North Africa are
sandstones which receive their water in areas
such as the Atlas Mountains and the Tibesti
and Ahaggar Highlands. In parts of the Sahara
it has been found that the water in the aquifer
flows about 50 m in a year. How long would
it take for water to travel from the surface
catchment area to an oasis 1000 km away?

SURFACE PROCESSES

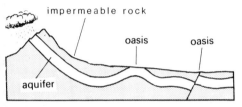

impermeable rock

oasis   oasis

aquifer

9 Conditions giving rise to oases. The aquifer
may come to the surface or the water may
rise up a fault.

Water in limestone regions

ainwater dissolves carbon dioxide from the air
nd from the soil atmosphere to form carbonic
cid. This weak acid dissolves limestone along
acture surfaces and bedding planes and a
mestone mass may become honeycombed by
averns and channels. On the limestone a
istinctive **karst landscape** is developed (figure
.10). Karst regions have little or no surface
rainage. Dry valleys are common. These valleys
ere probably cut by rivers which existed during
mes when rainfall was much heavier than at
resent. Alternatively, the rivers may have run
ver ground frozen during parts of the last Ice
ge. Streams may disappear into **swallow** or
nk holes then run through the limestone to
merge at the base of the limestone mass
erhaps in a gorge cut to the level of the water
ible. **Gorges** may form both by river erosion
nd by the collapse of cave roofs. **Dolines** are
epressions formed by dissolving of the lime-
one or by the collapse of cave roofs. On the
urface, limestone becomes grooved and pitted
rain water to give **lapiés** or **karren**. Lapiés
e furrows dissolved as the water trickles down
e rock. Exposed limestone which is fractured
jointed may form a **limestone pavement** con-
sting of blocks called **clints** separated by open
racks called **grikes**. Water which drips from
e roofs of caves may deposit **dripstone** on the
of and floor as **stalactites** and **stalagmites**
spectively. Banded **travertine** may be depos-
ed on cave walls by downward trickling water.
ripstone and travertine both consist of calcium
arbonate which is precipitated because the
ater evaporates slightly and gives off some
arbon dioxide on exposure to the air in the
ave. The water becomes less acidic so the
lubility of the calcium carbonate is reduced.
owstone is a deposit like travertine found in
nderground streams.

*4.10 Some features of a karst landscape formed
by the solution of limestone.*

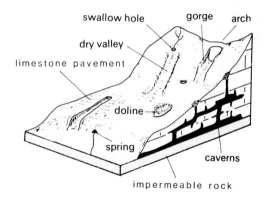

swallow hole   gorge   arch

dry valley

limestone pavement

doline

spring

caverns

impermeable rock

*A dry valley in limestone above Mal-
ham Cove, Yorkshire.*

*Limestone pavement, Malham Cove, Yorkshire.
Clints are separated by open grikes.*

Dripstone formations in the Hall of Giants, Carlsbad Caverns, New Mexico.

Hot springs and geysers

In volcanic areas water may be heated underground to leave the surface at **hot springs**. **Geysers** (gushers) are intermittent hot springs producing jets of steam and water usually between 30 and 60 m high. In a geyser, water is heated in a system of underground chambers (figure 4.11). The pressure of the crooked water column allows the water to be heated above its normal boiling point. Water may spill out of the mouth of the geyser because the water froths up or because the water expands by heating. Water loss causes pressure release on the water deep inside the geyser. The water

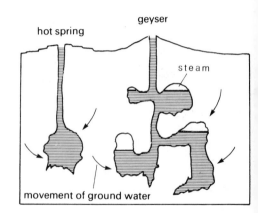

4.11 Hot spring (a) and a geyser (b). In a geyser, explosive expansion of steam in underground chambers causes an eruption.

turns to steam, expands explosively and causes an eruption. A well-known geyser is Old Faithful, Yellowstone National Park, Wyoming. It erupts for a few minutes every hour or so.

The water which emanates from hot springs and geysers is rich in dissolved calcium hydrogen carbonate or silica which are precipitated in mounds and terraces at the spring or geyser mouth as the emerging water is suddenly cooled. The hydrogen carbonate is precipitated as travertine (calcium carbonate) while the silica forms **siliceous sinter** or **geyserite**.

Old Faithful Geyser, Yellowstone National Park, Wyoming.

Travertine (calcium carbonate) deposits, Mammoth Hot Springs, Yellowstone National Park, Wyoming

SURFACE PROCESSES

*biling mud in the hot springs at Rotorua, New
aland.

ivers

a stream or river, water runs within the
onfines of a channel. Because of friction
etween the water and the channel walls the
elocity of the stream is zero against the channel
nd it increases to reach its maximum velocity
the middle, near-surface part of the stream.
ou can get a good idea of the average velocity
a stream by finding the velocity of a floating
oject then multiplying your answer by 0.8. The
scharge of a stream is a measure of the
mount of water carried. Discharge is given in
ubic metres per second ($m^3\,s^{-1}$) and it is found
y multiplying the average velocity by the cross-
ectional area of the stream. Discharge is a very
mportant property because studies of rivers
ave shown that it controls other stream char-
cteristics, e.g. the width, depth and velocity
a stream increase as discharge increases.
ischarge increases downstream so channel
idth and depth increase downstream. Surpris-
gly, perhaps, the average velocity also
creases downstream even though the slope
gradient down which the stream flows tends
decrease downstream. The increase in vel-
city comes about because in large channels
e water suffers less friction on the channel
alls. Also, the channel tends to be smooth in
e lower part of rivers so little turbulence is
roduced. Narrow, rough-walled upland
reams tend to be very turbulent and this
onstant churning means that the water spends
uch of its time flowing backwards or sideways.
Discharge can be measured at some point
a stream and it can be plotted against time

to give a **hydrograph** (figure 4.12). Hydrographs
may show discharge over a period of a few days
to find the effects of short-term weather conditions or they may show seasonal variations
in discharge.

Before entering streams water may run down
slopes in much the same way that rainwater
runs down windows. This unchannelled flow is
called **sheetwash**. On soft, easily eroded surfaces such as bare soil the water may erode
very small channels called **rills** which may then
enlarge to form deep, V-shaped **gullies**.

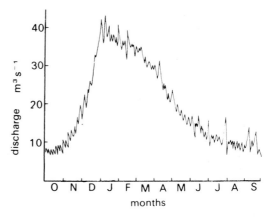

*4.12 Hydrograph showing the discharge of a
stream over a year.*

Erosion, transport and deposition by rivers

Erosion by rivers takes place in three ways.
Firstly, the water itself can wear away weak or
loose material. More effective is the process
of **abrasion** where particles carried by the water
strike the bottom and sides of the stream channel and slowly grind them away. Streams also
erode by dissolving, to various extents, the rocks
over which they flow. This dissolving process
is called **corrosion**.

The material carried by a river is its **load**. The
amount of material which can be be carried
tends to increase as discharge increases. Part
of the load consists of dissolved materials
making up about 120 parts per million (ppm)
of the river water. Hydrogen carbonate is the
most abundant dissolved material with calcium,
silica and sulphate in lesser quantities. Still less
abundant are chloride and sodium. The **suspended load** consists of very small particles

which are held up in the water so they travel without touching the bed of the stream. The **bed load** travels by bouncing, rolling and sliding along the stream bed. In general, the bed load is about one-tenth the mass of the suspended load.

The factors which cause particles to be moved or to be taken up into suspension are the forces of drag and lift generated mainly by turbulence in the flowing water. Water flow which is laminar or non-turbulent is much less effective at generating these forces. Non-turbulent, rapid water moves material more effectively than water which flows slowly since it generates uplift on the particles on the stream bed in much the same way that air flow over a wing provides the uplift which allows planes and birds to fly (figure 4.13). After being lifted a particle tends to sink back to the stream bed. While sinking it is carried along in the current so as it moves it describes a series of loops (figure 4.14). Large particles such as boulders may only suffer infrequent movement when the stream is in spate while smaller particles may be in nearly continuous transit. The removal of small particles means that many stream beds consist of pebbles and boulders. Some shallow, upland streams receive more sediment than they can

transport. In this case the channel fills up with sediment and the stream is separated by long bars of sand and gravel into numerous branches. Such a stream is said to be **braided**. In a braided stream the bed load may be more than half of the total load.

Deposition of transported material such as **alluvium** or river sediment takes place where turbulence and velocity decrease. Deposition takes place in various places. Where a stream runs suddenly from a steep mountain valley onto a plain it dumps its sediment in the form of an **alluvial cone** or **alluvial fan** (figure 4.15). Deposition commonly takes place on the insides of river bends because, here, the current flows much more slowly than it does on the outside of bends. Such deposits are **point bars**. Where a river runs into the sea or into a lake it may deposit sediment in the form of a **delta** which may extend into the water as sediment is added to its outer margin. In its lower course a river may deposit alluvium in the form of a flat **flood plain** (figure 4.18).

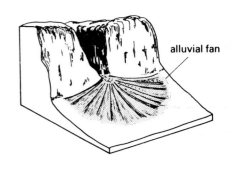

alluvial fan

4.15 An alluvial fan formed where a stream runs from a steep mountain valley onto a plain.

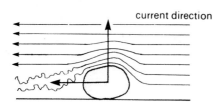

current direction

4.13 Water flowing over a particle generates forces which tend to lift the particle or to drag it along.

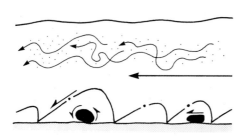

4.14 Particles carried by a stream may slide, roll, bounce or be carried in suspension.

River courses

River courses can be divided into three main parts. In the upper course the narrow stream channels lie in steep, V-shaped valleys characterized by the presence of interlocking **spurs**. **Pot-holes** may be present in the rock exposed in the bed of the stream. Pot-holes are cylindrical holes cut by swirling pebbles and boulders. The initial hollows which are later enlarged into pot-holes may form by a process called **cavitation** or bubble erosion. In very

SURFACE PROCESSES

The alluvial fan at Jullerstrasse, Switzerland, was deposited by a river running from a hanging glacial trough. It is possible to see scree slopes, truncated spurs, arêtes, cirques and horns.

urbulent water rapid increases in velocity cause ressure reductions which lead to the formation f bubbles. When the velocity falls the bubbles collapse violently producing shock waves which shatter the surface of the rock. Cavitation also lays a part in the erosion of deep pools (plunge ools) below waterfalls.

In its middle course the river channel is much wider than in the upper course and the river ows in a wide valley between rounded hills. In its lower course the river channel reaches its maximum width and the river flows in loops alled **meanders** on its own flood-plain alluvium. Meanders do not result from deflection f the stream by obstacles. Indeed, the waters f the Gulf Stream meander and initially straight aboratory streams develop meanders when hey run over uniform mud. Meanders owe their hapes to the operation of chance factors and he path taken by the river is statistically the most probable under the existing energy conditions. Meanders are fairly regular features in hat the wavelength of the meander is commonly about ten times the channel width. Also, eep pools and shallow stretches alternate with ach other and the channel section changes n a regular manner (figure 4.16). In a meandering stream the water flows in a corkscrew or elical path because water tends to be flung o the outside of the bends and to compensate

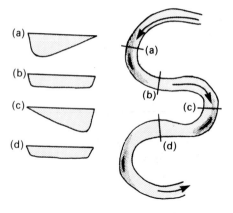

4.16 Changes in channel section of a meandering river.

for this a return flow develops over the stream bed towards the inside of the bends (figure 4.17). Meanders migrate a few metres downstream every year by continuous erosion from the outside of the bends and deposition on the point bars on the inside of the bends. In this way the flood plain alluvium is continuously reworked and transported downsteam. The scars on the flood plain left by advancing meanders are called **meander scrolls**. It often happens that the loops of a meander will intersect so the river is diverted through a short cutoff channel. The abandoned water-filled,

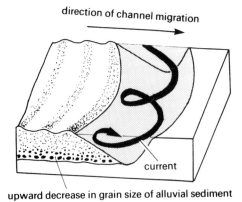

direction of channel migration

current

upward decrease in grain size of alluvial sediment

4.17 Water in a meandering river follows a cork-screw path.

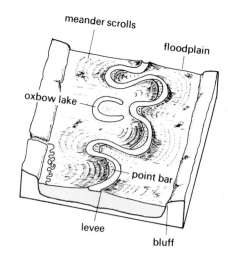

meander scrolls

floodplain

oxbow lake

point bar

levee

bluff

4.18 Features of a flood plain.

meander is left as an **ox-bow lake** (figure 4.18). When the river is in flood the water which runs over the river banks suffers a reduction in velocity and the coarser part of its suspended load is deposited adjacent to the river channel as banks called **levees**. It may happen, too, that deposition of sediment within the channel

causes the river bed to build up so the river confined by its levees, flows at a level above its surrounding flood plain. Such a situation may result in disastrous flooding so the levees may be built up and reinforced artifically.

Entrenched meander of the River Wear, Durham.

SURFACE PROCESSES

River profiles

A river profile is a curve which shows the slope of a river from source to mouth. A stream flowing over irregular terrain may have waterfalls, rapids and lakes along its course. Eventually, though, the stream will wear away the irregularities to leave a smoothly curving profile called a **graded profile** (figure 4.19). Such profiles are concave upwards with their steepest gradients near the source of the river. The gradient lessens downstream because the river gets bigger downstream and the water flows more efficiently in a large channel. The limit to which rivers can erode is called **base level**. It corresponds to sea level for rivers flowing to the sea.

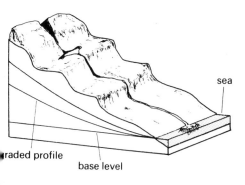

sea

graded profile

base level

4.19 Irregularities in a stream are worn down till a smooth graded profile is achieved.

Rejuvenation of rivers

If the land rises or if sea level falls a river begins to erode more actively down towards the lowered base level. When this happens the river is said to have been **rejuvenated** (made young again). A rejuvenated river may cut a gorge-like valley. It may also happen that flood-plain sediments are cut through and their remains may be left on the valley sides as **river** or **alluvial terraces**. Successive phases of rejuvenation may leave more than one set of alluvial terraces, e.g. study of the alluvial terraces and buried channels of the Thames have indicated the occurrence of about twelve changes of sea level during the last two million years.

It should be noted that alluvial terraces do not always result from rejuvenation, e.g. a stream may receive so much sediment from a melting glacier that the river valley may be filled by alluvium. Subsequently, the climate may change causing sediment supply to cease and the river may cut down through the alluvium to leave terraces along the sides of the valley.

The meanders of a rejuvenated river may cut down into hard rock and so become **entrenched**. The gorge of the River Wear in Durham is a well-known entrenched meander. Sometimes an entrenched meander is cut off and the short cut-off channel may run under an arch such as that of Rainbow Bridge, Utah, USA.

The sea

As the wind blows over the sea it generates waves in the surface water. The size of the waves depends on various factors such as wind speed, the length of time for which the wind has been blowing and the **fetch** or distance of open sea over which the wind has been blowing (figure 4.20). The water particles in a wave move in nearly circular paths which have a slight forward motion in the direction of the wind. The diameters of water particle orbits decrease very rapidly with depth. When the depth increases by one-ninth of the wavelength the diameter of the orbit is halved. This means that wave motions virtually die out at a depth of about half the wavelength.

When waves run from deep water into shallow water, movement of the wave base is retarded by drag on the sea floor so the velocity of the particles in the top of the wave exceeds that in the bottom. This causes the wave to acquire

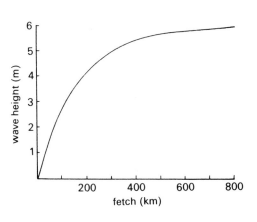

4.20 The relationship between wave height and fetch.

a higher, steeper form before it falls over or breaks (figure 4.21). You will know from having seen or taken part in surf riding that the water in breakers moves forwards. When a breaker strikes the shore, water runs up the beach as **swash** and back down as **backwash**.

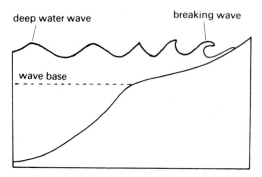

4.21 *As a wave approaches the shore it gets higher, steepens and breaks.*

You can learn a great deal about waves by studying their behaviour in a ripple tank, e.g. you can find out what happens to the speeds and directions of waves as they approach the shore. The speed of waves is given by:

$$\text{speed} = \text{frequency} \times \text{wavelength}$$

The frequency of waves in a ripple tank can be found by using a downward shining strobe lamp. The waves appear to stop when the lamp flashes with the same frequency as the waves. The wavelength can be measured directly or it can be calculated from measurements of wave shadows cast on the bench under the tank.

To find what happens when waves move into shallow water put a thin, rectangular, perspex plate on the floor of the ripple tank and pass the waves over the plate at right angles to its edge. What happens? The frequency of the waves is not changed but the wavelength decreases (figure 4.22). How does this affect the speed of the waves? Now use a perspex sheet which allows the waves to pass over an oblique boundary into shallow water. What happens? This time the waves are slowed down and their direction is changed. Such change of direction is called **refraction**. Similarly, in the sea waves are slowed when they run into

shallow water and when they approach the shore at an angle they are bent to become more nearly parallel to the shore. Indeed, waves approaching the shore at 45° or so may reach the shore at an angle of about 5°. Now in the ripple tank allow waves to pass over shapes like convex and concave lenses. What happens? The convex shape focuses the waves while the concave shape causes the waves to diverge. In the sea when waves approach a headland they run into an area of shallowing convex to the sea. This causes the waves to be focused on to the headland. On the other hand, waves approaching a bay are spread out because they run into a shallow area concave to the sea (figure 4.22). Because of these effects erosion is concentrated on headlands by the convergence and heightening of waves. Bays tend to be areas of deposition because wave energy is dispersed and the waves are very weak by the time they reach the shore.

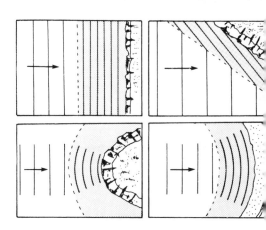

4.22 *Waves running into shallow water (shaded) slow down. Waves approaching the shore obliquely are bent to reach the shore at a lower angle. Waves running into a bay spread out while waves are focused onto head lands.*

Using a ripple tank you can also find out what happens when waves strike the end of a barrier. In this case the waves are bent round behind the barrier. The bending of waves around an obstacle is called **diffraction**. Waves with large wavelengths are diffracted more than waves with short wavelengths. Since sea waves have large wavelengths they bend a great deal behind breakwaters and harbour walls.

SURFACE PROCESSES

Now use your ripple tank to find out what happens when waves strike a barrier obliquely. Put some crystals of potassium permanganate close to the barrier to find out if any currents are produced. What do you find? In a similar way when waves strike the shore obliquely they generate currents called **longshore currents** which run parallel to the shore. These currents are found in the breaker zone and they result from the piling up of water close to the shore so the water here is slightly deeper than it would otherwise be. The focusing of waves on to headlands also makes water pile up in these areas causing longshore currents to flow from headlands into bays. Sometimes, too, the accumulation of water in the breaker zone sets up currents called **rip currents** carrying water away at a high angle to the shore.

Erosion, transport and deposition in the sea

Erosion by the sea takes place mostly by the action of the water itself and by the abrasive action of rock fragments carried by the water. The erosive power of breaking waves is well illustrated by the fact that in 1872 a 2600 tonne block from the breakwater at Wick, north-east Scotland, was lifted during a storm and dumped in the harbour. In addition to the force of the water and high speed spray the water traps and compresses air in crevices on the shore. When the wave retreats the compressed air is explosively decompressed and pieces of rock are plucked from the walls of the cracks. Shores also suffer from the effects of solution and from the activity of organisms which may bore into or loosen the rock surface. On the other hand, organisms such as barnacles may protect the shore from erosion. Above low tide level the evaporation of sea water which has soaked into rocks allows growing salt crystals to break the rock surface into small fragments.

Erosive features are best seen on steep coasts. Waves cut into the land forming a **wave-cut notch** which undermines the shoreline rocks. Collapse of the undercut rock leads to the formation of a cliff. Additionally, weak areas such as fractures or rocks of low resistance are preferentially eroded to give narrow inlets and bays. Headlands are quarried through by the development of caves which may cut through the headland to form an **arch**. Collapse of the arch roofs leaves isolated pillars called **stacks**. Continued erosion causes a cliff to retreat leaving a **wave-cut platform** which may have a **wave-built terrace** on its seaward side (figure 4.23).

A stack, Mainland, Orkney.

An arch near Portknockie, Banff.

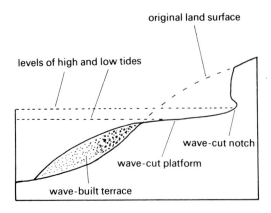

4.23 *Section through a steep coast.*

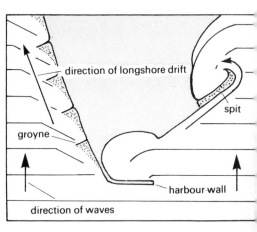

4.25 *Material moved by longshore currents can be trapped against groynes. A spit may be deposited across the mouth of a bay.*

Transport of sediment parallel to the shore is called **longshore drift**. It takes place in two ways. Firstly, in **beach drift** material is moved along a beach in a series of loops (figure 4.24). Oblique waves send material up the beach at an angle in the swash. The material then tends to move straight back down the beach in the backwash to be caught and moved again by the next wave. Secondly, in **littoral drift** sediment is transported by longshore currents. The speed at which sediment moves along the shore is very variable but rates of between 10 and 30m per hour are common. Beach drift may be slowed by building wall-like structures called **groynes** at right angles to the shore. Sediment collects against the groynes on the side from which beach drift comes (figure 4.25).

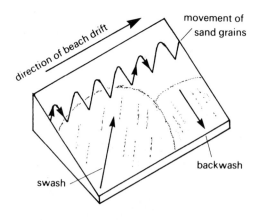

4.24 *Beach drift. Material is moved in a series of loops by the swash and backwash of waves oblique to the shore.*

Where there is an embayment in the coast longshore currents may not be maintained all the way across the bay. This results in the deposition of material across the mouth of the bay. Where the sediment is continuous with the land but ends in open water the resulting landform is a **spit**. The end of a spit is generally curved inwards because wave diffraction at the end of the spit causes longshore currents to curve round and deposit fine material behind the spit (figure 4.25). Spurn Head, Yorkshire, is a good example of a curved spit. If the sediment extends all the way, or nearly all the way, across the bay it is called a **bar** or **barrier beach**. Bars enclose lagoons, e.g. Chesil Beach in Dorset encloses a lagoon called the Fleet. A **tombolo** is a bar which runs between islands or from the mainland to an island. It should be noted that bars are not all built by longshore currents. On gently sloping coasts waves build offshore bars roughly parallel to the coastline. In Queensland, Australia, the offshore bars are roughly at right angles to the prevailing winds. On the east coast of the USA the offshore bars may represent ancient beaches left when sea level rose following the last Ice Age

Post-glacial rise in sea level has meant that coasts have been drowned and the sea has flooded pre-existing river valleys. Where only small amounts of sediment have been brought down by present day rivers or where the valleys are very deep the flooded valleys have survived as estuaries. A **ria** is a drowned river valley with a long, narrow, branching form. Good examples of rias are to be found in south-west England and in south-west Ireland. In some cases a river

SURFACE PROCESSES

A strongly curved spit, The Bar, Nairn. Note the structure of the spit and the direction in which sediment is being carried by longshore currents.

ria at the mouth of the River ...l, Cornwall.

rings down enough sediment to partly or completely fill the estuary. Where a great deal of sediment is brought down a delta may form. It should be noted that deltas can form in areas with high tidal ranges.

Types of coastline

Where the main structures of the land run into the sea at a high angle the coast is described as **tranverse** or **discordant**. This type of coast occurs in south-west Ireland. Where the main geological structures are parallel to the shore the coast is said to be of **longitudinal** or **concordant** type. The coast of Yugoslavia is largely of this type.

A coast suffering erosion is usually rocky with cliffs, headlands and stacks and with few beaches (figure 4.26). A coast where depostion is occurring would be characterized by the presence of features such as deltas, mud flats, bars, spits and extensive beaches (figure 4.27).

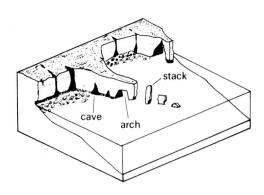

4.26 Features of a coast suffering erosion.

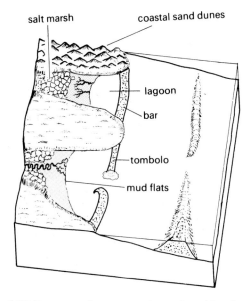

4.27 Features of a coast where deposition is dominant.

Coasts may also show signs of submergence or emergence. Submergence produces features such as estuaries and rias. There may be numerous near-shore islands which represent submerged hilly areas. Emergence tends to leave areas of sea bed as flat coastal plains.

Coasts in high latitudes such as those of Britain are often subjected to storm-generated waves. The waves are generally destructive and cliffs, wave-cut platforms and shingle beaches are common. In low latitudes, coasts are often affected by waves which have travelled a long way from persistent storm zones. Such waves constitute a **swell** and they tend to form depositional rather than erosive features.

Deposition on the ocean floor

Sediment derived from the land may be deposited in ocean trenches and on abyssal plains by **turbidity currents**. These are suspensions of sediment in water which flow like dense clouds along the sea floor. If you pour a milky suspension of calcium carbonate into water in a sloping tank you can produce your own turbidity currents. Turbidity currents may travel 1500 km and they may reach speeds of about 90 km h^{-1}. The currents may be submarine continuations of muddy rivers or, more often, they may be produced by earthquakes which shake sediment loose from the continental slope and set it flowing downwards. A well-known example occurred in 1929 when an earthquake off Newfoundland triggered a turbidity current which flowed south-east and cut telephone cables on the floor of the Atlantic. The cables were broken in sequence by the passing current and since the positions of the cables and their breakage times were known it was possible to work out that the current had reached a speed of about 70 km h^{-1}. The turbidity current deposited about 250 km^3 of sediment in a layer less than one metre thick over a large area of the sea floor.

Besides depositing sediment it is probable that turbidity currents have been responsible for the erosion of **submarine canyons** on the continental shelf and slope. Some canyons are virtually continuous with large rivers such as the Zaïre and Hudson but most are not directly related to rivers. Much of the sediment brought down the canyons is deposited as **submarine fans** at the canyon mouths. A **turbidite** is a sediment deposited by a turbidity current.

Where turbidity currents cannot reach the deep sea floor thin deposits are formed from the skeletons of surface living planktonic organisms and from atmospheric dust. Planktonic organisms live suspended in the water. The main ones contributing to organic deep sea sediments or **oozes** are diatoms (plants), foraminifera and radiolaria (unicellular animals) and pteropods (molluscs). Diatoms and radiolaria have siliceous skeletons, foraminifera and pteropods are calcareous. The various oozes have different distributions. Diatom ooze is found in high latitudes while radiolarian and pteropod oozes occur in tropical regions. The foraminifer *Globigerina* provides the most common type of ooze. *Globigerina* lives in both tropical and

nperate seas. Oozes are not found in very
ep water because the skeletons are progres-
ely dissolved as they sink. The more soluble
lcareous skeletons begin to dissolve fairly
pidly at depths of about 4000 m so they do
t reach the depths attained by siliceous
letons.

Volcanic, meteoritic and wind-blown dust
ovides a small amount of marine sediment.
nce the dust falls in very small quantities its
esence is usually obscured by planktonic
mains. However, planktonic remains do not
rvive into very deep water allowing the insol-
le atmospheric dust to accumulate as **red**
ay.

Deep sea sedimentation rates are very vari-
le. Turbidite deposition may take place at
tes of about 2000 mm per thousand years.
lcareous ooze may be deposited at a rate
60 mm per thousand years while up to 10
m of siliceous ooze may form in a thousand
ars. Red clay is usually deposited at rates of
ss than 2 mm per thousand years.

Large areas of the deep ocean floor are
tered with potato-sized **manganese nodules**
rmed by the precipitation of hydrated manga-
se oxides from sea water. Someday, the
dules may be collected economically for their
pper, nickel and cobalt contents.

Coral reefs

Corals are animals with calcareous skeletons
which are related to sea anemones and jellyfish.
Corals build reefs of three types: **fringing reefs**
are continuous with the shore, **barrier reefs**
grow offshore and **atolls** are roughly circular
reefs enclosing lagoons. Reef growth takes
place at rates up to about 2.5 cm per year.

Coral reefs are restricted to the warm region
between latitudes 30°N and S where the
temperature of the water is between 25° and
30°C. Reef corals only grow in clear, well-
oxygenated water of normal salinity. Best
growth occurs in well-lit water down to depths
of about 20 m. The reason for the apparent
requirement of light is that the coral organism
has unicellular algae living in its cells. The algae
provide the coral with photosynthetic oxygen
and they are thought to assist the coral in
obtaining calcium from the sea water. Since
corals are carnivorous they do not use the algae
as a source of food.

The calcium carbonate which makes up the
reef does not all come from the coral. A good
deal of the carbonate probably comes from
calcareous algae with smaller contributions
coming from organisms such as sponges, foraminifera, sea urchins and molluscs. Many animals such as starfish and fish act to destroy the
reef by feeding on the coral organism. Destruction also results from wave action and from the
activity of boring organisms. Destructive processes lead to the formation of coral sand which
may be deposited on or near the reef.

n atoll in the Cook Islands, West Pacific.

Chemistry of sea water

The amount of dissolved salts present in sea water is usually given as parts per thousand ($^0/_{00}$). Sea water normally contains $34.5^0/_{00}$ of salts with the most abundant ions being chloride and sodium. It should be noted that sea water is not just concentrated river water. The main ions in river water are calcium and hydrogen carbonate showing that weathering products alone do not determine the composition of sea water. In sea water the main positive ions come from the land but ions such as chloride and sulphate come from submarine volcanoes. The composition of sea water is also affected by organisms since they may extract materials such as calcium hydrogen carbonate and silica to make shells and skeletons.

The various substances present in sea water have varying solubilities so that evaporation of sea water leads to salts being precipitated in a definite sequence. When half of the water has been evaporated calcium carbonate is precipitated followed by calcium magnesium carbonate (dolomite). When 80 percent of the water has evaporated calcium sulphate precipitates, first as gypsum then as anhydrite. When 90 percent of the water has evaporated sodium chloride (halite) begins to precipitate followed by the very soluble potassium and magnesium salts when the water has almost gone. Sedimentary rocks formed by the salts left by the evaporation of water are called **evaporites**. In shallow, warm, turbulent water calcium carbonate may be precipitated as **ooliths**. Ooliths are rounded (diameter to 2 mm) with an internal concentric or radial structure. The calcium carbonate often begins to precipitate on a sand grain or shell fragment and agitation by wave action maintains the rounded shapes of the ooliths.

Ice

In cold regions and at high altitudes winter snow may not be entirely removed in summer. The snow which survives loses its fluffy form as the flakes melt and refreeze to give a sand-like snow called **firn** or **névé**. Firn is white because a great deal of air is trapped among the grains. As the firn is buried by later snow-falls it becomes glacier ice as it recrystallizes into a mass of interlocking grains. Since the ice has now lost most of its enclosed air it has acquired a pale blue colour.

The largest glaciers are **ice sheets** of the type found in Greenland and Antarctica. Smaller **ice caps** are found in places such as Iceland and Spitzbergen. **Valley glaciers** occupy valleys in mountain areas such as the Alps. A **piedmont glacier** is formed by the coming together of valley glaciers as they flow from a mountain area on to a lowland area. The Malaspina Glacier of south-east Alaska is a piedmont glacier.

The edge of the Greenland ice sheet showing 'elephant foot' glaciers spreading on to low ground

As ice accumulates it begins to flow like a very viscous liquid. Many processes are involved in producing ice movement including the deformation of ice crystals so that parts of the crystal slide over each other like playing cards in a pack. Melting and refreezing of ice, slip of ice on the underlying rock and movement on fractures also contribute to ice flow. Glaciers may also be lubricated by water. Pressure lowers the freezing point of ice and where two crystals are pressed against each other melting takes place along the contact and the water produced allows the crystals to slide over each other. Glaciers in temperate regions begin to melt when they come below the snow-line so they are lubricated by water running through and beneath them. Relatively thin glaciers in polar regions are solid throughout and, being frozen to the underlying rock, they flow less easily than temperate glaciers. The pressures under the thickest polar ice sheets are high enough, however, to cause the formation of thin films of water.

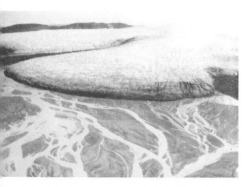

raided meltwater streams and glaciofluvial deposits at the margin of the Greenland ice sheet.

Like rivers, glaciers move fastest at the surface and in central regions away from the frictional drag exerted on the sides and floor of the glacier. Also, thick glaciers tend to move faster than thin ones. The rates at which glaciers move are very variable. While some glaciers move only a few millimetres in a year, rates of several kilometres in a year have been recorded. In the Alps glaciers usually move about 40 m in a year. In Antarctica the Beardmore Glacier moves about 300 m per year while the Ferrar Glacier has a flow rate of 18 m per year. In Greenland rates of 1.5 km per year have been measured. On occasions, Alaskan glaciers have been found to move at rates of 60 m per day and in Kashmir, India, glaciers have moved more than 100 m in a day. Very fast rates of ice movements (**surges**) are exceptional and seem to be caused by frictional ice melting at the base of the glacier. The water produced provides much more lubrication than previously existed.

The accumulation of ice at the top of a glacier is balanced by ice loss or **ablation** at the lower end. Ice loss takes place mainly by melting or by the calving of icebergs. The position of the end of a glacier depends on the balance between accumulation and ablation. In times of cold climate or heavy snow-falls the end or snout of the glacier would advance; in times of warm climate or light snow-falls the snout would retreat. In the last century or so most glaciers have shrunk, e.g. the Arctic ice sheet is now 1.5 m thinner than it was in 1890 and many valley glaciers have retreated several kilometres since last century. Ice loss has meant that since 1880 sea level has been rising at the rate of about 1 mm per year.

Erosion, transport and deposition by ice

Ice erodes partly by abrasion in which the ice and its load of rock debris act like sandpaper by scratching and scraping the underlying rock. **Striations** or **striae** are scratches on exposed rock which indicate the direction of ice flow. Where boulders in the ice were pressed very hard into the underlying rock **chatter marks** are produced. These are crescent-shaped gouges and fractures concave downstream to the flow. You can produce similar fractures by shoving a file or broken hacksaw blade hard over a glass block. Ice also erodes by **quarrying** or **plucking** in which rock fragments are pulled from bedrock which has fractures or joints running

Moraines and crevasses in the Kaskawulsh Glacier, Yukon.

The Aletsch Glacier, Switzerland. Note the shapes of the boulders and the vertical stripes of morainic material in the ice.

through it. Such fractures can be opened by water freezing in them. In this way blocks of rock are surrounded by ice so they become frozen to the base of the glacier.

Besides picking up material by erosion, glaciers receive fallen rock debris from higher mountain and valley sides. The rock material carried by glaciers is called **moraine**. **Subglacial moraine** is carried by the ice in contact with the bedrock while **supraglacial moraine** is carried on the surface of the ice. **Englacial moraine** is carried within the glacier. In valley glaciers debris from the valley sides forms **lateral moraines**. When valley glaciers join, lateral moraines come together to give **medial moraines**. Debris carried by ice covers a very wide range of grain size from very fine **rock flour** to very large boulders called **erratics**. Erratics often have flattened, scratched faces caused by their being rubbed along the bedrock under the glacier.

Drift is a general term applied to material deposited by ice and by meltwater running from the ice. Meltwater deposits are often referred to as **glaciofluvial** or **fluvioglacial deposits**. Besides meaning material carried by glaciers the word 'moraine' also refers to material deposited by glaciers. **Ground moraine** is deposited from the base of a glacier. It often gives rise to a gently sloping landscape of small hills and shallow valleys. Ridge-like **terminal** or **end moraines** are deposited at the edges of glaciers while **recessional moraines** mark successive

positions of the edge of a retreating glacie Morainic ridges may be accentuated by th bulldozing effect of a glacier during minc advances. **Till** or **boulder clay** is a mixture c rock flour, pebbles and boulders deposited b ice sheets.

Valley glaciers

The Tschierva Glacier, Switzerland. Note the crevasses and the ridge-like lateral and medial moraines.

SURFACE PROCESSES

mountain regions ice accumulates in hollows
ove the snow-line. By abrasion, quarrying and
st shattering the hollows may be enlarged
to large bowl-shaped **cirques**. (Cirques are
so known as corries and cwms.) Growth of
rques towards each other may result in their
eeting along sharp-edged ridges called
êtes. Cirques may also eat into the sides of
mountain to leave a pyramidal peak called
horn. Glaciers flow from the cirques out into
lleys. Since glaciers fill the valleys and since
ey erode over their entire area of contact with
e bedrock they cut river-formed V-shaped
lleys into U-shaped **glacial troughs** (figure
29). Spurs are cut away or truncated and
all tributary valleys are left to enter the glacial
ough high up on its sides. Such valleys are
lled **hanging valleys** and they may disgorge
terfalls. In a similar way tributary glacial
lleys enter the main trough as **hanging**
oughs. Valley glaciers often erode hummocky
sistant bedrock into streamlined forms called
ches moutonnées. Roches moutonnées have
ooth, oval shapes on their upstream sides
ere they have been abraded by the ice while
eir downstream sides have been steepened
ice plucking.

Irregularities in the floor of the glacial trough
ay be differentially eroded to give steep **rock**
eps with deepened **rock basins** between them.
hen the glacier crosses a rock step it forms
ice fall composed of ice heavily broken by
en fractures called **crevasses** running across
e glacier. If the ice is stretched by spreading

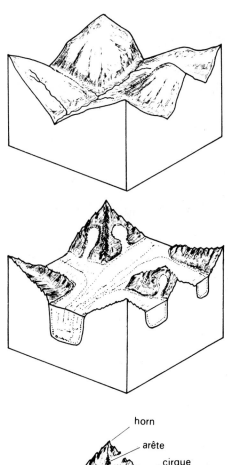

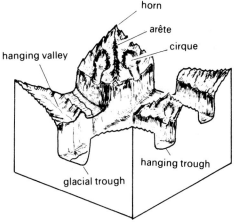

4.29 Mountain landscape before and after valley glaciation.

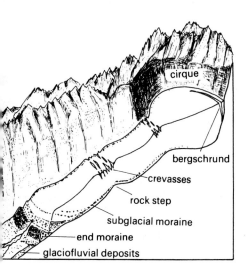

28 Section through a valley glacier.

out sideways crevasses form parallel to the
length of the glacier. A large crevasse called
a **bergschrund** develops in the ice close to the
head wall of a cirque. Where a glacier flows
through a narrow part of the valley the ice is
squeezed into **pressure ridges**.

After glaciation, glacial troughs may be occupied by long, narrow, deep lakes called **ribbon lakes**. There are numerous examples in the Scottish Highlands and in the English Lake District. Glacial troughs on the coast are flooded to give **fiords** or **sea lochs** which have relatively shallow rock barriers or **thresholds** at their seaward ends. **Tarns** are lakes left in cirques.

Ice sheets

Ice sheets tend to smooth off landscapes by erosion in upland areas and by deposition in lowland areas. A striking erosive feature called a **crag-and-tail** landform occurs where the glacier crosses a volcanic plug or a sill dipping in the same direction as the ice flow. The ice erodes the less resistant rocks from the front and sides of the igneous rock but leaves sedimentary rocks or till as a tail on the sheltered lee-side of the intrusion. Since a crag-and-tail has its steep side facing the ice flow it differs from a roche moutonnée which has its steep side facing downstream. Probably the best-known British crag-and-tail landform is provided by the Castle Rock and Royal Mile in Edinburgh.

In addition to leaving terminal and recessional moraines, ice sheets may deposit till as ground moraine. The till may be deposited or moulded in the form of mounds called **drumlins**. Drumlins are shaped like upturned boats lying in the direction of ice movement with their blunt ends

Crag-and-tail landform, Binny Craig, West Lothian (looking north). The ice sheet moved from west to east.

upstream and their sharp ends downstream. Drumlins are very variable in size but they are often about 0.5 km long and 45 m high.

If erratics consist of a distinctive rock type from one area their distribution in **boulder trains** leading away from the source outcrop indicates the direction of ice movement, e.g. Ailsa Craig in the Clyde consists of a distinctive microgranite containing blue amphibole. Boulders of Ailsa Craig microgranite occur in east Ireland and west Wales showing that Ailsa Craig lay in the path of a glacier which flowed from the Scottish Highlands down the Irish Sea. Similar evidence from distinctive igneous rocks shows that glaciers from Norway crossed the North Sea and impinged on the east coast of England.

SURFACE PROCESSES

Drumlins near Ribble Head, Yorkshire.

Glaciofluvial deposits

When a glacier melts, part of its load is carried away by water to be laid down as glaciofluvial deposits in the form of **stratified drift**. The sediment may be deposited away from the glacier in the form of an **outwash plain**. An outwash plain is built up like a system of coalescing alluvial fans by a large number of braided streams running from the ice front. Progressively finer material is deposited away from the glacier.

It often happens that glaciofluvial sediments are deposited against or within the ice (figure 4.30). When the support of the ice is lost by melting the deposits collapse so their bedding is often contorted. The main types of resultant landform are winding **eskers** deposited by rivers running under the ice and hummocky **kames** formed from collapsed alluvial cones and infilled ice hollows. **Kame terraces** form from sediment laid between a glacier and the side of its containing valley (figure 4.30).

The melting of ice blocks buried or partly buried in drift, leaves round depressions called **kettle holes** which may subsequently be occupied by lakes. Meltwater forms channels which, when the ice has gone, often take the form of flat-bottomed dry valleys. Such channels may form under the ice or away from the ice margin. Many British rivers were greatly swollen by meltwater at the end of the last glaciation. This allowed them to deposit large quantities of river gravel and to cut wide valleys and gorges now occupied by relatively small streams.

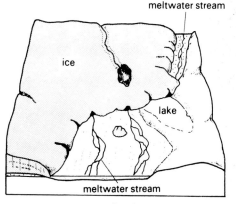

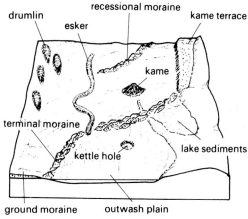

4.30 Deposition from an ice sheet.

Periglacial features

Periglacial regions border ice sheets. While they have not suffered glaciation they do show the effects of frozen ground or **permafrost**. Freezing of level ground causes the surface to contract and form domed **mud polygons**. Gaps between the polygons fill with ice to become **ice wedges**. In frozen ground, stones tend to move upwards because the build up of ice beneath the stones pushes them up. At the surface, stones tend to move down the sloping surfaces of the mud polygons to collect at the polygon edges as **stone** polygons or **stone circles** (figure 4.31 (b)). On slopes the polygons are drawn out to form **stone stripes**.

Freezing and thawing causes the layering of glaciofluvial sediments to be twisted into irregular, interpenetrating structures called **involutions** (figure 4.31 (c)). Since fine-grained sedi-ments hold more water than coarse-grained sediments the fine sediments expand more on freezing. The differential expansion produce pressures which can contort the bedding. Also surface freezing may trap fluid mud between the surface layer and the deep, permanently frozen layer. The liquid mud may then be squeezed as long flame-like extensions into the coarse non-fluid sediments.

Where valley sides consist of saturated clay overlain by sandstone or limestone freezing and thawing cause the clay to move down under the weight of the overlying rock. The clay is squeezed out into the valley to form **valley bulges**. Removal of the supporting clay causes the overlying rock to bend. Where it bends over parallel to the hillside the sandstone or limestone shows **cambering**. Cambering may cause the rock to break along deep fissures called **gulls**. Valley bulging and cambering are well developed in southern England and in the East Midlands. **Pingos** are small, steep-sided hills pushed up by growing internal cores of ice or frozen sediment. When the ice melts their remains appear as depressions surrounded by low ridges.

The wind blowing off an ice sheet may pick up fine outwash sediment and redeposit it further away as glacial **loess**. Loess forms extensive spreads in North America and in northern Europe.

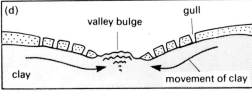

4.31 *Periglacial features: (a) ice wedges separating mud polygons; (b) stone polygons and stone stripes; (c) involutions; (d) valley bulge.*

Varves

With the spring thaw meltwater carries sediment into lakes close to the ice sheet. The coarse sediment settles fairly quickly but the finest sediment remains in suspension for a long time and only settles when the lake freezes over in winter. Continued sedimentation of this type results in the development of annual layers called **varves**. Each varve consists of a lower silty layer overlain by a thin layer of clay. Varves are typically only a few millimetres thick. Like the annual rings on trees, varves have been counted and used to date events towards the end of the last Ice Age. Baron de Geer (1858-1943) initiated the practice of varve counting and he used it to establish a history of the retreat of the last major European ice sheet during the last 17 000 years.

Arid lands

The rocks of arid or dry regions are not protected by a complete cover of vegetation so they are exposed to the full effects of wind and occasional rain-storms. The relative lack of water means that, while temperatures are often high, chemical weathering is very slow. The main type of physical weathering is probably salt weathering since the wind speeds evaporation and promotes salt crystallization. Temperature changes are probably not effective in breaking rock unless it has been weakened by chemical weathering.

Erosion, transport and deposition by wind

By itself, wind can only erode loose, dry materials such as dust, sand or soil. The pick-up or entrainment of grains takes place by a combination of processes. Because the pressure in a moving fluid is less than that in a stationary fluid, when wind blows over grains it tends to make them rise by a process like that which gives uplift to an aeroplane wing. Also, a grain projecting above adjacent grains is subjected to higher pressure on its upwind side than on its downwind side. The pressure difference tends to make the grain roll forward. In addition, the landing impact of already lifted grains knocks other grains up to be caught by the wind.

Transport of grains takes place in two main ways. Fine particles of clay or silt size can be kept in suspension by turbulent air currents. This wind-blown dust may be transported for long distances before being deposited. Very large deposits of desert **loess** occur in northern China where winds from the Gobi Desert have covered an area of about 800 000 km² to depths of up to 300 m. Sand-sized particles are transported by bouncing, rolling and sliding along the surface. In the bouncing motion or **saltation** sand grains are sucked up then they curve over in the wind to fall back at a lower angle. The impact of saltating grains moves other grains which are too large to be lifted by the wind alone. Most saltating grains do not jump above half a metre and only rarely do they rise above one metre.

Wind erosion takes place in two ways. Firstly, the wind removes loose material by a process called **deflation** (blowing away) and, secondly, transported grains give the wind an abrasive, sand-blast action.

Deflation starts from small depressions called **blowouts** cut into loose material. Deflation may proceed to cut enormous shallow depressions such as those of the Sahara. In Egypt, for example, the Qattara Depression is about 300 km long and it reaches to a depth of 135 m below sea level. Deflation ceases at the water table since water gives the grains enough adhesion to prevent their being picked up by the wind. Since this is the case oases are often found in deflation hollows. When the wind blows over loose sediment it selectively removes the smaller particles and leaves the pebbles and boulders as a surface accumulation called **desert pavement**. The desert pavement gives protection to the underlying sediment and helps to reduce the rate of subsequent deflation. The production of desert pavement is also aided by the washing away of fine materials following rain-storms.

The sand-blast action of the wind acts both on the transported grains and on exposed rocks. The grains move at relatively high velocities in wind and the air does not cushion their impacts. Continuous bombardment causes quartz grains to become well-rounded and to become chipped and frosted. Some desert sands consist of grains so nearly spherical that they are described as **millet-seed sand**. Bombardment also tends to break up minerals with well-defined cleavage. For this reason desert sandstones rarely contain mica because it is broken into very small particles and carried off as dust.

When sand-blasting attacks exposed rocks it removes weak areas and leaves resistant areas to protrude. The undercutting of exposures helps to maintain steep slopes. The efficiency of undercutting is shown by the fact that in desert regions the bases of telephone poles have to be protected by stones. Also, small isolated exposures may develop shapes like mushrooms. Larger exposures consisting of alternating hard and soft material may be cut into long whaleback or furrowed ridges called **yardangs** elongated parallel to the wind. Stones called **ventifacts** have had small faces or facets cut on them so they sometimes resemble Brazil nuts. The facets are cut on the side of the stone facing the wind. Sometimes, only one facet is developed and the stone is cut down to ground level (figure 4.32). On other ventifacts where the stone has been rotated, perhaps by undermining, other facets are formed. A **dreikanter** is a three-edged ventifact.

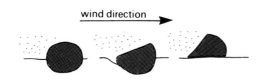

4.32 *Formation of a ventifact. Sand blasting cuts a flat face on an exposed stone. The stone may be rotated and other faces may be cut.*

Sand may be deposited in relatively smooth **sand sheets** such as those of the Kalahari Desert of south-west Africa. More often, though, the sand is deposited in **dunes**. Dune forms are of various types depending on factors such as the strength and direction of the wind, the supply of sand, the sizes of the sand grains and the site at which the dunes form. **Sand drifts** are stationary or fixed dunes formed by the accumulation of sand in sheltered areas behind cliffs, rock exposures or vegetation. The main types of moving or mobile dunes are **barchan dunes**, **transverse dunes** and **longitudinal** or **seif dunes** (figure 4.33). Barchan dunes are crescentic in plan with their concave sides downwind. The dune moves downwind because sand is constantly moving up the shallow upwind slope and being tipped off the steep downwind slope. The steeper slope can attain an angle of up to 34°. Barchans tend to form on firm desert floors with a limited supply of sand and under the action

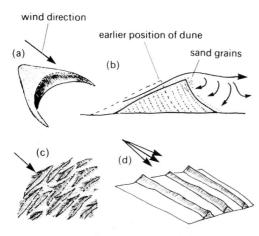

4.33 *Sand dunes: (a) barchan dune; (b) movement of sand in a barchan dune; (c) transverse dunes; (d) longitudinal dunes.*

of a wind blowing consistently in one direction. They reach heights of about 30 m and they move at rates of about 15 m a year. Transverse dunes resemble barchans in that their long-axes are at right-angles to the wind direction. They form where there is an abundant supply of sand so the simple crescent shape of the barchan cannot form. Ridge-shaped longitudinal or seif dunes are produced by winds blowing from two dominant directions so the dunes are parallel to the average wind direction. They form where there is a limited supply of sand. Longitudinal dunes are often very large reaching lengths of 100 km and heights of 200 m.

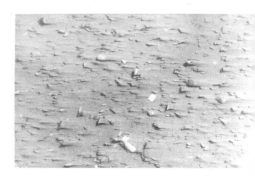

The scouring effect of wind on a sandy beach. The wind has blown from left to right.

Water in arid lands

Surprisingly, perhaps, the landforms of arid lands are largely the result of running water. The erosive effects of water are aided by the scarcity of protective vegetation and by the relatively impermeable ground surface. This allows the water to run off rapidly in flash floods carrying huge quantities of sediment. Between floods the landscape does not alter to any great extent. A few rivers such as the Nile, Colorado and Indus have sufficient volume to allow them to cross arid regions without drying up. Most desert streams, though, run only occasionally in steep-sided, flat-bottomed valleys called **wadis** or **box canyons**. Canyon sides remain steep because of the slow rate of mass wasting in dry areas. Where streams run from mountain areas out on to low ground they deposit most of their load in alluvial fans. Adjacent alluvial fans often overlap to form a continuous feature called a **bajada**. Following floods, drainage basins may contain short-lived lakes called **playa lakes**. When the lake dries up its bed is a **playa**

SURFACE PROCESSES

some playas salt is deposited while in others the sediment is mostly clay.

In some cases mountains in arid regions are not bordered by alluvial fans. Instead, between the mountains and the areas receiving sediment there is a gently-sloping, concave erosion surface called a **pediment** (figure 4.34). Pediments are cut in bedrock by water running in sheetwash or in rills.

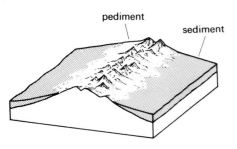

4.34 A pediment bordering mountains in an arid region.

Common features of arid lands are isolated hills called **inselbergs** (island mountains) which rise abruptly from the surrounding plains. They usually have steep sides and rounded tops. Well-known examples are Ayers Rock, Australia, and Sugar Loaf Mountain, Rio de Janeiro. Inselbergs may form by the wearing back of steep slopes until only a relatively small mountain is left. Alternatively, surrounding rocks may be deeply weathered then removed by erosion to leave the relatively resistant rock as an inselberg.

Where weak horizontal beds are overlain and protected by a resistant bed, recession of steep slopes leads to the development of flat, table-like mountains or small plateaux called **mesas**. Continued slope recession leads to the reduction of mesas to hills called **buttes**. Buttes are shaped like huge towers or columns.

An arid landscape, Utah. In the foreground are transverse dunes. In the background are eroded mountains, pediments and playas.

The Grand Canyon, Arizona. The canyon reaches a width of 24 km and a depth of 1.9 km.

The Devil's Golf Course, Death Valley, California. Salt deposits in the bed of a dried-up playa lake.

Buttes and mesas, Monument Valley, Arizona.

An inselberg, Ayers Rock, Australia.

SURFACE PROCESSES

Changing landscapes

W M Davis (1850 – 1934) put forward the theory that a landscape changes through a **cycle of erosion**. This idea suggests that a newly raised and near-level land area is progressively worn away through the three stages of **youth, maturity** and **old age**. In humid areas youthful landscapes are rapidly eroded by streams running in deep, V-shaped valleys with interlocking spurs. Mature landscapes have rounded hills and wide valleys with streams flowing down gentle slopes. By the time old age has been reached the landscape has been worn down to a flat **peneplain** with meandering rivers and isolated, residual hills called **monadnocks**. After passing through this sequence of stages the peneplain might be uplifted and the cycle of erosion could begin again (figure 4.35). Davis emphasized that landscapes could be described in terms of the kinds of processes at work, the structure of the rocks on which the landscape is developing and the stage which the landscape has reached in its development. The cycle of erosion originally described by Davis referred to humid, temperate regions. Later, a cycle of erosion was recognized for arid regions beginning with a young upland area the slopes of which retreat in maturity to leave gently sloping pediments at the slope bases. In old age the pediments have joined to form an extensive **pediplain** with inselbergs remaining as residual hills.

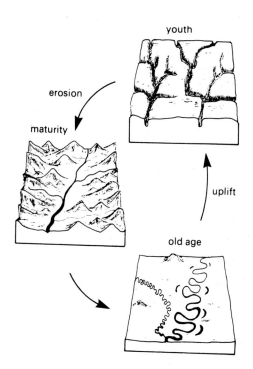

4.35 Cycle of erosion in a humid climate.

It should be realized that while landscapes certainly do evolve and change with time they are much too complex to be described simply in terms of the cycle of erosion. Besides Davis's main ideas of process, structure and stage we have to take into account the modifications caused by previous conditions.

SEDIMENTARY ROCKS

Sedimentary rocks are formed at the Earth's surface by deposition under air, water or ice. They may be formed from fragments derived from pre-existing rocks, by the chemical precipitation of dissolved substances or from the remains of plants and animals. Sedimentary rocks are classified in terms of their grain size, composition and origin.

Classification in terms of grain size

Fragments or **clasts** are named according to their size and the sedimentary rock is named according to the dominant fragment type (table 5.1).

The coarse-grained rudites or rudaceous rocks include **conglomerate** which consists of rounded fragments and **breccia** which consists of angular fragments. **Tillite** is a rock derived from glacially-deposited boulder clay or till. In a rudite the large fragments lie in a finer-grained **matrix**.

Arenites or arenaceous rocks may consist of mineral or rock (**lithic**) fragments. The mineral clasts are usually quartz. A **sandstone** which consists almost entirely of quartz is a **sedimentary quartzite** or **orthoquartzite**. Sandstones are usually brown, yellow, white, red or greenish in colour. A **grit** is a sandstone which consists of angular fragments. The term is also used to describe a coarse-grained sandstone. **Arkose** is a sandstone in which feldspar makes up more than 25 percent of the rock. Arkose is often red or grey. **Greywacke** is a lithic sandstone which consists of variously shaped rock and mineral fragments set in a muddy matrix. Mineral fragments are mostly quartz or feldspar while lithic fragments are often chert, mudstone or volcanic rock. The matrix may have a large amount of fine-grained chlorite and mica. Greywackes are usually grey, green or black in colour.

Siltstones are coarse-grained argillites or argillaceous rocks consisting mostly of quartz, feldspar and mica. They are usually grey, brown or yellow. The fine-grained argillaceous rocks are the most common of all sedimentary rocks. They consist largely of clay minerals and fine-grained quartz. **Mudstones** are usually coloured black, grey, white, red, brown or blue-green. The black colour of mudstones is often due to the presence of carbonaceous material while red or brown mudstones contain iron oxide. **Shale** is a mudstone which splits easily into thin, parallel sheets. The property of easy splitting

NAME OF FRAGMENT	DIAMETER	SEDIMENTARY ROCK	ALTERNATIVE ROCK NAME
Boulder	>256 mm		
Cobble	64 – 256 mm	Conglomerate	Rudite
Pebble	4 – 64 mm		
Granule or gravel	2 – 4 mm		
Sand	1/16 – 2 mm	Sandstone	Arenite
Silt	1/256 – 1/16 mm	Siltstone	Argillite or lutite
Clay or mud	< 1/256 mm	Claystone or mudstone	

Table 5.1   Grain size of sedimentary rocks

Unit 5

dimentary quartzite (crossed polars). The
ains are quartz with a few feldspars. Field
view 6 mm across.

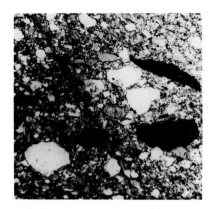

eywacke (crossed polars) consists
rock and mineral fragments in a
ddy matrix. Field 5 mm across.

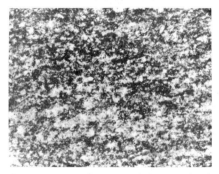

Shale (crossed polars) consisting mostly of
pale quartz and dark carbonaceous material.
Field 5 mm across.

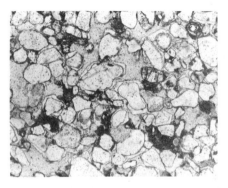

Sandstone (plane polarized light) showing
overgrowths of authigenic quartz on the original clastic quartz grains. Field 6 mm across.

described as **fissility**. **Clay** is mudstone which
becomes plastic and sticky when wet. A **marl**
a calcareous mudstone.

lassification in terms of composition
d mode of formation

mestones are sedimentary rocks which con-
st largely of the carbonate minerals calcite
d dolomite. The term 'limestone' is usually
plied to rocks consisting mostly of calcite.
agnesian limestone contains a small pro-
rtion of dolomite while the rock **dolomite** or
lostone contains a high proportion of the
ineral dolomite.

Limestones are a very variable group of rocks.
here they consist of carbonate fragments they
ay be described as **calcirudites** (fragments
rger than 2 mm diameter), **calcarenites** (frag-

ments $\frac{1}{16}$–2 mm) or **calcilutites** (fragments
smaller than $\frac{1}{16}$ mm). Fragmental limestones
may be described as being **clastic** or **detrital**.
Where the fragments are of organic origin the
limestone may be described as **bioclastic**.

Limestones rich in fossils may have names
such as **shelly, coral** or **crinoidal limestone**.
(Crinoids are animals commonly known as sea
lillies.) **Chalk** is a limestone which consists
largely of **coccoliths** (the skeletons of calcareous
algae) and foraminiferans. **Oolitic limestone** or
oolite is a limestone rich in ooliths. **Pisoliths**
(diameter greater than 2 mm) are large ooliths
and **pisolitic limestone** or **pisolite** consists
largely of pisoliths.

Calc tufa is a soft, porous form of calcium carbonate formed by precipitation from springs and ground water in limestone regions. **Travertine** is a compact, banded form of tufa which may form stalactites and stalagmites. Travertine may also be deposited as terraces round hot springs. **Caliche** is a soil rich in calcium carbonate or other soluble substances formed in arid regions by precipitation from ground water which has been drawn to the surface by capillary action.

Evaporites are sedimentary rocks which are formed by the evaporation of salty water. When sea water (table 5.2) evaporates the dissolved salts precipitate in order from the least to the most soluble. Complete evaporation of sea water would give the sequence and proportions

SALT	PERCENTAGE
NaCl	78.04
MgCl$_2$	9.21
MgSO$_4$	6.53
CaSO$_4$	3.48
KCl	2.11
CaCO$_3$	0.33
MgBr$_2$	0.25

Table 5.2   Percentages of salts in sea water. (Salts make up 3.5 percent by weight of sea water)

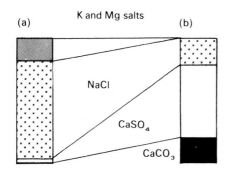

5.1 (a) Sequence and relative amounts of salts derived from the complete evaporation of sea water.
(b) Common proportions of salts found in natural evaporites.

of salts shown in figure 5.1. Because total evaporation may not be attained, evaporite sequences often have more CaCO$_3$ and CaSO$_4$ than would be expected. There may be less NaCl than expected and Mg and K salts may be absent. Thick evaporite sequences are not formed by the evaporation of deep sea water. Rather, they form under arid conditions in shallow, subsiding basins partly cut off from the sea by barriers which allow frequent influxes of sea water to be evaporated. At present gypsum is being precipitated in the Gulf of Kara Bogaz, an almost enclosed basin on the east of the Caspian Sea.

Precipitation of dissolved substances can take place by processes other than evaporation. During the early stages of the Earth's history, between about 3500 and 1700 million years ago **banded ironstones** were formed. The ironstone consists of thin alternating layers of haematite and chert which were probably precipitated by algae. It is probable that iron in the form of Fe^{2+} was carried into the sedimentary basin dissolved in reducing, acidic river water. The Fe^{2+} would then take up oxygen produced by photosynthesizing algae and be precipitated as haematite in its less soluble Fe^{3+} form.

Sedimentary ironstones formed within the last 600 million years are often oolitic with the commonest iron minerals being chamosite (iron silicate) and siderite. The iron was probably transported as Fe(OH)$_2$ embedded in colloidal organic particles. Chemical precipitation as chamosite and siderite takes place in the sea under reducing and slightly alkaline conditions. **Bog iron ore** forms by the bacterial precipitation of limonite in lakes and marshes.

Silica may be deposited as **bedded cherts** formed from the skeletons of radiolarians, diatoms and sponges. Radiolarian cherts are indicative of deep-water marine deposition. **Siliceous sinter** or **geyserite** is a porous form of silica deposited by hot springs and geysers.

Coal is formed from the remains of plants. In swamps, peat forms from partly decomposed plants. Burial of the peat removes volatiles and leads to the formation of **lignite** or **brown coal**, **bituminous** or **household coal** and **anthracite** as the proportion of carbon increases. **Oil shale** is rich in organic matter derived from algae (table 5.3).

SEDIMENTARY ROCKS

Chemistry of sedimentary rocks

Table 5.4 shows the composition and mineralogies of some common rocks. How do these rocks differ from each other? Firstly, you will see that, apart from quartz, the common minerals of igneous rocks are not the common minerals of sedimentary rocks. Secondly, the level of K_2O relative to Na_2O is higher in sedimentary than in igneous rocks. Among the sedimentary rocks you will see that limestone is very rich in CaO, shale has a high proportion of Al_2O_3 and sandstone is rich in SiO_2.

Differences such as these result partly from chemical weathering. The soluble products of chemical weathering reach the sea where they may be precipitated to form limestones and evaporites. The insoluble products may be transported and deposited to form rocks such as sandstone, siltstone and mudstone. Chemically unstable minerals decompose during transport so they tend to become less common with increasing distance from their source area. If transport goes on for a long time all unstable minerals may be removed and only quartz and clay minerals remain. Sediments made up of the insoluble end-products of chemical weathering are mineralogically **mature**, e.g. a sandstone consisting entirely of quartz is a mature sedimentary rock while arkose and greywacke are **immature** because they contain feldspars and rock fragments which have not been broken down by chemical weathering. Immature sediments generally result from rapid erosion and transport.

Changes in sediments after deposition

Diagenesis is the group of processes which change a sediment into a sedimentary rock. Diagenesis takes place at relatively low temperatures and pressures at or near the Earth's surface. **Lithification** is a diagenetic process in which loose sediment is converted to hard rock by **compaction** and **cementation**.

When a sediment is buried the increased pressure from the weight of the overlying material pushes the grains closer together. The volume of the sediment is reduced and fluids between the grains are squeezed out. When a mudstone is compacted the clay mineral flakes are pushed into nearly parallel alignment so a fissile mudstone or shale is formed. Deep burial

of 100 m of mud would give only about 20 m of shale. At the same time, the porosity of the mud would fall from about 50 percent to about 15 percent. Coarse-grained sediments are less affected by compaction than fine-grained sediments, e.g. 100 m of sand may give about 90 m of sandstone. Massive limestones of the type formed in reefs are not much affected by compaction though limestones formed from lime mud do suffer significant compaction. Also, as the sedimentary grains are squeezed together they may be bent or broken and the high pressure may cause them to dissolve at their points of contact. Grain-contact solution allows the grains to lock together and the porosity of the rock is further reduced.

If you mixed some plaster with sand you would be introducing a material which would hold the sand grains together. In a sedimentary rock such material is called **cement**. Cement may form in various ways, e.g. the mineral dissolved by grain-contact solution may be precipitated in the spaces between the grains. Again, sand grains may be cemented by minerals which are chemically precipitated at the time of deposition. Cementing material may also be precipitated from water percolating through the sediment. The water may be connate water squeezed from buried sediments such as shales or it may be water from the surface. The most common cementing minerals are quartz, calcite, haematite, limonite and dolomite. Quartz cement is often produced by grain-contact solution. It may grow over quartz sand grains in crystallographic continuity with the grains. Calcite cement may come from the solution and reprecipitation of shells or calcite grains. Iron oxide cement is indicative of deposition under oxidizing conditions such as those of deserts, alluvial fans and flood plains.

Diagenesis often results in the formation of new **authigenic** minerals which grow in the sediment or sedimentary rock, e.g. the green mica **glauconite** may grow in shallow marine sediments. **Greensand** is a sandstone with a high proportion of glauconite. Authigenic quartz often grows over quartz sand grains and calcite may grow over grains of detrital calcite. Limestones may show numerous changes in mineralogy since aragonite changes to calcite and calcite may be altered to dolomite. The change from calcite to dolomite is accompanied by a volume reduction so dolomite limestones which are derived from calcite limestones are

CONSISTING OF MINERAL AND ROCK FRAGMENTS		RICH IN ORGANIC MATERIAL	
MAIN ROCK TYPES	**RELATED ROCK TYPES**	**MAIN ROCK TYPES**	**RELATED ROCK TYPES**
CONGLOMERATE	BRECCIA — fragments angular TILLITE — derived from boulder clay CALCIRUDITE (LIMESTONE CONGLOMERATE) — fragments are limestone or shell	LIMESTONE — consists largely of calcite	SHELLY LIMESTONE CORAL LIMESTONE CRINOIDAL LIMESTONE ALGAL LIMESTONE CHALK — consists of skeletons of calcareous algae
SANDSTONE	ORTHOQUARTZITE — consists very largely of quartz GRIT — fragments angular GREYWACKE — rock and mineral fragments in muddy matrix ARKOSE — feldspar makes up >25% of rock CALCARENITE (LIME SANDSTONE) — carbonate grains	COAL — formed from plant remains	LIGNITE BITUMINOUS COAL ANTHRACITE Increasing carbon content ↓
SILTSTONE	CALCILUTITE (LIME SILTSTONE) — carbonate grains	OIL SHALE — rich in algal matter	
MUDSTONE	SHALE — fissile mudstone CLAY — plastic when wet MARL — calcareous mudstone CALCILUTITE (LIME MUDSTONE) — formed from carbonate mud	BEDDED CHERT — derived from organisms (e.g. radiolarians, diatoms, sponges) with silica skeletons	

Table 5.3 Sedimentary rocks

FORMED BY CHEMICAL OR BIOCHEMICAL PRECIPITATION	
MAIN ROCK TYPES	RELATED ROCK TYPES
VAPORITE — ormed by vaporation of ea water	LIMESTONE ROCK GYPSUM ROCK SALT
OOLITE — onsists of ooliths formed by precipitation n shallow, warm eas	OOLITIC LIMESTONE PISOLITIC LIMESTONE OOLITIC IRONSTONE
BANDED IRONSTONE — aematite and hert probably precipitated by algae	
BOG IRON ORE — limonite precipitated by bacteria	
CALC TUFA — calcium carbonate deposited from springs and ground water	TRAVERTINE — forms stalactites and stalagmites. Also deposited by hot springs
SILICEOUS SINTER — silica deposited by hot springs	

able 5.3 Sedimentary rocks (contd.)

FORMED BY POST-DEPOSITIONAL CHANGES	
MAIN ROCK TYPES	RELATED ROCK TYPES
DOLOMITE — formed mostly by the replacement of limestone	
CONCRETIONS — lumpy masses which grow in sedimentary rocks	FLINT NODULES — in chalk CHERT CONCRETIONS — in limestone IRONSTONE CONCRETIONS — in shale

feldspar to clay minerals or to white mica (sericite). In buried muds the change to mudstone or shale is accompanied by the change of other clay minerals to illite and chlorite.

Structures in sedimentary rocks

Sedimentary rocks are deposited in layers called **beds** or **strata** (singular stratum) separated from each other by **bedding** or **stratification planes** (figure 5.2). Beds which are less than 1 cm thick are sometimes called **laminae**. **Regular bedding** consists of beds of differing grain size lying parallel to each other. A **graded bed** shows a decrease in grain size from the bottom towards the top of the bed. Graded bedding often results from the settling of debris of variable size which has been transported by a turbidity current. The large particles sink faster than the small ones so the bed becomes finer towards the top. Varves show graded bedding on a small scale. **Cross bedding** results from deposition as current velocity falls on the sloping lee surface of a dune, sand bar, ripple or delta edge. The inclined layers are called **cross strata** or **foreset beds**. Topset beds are deposited on the up-current side of the foresets and bottomset beds are deposited on the down-current side of the foresets. In a delta, for example, topset beds are deposited on the upper surface of the delta while bottomsets are deposited off the delta front (figure 5.3). Strata

often porous. Fine-grained dolomite may form rom aragonite at the time of deposition by eaction of the aragonite with Mg^{2+} in the sea vater. Other mineral changes which take place n sedimentary rocks include the alteration of

OXIDES OR ELEMENTS (% weight)	IGNEOUS ROCKS		SEDIMENTARY ROCKS		
	GRANITE	GABBRO	SANDSTONE	MUDSTONE	LIMESTONE
SiO_2	70	48	78	58	5
Al_2O_3	15	15	5	16	1
Fe_2O_3	1	3	1	4	0.5
FeO	2	8	0.25	2.5	—
MgO	1	10	1	2.5	8
CaO	2.5	10	5.5	3	43
Na_2O	4	2	0.5	1.5	—
K_2O	3	1	1.5	3.5	0.25
TiO_2	0.5	2.5	0.25	0.5	—
H_2O	1	0.5	1.5	5	1
CO_2	—	—	5	2.5	42
C	—	—	—	1	—
MINERALS PRESENT	Quartz K-feldspar Na-feldspar Mica Hornblende	Ca-feldspar Pyroxene Olivine	Quartz	Clay mineral Quartz Mica Fe oxides	Calcite Dolomite

Table 5.4   Chemical compositions and minerals of some common igneous and sedimentary rocks

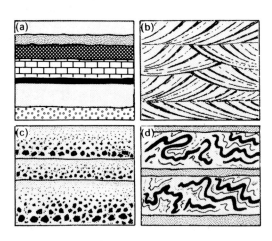

5.2 Types of bedding: (a) regular; (b) cross; (c) graded; (d) convolute.

which show **massive bedding** appear uniform and unbedded because they have no internal layering or partings. Massive bedding may result from water or wind deposition of particles with a fairly uniform grain size. It may also result from deposition by glaciers or mudflows. Reef limestones may also show massive bedding.

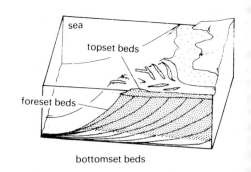

5.3 Internal structure of a delta.

SEDIMENTARY ROCKS

ded bedding in greywacke (crossed *ars). Field 5 mm across.*

oss bedding in sandstone.

Sedimentary rocks show numerous struc-
es formed mostly at the time of deposition
soon after deposition. Some structures are
diagenetic origin.
Structures formed on the tops of beds are
med by currents, by exposure to the atmos-
ere and by organisms. The movement of
ter or wind over loose sediment causes the
mation of **ripple marks** . **Current ripple marks**
ve shallow slopes on their up-current sides
d steep slopes on their lee or down-current
es (figure 5.4 (a)). Symmetrical **oscillation**
ple marks are formed by sea floor to-and-
water motion caused by passing waves.
erference ripple marks form when one set of
ple marks crosses another to give a choppy-
a appearance. **Linguoid** (tongue-like) **ripple**
arks point down-current. Rapid deposition of
nd may lead to the formation of a stack of
mbing ripples (figure 5.4 (b)). Erosional fea-
es include **rill marks** formed by water trickling
small channels and **crescent marks** formed
scouring round pebbles or shells.

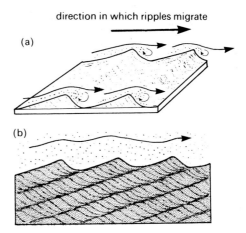

direction in which ripples migrate

(a)

(b)

5.4 (a) Ripple marks formed by a current. The
ripples migrate in the direction of the
current.
(b) Climbing ripples formed by rapid deposition of sand.

When a sediment is exposed to the atmosphere its surface may dry and split to form
polygonal **mud cracks** or **sun cracks**. The marks
of rain drops falling on soft mud may be
preserved as **rain prints**. The surface of a sediment may also be marked by organisms. Animals such as snails and crabs leave marks as
they crawl along and on coastal sand dunes
the drooping blades of marram grass cut circular grooves in the sand as they swing in the
wind.
Structures may be cut in mud which is then
covered by sand. When this happens the structures originally cut in the mud are preserved
in reverse as casts on the bottom of the sandstone bed. Such structures are called **sole**
markings. They are well-developed in greywackes where the muddy top of a graded bed
is marked by a passing turbidity current. The
marks are filled and preserved by the coarse
base of the next greywacke bed. **Flute casts** are
the tongue-shaped infillings of scour marks cut
by a turbidity current. The pointed end of the
flute cast is up-stream. The objects transported
by a turbidity current may also mark the underlying mud leaving a set of structures called **tool**
marks. **Groove casts** are the infillings of grooves
cut by boulders and pebbles being dragged
along the sea floor. Other marks may be left
by objects such as pebbles, shells or seaweed
being bounced, dragged or rolled along by
turbidity currents.

Ripples in beach sand. Small ripples have been superimposed on the large ripples.

Mud cracks in a dried-up lake bed.

Ripple marks in sandsto

Besides representing the infillings of structures already present in the underlying sediment, sole markings may be produced by the sinking of coarse sediment into the underlying mud. Such structures are called **load casts**. They usually have a bulbous form. As the lobes of coarse sediment sink, the mud is squeezed upwards to form jagged **flame structures**.

Within a bed the layering may be contorted to give **convolute bedding**. Such disturbed bedding may result from the sliding of newly deposited sediment down an underwater slope to give **slump structures** such as folds. Convolute bedding may result, too, from the loading effect of a coarse on a fine sediment. Bedding may also be deformed on a small scale at the time of deposition by suction forces generated by water currents flowing over ripples.

Concretions are lumpy masses which grow in sedimentary rocks during diagenesis. They are thought to form by the solution and pre-

cipitation of mineral material originally spre through the host rock. **Nodules** are round concretions. Examples include flint nodules chalk, chert concretions in limestone and pyr nodules in black shale. Concretions of c ironstone consisting of siderite and mudsto are often found in shales associated with co **Septarian nodules** are clay ironstone nodu which have internal polygonal and radiati veins of calcite. The calcite fills internal shrir age cracks possibly formed by the drying of the material making up the nodule.

Structures produced by organisms with sediment result mainly from burrowing. B rows may be marked by a rust colour becau they have allowed oxygen into the sediment that iron is oxidized. Burrowing may destr earlier structures such as lamination. If you visit a coastal area you can study the sedimen and their structures. You can see the effec produced by burrowing worms, arthropods a

Flute casts on the bottom of a bed of grey-wacke. The current has flowed from left to right.

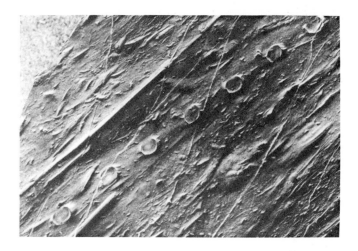

roove casts and marks left by a lling fish vertebra.

olluscs. Perhaps you can find which type of diment each organism prefers to live in and ow this relates to its method of feeding.
Some algae deposit calcite or aragonite or ey act as sediment traps to give an organically rmed layering in limestones. The algal owths generally form rounded masses.

rain shapes and surface textures

amine sand grains from various sources nder a binocular microscope. What do you e? You will find that the grains differ in shape, omposition, surface appearance and size. hat factors would affect the shapes and sur- ces of the grains? During transport and rework- g of the sediment the grains bump into each

other and into the rock over which they are travelling. The result of this is that the corners of the grains are constantly being chipped away so the grains tend to become smaller and rounder. In describing grain shapes use is made of terms such as 'angular' and 'rounded'. Note that 'rounded' does not necessarily mean 'spheri-cal', e.g. an egg-shaped grain is well rounded (figure 5.5). Transport by ice, wind or water has different effects on the grains. When sand is carried by glaciers the grains are often splin-tered into shiny, angular fragments. (Glacial sand is sometimes called 'sharp sand'.) Wind-blown sand grains collide violently because air does not cushion the impacts. The grains often become almost spherical in shape but the frequent impacts leave the grains chipped and frosted. Grains transported by water tend to

*Convolute bedding in fi[n]
sandstone.*

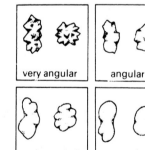

Ironstone nodules in shale.

The shape of a sedimentary particle is par[t]
controlled by its size. Large particles such [a]
pebbles and boulders quickly become round[e]
because their collisions are very violent. San[d]
sized particles require much more transport [
become rounded because their impacts are le[ss]
severe. Very small particles never becom[
rounded because their collisions are effective[
cushioned by the transporting medium. Sha[p]
is also affected by the internal structure of t[h]
mineral or rock being transported, e.g. quar[
lacks cleavage so it tends to form round grain[
Mica has one very good cleavage so it forn[
flaky particles. Igneous rocks readily form rou[r]
pebbles and boulders while rocks which ha[v]
well-defined layering or preferred grain orie[n]
tation tend to form flat or elongate pebbles ar[
boulders.

Grain size analysis

While the sizes of pebbles and boulders ha[v]
to be individually measured, you can find o[
a great deal about sand samples by passi[n]
them through stacks of sieves whose mesh siz[e]
show a regular decrease from top to botto[n]
You might have a set of sieves with the coarse[
sieve having a mesh made up of squares who[s]
sides all measure 4 mm (4000 μm). The me[s]
sizes decrease by half from sieve to sieve [
the complete stack would have mesh siz[
4000, 2000, 1000, 500, 250, 125 and [
μm. Beneath the finest sieve a pan catches t[
particles which come through.

You can study sand from places such [
beaches, coastal dunes, rivers and sand pi[
Some sandstones can be separated into th[
constituent grains by careful grinding or by t[

| very angular | angular | subangular |
| subrounded | rounded | well rounded |

5.5 Shapes of sedimentary grains.

develop polished, glassy-looking surfaces. They
are generally less well-rounded than wind-
blown grains. How do you think beach sand
would differ from river sand? Why do you think
immature sedimentary rocks such as greywacke
and arkose often consist of angular grains?

SEDIMENTARY ROCKS

se of acid. How would you collect samples
which are representative of the whole of a sand
deposit? How many samples should be collected, how much sand should be in each
sample and how should the sampling points
be distributed? The collected samples should
be dried and grain aggregates should be separated. Since you only need to sieve about 100g of
sand you now have to extract a small
amount of sand from your large sample. To
obtain a small representative sample the usual
procedure is that of coning and quartering. After
mixing up your sample pour it through a paper
funnel till it forms a cone on a sheet of paper.
Now quarter the cone using a ruler. If the
quarters have been reduced to the required size
you can sieve two diagonally opposed quarters.
If the quarters are not small enough mix two
opposite quarters then repeat the coning and

quartering.) Before sieving, weigh your sand
sample and make sure that your sieves are clean
and stacked in the correct order. Shake the
sieves till each fraction reaches a constant
weight. (This might take about 5 minutes.) After
sieving, weigh each fraction and express it as
a percentage of the total weight of sand in the
sieves and pan. (If your final and initial weights
of sand are not about the same you should start
again.) You can show your results in the type
of histogram shown in figure 5.6 (a). Alternatively, you can show the results as a cumulative
frequency curve by plotting the total percentage
of sand above any sieve against the mesh size
of the sieve. The cumulative percentage is found
by adding up the percentages as you go along
from the coarsest to the finest fractions. Note
that each point on the curve (figure 5.6 (b))
is plotted directly above each sieve size. Why
should this be so?

The graphs illustrate some characteristics of
sediments, e.g. your histogram will show you
the range of grain size and which grain sizes
are most common in terms of weight. Statistical
use of the cumulative frequency curve unfortunately requires that the micrometre size scale
be changed to a more useful geometric scale
called the **phi (ϕ) scale**. Phi values are related to
the mesh sizes by this equation:

$$\text{mesh size in micrometres } (\mu m) = \frac{1000}{2^{\phi}}$$

So, for a mesh size of 500 μm, $\phi = 1$ because

$$500 = \frac{1000}{2^1}$$

for a mesh size of 2000 μm, $\phi = -1$ because

$$2000 = \frac{1000}{2^{-1}}$$

Which ϕ values correspond to the other mesh
sizes (figure 5.6(b))?

When a sediment is sifted to and fro by water
currents or by wind, particles of the same size
tend to end up in the same place. A sediment
which consists of similarly sized grains is said
to be **well sorted**. Where there has been little
sifting of transported grains the sediment consists of a wide range of particle sizes. Such a
sediment is **poorly sorted**. Compare the histograms and cumulative frequency curves of the
two sediments shown in figure 5.7. Which
sediment shows the better sorting? In A you

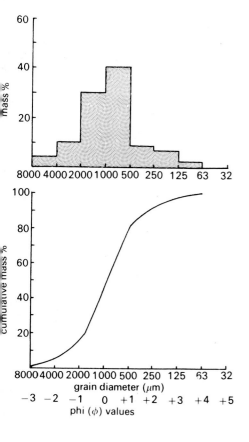

*(a) Histogram showing the percentage
weights of size fractions found by sieving.
(b) The same data shown as a cumulative
frequency curve.*

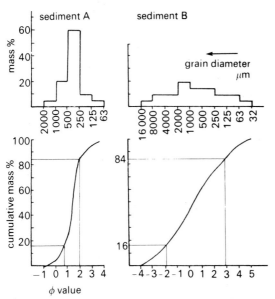

5.7 Histograms and cumulative size frequency curves for two sediments. Sediment A is quite well sorted (sorting coefficient 0.6) while sediment B is very poorly sorted (sorting coefficient 2.4).

will see that the grains are mostly of the same size so it is well sorted. You will see, too, that A has a steep cumulative frequency curve. On the other hand, sediment B is poorly sorted and its cumulative frequency curve has a shallow slope. A numerical value of sorting can be found by using the ϕ values which correspond to the 16 and 84 per cent levels. The coefficient (numerical value) of sorting is given by the following equation:

$$\text{sorting} = \frac{\phi_{84} - \phi_{16}}{2}$$

On a steep cumulative curve the values of ϕ_{84} and ϕ_{16} are close to each other so $\phi_{84} - \phi_{16}$ is a small number. In other words, the lower the numerical value of sorting the better the sediment has been sorted. On a gently sloping cumulative frequency curve the values of ϕ_{84} and ϕ_{16} are widely separated and the high numerical sorting value reflects the poor sorting. In general, sediments with sorting values less than 0.5 are well sorted while sediments with sorting values above 1.0 are poorly sorted. Sediments with sorting values between 0.5 and 1.0 are moderately sorted. Beach and dune sands are usually well sorted because they have been

sifted around by water and wind. River sediments tend to be poorly sorted because current velocities are very variable at different times and places. Turbidites and glacial deposits are also poorly sorted (figure 5.8). Can you see why?

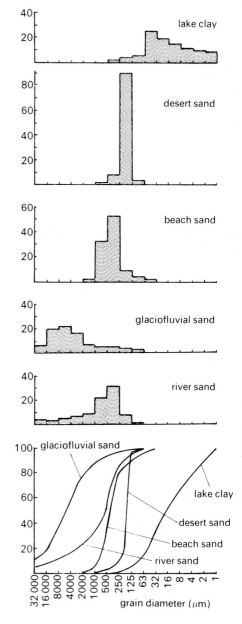

5.8 Representative histograms and cumulative size frequency curves for sediments from various environments.

SEDIMENTARY ROCKS

The grain size of a sediment gives some indication of the conditions of deposition, e.g. boulders are deposited by the strong currents of high-energy environments such as storm beaches while fine-grained sediment is deposited in low-energy environments such as lagoons and sheltered bays. Figure 5.9 shows the relationship between the velocity of moving air and water and the diameter of quartz grains carried in suspension. From figure 5.9 you can get an idea of the strength of currents which operated at the time of deposition. You will see that well-sorted sediments tend to be deposited over a narrow range of current velocities while poorly sorted sediments are deposited over a wide range of current velocities. In the case of a poorly sorted sediment this may mean that grains of various sizes were carried by a strong current which suddenly slowed down so that all the material was deposited at once. To get a fuller picture of the conditions of deposition grain size analysis must be used along with field evidence, study of sedimentary structures and examination of grain shapes and surface textures. Fossils, too, are very useful indicators of environmental conditions.

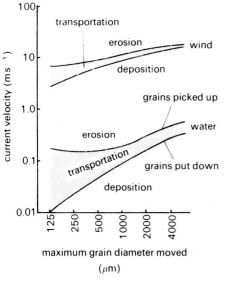

.9 The relationship between wind and water current velocity and the sizes of quartz grains carried in suspension.

Environments of deposition

A study of present day sedimentary environments helps us to work out the conditions under which sedimentary rocks were deposited because features of modern sediments may occur in rocks deposited under similar conditions.

Marine environments are divided according to depth. The **littoral** or **beach zone** lies between high and low tide. Deposits are often boulders, pebbles and sand though fine-grained material may collect in sheltered areas. In the **neritic zone** (0–200 m) the sediments are continental shelf sands, silts and muds. There may be a decrease in grain size away from the shore but this is not always the case. Present day shelf deposits are somewhat atypical because the continental shelves were partially exposed when the sea retreated during the last Ice Age. Changing shoreline positions meant that beach deposits were formed under what is now open sea. Also, moraines left on the exposed shelves are now seen as sea bed gravel banks. Limestones derived mostly from organic or chemically precipitated carbonate often form in the neritic zone. The **bathyal zone** (200–4000 m) corresponds to the continental slope. Deposition takes place from turbidity currents and by the settling of fine suspended muds. The **abyssal zone** (4000–5000 m) corresponds to the deep ocean floor. Abyssal deposits are mostly oozes and red clay. Turbidity currents deposit **abyssal fans** at the mouths of submarine canyons and they spread material out on to parts of the abyssal plain. The **hadal zone** (deeper than 5000 m) corresponds to the oceanic trenches. Many trenches have little sediment while those close to continents may have been partly filled by turbidites.

A wide range of sedimentary environments exists on the continents. Residual deposits such as soils or screes form by weathering. In deserts, wind-blown or **aeolian** sand is deposited in dunes while fine-grained material is carried away to be deposited as loess. Water running from highland areas into valleys deposits coalescing alluvial fans, and lakes evaporate to form salt deposits. River or **fluviatile** deposits consist mostly of boulders, pebbles, sand and silt. Mud may be deposited on the flood plain when a river overflows its banks. Deltas consist largely of cross-bedded sand though finer material is deposited in delta marshes. Estuaries are wide tidal river mouths.

Estuarine deposits are intermediate between fluviatile and marine types. **Lacustrine** deposits form in lakes. Lakes act as sediment traps and they may be partly filled by advancing deltas. Off the delta fronts finer material is deposited while beach deposits form round the lake.

Glacial drift may be deposited directly from the ice as unsorted till or moraine or it may be carried from the ice in meltwater streams. In glacial lakes, varved sediments form while the fine material of the outwash deposits may be blown away to form loess.

EARTH PHYSICS

The study of Earth physics or **geophysics** deals with properties of the Earth such as its gravity, magnetism and internal heat. The study of earthquakes and what they tell us about the Earth's interior is also a branch of geophysics.

Seismology—the study of earthquakes

Sudden fracturing in the Earth gives off energy which causes the Earth to shake or quake. The energy is given off in waves of three types: P-waves (push and pull or primary waves), S-waves (shake or secondary waves) and L-waves (long waves). The properties of P- and S-waves can best be shown by using a stretched 'Slinky'. Waves of P-wave type can be produced if the 'Slinky' is quickly pushed or pulled. This causes a wave of compression or decompression to pass along it. The wave makes the 'Slinky' shake backwards and forwards in the same direction in which the wave travels (figure 6.1 (a)). Waves of this type are called longitudinal waves. Shaking the 'Slinky' from side to side produces waves of S-wave type. The 'Slinky' vibrates at right angles to the direction of wave movement (figure 6.1 (b)). Such waves are called transverse waves. P- and S-waves can both travel deep into the Earth and for this reason they are sometimes called **body waves**. L-waves are quite like waves on the sea and in the same way that waves on water are restricted to the surface, L- waves are restricted to the surface of the Earth. Earthquake damage is largely due to the passage of surface waves.

The site of origin of an earthquake is its **focus** and the point on the Earth's surface directly above the focus is the **epicentre**. The strength of an earthquake is measured in two ways. **Intensity** is a measure of how hard the earthquake shakes the ground. Intensities are recorded according to their effects on the **Modified Mercalli** scale. Lines joining points of equal intensity are **isoseismal lines** (figure 6.2). Isoseismal maps show patterns of decreasing intensity away from the epicentre. Isoseismal lines

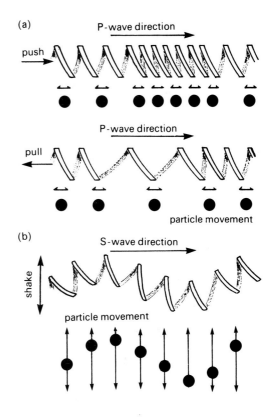

(a)

P-wave direction

push

P-wave direction

pull

particle movement

(b)

S-wave direction

shake

particle movement

6.1 (a) Waves like P-waves can be produced by pushing or pulling a Slinky. The particles move to and fro in the direction of wave movement.
(b) When the Slinky is shaken S-type waves are produced. The particles move at right angles to the direction of wave movement.

rarely form circles because the crust is not uniform so energy is not radiated out equally in all directions. The **magnitude** of an earthquake is a measure of the amount of energy given off. It is determined from the amplitude of the waves produced. In this respect different magnitudes may be likened to sounds of different volumes. Intensity would not be a measure of the sound itself—instead, it would be a measure of its effects. Magnitude is measured on a scale called the **Richter scale**

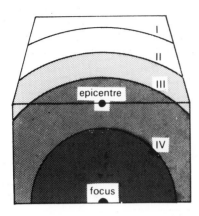

6.2 Isoseismal lines join points of equal intensity. Intensity decreases away from the
focus.

More than 3000 people died in the
earthquake which caused this
damage.

Rockfall caused by an earthquake in north-east
Italy, 1976.

This scale is logarithmic—in other words, an
earthquake of magnitude 4 gives off 30 times as
much energy as an earthquake of magnitude 3
which, in turn, gives off 30 times as much energy
as a magnitude 2 earthquake. Though intensity
and magnitude measure two different properties
of an earthquake it is possible to make a rough
correlation of the two scales of measurement. For
example, an earthquake of intensity I (Detected
by seismometers but felt by very few people.) has
a magnitude of 2; an earthquake of intensity VIII
(Weak buildings badly damaged; walls and
chimneys fall.) has a magnitude of 6; and an

earthquake of intensity XII (Total destruction;
waves seen in ground.) has a magnitude of 8.5.

Faults and earthquake waves

The way in which P- and S-waves leave a
moving fracture or fault can be found by attaching 'Slinkies' to a block as shown in figure
6.3. What kinds of waves are set up in the
'Slinkies' when the block is suddenly pushed
to one side? If the block is pushed to the left

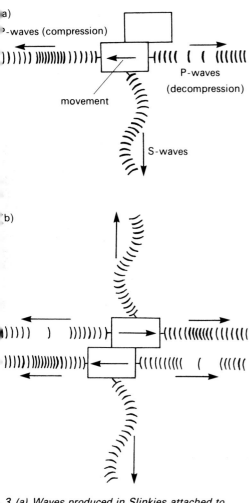

a)

P-waves (compression)

P-waves (decompression)

movement

S-waves

b)

3 (a) Waves produced in Slinkies attached to a block representing one side of a fault.
(b) P-waves of different types cancel out each other along the fault. S-waves move off at a high angle to the fault plane.

that the opposite waves cancel each other out in the direction of the fault plane. This means that no P-waves travel off parallel to the fault plane. The overall result of the opposite movements on each side of the fault is that the strengths of the P-waves build up from zero along the fault ot reach their maximum intensities at 45° to the fault plane. The P-wave intensities then decline to zero again at right angles to the fault. The intensities of S-waves reach their maximum at 90° to the fault and decrease to zero at 45° to the fault. The varying wave energies may be represented by loops where the length of each arrow in figure 6.4 gives the strength of the wave in the direction of the arrow.

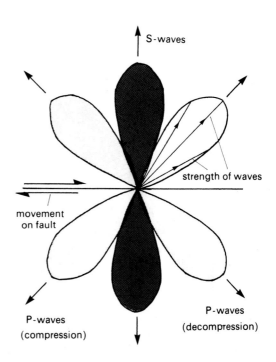

S-waves

strength of waves

movement on fault

P-waves (compression)

P-waves (decompression)

6.4 The strengths of P- and S-waves leaving an earthquake focus are represented by the lengths of lines from the focus to the edge of the loop. S-waves have their maximum intensities at 90° to the fault plane. P-waves reach their maximum intensities at 45° to the fault plane.

hen the 'Slinky' on the left is squeezed and wave of compression travels off to the left. he right hand 'Slinky' is stretched and a wave of decompression travels off to the right. Both vaves are of P-wave type. You can move the ight and left hand 'Slinkies' to other angles and epeat the experiment fo find if P-waves are iven off in other directions as well. The 'Slinky' it right angles to the block is neither compressed nor decompressed, so no P-waves are iven off in this direction. Instead the 'Slinky' s shaken sideways to give an S-wave. What appens when two blocks are used to represent he rocks moving on opposite sides of a fault? On each side of the fault P-waves of opposite ype are produced (figure 6.3 (b)) with the result

Recording earthquakes

The vibrations produced by an earthquake are recorded as a **seismogram** (figure 6.5) by an instrument called a **seismometer** or seismo-

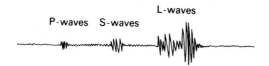

6.5 A seismogram is a recording of an earthquake.

graph (figure 6.6). Seismometers are usually laid out in sets of three to record vertical vibrations and horizontal vibrations in north–south and east–west directions. When vibrations pass the seismometer all parts of the apparatus vibrate except the heavy suspended weight. The differential movement is recorded as a wavy trace on the rotating drum.

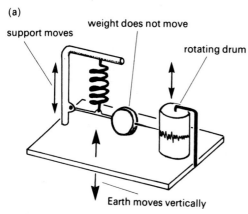

(a)

weight does not move

support moves

rotating drum

Earth moves vertically

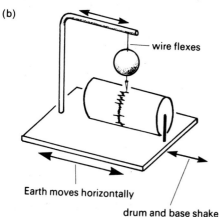

(b)

wire flexes

Earth moves horizontally

drum and base shake

6.6 Seismometers detect (a) vertical and (b) horizontal vibrations. The base of the instrument shakes but the heavy suspended weight with its attached pen does not move. The differential movement produces a trace on the rotating drum.

When faulting occurs P-, S- and L-waves are generated at the same time. How then, are P-, S- and L-waves recorded as separate peaks on a seismogram? This happens because the different waves have different velocities so they arrive at the seismometer at different times. P-waves travel fastest so they arrive first to be followed by S-waves then L-waves. How could you work out the wave velocities? (Velocity equals distance divided by time.) Besides knowing when the waves arrive at the seismometer you have to know where and when the earthquake occurred. From this information you know how long it took the waves to travel the known distance from the epicentre to the recording station so you can find the wave velocities. The time lag between the arrival of the P- and S-waves can also be used to find the distance from the earthquake focus. Figure 6.8 shows seismograms made at recording stations at different distances from an earthquake. What happens to the time interval between the arrival of the P- and S-waves as distance increases? The plot of travel time against distance gives a line called a **travel-time curve** whose slope gives the wave velocity. What are the velocities of the P- and S-waves in figure 6.8?

In earthquake studies distances are not usually given in kilometres. Instead, the distance between an earthquake epicentre and the recording station is given in terms of the **epicentral angle**. This is the angle subtended at

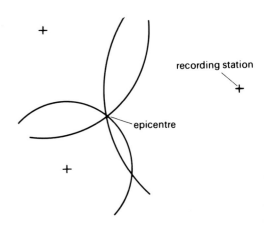

+

recording station

+

epicentre

+

6.7 Finding the position of an epicentre. Circles with radii equal to the distances from the recording stations are drawn. The point of intersection of the circles is the epicentre.

118   EARTH PHYSICS

Earth's centre by the arc of the Earth's circumference between two points on the Earth's surface (figure 6.9), e.g. the epicentral angle between the poles and the equator is 90° on the Earth's surface 1° of epicentral angle equals about 110 km.

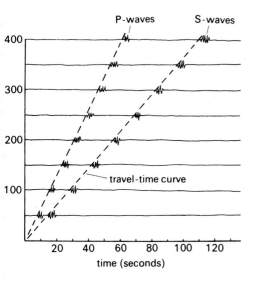

travel-time curve

Series of seismograms showing P- and S-waves recorded by stations at various distances from the focus. You can work out the wave velocities from the slopes of the travel-time curves.

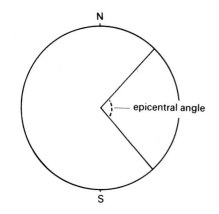

The epicentral angle is the angle at the Earth's centre subtended by part of the Earth's circumference.

Velocities of earthquake waves

The velocities of earthquake waves depend on the properties of the material through which they travel. In the case of P-waves, the denser the rock the more slowly they travel and the less compressible the rock the faster they travel. In this respect they behave just like sound waves. In air sound waves travel at about 330 metres per second (m s⁻¹) but in water the velocity is about 1400 m s⁻¹. Since water is much denser than air you might expect the sound waves to travel faster in air. That the waves travel faster in water is due to the fact that water cannot be compressed in the same way that air can be compressed. In the case of S-waves it is the rigidity of the rock along with its density that affect the velocity. The denser the rock the slower the S-waves; the more rigid the rock the faster the waves. Since liquids have zero rigidities S-waves cannot pass through them.

Earthquake wave velocities are not uniform throughout the Earth. Near the Earth's surface P-wave velocities are about 5.6 km s⁻¹ while S-wave velocities are about 3.4 km s⁻¹. Deep inside the Earth P-wave velocities may be as high as 13.6 km s⁻¹ while S-waves may have velocities as high as 7.3 km s⁻¹. What do these variations in velocity suggest to you?

What do earthquakes tell us about the Earth?

Earthquakes occur most commonly in well-marked **seismic zones** closely related to features such as oceanic ridges, young mountain ranges and island arcs. The association of earthquakes with these near-linear features indicates that the upper layers of the Earth are moving most actively in these areas. Between the seismic zones are more stable aseismic zones where earthquakes are much less common.

Earthquakes occur at depths down to a maximum of about 720 km. They are often classified into shallow (0–70 km), intermediate (70–300 km) and deep focus (300–700 km) earthquakes. The fact that earthquakes die out at depth shows that the properties of the Earth must change with depth. Above 700 km the rocks can fracture but below this depth the rocks are probably plastic and incapable of fracture.

Figures 6.10 and 6.11 shows the distributions of shallow, intermediate and deep focus earthquakes. You can see that shallow focus earthquakes are much more common than the other types and that the earthquakes associated with oceanic ridges are virtually all of shallow focus type. Intermediate and deep focus earthquakes occur most commonly in association with island arcs with the depth of focus increasing on the landward side of the ocean trenches. The steady increase in depth shows the foci to lie on a sloping zone called the **Benioff Zone**

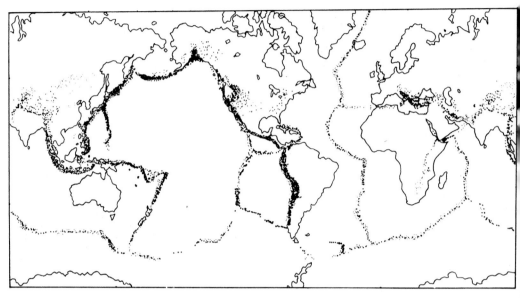

6.10 Distribution of shallow focus earthquakes.

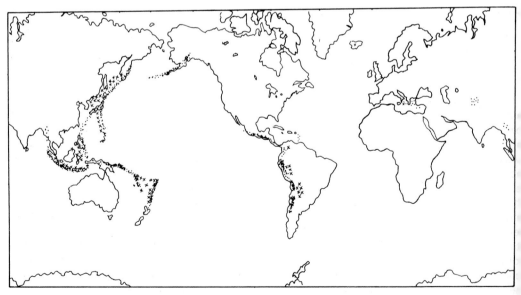

6.11 Distribution of intermediate (.) and deep (x) focus earthquakes.

EARTH PHYSICS

jure 6.12). What does the earthquake dis-
bution on the Benioff Zones suggest to you
terms of possible Earth movements close to
ean trenches?

A great deal of information about the interior
the Earth can be obtained from a study of
e behaviour of earthquake waves. In this
spect, P- and S-waves are most useful
cause they travel to great depths. We already
w that the velocities of P- and S- waves are
lated to the properties of the material through
ich they pass. The waves get slower as the
nsity of the medium increases but P-waves
t faster as the compressibility decreases and
waves get faster as rigidity increases.
anges of wave velocity, then, give us some
formation about the material through which
e waves pass.

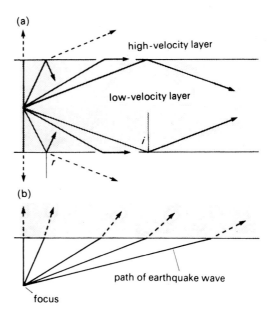

6.13 (a) Paths taken by waves from a focus in
a low velocity medium. Beyond the critical
angle of incidence the waves cannot enter
the high velocity media above and below.
(b) Waves from a focus in a high velocity
medium can always enter a low velocity
medium because they are refracted towards
the normal.

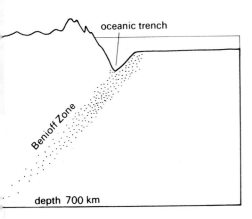

12 A Benioff Zone consists of earthquake foci
sloping from an oceanic trench beneath an
island arc or young mountain range.

In our study of the optical properties of
inerals we saw that light beams are refracted
wards the normal when they pass into a
edium which slows them down and they bend
way from the normal when they pass into a
edium which speeds them up. The rules of
fraction also apply to earthquake waves so
hanges in wave direction also provide us with
formation about the Earth's interior. Besides
eing refracted part of a beam striking a surface
: an angle is reflected. The angle between the
ormal and the reflected beam is the **angle of
eflection**. The angle of reflection is equal to
ie angle of incidence. When a beam moves
om a low-velocity medium into a high- velocity
iedium the beam is refracted away from the

normal (figure 6.13). As the angle of incidence
increases there comes a time when the angle
of refraction is 90° so no waves can enter the
high-velocity medium. This angle of incidence
is called the **critical angle**. At angles of incidence
equal to and greater than the critical angle the
waves are all reflected. Total reflection then, can
occur when waves try to pass from a low- to
a high-velocity medium. Could waves trying to
pass from a high- to a low-velocity medium be
affected in the same way? They cannot, because
the wave is bent towards the vertical and not
away from it. Overall, then, refraction, reflection
and changes of velocity are the sources of
information provided by study of earthquake
waves which allow us to work out the internal
structure of the Earth.

It has been found that earthquake waves
which do not travel vertically downwards follow
curved paths which become progressively less
steep with increasing depth until the waves
bend back towards the Earth's surface (figure
6.14). This means that the waves reach the
surface earlier than they would if they followed
straight paths. For a wave to bend in this way

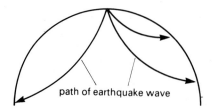

6.14 *Waves which travel deep within the Earth follow curved paths.*

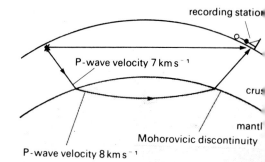

6.15 *The effect of the Mohorovicic discontinuity on earthquake waves. One set of waves remains in the crust. The other set enters the mantle, speeds up, re-enters the crust and is first to arrive at the seismometer.*

what must be happening to its velocity? Since the wave is continuously refracted away from the normal over the first half of its path its velocity must be increasing. After being reflected at the mid-point of its path it is continuously refracted towards the normal so it slows down on its way back to the surface. Since the density of the Earth increases with depth you would expect the waves to slow down with increasing depth. Why, then, do both P- and S-waves speed up as they go deeper? This can only happen because the incompressibility and rigidity of the Earth increase faster with depth than density increases.

Besides showing continuous refraction waves may suddenly change direction and velocity when they pass from one type of material into another. The surface separating materials of different properties is called a **discontinuity**. Such a discontinuity was discovered in 1909 by a Yugoslavian seismologist called Andrija Mohorovicic. He found that seismograms from shallow focus earthquakes had two sets of P- and S-waves. Mohorovicic reasoned that one set of waves had followed a direct path near the Earth's surface while the other set had gone down and been strongly refracted as it passed into a high velocity medium. The waves were then refracted back to the surface on striking the discontinuity once again (figure 6.15). This discontinuity is called the **Mohorovicic discontinuity** or the **Moho**. Above the Moho is the Earth's crust (figure 6.16) lying above another layer called the **mantle**. The thickness of the crust is very variable. Under the oceans the crust is generally about 7 km thick. Continental crust is usually about 33 km thick but it may be up to 90 km thick under major mountain ranges. In some places the continental crust is separated into lower and upper layers by the **Conrad discontinuity**. The oceanic crust is generally basaltic in character. Continental crust is very variable but, overall, it is thought to have a

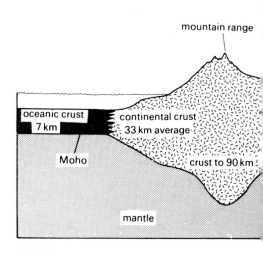

6.16 *The structure of the crust.*

composition like that of intermediate igneous rocks such as granodiorite.

It has also been found that P- and S-waves from an earthquake are not received all over the Earth. Up to epicentral angles of 103° both waves are received at recording stations. Between 103° and 142° no P- or S-waves are received. Beyond 142° only P-waves are received (figure 6.17). This situation is very similar to the focusing effect of a converging lens on light beams. Inside the Earth there is a central **core** which focuses earthquake waves in the way shown in figure 6.17. The depth to the core is about 2900 km and the surface separating the mantle from the core is called

EARTH PHYSICS

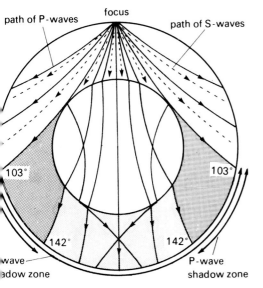

path of P-waves   focus   path of S-waves

103°   103°

142°   142°

wave   P-wave
adow zone   shadow zone

*7 Paths of P- and S-waves within the Earth.
P-waves are focused by the core. S-waves
do not pass through the core.*

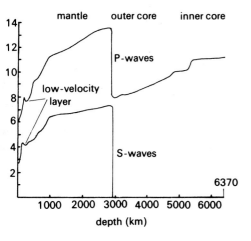

*18 Velocities of P- and S-waves within the
Earth.*

e core-mantle boundary or the **Taylor–Guten-
erg discontinuity**. Why do no S-waves pass
rough the core? You will remember that the
elocity of S-waves depends partly on the rigid-
y of the medium through which they pass and
at S-waves cannot pass through a substance
hose rigidity is zero. Since liquids have zero
gidity the indication is that the core is liquid.

P-waves passing straight through the core,
however, travel faster than they would if the
core was completely liquid and this suggests
that the core has a solid centre. The radius of
the core is 3470 km and the liquid outer core
has a thickness of 2255 km. The solid inner
core, then, has a radius of 1215 km.

The mantle is inaccessible but it is thought
to be composed of peridotite because lavas
sometimes contain xenoliths of peridotite pre-
sumably brought up from the mantle. Also,
mountain building processes sometimes bring
up wedges of peridotite again thought to be
from the mantle. In addition, the velocities of
earthquake waves are just those which would
be given by peridotite.

Travel-time curves of earthquake waves
which pass through the mantle show that the
properties of the mantle are not constant
throughout. Just below the Moho the P-wave
velocity is 8.1 km s^{-1}. Waves from earthquakes
at depths between 50 and 250 km, however,
take slightly longer than expected to arrive at
recording stations and P-wave velocities in this
zone drop to a minimum of about 7.8 km s^{-1}
at a depth of 100 km. S-wave velocities are
also reduced. It is thought that this low velocity
layer represents a zone in which the mantle
peridotite is about 5 percent molten. Since the
liquid would be basaltic this zone may be the
source of basaltic magmas. The low velocity
layer is sometimes called the **asthenosphere**
(weak sphere) or the **rheosphere** (flowing
sphere). All the material above the asthenosphere is part of the **lithosphere** (rock sphere).

At depths of about 400 and 700 km in the
mantle the velocities of earthquake waves rise
more steeply than normal. There is another less
obvious steepening of velocity at about 1050
km. The zone between 400 and 1050 km is
called the **transition zone** because in this area
it seems that the extremely high pressures
gradually change the peridotite to denser, less
compressible and more rigid material with the
same chemical composition. Below 700 km it
may be that the olivine and pyroxene of the
peridotite have changed to periclase (MgO) and
a dense form of quartz called stishovite. Alternatively, the changes may have led to the
formation of minerals unknown at the Earth's
surface. Such minerals would have their atoms
very tightly packed with six oxygen atoms clus-
tered round other atoms such as silicon, magnesium and iron.

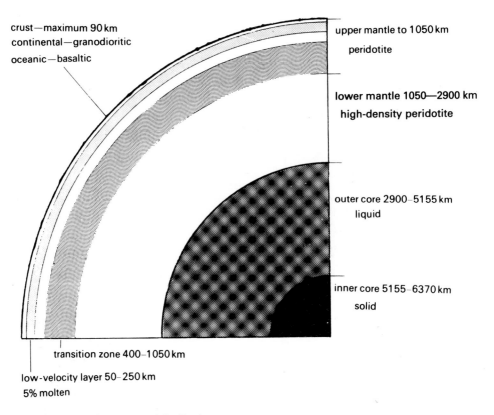

crust—maximum 90 km
continental—granodioritic
oceanic—basaltic

upper mantle to 1050 km
peridotite

lower mantle 1050—2900 km
high-density peridotite

outer core 2900—5155 km
liquid

inner core 5155—6370 km
solid

transition zone 400—1050 km

low-velocity layer 50—250 km
5% molten

6.19 The internal structure of the Earth.

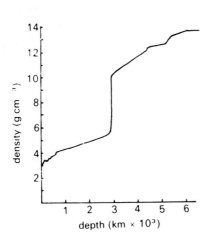

6.20 Changing density within the Earth.

At the base of the mantle P-wave velociti■ have risen to 13.6 km s^{-1} and the rock dens■ is about 5.4 g cm^{-3}. Across the core-man■ boundary the P-wave velocity drops to 8.1 km ■ and the density increases to 9.9 g cm^{-3}. In t■ inner core P-wave velocity is 11.3 km s^{-1} a■ the density is about 13.5 g cm^{-3}. The co■ is thought to consist of iron with about ■ percent nickel and 6 percent sulphur. T■ low-density sulphur is probably concentrat■ in the liquid outer core. On the other hand, t■ high-density inner core may contain as mu■ as 40 percent nickel (table 6.1).

The composition of the Earth

The layered structure of the Earth probab■ developed soon after it was formed. At this ti■ the Earth melted so dense materials could s■ and less dense materials could rise. Since mo■ of the materials of the Earth are inaccessi■ an estimate of the composition of the who■ Earth can only be made if we have some id■

EARTH PHYSICS

Table 6.1 Summary of Earth structure.

EARTH LAYERS AND DISCONTINUITIES	DEPTH (km)	VELOCITY OF P-WAVES (km s⁻¹)	DENSITY (g cm⁻³)	EARTH'S MASS (%)	EARTH'S VOLUME (%)	OTHER DETAILS
CRUST		6.0	2.7	0.7	1.5	Thickness variable. Continental crust 33 km average thickness. Oceanic crust 7 km average thickness. Continental crust granodioritic in composition. Oceanic crust basaltic
— Moho —	33	7.0	3.0			
MANTLE	50	8.0	3.3			Upper mantle peridotite
Low velocity layer	250	7.8				Low velocity layer 5% molten
Transition zone	400	8.2		68.0	82.5	
	1050	13.6	5.4			Lower mantle probably of peridotite composition but minerals in high density forms
Core-mantle boundary	2900	8.1	9.9			
OUTER CORE		10.1		31.3	16.0	Outer core probably consists of liquid iron and iron sulphide
INNER CORE	5155	11.3	13.5			Inner core probably consists of solid iron-nickel alloy
Centre of Earth	6370					

of the composition of the materials from which the Earth formed. Meteorites, which are thought to be the remains of broken asteroids or small planets in the area between Mars and Jupiter, provide us with a source of material of the type from which the Earth may have formed.

There are three kinds of meteorite. **Iron meteorites** or **irons** consist of iron–nickel alloy with nickel making up 4–20 percent of the total. They are thought to have formed at depths of about 200 km in the cores of large asteroids. Irons represent about 6 percent of meteorite falls. **Stoney-iron** meteorites consist of roughly equal proportions of iron–nickel alloy and silicate minerals which include olivine, pyroxene and plagioclase. They are thought to have formed close to the core-mantle boundaries of large asteroids. Stoney-irons are not common; they represent about 2 percent of known falls. **Stoney** meteorites or **stones** make up over 90 percent of falls. They are of two types. **Achondrites** consist of olivine, pyroxene and plagioclase. They resemble terrestrial igneous rocks and they are thought to have formed usually by the crystallization of molten material in the mantle regions of large asteroids. A few achondrites resemble basalts. **Chondrites** take their name from the presence of small globules or **chondrules** of olivine and pyroxene. Chondrites consist of olivine, pyroxene and plagioclase with some iron–nickel alloy and iron sulphide. The chondrules are thought to represent original condensed droplets of the nebular material

from which the solar system formed. Most chondrites show signs of metamorphism but they have never been molten. An important type of chondrite is the **carbonaceous chondrite**. This type consists of serpentine and olivine with a small amount of carbon and sulphur. Carbonaceous chondrites are the least altered of all meteorites and as such they probably represent the original material of the nebula from which the solar system was formed. Chondrites have probably come from asteroids which have not melted or from the cool surfaces of large asteroids which have melted internally.

In general, then, it appears that the Earth was formed by the coming together of material with the composition of carbonaceous chondrites. As it increased in size it heated up and became partly molten allowing the iron and nickel to sink to form the core while the remaining silicates were left as the mantle. In estimating the composition of the whole Earth the mass of the core (31 percent of the Earth) and of the mantle and crust (69 percent of the Earth) are found then their compositions are assumed to be similar to the constituents of chondrites. In the case of the core the materials are iron, nickel, cobalt and iron sulphide. The mantle and crust are thought to have the composition of the silicates, oxides and phosphates of the average chondrite (table 6.2). Other estimates of the composition of the mantle come from analyses of peridotite xenoliths brought up from the upper mantle by volcanoes. Another model

A meteorite crater, Wolf Crater, Western Australia. The crater has a diameter of 0.8 km.

EARTH PHYSICS

CHEMICAL CONSTITUENT	UPPER CONTINENTAL CRUST	LOWER CONTINENTAL CRUST	OCEANIC CRUST	AVERAGE GRANODIORITE	UPPER MANTLE	CORE	WHOLE EARTH	AVERAGE CHONDRITE
SiO_2	64.9	61.2	49.2	66.9	44.5		30.7	36.6
Al_2O_3	14.6	16.4	15.8	15.7	3.1		3.3	2.3
$FeO + Fe_2O_3$	4.2	5.8	9.4	3.9	7.9		5.0	10.5
MgO	2.2	3.0	8.5	1.6	39.1		21.9	23.7
CaO	4.1	4.4	11.1	3.6	3.2		2.7	1.8
Na_2O	3.5	4.0	2.7	3.8	0.3		0.2	0.8
K_2O	3.1	3.0	0.3	3.1	0.04		0.02	0.1
FeS						16.35	5.1	5.3
Fe metal						75.9	28.8	15.8
Ni metal						7.4	2.0	1.6

Table 6.2   Estimated compositions of the Earth and its layers. For comparison, compositions of chondrites and granodiorite are also given. All constituents given as percentages of total weight

for the composition of the mantle suggests that the upper mantle is peridotite only because it has been partly melted and so has lost constituents equivalent to basaltic magma. This idea is the **pyrolite** model and it suggests that, overall, the mantle is made up of pyrolite, a rock whose composition is equivalent to three-quarters peridotite and one-quarter basalt.

Since the crust is the accessible part of the Earth numerous crustal rock samples have been analysed. To obtain the overall composition of the crust estimates have to be made of the varying proportions and compositions of the different rock types. The ocean floors consist very largely of basalt and the composition of oceanic crust has been estimated simply by taking the average composition of basalts dredged up from oceanic ridges (table 6.2). The continental crust consists of more varied rock types and numerous estimates of its composition have been made. In general, though, it would appear that the upper continental crust has a composition very similar to that of granodiorite (table 6.2). The composition of the lower crust remains in doubt. It is possible that the lower crust is slightly more basic than the upper crust (table 6.2). Relative to the upper crust, it appears that the lower crust is depleted in elements such as potassium, uranium, thorium and rubidium. During evolution of the crust it is probable that these elements have been preferentially carried into the upper crust by granitic magmas.

Earthquake prediction and control

Every year earthquakes kill an average of about 14 000 people. At times, single earthquakes can cause very high death tolls, e.g. in 1556 about 830 000 people died in an earthquake in Shansi (China); in Tangshan, also in China, about 655 000 people were killed in 1976. Earthquakes also cause considerable damage. In 1906 San Francisco (USA) was badly damaged mostly by the fire which followed an earthquake and in 1960 the city of Agadir (Morocco) was destroyed. Submarine earthquakes may set off **tsunami** or seismic sea-waves. (Tsunami are often wrongly called 'tidal waves'.) Such waves may cause damage in coastal regions. In 1755 Lisbon (Portugal) was

destroyed by a combination of earthquakes, fire and huge waves up to about 9 m high. In 1923 Tokyo (Japan) was similarly destroyed by earthquakes and accompanying tsunami.

Because of their destructive nature it would be of great value if we could say where and when earthquakes were about to happen. For some time before rocks fracture to produce an earthquake forces build up and the rocks are strongly deformed or strained. Just before fracture the rocks swell up a little as numerous small cracks spread through them. Changes in rock volumes over large areas can be detected by repeated surveying, by observing changes in sea level and by using tiltmeters. A tiltmeter consists of two liquid-filled reservoirs connected by a long tube. When the land tilts the liquid levels in the reservoirs change with respect to each other allowing a tilt as little as 1 mm km^{-1} to be detected. Strain also affects the physical properties of the rocks and their magnetism and resistance to electricity change. Also, the velocities of seismic waves change. In one case, P-waves velocity was 5.3 km s^{-1} before a major earthquake and 6.3 km s^{-1} after the earthquake. It has also been observed that small earthquakes die out before a major earthquake then they increase just before the main shock. Yet another observed change is that the amount of radioactive radon increases in the water of deep wells just before an earthquake. Changes such as these begin at least ten years before a major earthquake.

The described changes along with other minor effects give warning of an approaching earthquake. Unfortunately, however, this does not mean that the exact time and place of the earthquake can be predicted. In only a few cases have earthquakes been successfully forecast. Some day, however, it may be possible to control or modify earthquakes. In 1965 at Denver, Colorado, it was found that waste water injected into deep wells triggered off small earthquakes. This happened because the water lubricated faults and allowed them to move. This finding led to the idea that it may be possible to inject water into major fault systems where damaging earthquakes could occur. The water would reduce friction allowing faulting to take place by a series of small movements giving off minor earthquakes. This would prevent the build-up of the large strains necessary to produce major earthquakes.

The Earth's gravity

The force of gravity is the force of attraction between objects. Where two masses (m_1 and m_2) are separated by distance r the force of attraction between them is:

$$F = \frac{G m_1 m_2}{r^2}$$

where G (the *gravitational constant*) has the value 6.67×10^{-11} N m² kg⁻².

We can use the relationship above to find the mass of the Earth by measuring the gravitational force on a known mass at the surface of the Earth so that the distance r becomes the radius of the Earth. The equation can be rewritten as:

$$\text{mass of Earth} = \frac{F \times (\text{radius of Earth})^2}{G \times \text{known mass}}$$

Since force equals mass times acceleration and the acceleration due to gravity (g) can be measured (g = 9.8 metres per second per second) we can find F. By these means it has been found that the Earth has a mass of 5.978×10^{24} kg. The volume of the Earth is about 1.08×10^{21} m³ and dividing the mass by the volume gives about 5500 kg m⁻³ (5.5 g cm⁻³) for the density of the Earth. Since very few surface materials have densities as high as this it would appear that the density of the Earth increases with depth.

The acceleration due to gravity can be accurately measured using an instrument called a **gravimeter**. It has been found that the force of gravity varies slightly from place to place. Why should this be so? The main reason is that the mass of material in the crust changes from place to place. Knowing the radius and mass of the Earth it is possible to say theoretically what the force of gravity at the Earth's surface should be. However, where there is an excess of material the force of gravity is slightly above normal and where there is a deficit of material the force of gravity is slightly less than it should be. These departures from the theoretical values are called **gravity anomalies**. A **positive anomaly** is caused by an excess of mass while a **negative anomaly** is caused by a deficit of mass. Anomalies are given in terms of **milligals** (mgal). A milligal is an acceleration of 10^{-3} cm s⁻². Gravity anomaly maps are prepared by joining up points of equal anomaly by lines called **isogals** (figure 6.21).

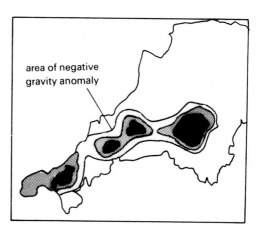

area of negative gravity anomaly

6.21 Negative gravity anomalies occur in S.W. England because of the presence of low-density granites. The darker the shading the stronger the anomaly.

Isostasy

In many ways the low density crust behaves as if it floats on the high density mantle. The concept of the floating crust is called the **principle of isostasy**. Since this idea seems to be true we can use the example of wooden blocks in water to help us understand the behaviour of the crust (figure 6.22). In condition A the block is floating normally. When the crust behaves like this it has no tendency to sink or rise and there is no gravity anomaly. In B the block is held up and denser water occupies the space once taken by the block. This means that there is an excess of material present and in the case of the crust this would give a positive gravity anomaly. If the wooden block were not held up it would tend to sink to position A. In C the block has been pushed down so the wood displaces some water. This produces a deficit of material which in the crust would give a negative gravity anomaly. Releasing the block in C would allow it to rise to position A. In the same way that blocks B and C tend to move to position A the crust tends to move by **isostatic movements** to a normal floating position so that gravity anomalies are removed. When the crust is in a normal floating position with no tendency to move up or down and with

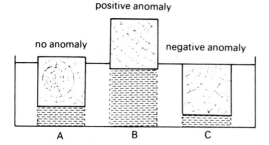

positive anomaly

no anomaly

negative anomaly

A   B   C

6.22 The principle of isostasy illustrated by wooden blocks in water. A is floating normally. If the block were the crust it would be in isostatic equilibrium and there would be no gravity anomaly. The raised block B has an excess of water underneath giving what would be a positive gravity anomaly. The depressed block C has a deficit of water underneath giving a negative gravity anomaly.

Raised sea cliffs near Crail, Fife. The present beach is in the foreground.

no gravity anomalies it is said to be in a condition of **isostatic equilibrium**.

A good example of isostatic adjustment is provided by the effects of the weight of ice sheets on land. At present, the ice sheets of Antarctica (ice 4 km thick) and Greenland (ice 3 km thick) have caused parts of these land masses to be depressed below sea level. Scandinavia was similarly depressed during the last Ice Age. When the ice melted about 10 000 years ago Scandinavia acquired a negative gravity anomaly because it remained relatively depressed. Melting of the ice caused sea level to rise and the depressed land was submerged. Later slow isostatic movements raised the land and caused the sea to retreat leaving **raised shorelines** as it went. Greatest isostatic recovery takes place where the ice was thickest because this was where the land was most depressed. In such areas of Scandinavia uplift is occurring at the rate of about 1 cm per year (figure 6.23). This means that uplift of about 100 m has taken place since the ice retreated. Another 200 m of uplift will have to take place before isostatic equilibrium is attained.

Isostatic adjustments also take place when the crust is loaded by deposition or unloaded by erosion. In an area such as the Mississippi delta where large quantities of sediment are being laid down on the sea floor a positive gravity anomaly would be expected to develop because of the extra mass of material being

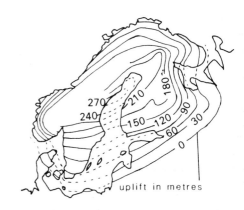

uplift in metres

6.23 Amount of isostatic uplift over Scandinavia during the last 10 000 years.

deposited. However, no anomaly has developed because the crust receiving the sediment has sunk to maintain isostatic equilibrium. Mountain areas lose large quantities of material by erosion. However, negative gravity anomalies do not usually develop because the mountains rise isostatically to keep pace with erosion. In the Himalayas, for example, rivers such as the Indus and Brahmaputra flow from north to south across the mountain ranges. This happens because the rivers existed before the mountains and they have cut down through more than 5000 m of rock to keep pace with uplift.

130   EARTH PHYSICS

In the oceans volcanic islands usually form less than about 5 Ma (million years). The mass of extruded material causes the development of a positive gravity anomaly and the islands subside isostatically to form sea mounts and flat-topped guyots. Guyots are flat because their tops were eroded by wave action before they sank. Where the original island lay in tropical or subtropical regions a fringing coral reef may have grown around it. As the island sinks coral growth keeps pace with subsidence and a barrier reef forms. (Coral reefs grow at an average rate of 1.4 cm per year. Rates may, however, be as high as 2.5 cm per year.) Further subsidence accompanied by coral growth leads to the eventual formation of a ring shaped atoll (figure 6.24). It should be noted that the formation of the Great Barrier Reef of Australia is not related to isostatic movements of the sea floor. It has grown on a block moved down on a huge fracture or fault running along the coast of Queensland.

Also in the oceans it has been found that large negative gravity anomalies are associated with the deep trenches (figure 6.25). This indicates that in such areas low density material is being forcefully held down so the trench is out of isostatic equilibrium.

When wooden blocks in water move up or down water flows sideways towards or away from the area under the block. It may be that a similar flow of material takes place inside the earth, perhaps in the asthenosphere. It could also be that isostatic movements are compensated by phase changes in the mantle. When part of the crust is loaded it may sink because the increased pressure may cause the minerals in the upper mantle to change to higher density forms with smaller volumes than before. Unloading the crust would cause the high density minerals to revert to their high-volume, low-density forms as the pressure is released.

The Earth as a magnet

The Earth behaves as if it had an internal bar magnet lying at an angle of about 11° to its axis. Since the north pole of a compass needle points north and since the opposite poles attract, it follows that it is the south pole of the Earth's internal magnet which is geographically north (figure 6.32). The field of a bar magnet is called a **dipole** because two poles are present. The Earth's magnetic field is almost

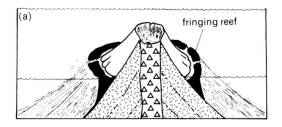

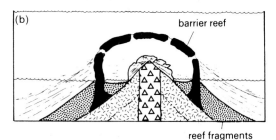

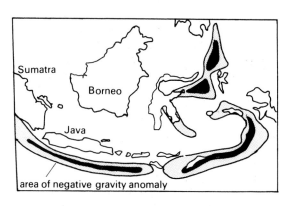

6.24 Atoll formation. Initially, a fringing reef grows round a new volcanic island. As the island sinks isostatically coral growth keeps pace to form a barrier reef then an atoll.

6.25 Strong negative anomalies associated with the oceanic trenches of the East Indies. (The darker the shading the stronger the anomaly.)

dipolar but it is not exactly so. Find the field of a large, strong bar magnet by sprinkling iron filings on a sheet of paper above the magnet. Now place some small, weak magnets in various positions next to the large magnet. You can embed the small magnets in Plasticine to prevent them from rotating. What is the new magnetic field like? You will have found that the field is less regular than before since it is made up of the regular field of the large bar magnet along with the irregular field of the small magnets. Now take away the large, strong magnet and find the field of the small, weak magnets. This irregular field is called a **non-dipole** field. Like the field of the large and small magnets together, the Earth's field may be considered as consisting of dipole and non-dipole elements. The irregular non-dipole field makes up about 5 percent of the total field of the Earth. The strength of the non-dipole field can be found simply by subtracting the dipole field from the total field.

6.26 *Map showing variation in the strength of the Earth's magnetic field for the year 1975. (The darker the shading the stronger the field.) The field strength at the poles is about twice that at the equator.*

We can partly describe the Earth's field by measuring the strength of the field at various places over the Earth's surface. We can then draw magnetic contour maps where the contours join points of equal field strength (figure 6.26). We can also determine the angle (**declination**) between geographic north and magnetic north at various places and again draw maps where contours join points of equal declination (figure 6.27). Finally, because the Earth's magnet is internally situated, a compass needle allowed to swing vertically will settle at an angle to the horizontal called the **inclination**. We can measure this angle at various points and draw contour maps showing equal inclinations.

The Earth's magnetic field changes with time (figure 6.28). Firstly, the strength of the field changes. At present, the field strength is decreasing by about 5 percent every 100 years. Secondly, the field drifts towards the west. Drift of the dipole field is shown by the north geomagnetic pole which has moved from 64°W to 70°W in the last 140 years. This represents a westward movement of about 0.04° longitude every year. Over the same period of time the latitude of the north geomagnetic pole has remained at 79°N. The irregular non-dipole

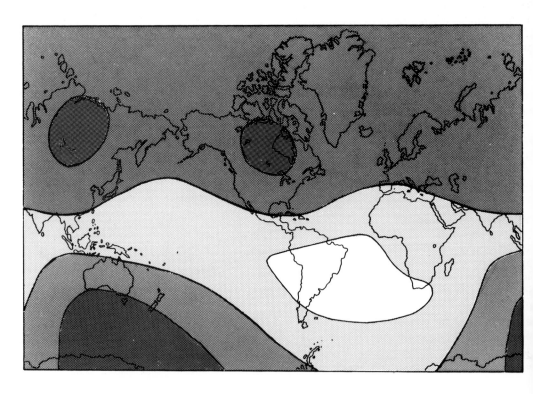

EARTH PHYSICS

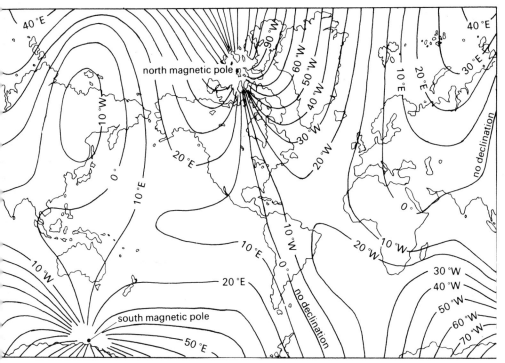

27 *Map showing variation in magnetic decli-*
nation over the Earth's surface for 1975.

ld changes much faster than the dipole field.
e non-dipole field is drifting west at about
2° longitude per year. Its strength also
anges relatively quickly.

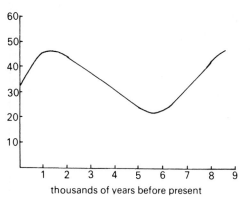

28 *Variation in the strength of the Earth's mag-*
netic field for the last 9000 years.

Origin of the magnetic field

Although the Earth's magnetic field looks as if
it is produced by a giant bar magnet at the
centre of the Earth this cannot be the case
because the very high temperatures near the
Earth's centre would prevent any material from
being magnetic. However, magnetic fields also
exist round wires which are carrying electricity
and a coil of wire carrying a current produces
a magnetic field of the type produced by a bar
magnet. It may be, therefore, that electric currents are flowing somewhere inside the Earth
and these currents produce the magnetic field.
Indeed, circular currents flowing from east to
west under the equator would produce a field
similar to the Earth's magnetic field. But where
could the currents be? Since the Earth's core
is largely metal it would seem to be the right
material to sustain electric currents. But how
could electric currents be produced? How does
a dynamo on a bicycle work? In a dynamo an
electric conductor is moved through a magnetic
field and a current is induced in the conductor.
In its turn, the current produces a magnetic field
round the conductor. It is thought that the
Earth's magnetic field is produced by a dynamo
effect in the outer core where movements of

conducting liquid metal could provide the energy needed to drive the dynamo. The **self-exciting disc dynamo** (figure 6.29) first designed by Michael Faraday (1791–1867) gives us a simple model of how the Earth's magnetic field might be sustained. In this dynamo a copper disc spins above a coil whose magnetic field generates electricity; in its turn, the electric current generates a magnetic field in the coil. The disc dynamo has to be started by inducing an initial magnetic field in the coil but, once started, the dynamo is self-sustaining. Similarly, in the outer core convection currents by themselves would not produce electricity or magnetism and it has been suggested that the magnetic field required to start the dynamo came from outside the Earth. The heat to drive the convection currents is thought to be derived from gravitational energy released as dense material freezes and sinks towards the inner core. The gravitational energy may be converted to electricity which is then converted to heat.

The rotation of the Earth seems to have a significant effect on the magnetic field by exerting forces on the moving liquid in the core. These forces produce effects like those seen on weather maps where the air in a cyclone moves round in a cylindrical form. In the core the liquid probably flows in forms like spiral staircases with the cylinders lined up parallel to the axis of rotation. This would explain why the Earth's geographical and geomagnetic poles are so close to each other.

The idea that the Earth's magnetic field results partly from convection currents in the core may also explain the observed changes in the magnetic field, e.g. the relatively rapid changes in the non-dipole field may reflect changes in the pattern and strength of the convection currents in the outer core. Indeed, the rate of westward drift of the non-dipole field indicates fluid flow at a rate of about 1 mm s^{-1} in the outer core.

Ancient magnetism

Evidence of the Earth's magnetic field through geological time is preserved in rocks because when rocks are formed iron-containing minerals are lined up like tiny magnets. The direction and strength of the ancient magnetism is related to the direction and strength of the Earth's magnetic field at the time when the rock was formed. Measurements of the inclination and declination of the ancient magnetic field allow the position of the ancient magnetic pole to be found relative to the position of the rock. Where the geomagnetic and geographical poles are in the same place the relationship between inclination and latitude is:

$$\tan I - 2 \tan \theta$$

where I is inclination and θ is latitude. In other words, if the magnetism of a rock sample gives a reading of zero inclination then the rock formed at 90° to the magnetic poles. If the inclination is 90° then the rock formed at magnetic pole. Steepening values of inclination occur as the rock position gets nearer the magnetic pole (figure 6.30).

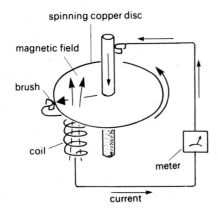

6.29 The self-exciting dynamo. Once the dynamo has been started by inducing a magnetic field in the coil it is self sustaining.

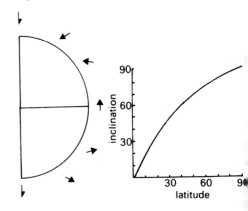

6.30 Variation of inclination with latitude.

EARTH PHYSICS

he study of ancient magnetism or **palaeo-gnetism** has shown two notable features.

irstly, pole positions from many ancient ks do not coincide with the position of the sent pole. This could be because the rock stayed in the same position and the pole moved or it could be because the rock has ved taking its ancient pole position with it so giving the false impression that the pole moved. Study of rocks of the same age from erent continents often give different pole sitions. This means that the continents have ved over the surface of the Earth because erent pole positions cannot exist at the same e and a single pole position can only be ained by moving the continents back to their jinal positions (figure 6.31). The strong indi-ion is, then, that the magnetic and geo-phic poles have been in similar positions ough geological time. This means that ding pole positions tells us the latitude of rock at the time of its formation. Note that can tell nothing about the longitude of a k when it was formed.

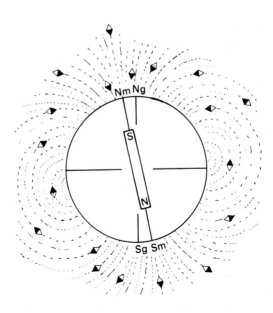

6.32 The Earth's magnetic field. (Note that there is no internal bar magnet.) This field is normal. In the reversed condition the N and S magnetic poles are the other way round.

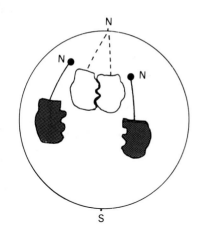

1 Ancient pole positions determined for rocks of the same age on separate continents (shaded) may differ. Moving the continents to their original positions (unshaded) gives coincident pole positions.

Secondly, palaeomagnetic studies have own that some rocks have been magnetized a direction opposite to that of the present agnetic field. This shows that the magnetic ld has switched itself around from its present rmal condition to a **reversed** condition (figure 32). Field reversals seem to take place fairly

regularly. It has been possible to erect a **polarity time-scale** showing times when the field was normal and reversed for about the last 4.5 Ma (figure 6.33). Beyond this time reversals did occur but the rocks cannot be dated with sufficient accuracy to allow the time scale to be extended. It seems that before a reversal the field dies away slowly over a period of about 10 000 years then the field reverses and begins to grow again. Various suggestions have been made to explain the mechanism of reversal. In the self-exciting disc dynamo reversing the current reverses the magnetic field even when the disc is spinning in only one direction. If electric currents in some convection cells of the outer core stopped for some reason they could be influenced to restart in the opposite direction by minor reversed magnetic fields from nearby convection cells. In this way the reversal might spread throughout the system of convection cells. It has also been suggested that reversals take place in constantly working dynamos. It is known, for example, that two disc dynamos coupled together with their coils con-nected to each other's brushes repeatedly reverse their fields. Perhaps in the core the electrical circuits of the dynamos are coupled together and field reversal is a property of the dynamo system.

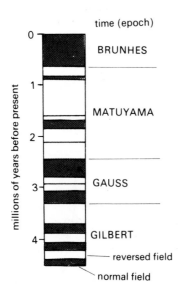

time (epoch)

BRUNHES

MATUYAMA

GAUSS

GILBERT

— reversed field

— normal field

6.33 Polarity time-scale showing changes in the condition of the Earth's magnetic field for the last 4.5 Ma.

The Earth's internal heat

The fact that volcanoes produce molten rock is a very strong indication that the inside of the Earth is much hotter than the surface. In general, temperature increases with depth at an average rate of 0.03 °C m⁻¹ so that at a depth of 1 km the temperature would be 30°C above that at the surface. The rate at which the temperature rises (the **geothermal gradient**) is very variable. In some parts of the crust temperature rises very slowly with depth while in other parts temperature rises very rapidly. Why should this be the case? Steep geothermal gradients are found in areas of igneous activity where magma chambers or cooling batholiths provide heat sources at depth.

Since the inside of the Earth is hotter than the outside it follows that heat must flow outwards. **Heat flow** is measured in joules per square metre per second (J m⁻² s⁻¹). Heat flow depends on the geothermal gradient (the steeper the gradient the greater the heat flow) and on how well the rocks conduct heat. Rocks which are relatively good conductors permit a high heat flow. Heat flow has to be measured at depths below about 30 m so that the Sun's heat will not affect the measurements.

Where does the heat come from?

The Earth's internal heat could come from fou possible sources. Some heat could still be le over from when the Earth formed. The energ derived from the impact of infalling particle and the compression of material as the Eart grew could have produced heat. The decay c short-lived radioisotopes could also have pro duced a lot of heat soon after the Earth wa formed. This early formed heat may still provid a small portion of the heat escaping from th Earth.

Another possible source of heat could be th result of the slowing of the Earth's rotation a loss of kinetic energy could be converted t heat. This would only contribute a small pa of the observed heat flow.

The formation of the Earth's core would hav released a lot of gravitational energy. It has bee calculated that the heat energy released by thi process could have raised the temperature c the whole Earth to 1500°C. If the temperatur of the Earth soon after its formation rose t this level then this early heat could be respons ible for 20 percent of the present heat flow.

By far the most important heat source is th decay of long-lived radioisotopes such as thos of uranium, thorium and potassium. Table 6. shows the amount of heat produced by th various isotopes.

RADIOISOTOPE	HEAT PRODUCTION Jkg⁻¹year⁻¹
^{238}U	2967.8
^{235}U	17 974.0
^{232}Th	836.0
^{40}K	877.8

Table 6.3 Heat production by radioisotopes

Since different rocks have different quantitie of these heat-producing elements, differen rocks have different heat producing qualitie (table 6.4).

Table 6.4 provides us with a strong indicatior that heat producing radioisotopes are concen trated at high levels in the Earth since low density, siliceous igneous rocks contain more

136   EARTH PHYSICS

ROCK	CONCENTRATION OF ELEMENTS (ppm)			HEAT PRODUCTION (J kg^{-1} year^{-1})
	U	Th	K	
Granite	4	20	40 000	3×10^{-8}
Basalt	0.5	2	15 000	0.57×10^{-8}
Peridotite	0.02	0.06	200	0.01×10^{-8}

able 6.4   Heat production by rocks

dioisotopes than basic igneous rocks. Also, e granodioritic continental crust would pear to have a higher concentration of radio- otopes than the basaltic oceanic crust.

eat flow over the Earth

ome regional variations in heat flow are shown table 6.5. Here you can see the general lationship of high heat flow being associated th the igneous activity of oceanic ridges and ung mountain ranges while the lowest values e found in ancient shield areas.

AREA OF EARTH'S SURFACE	HEAT FLOW (J m^{-2} s^{-1})
Whole Earth	0.069
All oceans	0.069
All continents	0.069
Ocean basins	0.053
Oceanic ridges	0.080
Oceanic trenches	0.049
Ancient shield areas (older than 570 Ma)	0.041
Platform areas younger than 570 Ma)	0.062
Old mountain areas (570–225 Ma)	0.060
oung mountain areas younger than 225 Ma)	0.074

ble 6.5   Heat flow over the Earth

We have seen that heat producing radio- isotopes are more abundant in continental crust than in oceanic crust. Surprisingly, though, average levels of heat flow from continental and oceanic crust are about equal. The observed heat flow from the continental crust could easily be produced by the rocks of the continental crust. The oceanic crust could not produce the observed heat flow so it would appear that heat comes largely from the underlying mantle. This indicates that the mantle under the oceans is hotter than the mantle under the continents. This may be because there are convection currents under the oceans but not under the continents. The currents bring heat from greater depths and they turn and flow under the oceanic crust giving off heat which escapes through the crust. The fact that the highest levels of heat flow occur at the oceanic ridges and the heat flow decreases across the ocean basins and reaches its lowest values in the oceanic trenches indicates that the convection currents rise under the ridges and flow off under the ocean basins towards the oceanic trenches (figure 6.34).

Temperatures inside the Earth

Trying to find how temperatures rise inside the Earth is like trying to find the temperature of hot tea inside a sealed vacuum flask. We can get some clues about the internal temperature of the Earth from measurements of surface temperatures and rates of heat flow. However, we cannot say exactly how temperatures rise within the Earth because we do not know enough about factors such as the distribution at depth of heat-producing radioisotopes or how much heat has been left over from the Earth's formation. Also, we do not know enough

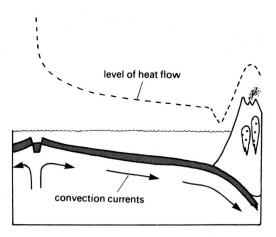

level of heat flow

convection currents

6.34 *Variations in heat flow across the oceans suggest that mantle convection currents ascend under the oceanic ridges and descend under the oceanic trenches*

It should be noted, however, that the melting point of the peridotite may be lowered by the presence of water. In the outer core the temperature must exceed the melting point of nickel-iron at the prevailing pressure. In the solid inner core the temperature is below the melting point.

Estimates of actual temperatures are very variable. Figure 6.35 shows a possible curve of temperature distribution within the Earth. From a surface temperature of about 20°C the temperature increases fairly rapidly to reach 1000°C at the top of the low velocity layer. At a depth of 400 km where phase changes begin in the mantle the temperature may have reached 1600°C. The temperature probably rises slowly thereafter to reach 3000 to 4000° at the base of the mantle and perhaps 5000° in the inner core.

about the ways in which heat escapes. It appears that most heat escapes by conduction but convection and radiation may also play a part in heat loss.

Despite these uncertainties, however, we can be reasonably sure of certain features. Firstly, because of the fact that radioisotopes are concentrated in the upper layers of the Earth it is very likely that temperatures rise very rapidly for about 200 km below the surface. Secondly, temperatures beneath the oceans are higher than those beneath the continents. At about 1000 km, however, the temperatures under both oceans and continents are probably the same. Thirdly, the melting points of rocks increase with pressure. In the partly molten low-velocity layer the temperature must approach the melting point of peridotite at this particular pressure.

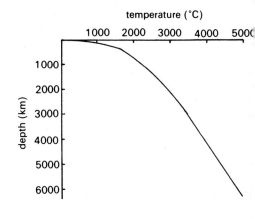

6.35 *Changing temperature within the Earth.*

EARTH PHYSICS

METAMORPHIC ROCKS

etamorphic rocks are formed by the solid-
ate recrystallization of pre-existing rocks
nder the action of heat and pressure. Meta-
orphism does not usually change the overall
hemical composition of the earlier rock and
e types of new minerals which form are
ctated by the conditions of temperature and
ressure. That is, the same kinds of rocks
etamorphosed under different conditions will
roduce metamorphic rocks containing differ-
nt mineral assemblages. Metamorphism may
ot completely destroy the structures of the
arlier rock and its sedimentary, igneous or
etamorphic nature may be recognized. Even
hen complete recrystallization has taken place
e chemistry of the metamorphic rock may
dicate the rock from which it was derived.

Metamorphism takes place in three ways: in
ermal or **contact metamorphism** the heat from
n igneous intrusion alters the adjacent country
ck; **regional metamorphism** takes place on a
rge scale in the roots of developing mountain
hains; **dynamic** or **dislocation metamorphism**
sults from localized deformation along zones
ch as fault planes.

hermal or contact metamorphism

hermal metamorphism results from the heat-
g of rocks close to an igneous intrusion. The
mount of heat which comes from an intrusion
epends largely on the size of the intrusion.
ery small intrusions have narrow zones of
etamorphic rocks adjacent to them while large
trusions may metamorphose a few kilometres
f country rock (figure 7.1). Low temperature
cidic intrusions do not have narrower zones
f metamorphism than higher temperature
asic intrusions because acidic magmas give
ff water which aids the process of metamorhism. The zone of metamorphic rocks round
large intrusion is called a **metamorphic** or
ontact **aureole**. Away from an intrusion the
emperature falls and the effects of metamorhism progressively decline and disappear (fig-
re 7.2). The different levels of metamorphism

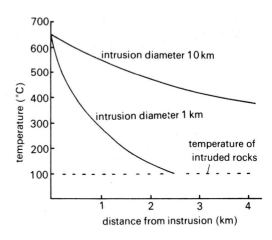

7.1 *Decreasing country-rock temperatures away
from large (10 km diameter) and small
(1 km diameter) granitic intrusions.*

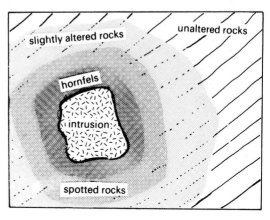

7.2 *Metamorphic aureole round a large
intrusion. The grade of metamorphism
decreases outwards.*

are described as differences in **metamorphic
grade**. High grade metamorphic rocks have
suffered intense metamorphism at high temperature while low grade metamorphic rocks
have been weakly metamorphosed at low temperature. Some rocks show the effects of metamorphism more easily than others. For example,

Unit 7

an intrusion in mudstones would produce a wide aureole while the same intrusion in sandstone would have a narrow aureole.

The various grades of metamorphism can be recognized by the successive appearance of distinctive **index minerals** as the intrusion is approached. On the outside of the aureole the country rocks suffer only partial recrystallization and structures such as bedding remain. At the low temperatures on the margin of the aureole, organic matter in argillaceous rocks is altered to form spots of graphite, Iron oxides such as limonite and haematite are also altered to form spots of magnetite. Chlorite and white mica also appear. With increasing temperature towards the intrusion some spots consist of large crystals or **porphyroblasts** which have grown in the otherwise unchanged rock. Initially, the porphyroblasts are indistinct, loose-knit crystals of chiastolite (a form of andalusite). At intermediate temperatures towards the intrusion the chiastolite porphyroblasts become more clearly defined. The mineral **cordierite** is often found in these parts of metamorphic aureoles. It looks very like quartz in thin section but it often shows a yellow alteration product. Cordierite often forms large crystals containing numerous small crystals of other minerals. This texture is **sieve** or **poikiloblastic texture**. Biotite also tends to appear at intermediate temperatures. A fairly typical rock of intermediate grade might have porphyroblasts of chiastolite and cordierite in a matrix of quartz, biotite, muscovite and opaque minerals.

At high temperatures on the inside of the aureole the structures in the original rock are almost completely destroyed and the metamorphic rock is hard and massive. The rock tends to break with a conchoidal fracture into sharp-edged splinters. Metamorphic rock of this type is called **hornfels**. Hornfels often has a fine- or medium-grained **granoblastic texture** consisting of equal sized, equidimensional grains. Hornfels formed from argillaceous rock may consist of andalusite, cordierite, biotite and quartz. At the highest temperatures the biotite and andalusite disappear and the hornfels consists of sillimanite, pyroxene (hypersthene), potassium feldspar (sanidine), cordierite and quartz.

Thermal metamorphism of pure quartz sandstone causes the quartz to recrystallize to give a granoblastic mosaic of interlocking grains. The grain boundaries often meet at about 120° because each quartz grain pushes on its neighbours with roughly equal force as it tries t grow. In impure sandstones the quartz an feldspar recrystallize while minerals such a muscovite, chlorite, haematite, calcite and cla minerals are altered to give biotite, magnetite epidote, garnet, andalusite, sillimanite and cor dierite. The metamorphism of sandstone lead to the formation of **metaquartzite**.

The thermal metamorphism of pure calcit limestone results in its recrystallization t **marble**. At low pressure, heating calcium car bonate gives calcium oxide and carbon dioxid (CO_2). In a metamorphic aureole the CO_2 doe not escape because the reaction takes plac under pressure. On heating, dolomite decom poses to give calcite, periclase (MgO) and CO_2. In this case the CO_2 can escape because th reaction is less inhibited by pressure. The peri clase is often changed to brucite, $Mg(OH)_2$, b the addition of water. Quartz in limestone react with calcite to give wollastonite ($CaSiO_3$) an CO_2 which escapes. Quartz reacts with dolomit to give magnesium and calcium silicates suc as talc.

When basic igneous rock is metamorphose at low temperature augite is hydrated and con verted to hornblende. At higher temperatur plagioclase recrystallizes and a hornblende plagioclase hornfels results. At very high tem perature pyroxene forms from the hornblende and the resulting hornfels may look like the original igneous rock. When acidic igneou rocks are thermally metamorphosed the quart and feldspar may recrystallize to form an inter locking mosaic. At low temperatures horn blende is altered to biotite while at high tem perature augite forms from hornblende and biotite. **Halleflinta** is a flint-like hornfels formed by the metamorphism of rhyolite or ignimbrite

Chemically, the rock generally shows a pro gressive reduction in H_2O and CO_2 as the grade of metamorphism increases. Sometimes, gases and fluids from the magma carry elements such as chlorine, fluorine, sodium, potassium and boron into the surrounding rock producing changes by **contact metasomatism**. Contact meta somatism is more common around the rela tively wet acidic magmas than around the dr basic magmas. The slightly acidic fluids from the magma react with limestone to form rock called **skarns** which may contain ores (oxide and sulphides) and a range of magnesium calcium, boron and manganese silicates.

	ROCK NAME	COLOUR	GRAIN SIZE	MAIN MINERALS	ORIGINAL ROCK
UNFOLIATED	Hornfels	Grey, black, bluish, greenish	Fine – medium	Variable — feldspar, quartz, andalusite, biotite, cordierite, sillimanite, pyroxene	Mudstone or other fine-grained rock
FOLIATED OR UNFOLIATED	Marble	White, grey, black, red, green, yellow	Medium – coarse	Calcite, calcium and magnesium silicates	Limestone, dolomite
	Metaquartzite	White, grey	Medium – coarse	Quartz	Sandstone
FOLIATED OR BANDED	Slate	Black, grey, brown, greenish, bluish	Very fine	Quartz, muscovite, chlorite, feldspar	Mudstone, tuff, marl
	Phyllite	Grey, green, silvery	Fine	Quartz, muscovite, chlorite, feldspar	Mudstone, tuff, marl
	Schist	Variable — white, grey, green, black, brown, bluish. Often shiny	Medium – coarse	Variable — quartz, mica, chlorite, feldspar, garnet, hornblende, kyanite, staurolite, epidote, sillimanite	Mudstone, greywacke, tuff, basalt, andesite, rhyolite
	Gneiss	Variable — pink, grey, black. Often banded	Medium – coarse	Feldspar, quartz, mica, hornblende, garnet, pyroxene	Mudstone, greywacke, igneous rocks, other metamorphic rocks
	Migmatite	Mixed dark and pale. Coarsely banded	Medium – coarse	Feldspar, quartz, hornblende, mica, garnet	Gneiss which has partly melted
	Amphibolite	Black, green	Medium – coarse	Hornblende, feldspar, garnet, quartz	Basic igneous rocks
	Granulite	Grey, brown	Medium – coarse	Pyroxene, feldspar, quartz, garnet	Mudstone, greywacke, igneous rocks
	Serpentinite	Green, grey, black	Medium – coarse	Serpentine	Ultrabasic igneous rocks

Table 7.1   Some metamorphic rocks

Regional metamorphism

Regional metamorphism is a large scale process resulting from mountain building or orogenesis. The rocks are generally subjected to high stresses as well as high temperatures. The rock types which form depend on the composition of the original rock and on the conditions of temperature and pressure at the time of metamorphism.

Under conditions of high stress and relatively low temperature fine-grained rocks such as shales, tuffs and marls are converted to **slate**. Slate has a well defined cleavage (slaty cleavage) which allows it to be split into thin sheets. Slates are usually grey, black or shades of blue, green and brown. They consist mainly of quartz, muscovite and chlorite oriented parallel to the cleavage. Pyrite is often present. Since metamorphism has taken place at low temperature the rock has suffered only partial recrystallization. Under the microscope many of the quartz grains can be seen to be deformed sedimentary grains. The original bedding may form layers of different colour oblique to the cleavage and highly deformed fossils may be present. **Phyllite** is similar to slate but it has suffered more recrystallization so it is coarser grained and it has less perfect cleavage than slate. Phyllite tends to be shiny and it is usually grey or green in colour.

As the temperature of metamorphism increases medium- or coarse-grained **schists** form. The planar alignment of the mineral grains gives a type of foliation called **schistosity**. (**Foliation** is a planar structure found in metamorphic rocks formed under stress.) At relatively low temperatures phyllite grades into **chlorite schist**. Chlorite schist is green or grey and its main minerals are quartz, chlorite, white mica, epidote and feldspar. At higher temperatures **mica schist** forms. Mica schists consist mostly of muscovite, biotite and quartz. Feldspar and chlorite may be present. Mica schist rich in garnet is called garnet mica-schist. Other schists named from the presence of distinctive minerals include staurolite schist, kyanite schist and sillimanite schist.

Gneiss is formed as the grade of metamorphism becomes still higher. The foliation acquires a banded form (**gneissose banding**) which may show dark layers rich in hornblende, biotite, pyroxene or garnet and pale layers rich in quartz and feldspar. **Augen** (eyed) **gneiss** has

oval porphyroblastic quartz-feldspar masses s[...] in a finer matrix. Gneissose banding may ori[...] inate in various ways. Sometimes the bands a[...] the remains of pre-existing bedding. In som[...] cases, low-melting point minerals such a[...] quartz and feldspar may have melted durin[...] metamorphism and become segregated fro[...] the high-melting point dark minerals. Again, th[...] bands may result from the diffusion or slo[...] spreading of sodium and potassium in on[...] direction and the diffusion of iron and ma[...] nesium in the other direction. Finally, the band[...] ing may result from the separation of differe[...] layers during intense folding.

At very high grades of metamorphism parti[...] melting produces **migmatites**. Migmatites lo[...] like mixtures of granite and dark gneiss. Th[...] granitic part represents the low-melting poi[...] fraction of the rock which has separated o[...] during metamorphism. The dark gneiss has n[...] melted during metamorphism. Migmatites ind[...] cate that granite magma can be produced b[...] partial melting during metamorphism.

The metamorphism of sandstone gives ri[...] to metaquartzite. At low temperature chlor[...] and white mica (sericite) are formed from de[...] rital clay and biotite. The quartz grains a[...] deformed with only minor recrystallization. [...] higher temperatures the rock may become di[...] tinctly foliated as the quartz recrystallizes [...] form a mosaic of interlocking grains. Biotite ar[...] muscovite grow at the expense of chlorite ar[...] sericite. Magnetite may be present if the origin[...] sandstone was rich in iron oxide. At the highe[...] grades of metamorphism the metaquartzite m[...] develop banding. Sometimes, metamorphose[...] sandstones are called **psammites** while metar[...] orphosed shales are called **pelites**.

The regional metamorphism of limesto[...] gives marbles which are generally similar [...] those produced by thermal metamorphis[...] However, the high pressure of regional met[...] morphism prevents the reaction of quartz a[...] calcite so wollastonite is not usually found. [...] low grades of metamorphism, impurities [...] calcite limestones may crystallize as chlor[...] and white mica. At higher grades biotite m[...] appear. At still higher grades, garnet and py[...] oxene may be present. In impure dolomit[...] limestones, low grade metamorphism caus[...] quartz to react with dolomite to give amphibo[...] At higher grades, pyroxene and olivine repla[...] amphibole.

At low temperatures, basic igneous rocks a[...]

...n early stage in the regional meta-
...orphism of quartzite. The quartz
...ains have been deformed and partly
...crystallized. Field of view 4 mm
...ross (Crossed polars).

Metamorphosed gabbro (crossed polars). The
pyroxene has recrystallized to give chlorite
and opaque mineral. Some of the original
feldspar has survived. Field 4 mm.

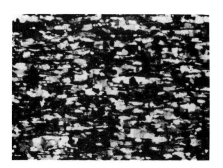

Quartz-mica schist formed by the complete
recrystallization of sandstone during regional
metamorphism. Opaque mineral is also present. Field 6 mm across. (Crossed polars).

...egionally metamorphosed shale showing
...e growth of large mica crystals. Field
...mm. (Crossed polars).

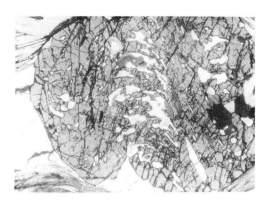

Garnet crystal which has grown over and preserved
an earlier foliation. Quartz and mica are also
present. Field 4 mm. (Plane polarized light.)

...onverted to **greenschists** consisting of albite,
...hlorite, calcite, epidote and some quartz. At
...igher temperatures hornblende forms from
...hlorite, calcite and epidote and the rock
...ecomes an **amphibolite** consisting of horn-
...lende, andesine, garnet and quartz. At very

high temperatures **granulite** is formed; it consists of pyroxene, labradorite and quartz. **Eclogite** consisting of green pyroxene and red garnet
forms at extremely high pressures. Eclogite has

a density of 3.5 g cm^{-3} compared with densities of about 3.0 g cm^{-3} for basic igneous rocks. Eclogite can be classified as a metamorphic or as an igneous rock. At high pressure a basic igneous rock recrystallizes in the solid state to eclogite while a magma crystallizing at high pressure, e.g. in the Earth's mantle may crystallize as eclogite. **Serpentinite** consists largely of serpentine formed by the hydration of ultrabasic rocks such as peridotite. At low grades of metamorphism acidic igneous rocks recrystallize as **sericite albite schists**. At intermediate grades muscovite schists form and at very high grades muscovite is converted to feldspar.

Zones of regional metamorphism

In some areas of regionally metamorphosed rocks progressive increase in grade can be recognized by the successive appearance of index minerals. In 1912, George Barrow described metamorphic zones in pelitic rocks of the south-east Scottish Highlands (figure 7.3). In order of increasing grade the zones are:

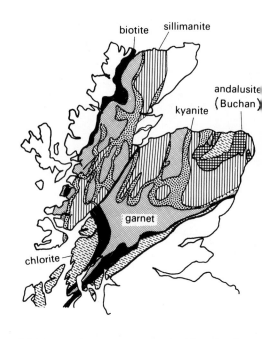

7.3 Zones of regional metamorphism in the Scottish Highlands.

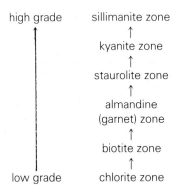

The assemblage of minerals which develops at any grade depends on the composition of the rock being metamorphosed, e.g. at garnet grade metamorphism a typical pelite would contain garnet, mica, quartz and plagioclase while a metamorphosed basic igneous rock would contain chlorite, albite and epidote. This means that the index mineral for any particular zone is not present in all rocks of that zone. Also, a mineral may appear then survive into higher grades, e.g. garnet first appears in rock metamorphosed at garnet grade but it also occurs in rocks formed at all grades above garnet grade.

In the north-east of Grampian region a different set of zones is found in rocks metamorphosed at relatively low pressure following the main phase of mountain building which produced the Barrovian Zones. Such low pressure regional metamorphism is sometimes called **Buchan-type metamorphism** and its sequence of index minerals resembles that found in aureoles round igneous intrusions.

Another type of regional metamorphism is high-pressure, low-temperature type sometimes called **burial metamorphism**. It is characterized by the presence of **blueschists** containing a distinctive blue amphibole called glaucophane. Jadeite (pyroxene) formed from albite may also be present. Glaucophane schists are found in places such as Anglesey, south west Scotland and in a ring around the Pacific. Japan shows parallel zones of high and low pressure metamorphism. The zone on the Pacific side contains glaucophane schist

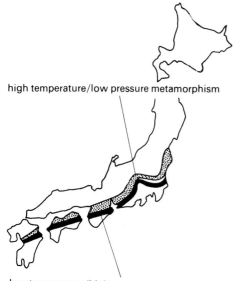

high temperature/low pressure metamorphism

low temperature/high pressure metamorphism

7.4 Zones of high and low pressure metamorphism in Japan.

formed at high pressure while on the continental side the rocks were metamorphosed at low pressure. This distribution results from the movement of the oceanic crust under Japan (figure 7.4)

Dynamic or dislocation metamorphism

Dynamic metamorphism results from the intense deformation associated with faults or deep-seated movement zones. At relatively shallow depths the rocks suffer brittle fracture with little recrystallization. The process of rock break-up is called **cataclasis**. In a fault zone the broken rock (**fault breccia**) consists of angular fragments set in a matrix of finely broken rock. More intense deformation gives an unfoliated rock called **cataclasite** which consists of fine-grained crushed material. Fragments of pre-existing rock which have survived cataclasis are called **porphyroclasts**. **Mylonite** is a fine-grained, foliated and usually banded rock produced by extreme deformation in deep-seated movement zones. Mylonite consists of lens-shaped porphyroclasts in a very fine-grained streaky matrix which may show signs of recrystallization. Myl-

onites may form along thrust planes during the emplacement of nappes. (A nappe is a large mass of rock which has moved along a low-angle thrust fault.) e.g. in the Alps the Glarus Nappe has moved about 35 km over a thrust plane marked by a thin layer of mylonite. On the other hand, mylonites found in the thrust zone of the north-west Highlands of Scotland have not been formed during thrusting. The mylonites were formed before thrusting by intense squeezing in deformation or shear zones.

Metamorphic facies

When rocks of different chemical composition are metamorphosed under the same conditions of temperature and pressure the metamorphic rocks which form have different mineral assemblages. Depending on their conditions of formation, metamorphic rocks can be placed in groups called **facies** (figure 7.5). The rocks in a facies may have different minerals but they have all formed at similar temperatures and pressures. The main metamorphic facies with typical mineral assemblages and with their conditions of formation are shown in table 7.2.

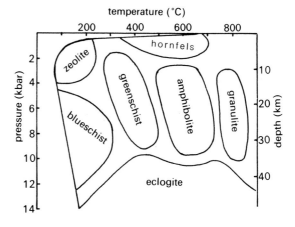

7.5 Pressure and temperature fields of metamorphic facies.

FACIES	CONDITIONS OF METAMORPHISM	MINERAL ASSEMBLAGE IN PELITIC ROCKS	MINERAL ASSEMBLAGE IN METAMORPHOSED BASIC IGNEOUS ROCKS
PYROXENE HORNFELS	Low pressure, high temperature on the inside of metamorphic aureoles	Quartz, cordierite, andalusite, biotite	Pyroxene, plagioclase, quartz
GREENSCHIST	Low pressure and low temperature zones of regional metamorphism	Quartz, chlorite, muscovite	Amphibole (actinolite), albite, chlorite, epidote
AMPHIBOLITE	Medium pressure and medium temperature zones of regional metamorphism	Quartz, biotite, muscovite, garnet, sillimanite	Hornblende, plagioclase, quartz
GRANULITE	High pressure and high temperature zones of regional metamorphism	Quartz, sillimanite, cordierite, garnet	Pyroxene, plagioclase
ECLOGITE	Very high pressure and high temperature deep inside the Earth	—	Pyroxene, garnet
GLAUCOPHANE SCHIST	High pressure and low temperature zones of regional metamorphism	Quartz, garnet, chlorite, muscovite	Glaucophane, quartz

Table 7.2 Metamorphic facies

THE MOVING EARTH

Forces acting within the Earth bend and break rocks, push up huge mountain ranges and pull oceans apart. **Structural geology** is the study of rock deformation and the resulting structures. **Tectonics** is the study of large-scale processes such as mountain building.

Deformation

Examine the effects of pulling, squeezing and twisting a variety of materials such as rubber, Plasticine and blackboard chalk. You will see that some materials change their shapes when they are subjected to forces. This change of shape is called **deformation** or **strain**. What happens to the materials when the forces are removed? Rubber goes back to its original shape. Such a substance is said to be **elastic** and the deformation, which disappears when the force is removed, is called **elastic strain**. Substances such as Plasticine and putty remain deformed when the forces are removed. Such substances are **plastic** and the strain produced in them is **plastic strain**. What happens when you pull a piece of Plasticine? Eventually, the Plasticine comes apart. This breaking is called **fracture** or **rupture**. With the Plasticine a good deal of plastic strain comes before rupture. Substances such as blackboard chalk which break without deforming plastically are described as being **brittle**. A material such as chewing gum which shows a great deal of plastic strain before fracture is said to be **ductile**. Liquids show **viscous** behaviour. This means that they begin to flow even under the influence of very small forces. Highly viscous liquids such as tar and syrup flow less readily than liquids of low viscosity such as water.

The forces which cause strain and fracture are of three types: **compressive** forces are squeezing or pushing forces; **tensile** forces are pulling or stretching forces; and **shear** forces tend to make one part of an object slide over the part next to it. In fig. 8.1 compression and tension both turn a square into a rectangle. You

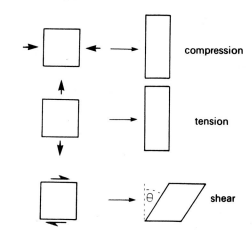

8.1 The effects of compressive, tensile and shear forces on a square.

will see that compression is equivalent to tension at right angles to the compression. A square deformed by shear forces becomes a parallelogram.

When a force acts on a surface we can think of the effects of the force as being spread out over the surface. A measure of how the force is spread out is given by the quantity pressure, which is the force divided by the area over which it acts. But a force also produces effects inside an object so we can imagine the inside of a body being subjected to something we could call internal pressure or **stress**. Stress is measured in the same units as pressure (that is, in newtons per square metre [$N\ m^{-2}$]). As with forces, stresses may be described as compressive, tensile or shear stresses.

Strain

Strain is the change of shape in a body subjected to stress. **Unit strain** is a measure of how lines change in length:

$$\text{unit strain} = \frac{\text{change of length of line}}{\text{original length of line}}$$

Unit 8

Note that the unit strain can be positive or negative depending on whether the line becomes longer or shorter during strain. **Shear strain** is a measure of how angles change. Imagine we have two lines at right angles to each other on an undeformed object. If, after strain, the lines come to be at 70° to each other then the change of angle is 20°. The shear strain is the tangent of the change of angle, that is, tan 20°. Unlike stress, strain has no units, it is given simply as a number.

Strains can be described in two ways. In **homogeneous strain**, straight lines before deformation are still straight after deformation. Also, circles become ellipses and spheres become ellipsoids. Where strain is **inhomogeneous** straight lines do not remain straight and circles and spheres are not deformed to become ellipses and ellipsoids.

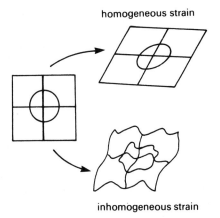

homogeneous strain

inhomogeneous strain

8.2 In homogeneous strain, circles become ellipses and straight lines remain straight. In inhomogeneous strain, circles do not become ellipses and straight lines do not remain straight.

How is strain related to stress?

Progressively load a length of thin elastic. As loading proceeds measure the distance between two markers on the elastic. Plot a graph of load against extension. What do you find?

You should have found your graph—at small loads anyway—to be a straight line. This means that the extension is proportional to the load. Another way of saying this is that for elastic materials such as rubber, strain is proportional to stress. This relationship is known as **Hooke's Law**. Hooke's Law also holds for elastic materials deformed by compressive and shear stresses. You can repeat the previous experiment using springs, copper wire and PVC flex cover. Plot graphs as before.

The graphs you have drawn are called **load-extension curves**. Fig. 8.3 (a) shows the type of load-extension curve commonly obtained for a ductile material. You will see that the curve can be divided into three parts. The first part is straight. Here, extension is proportional to load so the material is showing elastic behaviour. Following the region of elastic behaviour the curve starts to bend. This means that the extension is no longer proportional to the load and the material has stopped behaving elastically. When a stressed material ceases to behave elastically it is said to have reached its **elastic limit** or **yield point**. After bending, the curve straightens again and becomes nearly horizontal. This is the region of plastic behaviour in which the material is deforming with little extra load being applied. Following plastic deformation the material breaks. The stress causing rupture gives a measure of the strength of the material. Different materials show these different forms of behaviour to different extents. Brittle materials such as rock show little or no plastic deformation before fracture. Ductile materials such as copper may show little elastic strain but a lot of plastic strain before rupture.

So far, we have applied stresses which produce strains fairly rapidly. But deformation in the Earth is usually produced very slowly over millions of years by a process called **creep**. Creep produces plastic strain at stresses below the elastic limit of the deforming material. What happens to pitch and silicone putty when they are slowly and rapidly strained? In general, high strain rates lead to brittle behaviour while slow strain rates lead to ductile behaviour. Changes in pressure and temperature also affect the way in which a material responds to stress. Increased pressure caused by burial within the Earth tends to increase the strengths of rocks. Increased temperature and pressure both make rocks less brittle and more ductile.

THE MOVING EARTH

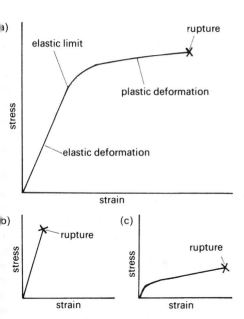

(a) elastic limit · rupture · plastic deformation · elastic deformation · stress · strain

(b) rupture · stress · strain (c) rupture · stress · strain

Load-extension curves.
(a) Ductile material. With increasing load the material shows elastic then plastic deformation before rupture.
(b) Brittle material. The material shows little or no plastic deformation before rupture.
(c) Very ductile material. A small load produces plastic deformation.

rike and dip

e position in space of any tilted planar struc-
re such as bedding or foliation can be defined
 the **strike** and **dip** of the plane (fig. 8.4). The
rike is the geographical direction of a hori-
ntal line on the planar structure. The position
 the horizontal line on a plane is found by
ing a spirit level and the direction is taken
th a compass. The dip or true dip is the
aximum angle which the plane makes with
e horizontal. It is measured with a **clinometer**
 the direction at right angles to the strike.
Your clinometer may be built into your geo-
gical compass as a pendulum which swings
ver a graduated scale. Alternatively, a clinome-
r rule can be used. The rule hinges round
 graduated scale and it has a spirit level built
to one arm. The spirit level makes it very easy
 find the strike direction. When recording
rike and dip in the field the strike is given
 a compass bearing and the amount and
rection of dip are noted, e.g. in a quarry you
ight record the strike and dip of bedding as

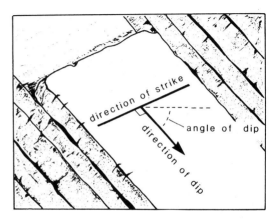

8.4 Strike and dip. The strike is the direction of a horizontal line on the planar structure. The dip is the maximum angle the plane makes with the horizontal.

follows: Bedding: strike 130°; dip 50°N.E. Any angle of dip measured in a direction at less than 90° to the strike gives an **apparent dip** which is less than the true dip. What happens to the magnitude of the apparent dip as the angle is measured at progressively higher angles to the strike?

Joints

If you pull or bend Plasticine you will find that it develops small cracks. In the same way, rocks which are subjected to stress very often split along cracks called **joints**. The cracks you made in the Plasticine were produced by tensile stresses. In the case of the folded Plasticine you may have found cracks formed by tension on the outside of the fold and small wrinkles formed by compression on the inside of the fold (figure 8.5(a)). Can you see how these tensile and compressive stresses are developed? Paint a round area of type correction fluid on a piece of ballon rubber. Allow the fluid to dry then stretch the rubber and watch how cracks develop. Many of the cracks open at right angles to the extension while some cracks form at angles between the directions of maximum extension and compression. The angled cracks have been opened, in part at least, by shear stresses.

When rock specimens are compressed they tend to break along paired sets of shear fractures commonly at about 30° to the compressive stress (or at 60° to the direction of exten-

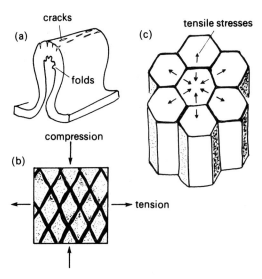

The fractures often intersect along lines at right angles to the directions of maximum compression and extension. Joints which form at angles to the compressive stresses are called **shear joints**. They may divide a rock into diamond shaped blocks (figure 8.5(b)). Shear

8.5 Joints.
(a) Joints formed by tension on the outside of a fold.

(b) Shear joints formed at an angle to the compressive stress.

(c) Columnar joints formed by contraction during the cooling of an igneous rock.

Compression parallel to the hammer has generated shear forces which have opened gashes in the rock. The gashes have been filled by a later mineral.

Shear joints in dolomite. Mud cracks are visible on the left.

Columnar jointing in a volcanic plug, Devil's Tower, Wyoming.

THE MOVING EARTH

nts can sometimes be recognized by the
esence of slight sideways displacements
tween the opposite sides of the fractures.
nsion joints are formed at right angles to the
in direction of extension by pulling apart of
e rock.
Sills and lava flows often have **columnar joints**
ulting from contraction during cooling. The
eous rock is held above or below by rock
ich will not contract along with the hot
eous rock. This causes the igneous rock to
it into columns which usually lie at right
gles to the contact with the adjacent rock.
litting occurs across polygonal cracks pulled
art by tensile stresses acting towards the
ntres of the columns (figure 8.5(c)). You can
ke fairly similar structures if you allow mud
dry. In this case, though, shrinkage is due
water loss and not cooling.
n intrusions such as stocks and batholiths
eet joints often form nearly parallel to the
und surface. The removal of overlying rocks
denudation reduces the pressure on the
ruded rock and allows it to expand. The
pansion sets up tensile stresses which split
e rock. Other joints in plutons often result
m contraction during cooling.
t may happen that many joints are formed
the same time, e.g. when rocks are folded
shallow depths they often break to give sets
joints like those in figure 8.6.

Faults

A **fault** forms when rocks break then move past
each other along the fracture surface or **fault
plane**. Movement parallel to the strike of the
fault plane is **strike slip** while movement parallel
to the dip direction is **dip slip**. The **net slip** is
the overall or total displacement; it may consist
of strike and dip slip components (figure 8.7).
The **throw** is the total vertical displacement of
a fault and the **heave** is the total horizontal
displacement. The **downthrown** side of a fault
has been displaced downwards relative to the
upthrown side. In a fault which is not vertical,
the **footwall** is the rock face below the fault and
the **hanging wall** is the rock face above the fault.

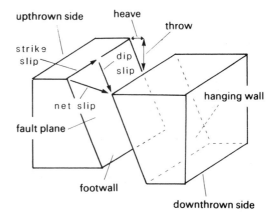

8.7 Components of a fault.

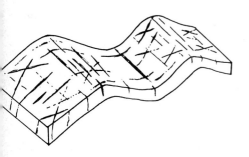

*Joint sets formed during the folding of rocks
at shallow depths.*

Faults may be described in terms of the
displacements which have taken place (figures
8.8 and 8.9). A **normal fault** is a dip slip fault
in which the hanging wall has moved down
relative to the footwall. A **reverse fault** is a dip
slip fault in which the hanging wall has moved
up relative to the footwall. A **tear fault** is a strike
slip fault. (Tear faults are also called wrench
or transcurrent faults.) In an **oblique slip fault**
movement has taken place in a direction about
half-way between the strike and dip directions.
Normal faults are formed by tensile forces
so they reflect extension of crustal rocks. They
commonly dip at angles of between 45 and 70°.
Step faults consist of a set of parallel normal
faults which all downthrow in the same direction. **Block faults** divide the crust into blocks
which may form mountains like those of the
Basin-and-Range Province of western USA.

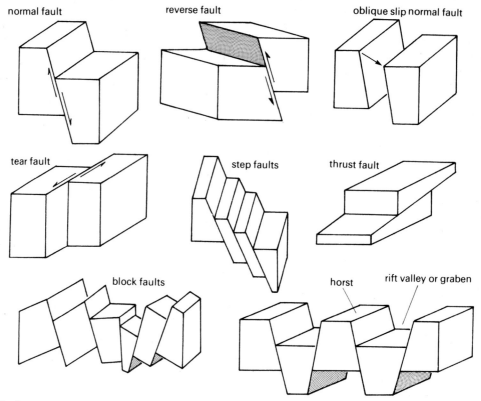

8.8 Fault types.

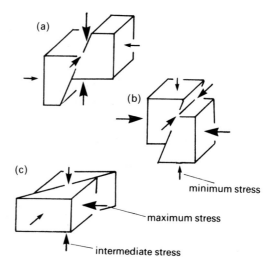

minimum stress

maximum stress

intermediate stress

8.9 Fault-producing stresses can be considered in terms of three unequal compressive stresses at right angles to each other.
In a normal fault (a) the major compressive stress is vertical. Crustal extension results. In a reverse fault (b) the strongest compressive stress is horizontal and the weakest is vertical. Crustal shortening results. In a tear fault (c) the strongest and weakest compressive stresses are horizontal. The crustal blocks slide past each other.

horst is an upraised fault block bounded by normal faults. The Vosges and Black Forest mountains of France and Germany respectively are horsts. A **graben** or **rift valley** is a long fault trough bounded by normal or step faults. Well known rift valleys include the East African rift valleys (figure 8.10), the Rhine rift valley and the Midland Valley of Scotland (figure 8.12(b)). Oceanic ridges have rift valleys running along their spines.

Reverse faults are caused by compression so they are indicative of crustal shortening. The fault planes may dip at high angles but usually the dip is less than 45°. Low-angle reverse faults are called **thrust faults** or **thrusts** and the rock mass which moves over such a fault is a **thrust nappe**. Thrusts are common in mountain areas (figure 8.12(a)). In many cases the thrust nappes have moved for many kilometres, e.g. displacement on the Moine Thrust of the north-west Highlands of Scotland has been at least 10 km from east to west. In the oceans,

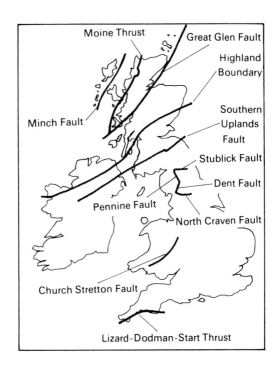

8.11 Major faults in the British area.

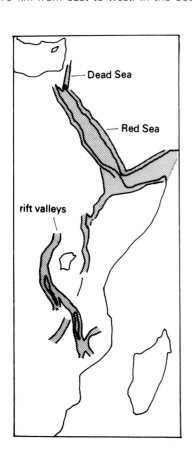

8.10 The East African rift valleys.

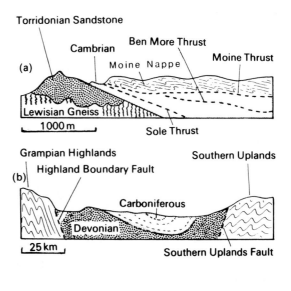

8.12 (a) Section through the Moine Thrust zone, N.W. Scotland.
(b) Section across the Midland Valley of Scotland.

the trenches mark the sites where ocean crust is thrust under a continent or island arc.

Tear faults are formed by shear forces which cause the rocks to slide horizontally past each other. The crust is neither shortened nor extended. Movement on a tear fault is described in terms of whether the opposite side of the fault has moved relatively to the left (**sinistral** or **left-lateral** movement) or to the right (**dextral** or **right-lateral** movement) when you stand looking over the fault. In the oceans there are special types of strike-slip faults called **transform faults**. They have this name because they end by running into and appearing to change or transform into other structures such as oceanic ridges or trenches. In the oceanic ridges the crust is pulling apart while in the trenches oceanic crust is being pushed down. This means that transform faults connect structures where movement is different from that on the fault itself. Transform faults may also appear on continents, e.g. the San Andreas Fault of California is a transform fault. It is carrying part of the Pacific crust in a northerly direction past North America. So far, displacement on the San Andreas Fault may have exceeded 600 km. The present rate of movement seems to be 1 or 2 cm a year. In Scotland, the Great Glen Fault has moved the north-west Highlands about 100

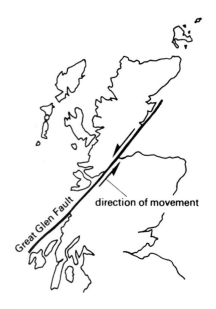

8.13 The Great Glen Fault has moved N.W. Scotland about 100 km to the south-west.

km towards the south-west (figure 8.13). The fault may be an ancient transform fault. The reason for believing that very large strike-slip faults may be transform faults is that it is no easy to see how such faults can die out unless

The line of the Great Glen Fault

THE MOVING EARTH

ey run into other major structures. More
tails of transform faults are given on p.176.
Movement on a fault may shatter the rock
the fault zone to produce a **fault breccia** made
of angular rock fragments. Sometimes the
ck may be ground up into a fine-grained,
nded rock called mylonite. The surface of a
ult plane may become polished to form **slick-
sides** which may have streaks or striae parallel
the movement direction. Slickenside striae
one are indicative of movement in one of two
ections. However, the striae may show steps
nich allow the actual movement direction to
determined (figure 8.14). It should be noted
at slickenside striae indicate the direction of
ly the last movements on the fault. These late
ovements may not have been in the same
ection as earlier, more important movements.
e movement direction on a fault may also
indicated by folds adjacent to the fault plane.
fault may develop by brittle fracture after early
ding and the movement direction is indicated
the fold orientation (figure 8.15). It should be
noted that movement on a curved fault
rface may produce folds which are bent in
e opposite direction to fault movement. Move-
ent on fault planes may be continuous or jerky.
rky behaviour is called **stick-slip** movement
d it results from the build-up of stress which
released by a sudden movement on the fault.
hallow focus earthquakes are commonly
used by stick-slip movements on faults.

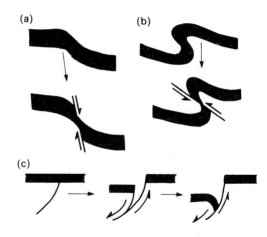

8.15 *(a) and (b) Faults may develop during folding.
The fold orientation indicates the direction
of fault movement.
(c) Movement on a curved fault plane may
produce folds bent so they do not give a true
indication of fault movement.*

Folds

Rocks are often bent to form **folds** (figures 8.16
- 8.18). In a fold, the area where the rocks are
most strongly bent is called the **hinge** or **fold
closure**. The areas between the hinges are the
fold **limbs**. The fold closes in the direction in
which the limbs converge. In the hinge, the line
joining points of maximum bending is called
the **hinge line**. The surface containing the hinge
lines of adjacent folded surfaces is the **axial
surface**. The **fold axis** is a line on the folded
surface parallel to the hinge line. The **fold core**
is the central area of the fold. The **wavelength**
of a fold is the distance between the fold crests
or between the fold troughs. The **amplitude** is
half the vertical distance between the crest and
trough. Where the fold hinge line is not horizontal the angle between the hinge line and
the horizontal is the **plunge** of the hinge line.

Folds may be partly described using properties such as their interlimb angles, relative
limb lengths, direction of closure and position
of the axial surface. An upfold is an **antiform**
and a downfold is a **synform**. An anticline is
an antiform in which the beds get younger away
from the fold core while a **syncline** is a synform
in which the beds get younger towards the core.
A **dome** is an antiform shaped like an upturned
bowl so the beds dip outwards in all directions.

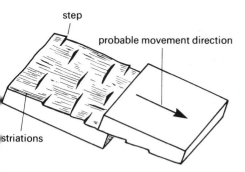

step

probable movement direction

striations

14 *Slickensides on a fault plane.Slickensides
alone indicate movement in one of two
directions. If steps are present the movement direction is probably that indicated.*

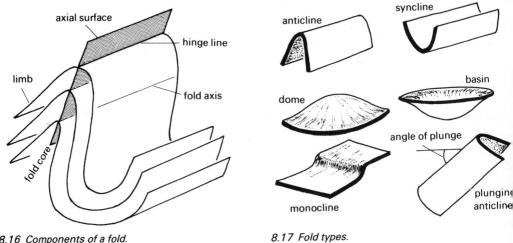

8.16 Components of a fold.

8.17 Fold types.

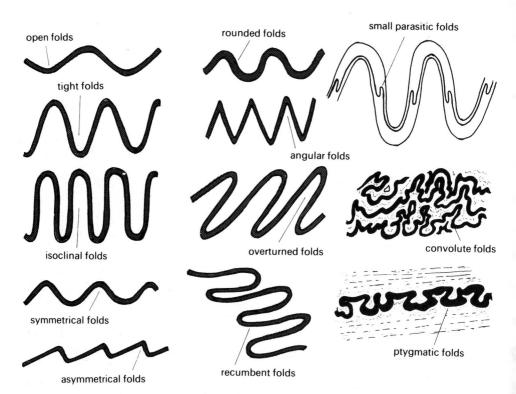

8.18 Some terms used to describe folds.

A **basin** is a saucer-shaped synform. A **monocline** is a step-shaped fold.

As the intensity of folding increases and the angle between the fold limbs decreases the folds may be described as **gentle, open** and **tight**.

When the limbs are parallel or nearly parall to each other the folds are **isoclinal**. In **syn metrical** folds the opposite limbs are abo equal in length so that one side of the fo mirrors the other side. **Asymmetrical** folds ha

THE MOVING EARTH

An anticline, Kuh-I-Pabda, Iran.

lop-sided appearance. An **overturned** fold has n inverted limb while a **recumbent** fold has near-horizontal axial surface. Folds may also e described as being **rounded** or **angular**.

Large folds often develop small **parasitic** folds n their limbs and in their cores. The parasitic olds are often asymmetrical and their Z- and -shapes point in the directions of the closures f the large folds. In figure 8.18 the upper parts f the parasitic folds point towards large anticlinal closures while the lower parts of the arasitic folds point towards large synclinal osures.

Parallel folds consist of layers whose thick-esses (measured at right angles to the layers)

do not change throughout the fold. **Concentric** folds are parallel folds whose layers lie on arcs of circles. You will see from figure 8.19 that the shapes of parallel folds must change vertically through the folded sequence. Parallel folds are generally impersistent and changeable structures. In **similar** folds each layer has a constant thickness when measured parallel to the axial surface. Similar folds are persistent

Similar folds in gneiss.

lylonite showing fractured folds, Width 1 cm.

THE MOVING EARTH

157

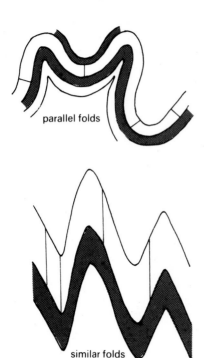

parallel folds

similar folds

concentric folds

8.19 The layers of parallel and concentric folds are of constant thickness. The layers of similar folds are of constant thickness measured parallel to the axial surface.

structures. **Convolute** folds are highly contorted and they are of very variable shape. **Ptygmatic** folds are again highly contorted but tend to affect single layers in highly metamorphosed rocks.

Folding mechanisms

Mark circles on one side of a thick sheet of foam rubber and on the end of a telephone directory. Fold the rubber and the book. Do they deform in the same way? The rubber deforms by a process called **buckling** (figure 8.20(a)). When the book deforms the pages slide over each other. This sliding process is called **flexural slip** (figure 8.20(b)). Buckling and flexural slip tend to produce parallel folds. Now draw parallel lines on the side of a pack of cards and push the cards in at the bottom (figure 8.20(c)). Here, deformation has taken place without compression along the layers by slip on the axial surface on the fold. This process is called **shear folding** and, ideally, it would lead to the formation of similar folds. You can also produce folds by allowing different coloured paints to mix on a lid which you can slowly move about.

Convolute folds may develop during metamorphism in rocks which behave in a viscous manner. Ptygmatic folds are often of parallel type. They may form by the buckling of a relatively stiff layer surrounded by weaker rock. You can see how this happens by squeezing a thin line of Vaseline from a syringe on to water

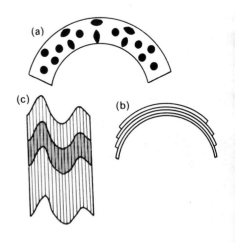

8.20 Folding by (a) buckling (b) flexural slip and (c) shear folding.

THE MOVING EARTH

egin the Vaseline line on the wall of a trough
nd maintain a gentle pressure on the line as
e rest of the Vaseline is squeezed out. You
ould be able to produce some good folds.

Folding in rocks is generally more compli-
ted than these simple models suggest, e.g.
cks often consist of layers with different
operties. The stiffer, more resistant layers are
scribed as being **competent** whereas the
ak, easily deformed layers are **incompetent**.
uring folding the behaviour of the competent
yers, e.g. sandstone, dictates the way in which
e incompetent layers deform. Also, the wave-
ngths and amplitudes of the folds are deter-
ned by the properties of the competent layers.

in the rock before metamorphism or it may have
developed during metamorphism by the separation of an originally uniform rock into layers
of different composition.

Foliation is formed by the deformation and
recrystallization of rocks under stress. If you
embed some rice grains in the surface of a
Plasticine block and then squeeze it you will
find that the grains tend to rotate until they are
roughly lined up at right angles to the compression. Also, when a rock recrystallizes under
compression the mineral grains tend to crystallize as elongate grains at right angles to the
compression. Since folds often result from compression, foliation may develop in the fold axial
surfaces (figure 8.22). It should be noted that
foliations are not always at right angles to the

oliation

eformation and metamorphism very often lead
the development of new planar structures
lled **foliations** (figure 8.21). **Fracture cleavage**
nsists of closely spaced, microscopic frac-
res. **Crenulation cleavage** is formed by the
icroscopic wrinkling of material between
eavage planes which may be fractures or the
reaked out limbs of microscopic folds. In **slaty
eavage** the microscopic grains lie in parallel
anes. In **schistosity** the mineral grains are also
gned in parallel planes. The grains are gener-
y visible to the naked eye. In some rocks the
liation is represented by distinct, separate
yers making up **gneissose banding**. The band-
g may represent bedding which was present

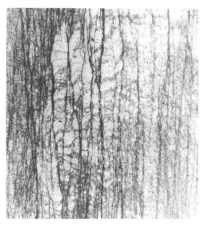

*Crenulation cleavage. Note the folds
between the parallel fractures. Width
3 mm.*

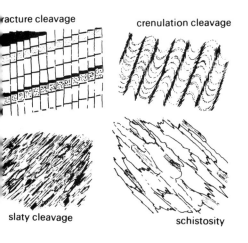

*21 Types of foliation seen under the
microscope.*

*Foliation induced by the compression of
pebbles in a conglomerate.*

compression nor are they always in the axial surfaces of associated folds. Shear joints and faults tend to develop at angles to the main compressive or tensile forces. Foliation may also develop at an angle to the compression then it may be rotated under compression towards the direction of maximum extension.

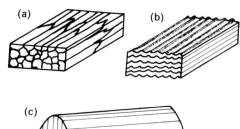

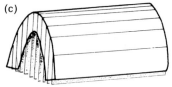

8.23 Types of lineation: (a) grain elongation; (b) small scale folding; (c) cleavage-bedding intersection.

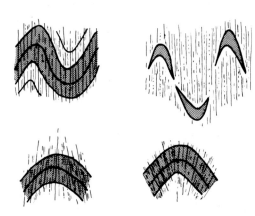

8.22 Relationship of foliation to folds. The foliation may lie in the fold axial surface.

Lineation

A **lineation** is a linear structure in rocks (figure 8.23), e.g. during deformation pebbles, sand grains or ooliths may be drawn out into elongate shapes. During metamorphism, too, mineral grains may crystallize in elongate forms. Lineations also result from the intersection of planar structures, e.g. where a fold has a cleavage in its axial surface, the intersection of the cleavage and bedding gives a lineation parallel to the fold hinge. Lineation may also result from small-scale folding so the surface of the rock looks like a piece of corrugated paper.

Unconformity

Earth movements may bring deeply buried rocks to the surface. Here, the rocks are broken down by weathering and erosion and they may be covered by much younger loose sediment. On

reburial, the young sediment is converted to hard rock lying discordantly on the older rock. The discordant relationship is called **unconformity** and it represents a break in deposition. The older and younger rocks are separated by a **surface** or plane of **unconformity** (figures 8.24 and 8.25). The unconformable relationship may be recognized by a change of dip or rock type at the surface of unconformity. A **basal conglomerate** representing, perhaps, the shingle beach of an advancing shoreline may occur above the surface of unconformity. Where there is little or no dip discordance across the unconformity, study of fossils may allow the different

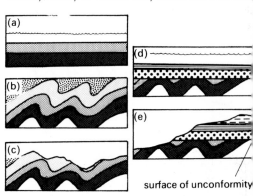

surface of unconformity

8.24 Formation of an unconformity. (a) The early rocks are deposited. (b) and (c) The early rocks are deformed, uplifted and partly eroded. (d) Later rocks are deposited. (e) Uplift and erosion expose the surface of unconformity.

THE MOVING EARTH

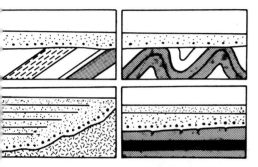

.25 Types of unconformity showing various degrees of discordance between the older and younger beds.

ock ages to be recognized. Structurally, a urface of unconformity may resemble a thrust ault. How would you tell them apart?

nliers and outliers

\n **inlier** is an outcrop of older rock completely urrounded by younger rock (figure 8.26). It nay result from erosion along the crest of an nticline to expose the older rock in the core r from erosion through the rocks above an nconformity. An inlier formed by erosion hrough a nappe is sometimes called a **window**. \n **outlier** is an outcrop of younger rocks comletely surrounded by older rocks. An outlier s a remnant of a more extensive area of rock vhich has been mostly removed by erosion. A **klippe** (plural klippen) is an outlier of a thrust appe.

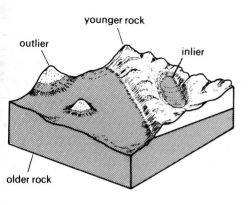

3.26 An inlier is surrounded by younger rocks. An outlier is surrounded by older rocks.

Geological maps

When a body of rock comes to the surface it is said to **crop out** even though it may be covered by materials such as peat, soil, glacial deposits or alluvium. An **outcrop** is the area over which the rock occurs at the surface. (The word 'outcrop' is also used as a verb so rocks are often said to outcrop). Where the surface rock can be seen it is said to be **exposed**. Outcrop patterns depend on various factors such as the angle of dip, the presence of folds and faults and the form of the ground surface. Layered rocks also give outcrop patterns which are different from those of massive intrusions such as plugs and stocks.

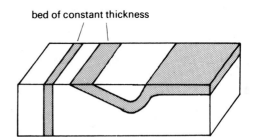

8.27 On flat ground the width of outcrop depends on the angle of dip.

To begin with we can look at outcrop patterns on flat ground. Figure 8.27 shows that the steeper the dip the narrower the outcrop. The outcrop width of a vertical bed is the same as the thickness of the bed. Otherwise, the width of the outcrop exceeds the bed thickness. Can you establish a relationship between the width of the outcrop (w), the thickness of the bed (t) and the angle of dip (θ)? In figure 8.28:

$$\sin \theta = \frac{t}{w} \quad \text{so} \quad t = w \sin \theta$$

We can also see that a borehole through an inclined bed will penetrate an apparent thickness (t') greater than the true thickness (t). Here,

$$\cos \theta = \frac{t}{t'} \quad \text{and} \quad t = t' \cos \theta$$

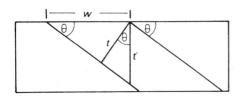

8.28 *Showing the relationships between width of outcrop (w), angle of dip (θ), thickness (t) and vertical thickness (t')*

Faults produce displacements which depend on the type of fault, the orientation of the fault and the inclination of the faulted beds. When horizontal beds are moved up or down by normal or reverse faulting, rocks of different ages are brought into contact across the fault plane. Tear faulting does not change the out-crop pattern of horizontal beds (figure 8.29). A fault whose strike is parallel to the strike of the faulted beds is called a **strike fault**. A **dip fault** strikes parallel to the dip of the faulted beds. Figure 8.30 shows a normal fault running parallel to the strike of inclined faulted beds. Where the fault dips in the opposite direction to the beds the outcrops are repeated. Where the fault dips in the same direction as the beds some beds may not outcrop. Where a reverse strike fault (figure 8.31) dips in the opposite direction to the beds some beds are concealed. If the reverse fault dips in the same direction as the beds outcrops are repeated. Tear faults

running in the same direction as the dip of the beds move the outcrops sideways. The outcrop patterns produced by normal and reverse dip faults are like those of tear faults when inclined strata are affected (figure 8.32). Normal strike

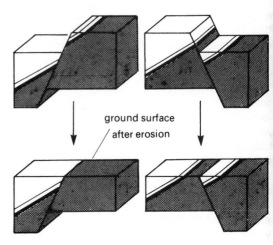

ground surface after erosion

8.30 *Normal faults running parallel to the strike of inclined beds. If the fault dips in the same direction as the beds outcrops may be concealed. If the fault dips in the opposite direction to the beds outcrops may be repeated.*

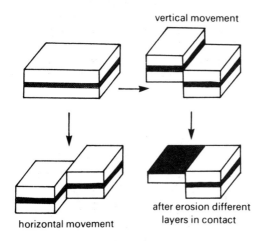

vertical movement

horizontal movement

after erosion different layers in contact

8.29 *Faulting of horizontal beds. Vertical movements bring together rocks of different ages. Horizontal movements do not alter age relationships across a fault.*

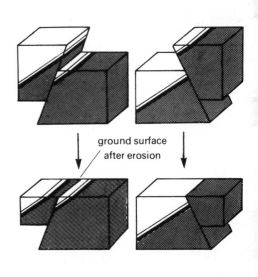

ground surface after erosion

8.31 *Reverse faults running parallel to the strike of inclined beds. If the fault dips in the same direction as the bedding, outcrops may be repeated. If the fault dips in the opposite direction to the beds, outcrops may be concealed.*

THE MOVING EARTH

ults cause vertical beds to be repeated while
verse strike faults may conceal vertical beds
gure 8.33). Normal and reverse faults at right
ngles to the strike of vertical beds do not alter
e outcrop pattern. The outcrops of vertical
eds are displaced by all tear faults except those
nning parallel to the strike.

The changes in outcrop patterns which are
roduced by faulting are usually more complex
an those which have been described, e.g.
lique faults cut across beds at angles between
eir strike and dip directions so the faults
ehave partly as strike and partly as dip faults.
hen oblique normal and reverse faults cut
clined beds the faulted beds are shifted and
artly concealed or repeated depending on the
pe and attitude of the fault (figures 8.34 and
35). Because the outcrops are shifted these
ults may look like tear faults. Oblique slip faults
roduce effects equivalent to tear faulting fol-
wed by normal or reverse faulting. In this case
may not be possible to detect both compo-
ents of the movement. If a fault block moves
turning or rotating on the fault plane the

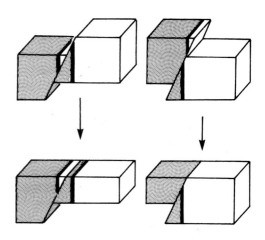

8.33 Normal faults parallel to the strike of vertical
beds cause outcrops to be repeated. Reverse
faults parallel to the strike of vertical beds
may conceal outcrops.

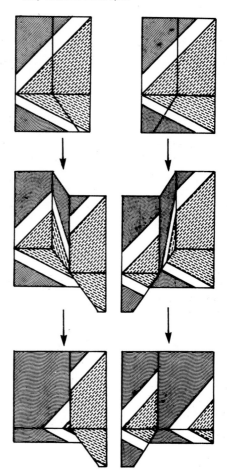

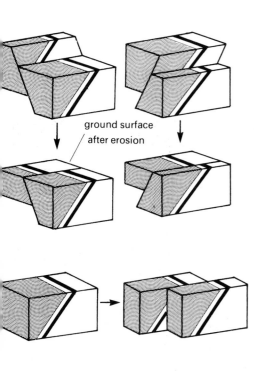

ground surface
after erosion

.32 Normal and reverse faults running parallel
to the dip of inclined beds produce outcrop
patterns like those resulting from tear
faulting.

8.34 Normal faults at an angle to the strike of
inclined beds. Compare the outcrop patterns
with those produced by faults parallel to the
strike or dip of inclined beds.

THE MOVING EARTH   163

strike and dip of its beds may be changed. Also, complex outcrop patterns may be seen among rocks which have been repeatedly displaced by faults of different ages (figure 8.36). The ways in which faults affect outcrop patterns can best be studied by using Plasticine models. Cut blocks of layered Plasticine in various ways and move the parts in different directions. Level off the tops of the blocks to see the outcrop pattern which would be left after erosion.

In general, folding causes outcrops to be repeated without their having been displaced. The fold type can be recognized from its outcrop pattern, e.g. an anticline has relatively old rocks in its core while a syncline has relatively young rocks in its core (figure 8.37). Sometimes, the

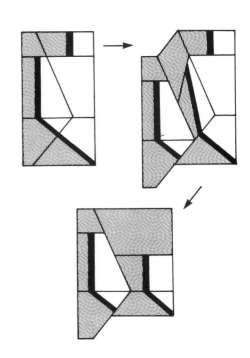

8.36 Complex outcrop patterns may be produced by repeated faulting.

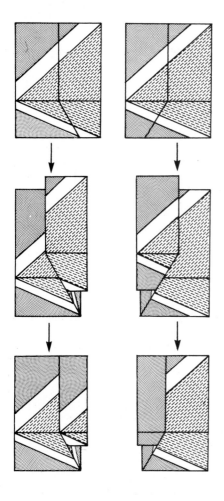

8.35 Reverse faults at an angle to the strike of inclined beds. Compare the outcrop patterns with those produced by faults parallel to the strike or dip of inclined beds.

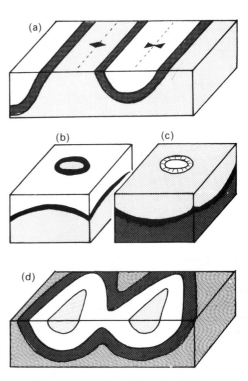

8.37 Outcrop patterns produced by folding: (a) anticlines and synclines; (b) dome; (c) basin; (d) plunging folds.

THE MOVING EARTH

ersection of the fold axial surface with the ound (the **trace** of the axial surface) is used indicate the presence of a fold. Triangles or rows on the trace indicate whether the fold an anticline or a syncline. On flat ground, omes and basins have rounded outcrops hereas plunging folds have loop-shaped tcrops.

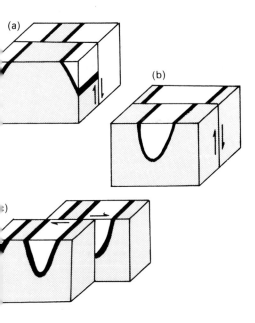

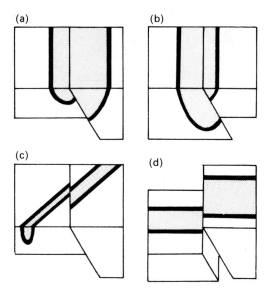

8.39 *Synclines affected by (a) normal faulting and (b) reverse faulting parallel to the fold hinge. In (c) a normal fault cuts across the fold hinge. Oblique slip has occurred in (d).*

38 *Faults at right angles to fold hinges.*
(a) In an anticline repeated outcrops are closer on the downthrown side.
(b) In a syncline repeated outcrops are closer on the upthrown side.
(c) On opposite sides of a tear fault the distances between repeated outcrops are not changed.

Folds affected by normal or reverse faults at ght angles to the fold hinges (dip faults) have eir closures raised or lowered relative to each her. In a syncline which has been faulted and oded repeated outcrops are closer together the upthrown side of the fault and further art on the downthrown side. The opposite fect occurs with an anticline. Here, down-row brings repeated outcrops closer together hile upthrow causes repeated outcrops to be rther apart. Tear faults simply displace out-

crops sideways (figure 8.38). Use Plasticine models to find how folds are affected by a variety of faults: you could find the effects of faults parallel to the fold hinges; faults oblique to the fold hinges; faults on which there has been oblique slip; and faults on which a fault block has rotated.

Unconformities and thrust faults may resemble each other on maps. Provided the rocks have not been inverted, all of the rocks above an unconformity are younger than those below. The rocks above a thrust fault may be older or younger than those below (figure 8.40).

Outcrop patterns are affected by the form of the ground surface (figure 8.41), e.g. on flat ground wavy outcrops mean that the rocks have been folded but on hills and valleys the presence of wavy outcrops does not necessarily mean that folds are present. Wavy outcrops can result from the way in which unfolded strata intersect an uneven surface. The ups and downs of the ground surface are shown on maps by **topographic contours**. These are lines on the land surface joining points of equal height above sea level. Before studying geological maps you must be able to interpret contours in terms of

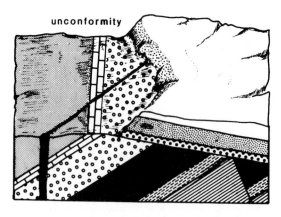

unconformity

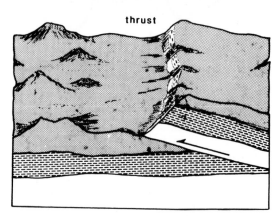

thrust

8.40 *The rocks above an unconformity are younger than those below. The rocks above a thrust may be older than those below.*

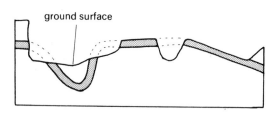

ground surface

8.41 *Outcrop width is affected by dip and by the form of the ground surface.*

wavy outcrops which cut contours. As the beds become steeper the outcrops become less wavy and cut more contours. In valleys, beds which dip up valley have V- shaped outcrops which point up the valley. Beds which dip down valley have V-shaped outcrops which point down the valley. However, if the valley slopes down more steeply than the down-valley dip the outcrop points up the valley (figure 8.42).

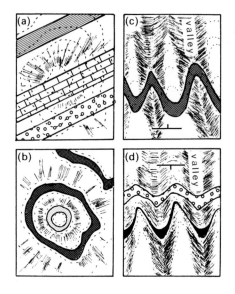

8.42 *Outcrops on uneven ground.*
(a) Vertical beds have straight outcrops.
(b) Horizontal beds have outcrops parallel to contours.
(c) Beds dipping down a valley have V-shaped outcrops pointing down-valley.
(d) Beds dipping up a valley have V-shaped outcrops pointing up the valley.

the topography which they represent. You must also be able to draw topographic profiles from contour maps.

Horizontal beds have outcrops which are parallel to contours while vertical beds have straight outcrops which run across contours without deviating. Inclined unfolded strata have

In the same way that contours can be drawn on the ground surface, **structure contours** can be drawn on geological surfaces such as the top or bottom of a bed, a fault plane, or an unconformity. (Structure contours are also called strike lines and stratum contours.) Figure 8.43 shows how structure contours can be drawn on the base of an unfolded bed. First of all, the points where the base of the bed crosses the topographic contours are marked in. Here, the base of the bed is at the same height as the contour. If the bed crosses the

me contour twice the two points can be
ined. The line obtained is the structure con-
ur whose height is the same as the topo-
aphic contour cut by the base of the bed.
ther contours may be added parallel to the
st. These are drawn through other points
here the base of the bed cuts topographic
ntours. Additional structure contours can
en be drawn equidistant from and parallel to
ose established by the use of the topographic
ntours. You will see that flat surfaces such
unfolded beds have straight, equally spaced
ructure contours. The dip of the bed can be
und from the structure contours. Measure the
stance between two contours and convert this
a true distance (d) from the map scale. The
rtical drop (v) is found by subtracting the
ntour heights. The tangent of the angle of
p is v/d. Note that widely spaced contours
dicate shallow dip while closely spaced con-
urs indicate steep dip. If the dip of a bed
nanges the spacing between the structure
ntours also changes (figure 8.44).
On folded surfaces the changing dip means
at the structure contours are not equally
paced. Also, in plunging folds and in domes
nd basins the contours are not straight. The
ld type can be determined from the sequence
structure contours. In anticlines the highest
ntours are in the middle while in synclines
e lowest contours are in the middle (figure
44). Take care when drawing contours on

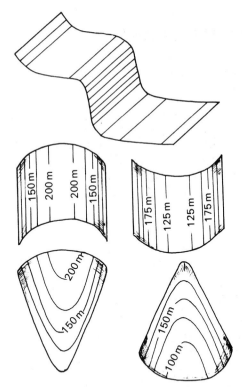

*8.44 Structure contours on folded surfaces.The
contours are closest where the dip is steepest. In anticlines the highest contours are
in the middle. In synclines the lowest contours are in the middle.*

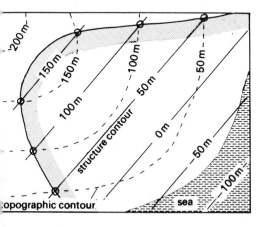

*43 Drawing structure contours (strike lines) on
the base of an unfolded bed.Mark the points
where the base of the bed cuts the topographic contours.Join up points where the
bed crosses the same contour.*

folds that you treat each fold limb separately.
If the base of a bed is at the same height on
each limb of a fold you cannot draw a structure
contour in the dip direction to connect the two
points. The contours must be drawn parallel
to the strike.

Finding strike and dip by
the three-point method

If a planar structure is picked up at three points
by boreholes, structure contours (strike lines)
can be drawn on the surface. The dip can also
be found and if the structure is covered by some
surface deposit the position of its outcrop can
be found. In figure 8.45 the top of a sandstone
is struck at depths of 70 m in borehole A, 20 m in
B and 40 m in C. Since boreholes A,B and C were
sunk from heights of 60, 40 and 40 m above sea

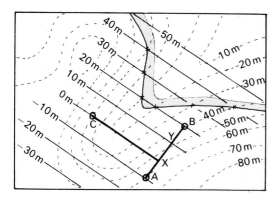

8.45 Finding strike and dip by the three-point method. If three positions of a bed are found in boreholes structure contours can be drawn in. If the bed is not exposed the position of its outcrop can be found.

level the height of top of the sandstone relative to sea level is −10 m in A, 20 m in B and 0 m in C. The structure contours for −10 m, 20 m and 0 m must pass through A, B and C respectively and the 0 m and 10 m contours will pass between A and B. If the dip is regular the structure contours will be equidistant so the 0 m and the 10 m contour will be one-third and two-thirds of the way along the line joining A and B. Since the 0 m contour passes through C the 0 m contour can be drawn in from C to X. This contour gives us the direction of other contours which can be drawn in parallel to CX through points A, Y and B. Since the structure contours are parallel and equidistant they can be drawn to cover the map beyond A and B.

The outcrop of the top of the sandstone can now be found. Where the structure contours meet topographic contours of the same height the top of the sandstone must be at the ground surface. These positions can be marked on the map and the outcrop can be drawn in. For the base of the sandstone a similar procedure is used. Since the top and bottom of the bed are parallel, the direction and spacing of the structure contours on the base are the same as those on the top of the bed. However, the contours on the base are displaced relative to the contours on the top. In figure 8.45 if the base of the sandstone is found 7 m below the top how would the contours on the lower surface lie in relation to the contours on the upper surface? Since the contour interval is 10 m, the lower

contours appear to be displaced ⁷⁄₁₀ of the dis tance between the contours in the up-di direction.

Mapping the thicknesses of beds

Variations in the thickness of beds are show on maps by means of **isopachytes** or **isopachs** An isopachyte is a line joining points of equa thickness. In figure 8.46 boreholes have bee sunk into a reef limestone. The thickness o limestone found in each borehole is showr Contour-like isopachytes drawn at selecte thickness intervals show the three-dimensiona form of the limestone.

Isopachyte maps allow us to estimate th volumes of rock bodies. In sedimentary an stratigraphical studies the maps can be use to show how rates of sedimentation have varied from place to place. In deltaic sedimentary rock variation in thickness may indicate the genera

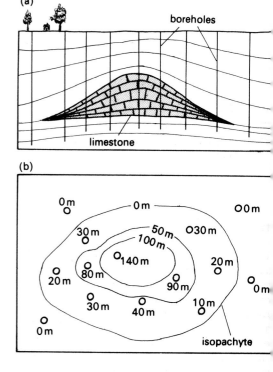

8.46 Constructing an isopachyte map from bore-hole data. The isopachytes show thickness variation in the reef limestone.

rection of sediment transport. In the study of
olcanoes, isochyte maps allow the volume
ejected material to be estimated. When large
alderas are studied the volume of material
ected is found to be less than the volume of
e original cone. This indicates that such cal-
eras are formed by sinking of volcanic cones
to magma chambers rather than by cones
eing blown away. Since ash is blown down-
nd isopachyte maps may also indicate the
nd direction at the time of the eruption. Ash
stribution from the eruption of Vesuvius in
9 AD indicates that the wind was blowing
om north-west to south-east (figure 8.47). In
onomic geology isopachyte maps are used
making estimates of coal, oil and ore reserves.
e volumes of water-bearing strata can also
e estimated.

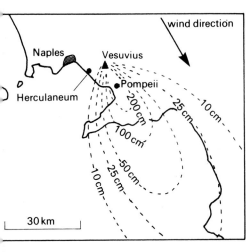

47 *Thickness variation in ash from the Vesuvius
eruption of A.D. 79.*

tructure and scenery

e have already seen that a relationship may
ist between landforms and rock type and
 structure, e.g. karst topography develops on
mestone. However, similar landscapes may
evelop on different rock types so there is no
mple relation between the two. Rocks which
e resistant to weathering and erosion tend
protrude so the presence of igneous rocks
ay be indicated by a hill or ridge while rocks
uch as clay may occupy low ground. How is
crag-and-tail landform produced? The angle

at which a resistant bed meets the ground
surface may determine the shape of the landform. Where the resistant bed is horizontal or
nearly so mesas and buttes develop under arid
or semi-arid conditions. A gently dipping bed
may have a steep **scarp slope** running roughly
in the direction of the strike and a shallow **dip
slope** down the dip of the bed. The combination
of scarp and dip slope is a landform called a
cuesta (figure 8.48). Where the bed dips at a
high angle a triangular ridge called a **hogback**
or **hog's back** results (figure 8.49).

*8.48 A steep scarp and a shallow dip slope form
a cuesta.*

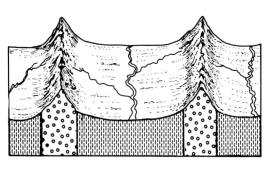

*8.49 A vertical or near vertical resistant bed may
protrude as a hogback landform.*

Joints and faults provide planes of weakness
along which rocks may easily be attacked by
weathering and erosion, e.g. the rounded tops
and steep sides of inselbergs may result from
exfoliation parallel to sheet joints. **Tors** are hill-
top masses of weathered joint blocks shown,
for example, by the granites of the moors of
Devon and Cornwall. Deep weathering along
joint planes followed by removal of the weathered material mostly by solifluction leaves the

granite blocks exposed as a mass of huge slabs (figure 8.50). Faulting may leave a fault plane exposed at the surface as a steep slope called a **fault scarp**. Faulting may bring rocks of varying resistance to erosion into contact. The weaker rock may be quickly removed to leave a **fault-line scarp** of resistant rock. Since fault breccia may be easily eroded the line of a fault may be marked by a depression. Fiords often lie along weak zones formed by jointing and faulting which are followed by valley glaciers.

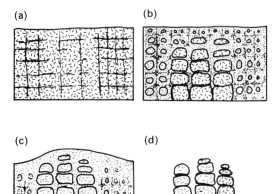

(a) (b)

(c) (d)

8.50 Formation of a tor. Granite is deeply weathered along joint planes. The weathered material is then removed.

Drainage patterns are affected by rock structure because rivers tend to follow weak zones delineated by soft beds, faults and large joints (figure 8.51). **Dendritic** (tree like) drainage tends to develop on uniform rocks while **radial** drainage develops on dome-shaped uplands. A rectangular pattern called **trellised** drainage develops on uniformly dipping strata which consist of alternating hard and soft layers. The streams are at right-angles to each other because some of them run parallel to the strike while others run parallel to the dip. **Superimposed** drainage bears no relationship to the underlying rock structure because the drainage pattern was initially established on rocks above a surface of unconformity. As the land surface is lowered by denudation the drainage pattern is imprinted on the rocks below the unconformity. The radial drainage of the Lake District is of superimposed type since it was developed on a dome of younger rocks which once covered the Lake District. The drainage patterns of east Glamorgan and the Hampshire Basin are also thought to have been superimposed. **Antecedent** drainage predates the rock structures over which it flows.

Geological field work

Field work is an essential part of geological studies. It normally entails making geological maps and visiting sites such as quarries, mines

A tor in the Scilly Isles showing weathered joint blocks.

THE MOVING EARTH

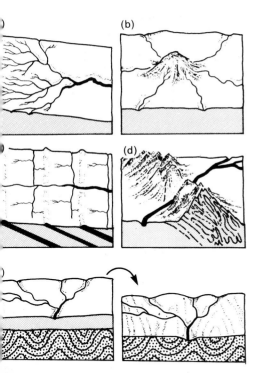

(b)

(d)

51 Drainage patterns: (a) dendritic; (b) radial; (c) trellised; (d) antecedent; (e) superimposed.

d coastal areas where particular features can
 seen. Before embarking on field work you
ould be familiar with the sound advice con-
ned in the leaflet A Code for Geological Field
ork issued by the Geologists' Association. In
 sence it states that you must be seen to be
sponsible and considerate. You should not
use damage or disturbance of any kind and
rmission should be obtained from land-
vners and quarry managers before visits are
ade. It is important, too, that you take sensible
fety precautions.

Your field equipment will include a geological
ammer, a compass, a clinometer, maps, a hand
ns, a penknife, a notebook, pens and pencils
d a chisel. You may need a protractor and
 felt marker can be used to label rock and
ssil specimens. Newspaper can be used for
rapping specimens and loose material can be
rried in polythene bags. The maps should be
 a scale of about 1 in 10 000 and they can
 augmented by aerial photographs. Aerial
otographs can be obtained in pairs which
ve a three-dimensional view of the country-
de when looked at through a stereoscope.

Maps and photographs should be carried in a map case.

When making a geological map, exposures should be found and drawn in on the map. The exposure should be carefully examined and observations and measurements recorded. On the map, different rock types can be shown in different colours and visible geological boundaries can be shown by solid lines. Hammering and specimen collecting should be kept to a minimum. You may be able to obtain specimens from fallen material. At the exposure you can measure the strike and dip of bedding, foliation, joints or fault planes. You can also measure the direction and plunge of fold hinges and lineations. Drawings should have an indication of scale and an object such as a hammer or clinometer rule should be included in a photograph to show scale. Fossil types should be carefully noted and some may have to be collected for later identification. Before leaving an exposure make sure that your observations and recordings are complete. You will find that a picture of the geology of an area can only be built up after a large number of exposures have been examined. At any exposure you may be uncertain of the geological relationships, e.g. you may not be sure if you are looking at a sill or a lava flow. Despite this you should try to make some interpretation of what you have seen. Possible interpretations, uncertainties and questions should be written down. Later, key exposures can be re-examined if problems remain.

Topographic features should be carefully observed because they provide clues about the underlying geology. Ridges may indicate the positions of dykes or steeply dipping beds. Depressions, valleys and gullies may signify the presence of faults or beds with a low resistance to erosion. However, soils migrate downslope so different soil types do not necessarily coincide with different rock types. Plants may grow under limited pH ranges, e.g. heather, foxglove, broom, whortleberry, sheep's sorrel and heath bedstraw do not grow very well on the calcareous soils of limestone areas. On the other hand, plants such as traveller's joy, way-faring tree, dark mullein, dogwood, whitebeam, mountain avens, dark-flowered helleborine and many others are characteristic of calcareous soils. If you live in a limestone or chalk area it is worthwhile finding out about your local calcicole (chalk living) plants.

Field work is followed up by laboratory studies, e.g. you can study your hand specimens in detail and you may be able to have some thin sections made. Study of thin sections may tell you a great deal about how the rocks have formed. You can also identify your fossils. Since different fossils are found in rocks of different ages you may be able to establish age relationships among the rocks. Your field map can be completed by drawing in geological boundaries and faults between the outcrops. Where the boundary cannot be seen at the surface a dashed line is drawn on the map. The information on the field maps can then be transferred to a new map. The different rock types can be coloured in and a key can be given to explain the map symbols and colours. You should then write a report outlining the geology of the area.

Continental drift

The idea that the continents have moved or drifted over the surface of the Earth probably arose during the 17th century. In 1668, François Placet suggested that the Old and New Worlds were separated by Noah's Flood. In 1858, Antonio Snider-Pelligrini showed how the Americas and Europe and Africa could have fitted together before separation. In 1915, Alfred Wegener wrote a book called *The Origin of Continents and Oceans* in which he set out evidence for continental drift partly in terms of continental fit, past climate and ancient glaciation. He also suggested that the two distinct crustal levels shown by the hypsographic curve indicated that oceanic and continental crusts were fundamentally different. At this time most Earth scientists did not believe in continental drift because they could see no mechanism by which continents could be moved. Even when Arthur Holmes in 1927 suggested that convection currents in the mantle could provide the necessary movements geologists and geophysicists remained sceptical. It is only since the 1950s that evidence from exploration of the sea floor and palaeomagnetism has led to widespread acceptance of continental drift. Let us now look at the evidence which suggests that such continental movements have taken place.

Continental fit

Figure 8.52 shows how the continents roun the Atlantic may be assembled to form a sing land mass. The best fit is obtained not by usin present coastlines but by using the 1000 depth contour. That is, the edge of the contine is taken to be part of the way down the co tinental slope. The fact that overlaps and ga are very small (less than 90 km) indicates th the continents were originally together.

1000 m submarine contour

8.52 Fit of the Atlantic continents along the 1000 submarine contour. The black areas show where overlap occurs.

Matching geology

The rocks of Africa and South America sh many similarities. Cratons older than 2000 and ancient orogenic belts (2000–600 Ma o match up very well (figure 8.53). Sediment sequences 140–100 Ma old on the Atlan margins of both continents are very simi indicating that the rocks were deposited in la and narrow seas between the separating c tinents (figure 8.54). The appearance of t marine conditions about 110 Ma ago sho that distinct separation had been achieved this time. In the North Atlantic the Caledon

THE MOVING EARTH

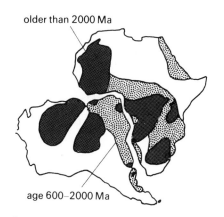

8.53 Match of cratons (dark shading) and ancient orogenic belts (dotted) between South America and Africa.

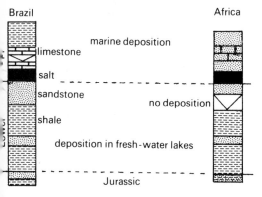

8.54 Match of sedimentary sequences (140-100 Ma old) on the Atlantic margins of South America and Africa.

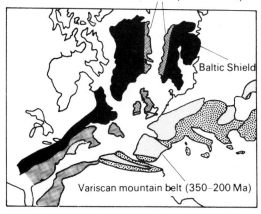

8.55 Match of orogenic belts across the North Atlantic.

After 'The Confirmation of Continental Drift,' by Patrick M. Hurley. Copyright © 1968 by Scientific American, Inc. All rights reserved.

Past glaciations

India and the southern continents show signs of having been glaciated about 300-250 Ma ago. It seems that all of these land masses lay near the South Pole at this time. The direction of ice movement can be found by study of striae and erratics (figure 8.56), e.g. erratics found in Brazil are of rock types found only in South Africa. When glaciation took place South Africa and Brazil were apparently side by side.

Mountains (500-400 Ma old) can be traced from Greenland and Norway through the British Isles to North America (figure 8.55). The younger Variscan orogenic belt (400-300 Ma old) also appears to continue from Europe and north west Africa into North America.

South America, Africa, India, Australia and Antartica all have a similar Devonian to Triassic sequence (the Gondwana Succession) of sedimentary rocks containing coals and tillites. The Gondwana Succession suggests that these continents were part of a single land mass (Gondwanaland) which began to break up about 160 Ma ago during the Jurassic.

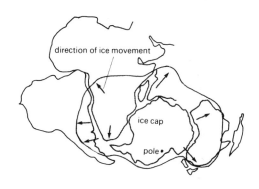

8.56 Position of the ice sheet over the southern continents 300-250 Ma ago.

THE MOVING EARTH

173

Ancient plants and animals

Before the theory of continental drift became accepted, similarities of fossil organisms on widely spaced continents were explained by saying that organisms would migrate from one continent across long land bridges. Such bridges, for example, crossed the Atlantic and went from South Africa through Madagascar to India. Wegener said that such large land bridges could not have existed. He thought that, because of the principle of isostasy, bridges could not sink without leaving gravity anomalies. Ocean gravity surveys have shown no sign of sunken, low density material.

Fossil studies may provide evidence which supports continental drift, e.g. *Mesosaurus* was a crocodile-like reptile about 45 cm long whose remains are only found in lacustrine shales about 270 Ma old in southern Africa and Brazil. Since *Mesosaurus* could not have crossed wide seas the fossils suggest that Africa and South America were joined 270 Ma ago. India and the southern continents all have fossils of ferns called *Glossopteris* and *Gangamopteris*. The fossils are so distinctive that the plants are thought to have lived on a single continent which existed for a time up to about 200 Ma ago.

Polar wandering curves

We have already seen that the inclination and declination of the remanent magnetism of a rock can be used to find the magnetic pole positions when the rock was formed. Study of rocks of various ages on the one continent give different pole positions. This seems to indicate that the pole has changed position and, indeed, the line joining the pole positions through time is called a **polar wandering curve** (figure 8.57). If the poles had wandered then rocks of the same age on different continents would give the same pole positions. However, since different continents have different polar wandering curves, it follows that the continents and not the poles have wandered. The term 'polar wandering curve' is misleading because the magnetic and geographic poles have apparently occupied similar positions through geological time.

Besides showing that drift has occurred polar wandering curves indicate when continents separated. The curves of different continents

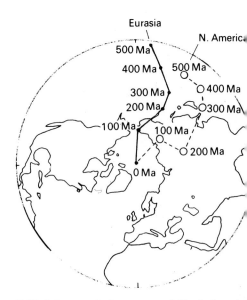

8.57 Polar wandering curves of North America (dashed line) and Eurasia (solid line).

are similar until the time of separation. A[fter] separation, the polar wandering curves diver[ge] (figure 8.58). Moving separate continents [so] that their polar wandering curves overlap brin[gs] the continents back to their original position[s].

Movements of the ocean floor

Magnetic surveys have shown that parts of [the] sea floor have strip-like magnetic anomal[ies] lying roughly parallel to the ocean ridges. [In] 1963 Fred Vine and Drummond Matthe[ws] suggested that the linear anomalies had be[en] produced by reversals of the Earth's magne[tic] field. The positive anomalies were thought [to] have been produced by rocks 'magnetized [in] the same direction as the Earth's field is [at] present. The negative anomalies resulted fro[m] rocks magnetized when the Earth's field w[as] reversed so their remanent magnetism oppo[ses] the present field. In 1960 Harry Hess h[ad] suggested that convection currents in t[he] mantle rose under oceanic ridges before flo[w]ing off to each side. As a result, new crust [is] formed as each side of the ridge moves ap[art]. In 1961 Robert Deitz called this process s[ea] **floor spreading**. The Vine–Matthews hypothe[sis] or supposition provided strong evidence [in] favour of sea floor spreading. As basic ignec[us]

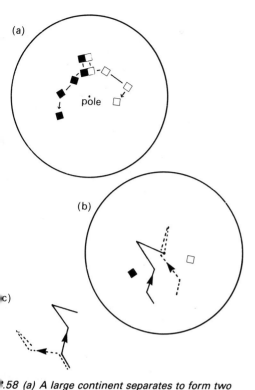

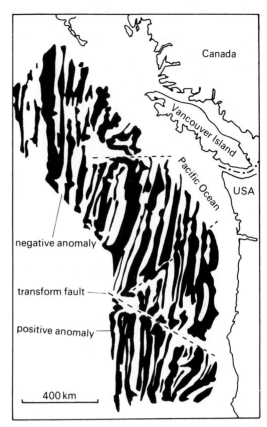

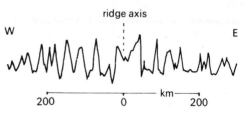

8.58 (a) A large continent separates to form two smaller continents.
(b) Polar wandering curves for the two continents show pole positions relative to the continents.
(c) Superimposed polar wandering curves diverge at the time when the large continent separated.

8.59 Linear magnetic anomalies in part of the floor of the N.E. Pacific Ocean.

8.60 Plot of magnetic anomalies across the East Pacific Ridge. The anomalies are symmetrical about the ridge.

rock is added to the oceanic ridge it is magnetized in the direction of the Earth's field at that time. Continued addition of new material along with repeated reversals of the Earth's magnetic field result in the build up of linear anomalies situated symmetrically on each side of the oceanic ridge (figure 8.59 and 8.60).

By comparing the pattern of ridge anomalies with the magnetic polarity timetable derived from study of continental lavas it is possible to work out the spreading rates of oceanic ridges. Spreading rates vary considerably, e.g. the North Atlantic ridge is spreading at about 1 cm per year on each side whereas the East Pacific rise spreads at about 5 cm a year on each side. Spreading rates such as these suggest that all of the ocean floors could have been produced within the last 300 Ma. The Deep-Sea Drilling Project begun by the drillship *Glomar Challenger* in 1968 has confirmed that the ocean floors are relatively young. Drilling has shown that the ocean floor becomes progressively older away from ocean ridges. The oldest part of the ocean floor so far found is only about 150 Ma old.

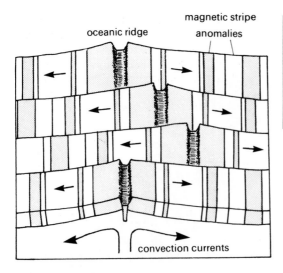

oceanic ridge

magnetic stripe anomalies

convection currents

8.61 *Movement of the sea floor away from an oceanic ridge. Reversals of the Earth's magnetic field produce the symmetrical pattern of anomalies across the ridge.*

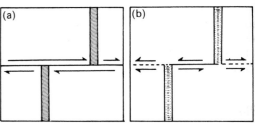

8.62 *(a) Movement on a tear fault.*
(b) Movement on a transform fault.
How do they differ?

Transform faults

Oceanic ridges often appear to have been displaced sideways along major faults in the sea floor. The faults appear to be simple tear faults with the direction of displacement shown in figure 8.62(a). However, sea floor spreading shows that movement takes place away from ridges so that movement on the faults should be the opposite of that expected (figure 8.62(b)). This was shown to be the case by study of earthquake waves coming from the faults. The fact that the faults between oceanic ridges are not tear faults was recognized by Tuzo Wilson. In 1965 he called them **transform faults** because they end by seeming to change or transform into other structures such as oceanic ridges, island arcs or mountain belts (figure 8.63). It should be noted that movement of material away from an oceanic ridge is not necessarily at right angles to the ridge. Movement is, however, parallel to the associated transform faults.

Benioff Zones

So far we have seen that material is being added to the solid Earth's surface at oceanic ridges. Since the Earth does not seem to be getting

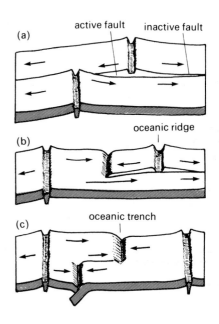

active fault   inactive fault

(a)

oceanic ridge

(b)

oceanic trench

(c)

8.63 *Transform faults running (a) from a ridge to a ridge (b) from a ridge to a trench and (c) from a trench to a trench.*

any bigger it would appear that there must be areas where material is being consumed at the same rate as it is being formed. Such areas are thought to exist at oceanic trenches. Here, oceanic crust slides under island arcs or mountain ranges giving rise to associated earthquake and igneous activity. Study of earthquake foci shows them to lie at progressively greater depths in a zone called the **Benioff Zone** which slopes down on the landward side of the trench. The earthquakes generated by the sinking crust indicate an angle of descent which is often about 45°. Partial melting of both the descending crust and overlying mantle gives rise to intrusive and extrusive igneous activity above the Benioff Zone.

Plate tectonics

The ideas of continental drift, sea floor spreading at oceanic ridges and destruction of oceanic crust at oceanic trenches have been brought together into a single theory which says that all these processes are parts of one process called **plate tectonics**. This theory considers the surface of the Earth to be made up of rigid blocks called **plates**. There are six major plates along with a few smaller ones (figure 8.64). The plates are thought to slide on the partially molten and weak asthenosphere or rheosphere. The relatively rigid outer shell of the Earth above the asthenosphere is called the **lithosphere**. The asthenosphere is about 100 km thick so the lithospheric plates are much thicker than the crust. Plates meet along **plate boundaries** and the areas close to plate boundaries are called **plate margins**.

Plates move away from each other at oceanic ridges. Since material is added to the edges of the moving plates such areas are called **constructive margins**. Plates move past each other along transform faults. Since material is neither added nor lost such margins are described as being **conservative**. Plates collide in the regions of oceanic trenches and since the oceanic plate is consumed such margins are described as **destructive**.

The structure of a constructive margin is shown in figure 8.65. The uppermost layer consists of about 2 km of basaltic pillow lavas. Can you recall how pillow lavas are formed? On the ridge flanks the lavas are overlain by thin sediments formed from organic remains, chemical precipitates and volcanic ash. None of the sediment has come from the continents. Beneath the lavas are basaltic dykes which are underlain by gabbro. It is thought that this sequence of igneous rocks forms above uprising convection currents in the mantle. The existence of deep seated magma chambers is indicated by reduced P-wave velocities in the base of the crust. Slow cooling in the magma chambers produces gabbro. Magma leaving the chambers forms dykes which feed lava to the surface.

Oceanic ridges generally rise about 3 km above ocean basins because they consist of relatively hot, low-density rock. As the crustal material moves away from the ridge it cools and becomes lower as it contracts. Because of this the ocean becomes deeper away from the ridge, e.g. in the Atlantic the ridge axis is about

8.64 Map showing the positions of the major plates. The arrows indicate the directions of plate movement.

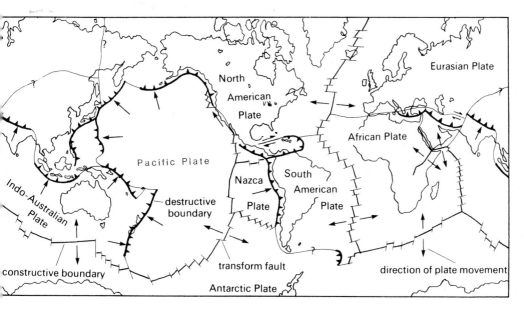

Eurasian Plate

North American Plate

African Plate

Pacific Plate

Nazca

South American Plate

Indo-Australian Plate

destructive boundary

Plate

constructive boundary

transform fault

direction of plate movement

Antarctic Plate

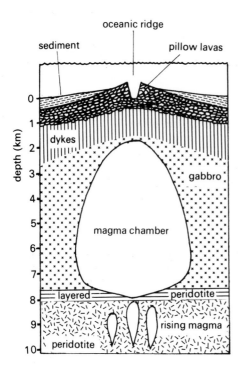

8.65 *Structure of a constructive plate margin.*

2500 m below sea level while ocean floor with an age of about 50 Ma is at a depth of 5000 m (figure 8.66).

Destructive plate margins form by three types of plate collision. Where oceanic plates collide an island arc is built up by igneous activity in the region above the sinking plate (figure 8.67). Island arcs are well-developed in the eastern Pacific, in the Java-Sumatra area of the Indian Ocean and in the Caribbean. When an oceanic plate meets a continental plate the oceanic plate sinks or is **subducted** beneath the continental plate. The relatively low-density continental plate is compressed and thickened to form a mountain range of Andean type. Continents

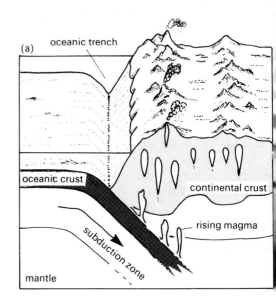

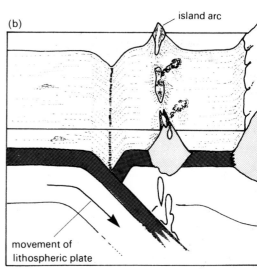

8.67 *Destructive margins.*
(a) Collision between oceanic and continental plates produces Andean type mountains.
(b) Collision between oceanic plates produces an island arc.

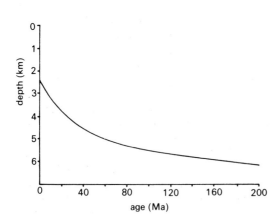

8.66 *Increasing depth of the sea floor with age as it moves away from the oceanic ridge.*

THE MOVING EARTH

ay collide when oceanic lithosphere between em is completely removed by subduction gure 8.68). A collision of this type forms ountains such as the Himalayas where there e no volcanoes or deep-focus earthquakes.

Gravity anomalies associated with destructive argins are distinctive in that negative anomies exist over the trenches while positive iomalies exist over island arcs and mountain nges (figure 8.69). A positive anomaly seems occur because the sinking plate is cold so is denser than the surrounding mantle. This eans that there is an excess of mass on the ndward side of the oceanic trench. The negae anomaly associated with a trench occurs ecause the crust is pulled down to form a epression which is occupied by low density ater instead of high density rock.

As the lithospheric plate sinks at a subduction ine it is heated by conduction from the surounding mantle and by friction between the ate and the mantle. The increased pressure so makes it hotter and the phase change of minerals to higher density forms also produces heat. The heating causes partial melting the sinking plate and magma of dioritic or ndesitic type is produced. The melting of

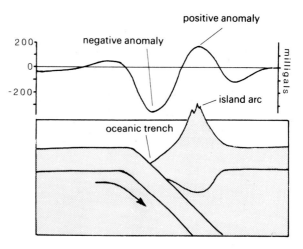

8.69 Gravity anomalies at a destructive margin. There is a negative anomaly over the trench and a positive anomaly over the island arc or mountain range.

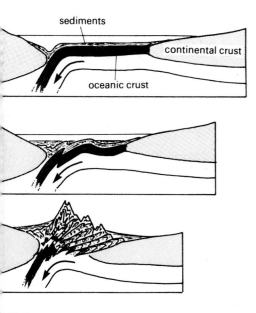

.68 Destructive margin formed by the collision of continental plates. Mountains of Himalayan type result.

trench sediments dragged into the subduction zone also contributes to the magma. Also, any water carried down by the subducting plate would tend to lower the melting point of the plate and surrounding mantle. Initially, the mantle above the sinking plate is relatively cool and the magma does not rise very far. As more and more heat is produced the early-formed diorites are partly melted to give more siliceous magmas of granodioritic or granitic type. These magmas rise as diapirs to form batholiths often at high levels in the crust. Andesitic magma which reaches the surface gives rise to explosive volcanic activity. Igneous activity results in the build-up of island arcs and in the thickening of continental crust. In this way continental crust is constantly being formed because it is not dense enough to be subducted. The absence of earthquakes below a depth of about 700 km indicates that the descending plate has been totally consumed and its remains have merged with the mantle.

The heat generated by plate collision also gives rise to regional metamorphism. Away from the subduction zone metamorphism is of low pressure type while close to the subduction zone metamorphism takes place under high pressure. Round the Pacific the metamorphic zones lie in pairs. Near the oceanic trench the metamorphic rocks are high pressure glaucophane schists while away from the trench the low pressure metamorphic rocks contain andalusite and sillimanite (figure 7.4).

Ophiolites are ocean floor rocks which have been moved up or **obducted** at destructive margins. A fragment of oceanic crust occurs in the Troodos Mountains of south-west Cyprus. Here, peridotite derived from the mantle is overlain by gabbros probably formed in magma chambers at a constructive plate margin. Above the gabbros are dykes formed by magma from the gabbroic chambers. Above the dykes are pillow lavas formed by ocean floor extrusion of magma through fissures now occupied by dykes. The pillow lavas are overlain by marine sediments. Another unusual rock type found at destructive margins is **serpentinite**. It is formed by the hydration of mantle peridotite which has been squeezed into trench sediments. The chemically added water produces an increase in the volume and reduction in the density of the serpentinite compared with the original peridotite. The reduced density allows the solid serpentinite to rise to higher levels in the crust.

Geometry of plate movement

In figure 8.70 the plates have moved apart along circular paths. The plates move around a line through the centre of the Earth called the **axis of rotation**. The axis meets the Earth's surface at points called the **poles of rotation**. You will see that spreading reaches its maximum rate at right angles to the axis of rotation and that

spreading rates decline towards the poles of rotation. The positions of poles of rotation can be found because great circles drawn at right angles to transform faults pass through them. (A great circle is the same size as the Earth's circumference.) For example, the equatorial Atlantic is spreading about an axis whose pole lies south-east of Greenland (figure 8.71).

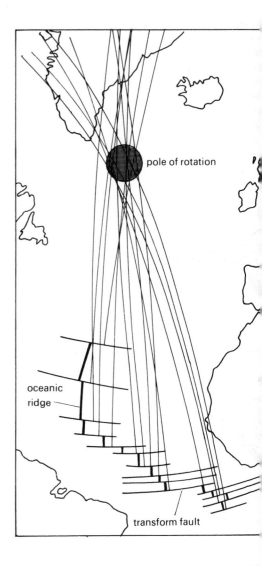

8.71 Great circles drawn at right angles to transform faults intersect at the pole of plate rotation. The equatorial Atlantic is spreading about an axis whose pole lies near S.E. Greenland.

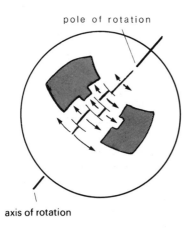

8.70 Plates move apart along circular paths about an axis of rotation.

THE MOVING EARTH

Mechanisms of plate movement

The small quantity of molten material present in the asthenosphere is thought to provide the lubrication necessary to allow plates to move. The driving mechanism may be that of convection currents which rise at oceanic ridges and sink at destructive margins. Such convection currents may flow through the whole mantle or they may be contained within the asthenosphere. The sinking plate may even set up convection cells by cooling the surrounding mantle. Gravity may also play a part in plate movement. Plates may slide off the elevated oceanic ridges under the action of gravity and, when the plate sinks at a destructive margin, may pull the rest of the plate with it (figure 8.72). It has also been suggested that injection of material at oceanic ridges simply shoves the plates apart.

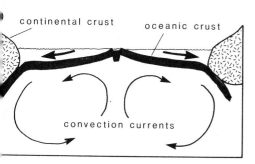

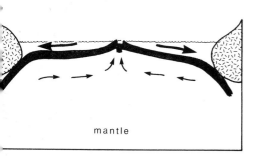

continental crust   oceanic crust

convection currents

mantle

8.72 (a) *Plates may be moved by mantle convection currents.*

(b) *Alternatively, the weight of the sinking plate may pull the rest of the plate behind it. Such plate movements would cause reverse movements in the mantle.*

History of plate tectonics

Plate tectonic processes have probably been operating through much of geological time. We cannot be certain about what happened at the Earth's surface soon after its formation, e.g. it has been suggested that continental crust formed all over the Earth about 4500 Ma ago and that the present continents are the remnants of this original crust. It is more likely, however, that the continents have been growing through geological time. Initially, the heat generated by short-lived radioisotopes would drive strong convection currents in the mantle. Island arcs would form above the descending limbs of the convection cells and continents would form by the accretion of island arcs. Continental crust does not return to the mantle because its low density prevents it from sinking. Since andesitic volcanism at destructive margins adds material to the continental crust, the continents are still growing.

In many parts of the world ancient plate movement is indicated by metamorphic rocks, andesites, ophiolites and granites which mark the positions of old mountain belts probably formed by plate collision. Such evidence suggests that Britain has suffered two phases of plate collision. About 450 Ma ago the Caledonian Mountains may have been formed by the closing of an ocean which covered much of Britain. About 300 Ma ago a subduction zone of the Variscan Mountains may have run across south-west England. On a larger scale it is thought that about 300 Ma ago the continents formed a single landmass called Pangaea (figure 8.73). Pangaea consisted of a southern part called **Gondwanaland** and a northern part called **Laurasia** separated from each other by the **Tethys Ocean**. Gondwanaland was made up of South America, Africa, India and Antarctica. Part of Gondwanaland lay under ice sheets at the south pole. Laurasia was made up of North America, Europe and Asia. It lay close to the equator. About 160 Ma ago Pangaea began to break up along spreading plate boundaries which seemed to affect Gondwanaland before Laurasia. Narrow, shallow seas similar to the Red Sea and the Gulf of California cut across parts of Gondwanaland. Evaporites formed in these seas now lie on the margins of the continents. By about 100 Ma ago the Atlantic Ocean between Africa and North America was well formed and South America and Africa were

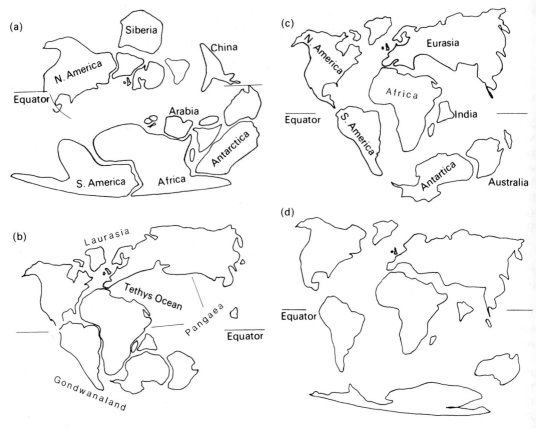

8.73 Positions of the continents over the last 400 Ma.
(a) 400 Ma ago.
(b) 240-200 Ma ago.
(c) 90-80 Ma ago.
(d) 60 Ma ago.

moving apart. The Indian Ocean was beginning to form as India moved north-east away from Africa and Antarctica. Africa was swinging round to begin closing the western end of Tethys. About 50 Ma ago Australia separated from Antarctica while Greenland and Europe moved apart to form the North Atlantic. The closing of the eastern end of Tethys by India led to the formation of the Himalayas within the last 10 Ma. Similarly, the Alps were formed as the African plate moved north towards Europe.

GEOLOGICAL TIME

ur study of geology so far will probably have
en you some impression of the long time
ans over which changes on the Earth take
ace. While some processes such as landslides
d volcanic eruptions produce their effects
ry quickly other processes such as the build-
g and wearing away of mountains, the open-
g and closing of oceans and the depostion
thick sediments take a very long time.

Estimates of the scale of geological time have
en made in various ways. A non-geological
timate was made by Archbishop James Usher
581-1656) who studied the chronology of
e Old Testament and concluded that the Earth
d been created in 4004 BC. Geological esti-
ates stemmed from the work of James Hutton
726-97) who believed that features he
served in rocks could be produced, if enough
ne were available, by processes operating
day. Hutton could not give an estimate in years
t he did say that 'a boundless mass of time'
d already passed.

Charles Lyell (1797-1875) was first to try
measure the passage of time by using the
te at which sediment accumulates. He esti-
ated both the volume of the Mississippi delta
d the volume of sediments added to it every
ar. By dividing one figure by the other he
timated the delta to be 70 000 years old.
nce the delta lay on rocks which must be older
ell concluded that the Earth was many mil-
ns of years old. Rates of sedimentation were
er used by other geologists who estimated
e total thickness of sedimentary rocks laid
wn through all of geological time and the
erage annual rate of sedimentation. This
ethod gave a very wide range of estimates
r the age of the Earth from 1500 million years
ven by Haughton in 1871 and McGee in 1893
3 million years given by Winchell in 1883.

A different approach to finding the age of
e Earth was used by John Joly (1857-1933).
e assumed that the oceans had originally been
esh water and that they had slowly become
lty. He estimated the amount of salt added
ery year and divided this into his estimate
the total salt in the oceans to get a figure

of 90 million years for the age of the Earth.
It is now known that Joly's method is invalid
because the salt is recycled so it does not
remain permanently in the ocean.

Lord Kelvin (1824-1907) assumed that the
Earth had been cooling steadily from its original
molten state. From his estimate of the rate of
cooling he concluded that the Earth was
between 20 and 40 million years old. Kelvin
was unaware of the fact that heat is produced
by radioactive elements within the Earth so the
heat presently coming from the Earth has not
all come from its original molten condition.

The discovery of radioactivity by Henri Bec-
querel in 1896 led to the use of radioactive
elements as geological clocks. In 1902 Ernest
Rutherford and Frederick Soddy showed that
when radioactive elements decay they change
into other elements and in 1905 Bertram Boltwood showed that lead was an end-product
of the decay of uranium. Boltwood went on to
calculate a range of geological ages from the
lead/uranium ratios in minerals based on the
idea that the older the mineral, the higher the
proportion of lead to uranium. Boltwood's work
was extended and fully developed by Arthur
Holmes (1890-1965) who in 1913 produced
the first detailed geological time scale. We shall
now take a look at the principles of dating rocks
using their contained radioactive elements.

Radiometric dating

Radioactive elements change by giving off particles and rays from their nuclei. Alpha- particles
are the same as helium nuclei in consisting of
two protons and two neutrons. When an alpha-
particle is emitted the mass number of the
parent radioactive isotope falls by four and its
atomic number falls by two. A beta-particle is
an electron given off when a neutron changes
to a proton. When this happens the mass
number of the isotope stays the same but the
atomic number is increased by one. Change

also takes place by a process called electron capture in which a proton takes in an electron and changes to a neutron. This causes the atomic number to decrease by one but it leaves the mass number unchanged. The result of the decay of a radioactive parent isotope is a stable daughter isotope which does not decay. Very often there is a complex series of intermediate radioactive isotopes between the parent and daughter elements.

The way in which radioactive elements are used to measure time is vaguely similar to the use of an hour-glass or a candle clock. In an hour-glass the sand runs through at a constant rate and in a candle clock the candle burns away at a constant rate so giving a measure of time. Suppose we had a candle which could burn for five hours. What percentage of the candle would be left at the end of every hour's burning? Plot your results on a graph. Radioactive decay differs from candle burning in a way which you can find from a simple experiment. Get a large number of coins—say 64 or 128—to represent the atoms of a radioactive element. Toss the coins and let those which come down heads represent atoms which have decayed while those which land tails are atoms which have not changed. After the first tossing discard the heads and find the percentage of tails. Again toss all those which came down tails and discard the heads. What percentage of the original number of coins is left now? Repeat the procedure until the coins have gone and plot the percentage of tails (that is, unchanged atoms) left after each set of coins has been tossed. What shape is the graph? How does it differ from the graph of a candle burning?

Radioactive isotopes decay in the way shown by the coins. That is, over a fixed period of time half of the atoms decay. This time interval, which is different for different isotopes is called the **half-life**. If we began with 64 radioactive atoms, 32(50 percent) would be left after one half-life; 16(25 percent) would be left after two half-lives; 8(12½ percent) would be left after three half-lives and so on. Your teacher may be able to show you experiments to verify the half-lives of short-lived radioisotopes such as thoron (half-live 54.5 s) and protactinium (half-life 68 s). You can plot graphs of counts per second against time. What shape are your graphs?

How can we use information from radioactive decay to measure time? Suppose we begin with 32 coins and toss them as before leaving 10 minutes between every set of tossings. How long does it take to get to a stage where we have 4 coins showing tails and 28 showing heads? After 10 minutes there would be 16 tails, after 20 minutes there would be 8 tails and after 30 minutes there would be four tails. In other words, it has taken three 10 minute intervals to get to the 4 surviving coins. A similar argument can be applied to radioactive isotopes. Suppose we begin with a parent isotope of half-life 1000 years which decays to a stable daughter isotope and we find that decay has reached a stage where 15 000 atoms are daughter atoms and 1000 atoms are parent atoms. Here, we began with 16 000 atoms of which 1000 have survived. To reduce the parent atoms to $\frac{1}{16}$ of what they were requires four half-lives or 4000 years.

The half-lives of radioactive isotopes can be measured in the laboratory. Half-lives range from many millions of years to much less than a second. We have to use a variety of radioisotopes with long half-lives to measure the wide range of geological time. Table 9.1 shows some of the more common radioisotopes with their half-lives, daughter products and dating ranges.

Problems of radiometric dating

Radiometric dating is based on certain assumptions. It is assumed, correctly, that the rate of decay does not change with changing conditions. It is also assumed that decay has taken place in a closed system so that no parent atoms have been removed or added and the daughter atoms have all been produced by decay of the parent atoms. This assumption is usually valid. Sources of error arise from the fact that the rates of decay and so the half-lives of the isotopes may not be precisely known, e.g. the half-life of ^{87}Rb is variously given as 47 000 or as 50 000 Ma. Fortunately, it is possible to use dates obtained from one method to check dates from another method. Because dates using the higher ^{87}Rb half-life agree better with potassium-argon and uranium-lead dates for the same rock the figure of 50 000 Ma is more often used. Dating by ^{14}C was checked against tree rings from the bristlecone pine of the USA. The oldest bristlecone pine is about 4500 years old but by using dead trees it was possible to check the timescale back to about 8000 thou-

ISOTOPE	ISOTOPE			IN DATING	
Uranium-238 (^{238}U)	Lead-206 (^{206}Pb)	4500 Ma	10–4600 Ma	Zircon ($ZrSiO_4$), Uraninite (UO_2)	Zircon is common in acid igneous rocks. It is also found in some metamorphic rocks. Zircon contains about one part per thousand of uranium
Uranium-235 (^{235}U)	Lead-207 (^{207}Pb)	710 Ma			
Potassium-40 (^{40}K)	Argon-40 (^{40}Ar)	11 900 Ma	0.1–4600 Ma	Muscovite, biotite, hornblende, lava, slate, phyllite, some sedimentary rocks	Loss of argon may lead to errors in dating. Can be used to date Mesozoic and Tertiary rocks which contain glauconite (green mica). Glauconite is formed at the time of deposition. Orthoclase is not used in dating because it loses argon too easily
Rubidium-87 (^{87}Rb)	Strontium-87 (^{87}Sr)	50 000 Ma	10–4600 Ma	Muscovite, biotite, orthoclase, gneiss, granite	Often used to date Precambrian metamorphic rocks
Carbon-14 (^{14}C)	Nitrogen-14 (^{14}N)	5730 years	100–64 000 years	Peat, wood, bone, shell, dripstone, some water samples	^{14}C is formed from ^{14}N in the atmosphere by cosmic ray bombardment. ^{14}C in carbon dioxide enters plants by photosynthesis then animals by feeding. Radiocarbon dates are given in terms of 'before present' or B.P. where the present is 1950. Used to date part of the Quaternary

Table 9.1 Isotopes used in radiometric dating.

sand years before present. It was found that when tree rings of known age were dated, the ^{14}C dates older than 1000 BC were too young so the half-life of ^{14}C had to be revised.

Problems also arise from the fact that daughter atoms may have been included in a mineral when it was formed and some allowance may have to be made for this when finding daughter/parent ratios. Errors arise during analysis because of the very small quantities of material being measured and because of variation between samples. Analytical errors are indicated along with the radiometric date, e.g. a date of 100 ± 5 Ma means that a repeated measurement would very probably give a date between 95 and 105 Ma. Errors are usually between 2 and 5 percent of the calculated age. Another problem is that sedimentary rocks cannot often be dated. The most accurate ages come from igneous rocks whose age relationships to other rocks may not be accurately defined. All we can say is that igneous rocks cut through rocks older than themselves.

Age of the Earth

Since the Earth formed, uranium has been changing to lead 206 and 207 so if we can estimate the concentrations of uranium and the lead formed from it we can get an approximate age for the Earth. It is thought that deep-sea sediments give isotopic abundances most representative of the whole Earth because they receive material from wide source areas. Using such isotopic abundances gives ages for the Earth of 5460 Ma for the ^{235}U – ^{207}Pb method and 6750 Ma for the ^{238}U – ^{206}Pb method. Can you suggest why these figures may be inaccurate? Firstly, the ages are derived from what may be inaccurate estimates of the Earth's uranium and lead concentrations. Secondly, in calculating the ages it was assumed that all of the ^{207}Pb and ^{206}Pb had come from uranium. However, some ^{207}Pb and ^{206}Pb could have been present when the Earth formed. To improve on our estimate of the age of the Earth we would have to subtract the amount of lead which was originally present. The quantity of original lead can be estimated by analysing meteorites. Subtracting the amount of original lead from the lead found in deep sea sediments and repeating the calculation gives Earth ages of 4590 Ma from the ^{235}U – ^{207}Pb method and 4630 Ma

from the ^{238}U – ^{206}Pb method. The proximity of these answers indicates the age of the Earth to be about 4600 Ma.

Meteorites can be dated directly and they give ages of about 4600 Ma. Since the oldest Moon rocks give the same age it is probable that the Earth and the rest of the solar system formed about 4600 Ma ago.

Relative dating

The relationships between rocks and structures allow us to place them in order of age. Nicolas Steno (1638–1686) was first to recognize such relationships. He formulated the **principle of superposition** which says that younger rocks are deposited on top of older rocks. This means that in a sequence or succession of sedimentary rocks which has not been inverted by folding the youngest beds will be at the top and the oldest at the bottom. Steno also realized that sedimentary rocks were originally laid down in horizontal or near-horizontal layers.

Relative ages of rocks are also indicated by cross-cutting relationships, e.g. joints, faults and intrusions are younger than the rocks which they cut. Also, where there has been no inversion, the rocks above an unconformity are younger than those below. Again, if a conglomerate contains pieces of granite then the conglomerate must be younger than the granite. In other words, a rock must be younger than the fragments it contains.

While geological relationships do not allow us to date rocks in years we can use radiometric dates as a means of calibrating relative ages. Of all igneous rocks, lavas are the most useful time indicators since they have ages between those of the rocks above and below. Lavas are often interbedded with sediments so their ages may differ very little from the sedimentary rock above and below.

Geological column

The **geological** or **stratigraphical column** (table 9.2) shows the sequence in which rocks have been formed through geological time. The geological column has been built up by accumulating evidence from many different places;

ERA	PERIOD OR SYSTEM		MILLIONS OF YEARS BEFORE PRESENT
CAINOZOIC (recent life)	Quaternary	Holocene or Recent Pleistocene	
			— 2.5 —
	Tertiary	Pliocene Miocene Oligocene Eocene Palaeocene	
			— 65 —
MESOZOIC (middle life)	Cretaceous		— 135 —
	Jurassic		— 195 —
	Triassic		— 235 —
PALAEOZOIC (ancient life)	Permian		— 280 —
	Carboniferous		— 370 —
	Devonian		— 415 —
	Silurian		— 445 —
	Ordovician		— 515 —
	Cambrian		— 590 —
PRECAMBRIAN	Origin of Earth		— 4600 —

Table 9.2   The Geological or Stratigraphical Column

ny one area only parts of the column are represented. After the column had been conructed it was dated radiometrically. This eans that the geological column can be divled on the basis of the order in which the rocks ave been formed or in terms of time.

The largest time units are the four **eras**. These are the **Precambrian** era which lasted for about 4000 Ma from the origin of the Earth at 4600 Ma till 590 Ma ago. The Precambrian is followed by the **Palaeozoic** (old life) era from 590 to 235 Ma ago, the **Mesozoic** (middle life) era from 235 to 65 Ma ago and the **Cainozoic** (new life) era from 65 Ma ago until the present day. The last 590 Ma is divided into eleven shorter time units called **periods**. Periods lasted for variable times from the 90 Ma of the Carboniferous to the 2.5 Ma of the Quaternary.

The rocks of the geological column can be divided into **systems**. A system consists of all the rocks formed during a period. Systems and periods have the same names so the rocks of the Carboniferous system were deposited during the 90 Ma of the Carboniferous period. Similarly, all Cretaceous rocks were formed during the Cretaceous period (135-65 Ma ago). Since the rocks of a system have been formed during a given time interval the system is an example of a **time-stratigraphical** unit. Systems can be divided into shorter time-stratigraphical units called **series, stages** and **chronozones**. A series consists of the rocks deposited during a length of time called an **epoch**; a **stage** is deposited during a shorter time called an **age** and a chronozone is deposited during a still shorter time called a **chron**.

In addition to time-stratigraphic units such as the system, series and stage we can divide up the geological column into convenient rock units which have no time connotations. **Formations** are locally recognized, distinctive bodies or sets of sedimentary rocks which are often used to construct geological maps. Formations may be combined into **groups** or divided into **members**. Members are made up of a few distinctive **beds**.

PALAEONTOLOGY

Palaeontology is the study of **fossils**. Fossils are the remains or traces of organisms preserved in rocks. Most fossils are found in sedimentary rocks though a few are found in extrusive igneous rocks and in weakly metamorphosed rocks.

Taxonomy is the study of classifying organisms. Organisms may be placed in large groups (plants, animals and protists) called **kingdoms**. Protists include bacteria, blue- green algae, radiolarians and foraminiferans. Within each kingdom organisms which have a general resemblance to each other are grouped into **phyla** (singular phylum). Phyla are divided into **classes** and classes are divided into **orders**, e.g. animals with backbones are all placed in the phylum chordata or vertebrata. The mammals constitute a class of the phylum chordata. Orders of mammals include carnivores (cats, dogs, bears, etc.) and primates (monkeys, apes, humans, etc.). Orders are divided into groups of closely related organisms called **families**, e.g. chimps and gorillas are members of the ape family (Pongidae). Families consist of groups called **genera** (singular genus). Members of the same genus are fairly similar, e.g. the rook, the raven, the jackdaw and the crow are all members of the genus *Corvus*. Genera can be divided into **species**. A species is a group of organisms which are all of the same type. Organisms within a species can interbreed and produce fertile offspring. The name of an organism is in two parts. The first part (the generic name) gives the genus and the second part (the specific name) gives the species, e.g. the rook is *Corvus frugilegus* and the jackdaw is *Corvus monedula*. Note that the generic name begins with a capital while the specific name begins with a small letter.

Fossil organisms are placed in the same taxonomic groups as living organisms but, since their breeding behaviour can hardly be tested, they have to be classified in terms of their appearance and structure. While the forms of organisms generally give enough information to allow species to be separated this means that the classification of fossils is less accurate than the classification of living things.

Preservation of fossils

Fossils do not necessarily give us a complete record of life in the past firstly because an organism's chances of being preserved are very small and secondly because fossils may be destroyed by weathering, erosion and metamorphism. The chances of preservation depend on various factors. Most fossils are the remains of hard parts such as shells. Soft tissues are usually eaten or decomposed before they can be preserved so fossils of organisms such as jellyfish and worms are rare. An organism has an improved chance of being preserved if it lives in an area of deposition so it can be buried rapidly. This means that land organisms are not preserved very often since they have little chance of burial after death. In the sea, organisms which live on rocky eroding shores have less chance of being preserved than those which live buried in sediment. When rocky-shore molluscs such as limpets, winkles, whelks and mussels die their shells are transported, partly broken and deposited in masses of mixed shells. When such an accumulation is preserved it is called a **death assemblage** because the fossils are not in their living positions. On the other hand, burrowing organisms are often preserved in their living positions. Fossils found in their living positions constitute a **life assemblage**.

The type of sediment being deposited affects the chances of preservation. Fossils are most common in rocks such as mudstones, shales, siltstones and limestones. They are much less common in sandstones and conglomerates. One reason for this is that many more organisms live in fine-grained sediments because their high contents of organic matter mean that more food is available. Also, if planktonic organisms settle into mud they will not be moved and broken after landing. Organic remains which are washed into areas where conglomerates are

eing deposited will be rapidly broken up by
ne moving pebbles and boulders.

Some fossils are unaltered remains. Soft parts
re not often found unaltered though frozen
mammoths are notable examples. Unaltered
ard parts such as teeth and shells are only
ound in rocks younger than the Palaeozoic. The
changes that can take place include **petrifaction**
(urning to stone) in which the original material
may be **impregnated** or **replaced** by substances
uch as calcite, silica and iron minerals. In
mpregnation, spaces in the tissue are filled by
minerals. Petrifaction may destroy the fine struc-
ire of the organism but sometimes, e.g. where
ood is replaced by opal, the cellular structure
f the organism is almost perfectly preserved.
lineral **alteration** occurs in aragonite shells
hich are slowly converted to the more stable
alcite. Aragonite fossils are only found in rocks
ounger than the Palaeozoic. Another form of
teration occurs when organic matter loses its
olatile components to leave only carbon, Plant
ossils are often preserved as carbon.

Fossils often occur as **impressions**. If you
ress a shell into clay and then remove it you
ill have left an impression of the shell on the
ay. This type of impression which has come
om the original shell is called a **mould**. If you
l the mould with plaster of Paris, the plaster
ill give an impression called a **cast**. It often
appens, especially in sandstones, that ground
ater dissolves shells away to leave moulds of
ie outsides and insides of shells.

The burrows, tracks and other marks left by
nimals are often preserved as **trace fossils**.
ertebrate excrement may be fossilized as phos-
natic **coprolites** while **gastroliths** are polished
ebbles thought to have helped mechanical
gestion in the stomachs of reptiles.

cology

:ology is the study of organisms in relation
 their **environment** or surroundings. The place
 which a plant or animal lives is its **habitat**.
 community consists of all the organisms in
ny particular habitat while the habitat and
ommunity together constitute an **ecosystem**.
Since green plants make food by photosyn-
esis they are called **producers**. Animals are
 consumers since they cannot produce their
vn food. Food relationships may be shown
in a **food chain** which is the sequence:

tertiary consumer	(e.g. hawk)
↑	
secondary consumer	(e.g. blackbird)
↑	
primary consumer	(e.g. caterpillar)
↑	
producer	(e.g. cabbage)

A **food web** shows feeding relationships
among a large number of producers and consumers. Going up a food chain the mass or
number of organisms at each stage declines
sharply giving a relationship called the **pyramid
of biomass** or the **pyramid of numbers** (figure
10.1).

An organism's place in the community is
called its **niche**. The niche describes all of the
relationships between a species and its environment but it is mainly concerned with how an
organism gets its food or 'earns its living'.
Because of this an organism's niche can be
thought of as being roughly equivalent to a
person's occupation or job. No two species
occupy the same niche though there may be
a lot of overlap between niches.

Organisms may live together in a relationship
known as **symbiosis**. In **mutualism** the relationship is beneficial to both organisms; in **com-
mensalism** one organism benefits while the
other is not harmed; in **parasitism** one organism
lives off and damages another organism.

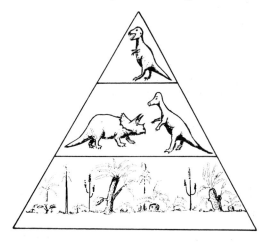

10.1 *An ancient pyramid of biomass (pyramid of
numbers). The mass of organisms decreases
up the food chain.*

Organisms and environments

The main types of environments in which organisms live are **aquatic** (in water) or **terrestrial** (on land). In the sea, environments are classified in terms of water depth into **littoral** between high and low tide; **neritic** down to about 200 m; **bathyal** between 200 and 4000 m; **abyssal** between 4000 and 5000 m and **hadal** below 5000 m. Fresh-water environments include lakes and ponds (**lacustrine**), rivers (**fluvial**) and marshes and swamps (**paludal**). Terrestrial environments include those of deserts, forests, grasslands and tundra. They tend to be more variable and to have more extreme conditions than aquatic environments.

Organisms are often grouped according to their life styles, e.g. organisms which live floating or suspended in water are described as **planktonic**. Plant plankton is **phytoplankton** and animal plankton is **zooplankton**. In the sea, planktonic organisms live mostly in the neritic zone because the phytoplankton need light for photosynthesis. Swimming animals are called **nekton** while bottom-living organisms are **benthos**. Among benthonic animals, those which live within the sediment are **infauna** while those which live on the surface of sediment or rocks are **epifauna**.

Palaeoecology

Palaeoecology is the study of ancient organisms in relation to their environments. In studying present-day ecosystems it is possible to measure or evaluate factors such as temperature, light intensity, humidity, oxygen levels, turbulence, population sizes and predator/prey ratios. In studying ancient ecosystems such measurements cannot be made so we have to rely on indirect indications of ecological factors. The ways in which fossils and sedimentary features can be used to reconstruct past environments have been described on pages 229 to 232.

Evolution

The theory of evolution is the idea that the characteristics of plant and animal populations change with time leading to the appearance of new and perhaps more complex life forms.

There is a great deal of evidence which indicate that evolution has taken place.

Fossils show that life forms are different rocks of different ages and that types of organism have often become extinct. The embryo of vertebrates are very similar especially durin their early development. Indeed, the huma embryo has a tail, muscle segments, g pouches and gill arteries quite like those of fish. Similarities such as these indicate a com mon ancestry for all vertebrates. Young anima may show ancestral traits. In South America th young hoatzin bird has claws projecting fro its wings. The claws are used to help it to clim until it is old enough to fly. Such a featur indicates that bird wings evolved from clawe fore limbs. Many organisms have reduce organs called vestigial organs which may n now have any function but which were presum ably used normally by their ancestors. Example include the reduced pelvis in whales and snake and the wings of flightless birds. The limbs vertebrates may be very different but they a all built on the same plan. The varied limb form are all modifications of the original five-finger or pentadactyl limb which first appeared Devonian lobe-fin fish.

There are many explanations of how evolutic may have come about. Georges Cuvier (176￼ 1832) suggested that life was regularly de troyed then recreated. Jean-Baptiste d Lamarck (1744–1829) thought that characte istics acquired during an animal's lifetime cou be passed to its offspring. The theory whic has gained widest acceptance was propose by Charles Darwin (1809–82) and Alfred Russ Wallace (1823–1913) in 1858. In 1859, Da win elaborated the idea in a famous book c *The Origin of Species by Means of Natur Selection or the Preservation of Favoured Rac in the Struggle for Life*. Darwin had been infl enced by the geological writings of Charles Lye (1797–1875), by the study of populations t Thomas Malthus (1766-1834) and, perhap by the economic writings of Adam Smi (1723-90). Lyell's work the *Principles Geology* told Darwin 'how vast have been th past periods of time' which would allow for th slow evolutionary changes suggested by Da win. Malthus showed how organisms tend produce many more offspring than can surviv A geometric rise in the population is prevente by the deaths of the great majority of organism before they are old enough to breed. Smi believed in a capitalist economic system base

competition among people motivated by self
~~interest~~. Darwin was also strongly influenced
~~by~~ his observations of the varied products of
~~artificial~~ selection and by what he had seen
~~during~~ his voyage (1831–36) as naturalist on
~~the~~ survey ship *HMS Beagle*.

The theory of evolution by natural selection
~~has~~ sometimes been summarized as meaning
~~survival~~ of the fittest'. Fitness is a measure of
~~an~~ organism's survival and reproductive ability.
~~A fit~~ organism can survive to produce offspring
~~which~~ can also survive and reproduce. Darwin
~~and~~ Wallace said that organisms produce many
~~more~~ offspring than can possibly survive.
~~Because~~ of this, there is competition between
~~the~~ offspring and since the members of a
~~population~~ are all different those which are fitter
~~will~~ survive at the expense of the less fit. In
~~the~~ process of natural selection, the environ-
~~ment~~ acts as a kind of 'quality control' which
~~favours~~ those organisms with advantageous
~~characteristics~~. An organism's degree of fitness
~~depends~~ on its environment so if its environ-
~~ment~~ changes so will its level of fitness.

~~In~~ addition to changes caused by natural
~~selection~~, alteration in the characteristics of
populations comes from **mutations**. A mutation
is a change in an organism's genetic material.
Mutation provides a source of new features
within a species.

The following sections outline the main fossil
types.

Brachiopods

Brachiopods are shelled, bottom-living marine
organisms. The shell consists of two **valves**
usually of different size which are symmetrical
about a **median plane** running from one end
of the shell to the other (figure 10.2). Brachiopods are found mostly in sedimentary rocks
(Cambrian—Recent) deposited in shallow
water. About 70 genera exist today mostly in
warm, shallow eastern seas, e.g. round Japan,
Australia and New Zealand but some live in
colder water to depths of about 5000 m. Adult
shells are usually 2–7 cm in length.

The phylum Brachiopoda is divided into two
classes: the **Articulata** and the **Inarticulata**. The
Articulata have calcareous shells hinged by

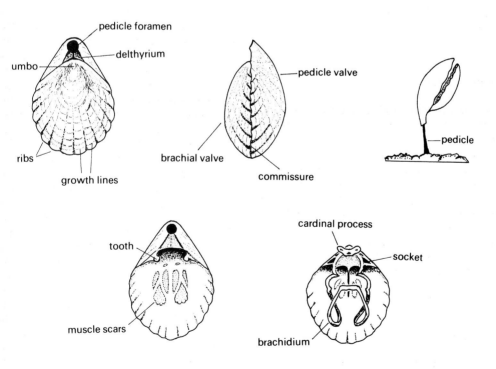

2 *Morphology of a brachiopod.*

teeth and sockets. The Inarticulata have horn-like shells made from a protein called chitin. The valves are not hinged by teeth and sockets.

Articulate brachiopods

In articulate brachiopods the valves are not equal in size. The larger valve is called the **pedicle** or **ventral valve** and the smaller valve is the **brachial** or **dorsal valve**. The shell is hinged along a **hinge line** at its posterior end so the shell opens anteriorly. The posterior end of each valve is pointed to form a projecting region called an **umbo** (plural umbones). The valves may be marked by radial **ribs** and by concentric **growth lines**. The umbo of the pedicle valve usually has a round opening called the **pedicle foramen**. From the foramen comes a horny stalk called the **pedicle** which attaches the brachiopod to the sea floor. Some forms have no pedicles and they have their pedicle valves cemented to the sea floor or they may be attached by means of spines. Between the pedicle foramen and the hinge line is a nearly triangular gap called the **delthyrium**. The delthyrium may be open or it may be closed by two plates or by a single plate called the **deltidium**. The brachial valve may have a gap called the **notothyrium** opposite the delthyrium so making the pedicle opening diamond shaped. The hinge line of the pedicle valve has two projections called **teeth** which fit into **sockets** on the hinge line of the brachial valve.

The brachial valve holds the **lophophore**. The lophophore is used for gas exchange and for feeding. It consists of two arms or **brachia** supported by a long, loop-shaped structure called a **brachidium**. Sometimes the brachidium takes the form of two short prongs called **crura** (singular crus).

Inside the shell are three types of muscle. **Adjustor muscles** from the pedicle valve to the pedicle turn the shell into or out of water currents. The other two muscle sets run between the valves. The **adductor muscles** close the valves and the **diductor muscles** open the valves. The diductor muscles are attached to a projection called the **cardinal process** on the posterior side of the hinge. ('Cardinal' means 'hinge'.) The points of attachment of the muscles to the insides of the valves leaves marks called **muscle scars**. In some brachiopods the muscles are attached to projections rising from the valve floors. In the pedicle valve the Y-shaped pro-

jection is called a **spondylium**. In the brachial valve there is a pair of vertical projections called a **cruralium**.

Inarticulate brachiopods

Inarticulate brachiopods are often chitinous but some are calcareous. The lack of hinge structures means that the valves cannot be opened in the same way as those of the articulate brachiopods. Another difference from articulate brachiopods is that the lophophore has no supporting structures. Where a pedicle is present it comes out between the two valves though a few have a pedicle foramen.

Some examples of brachiopods from various orders within the classes Articulata and Inarticulata will now be described and illustrated.

Phylum Brachiopoda

Class Articulata

Orthides (Lower Cambrian–Upper Permian)

Hinge straight. Both valves convex. Delthyrium and notothyrium usually open. No brachidium. Cardinal process usually present.

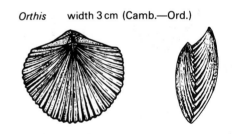

Orthis   width 3 cm (Camb.—Ord.)

10.3 Orthide.

Strophomenides (Lower Ordovician–Lower Jurassic)

Hinge straight. Brachial valve often flat or concave. Pedicle opening closed or small. Spines may be present. Cardinal process well developed and often bilobed.

Strophomena   width 5 cm (Ord.)

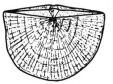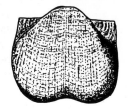

Dictyoclostus [Productus]   width 7 cm (Carb.)

Spiriferides (Middle Ordovician-Jurassic)

Spiral brachidium. Hinge line straight or curved.

Spirifer   width 15 cm (Carb.)

spiral brachidium

10.7 Spiriferide.

).4 Strophomenides.

entamerides (Middle Cambrian-Upper evonian)

iconvex. Spondylium well developed.

Kirkidium [Conchidium]   height 6 cm (Sil.)

0.5 Pentameride.

Terebratulides (Lower Devonian-Recent)

Hinge curved. Pedicle present.

Dielasma [Terebratula]   height 4 cm (Carb.)

10.8 Terebratulide.

Rhynchonellides (Middle Ordovician-Recent)

inge curved. Umbo of pedicle valve often harply pointed to form a beak-like structure. edicle usually present. Crura present. Shells sually coarsely ribbed meeting along a zig-ag line.

Trigonirhynchia   width 2.5 cm (Sil.)

).6 Rhynchonellide.

Class Inarticulata

Lingulides (Lower Cambrian–Recent)

Shell usually chitinous. Pedicle comes out between valves.

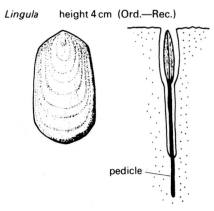

Lingula   height 4 cm (Ord.—Rec.)

pedicle

10.9 Lingulide.

Evolution of brachiopods

Inarticulate brachiopods and orthides appeared in the Lower Cambrian while pentamerides evolved from the orthides during the Middle Cambrian. During the Ordovician strophomenides and spiriferides evolved from the orthides and rhynchonellides evolved from the pentamerides. The terebratulides evolved, probably from the spiriferides, at the end of the Silurian. The pentamerides became extinct during the Devonian while the orthides and most of the strophomenides became extinct at the end of the Permian. Spiriferides became extinct during the Jurassic. Surviving forms are the inarticulate lingulides and the articulate rhynchonellides and terebratulides.

Graptolites

Graptolites are largely Lower Palaeozoic fossils which often look like pencil markings on the rock. They were colonial, marine organisms which were mostly planktonic. Their skeletons were made of tough protein. Graptolites are classified as simple chordates (subphylum Hemichordata). The class Graptolithina is divided into the orders **Graptoloidea** and **Dendroidea**.

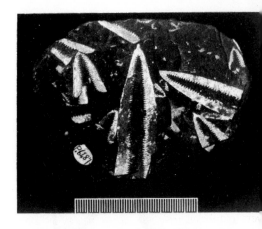

The graptoloid Didymograptus.

Graptoloids

Graptoloids consist of a series of hollow, linked tubes. The first part of the graptoloid to form is a hollow cone called a **sicula** which may have an upward projecting spine called a **nema** and a downward projecting spine called a **virgella**. Small cups called **thecae** (singular theca) grow from the sicula. The thecae were occupied by simple animals called zooids each of which was connected to a common canal so that food caught by a zooid could be shared by the whole colony. During food gathering the zooid extended from the thecal apertures. The thecae have various shapes, e.g. straight, S-shaped or

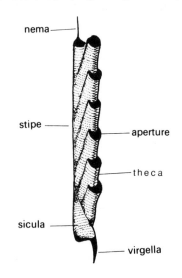

nema

stipe

aperture

theca

sicula

virgella

10.10 Morphology of a graptoloid.

ooked and they may overlap or be widely
eparated. Apertures also have various shapes
nd some have spines extending from them
igure 10.10).

The complete graptoloid colony is called a
habdosome while branches of the rhabdosome
re called stipes. Rhabdosomes may have up
o eight stipes. Stipes with one row of thecae
re described as being **uniserial**. A rhabdosome
ith a double row of thecae is **biserial**. The
habdosome is described as **pendent** if the
tipes hang down with the thecae on the inside
r **scandent** if the stipes grow up from the sicula
ith the thecae facing out. Most graptoloids
ere planktonic organisms though some may
ave been able to swim.

Dendroids

Unlike the planktonic graptoloids most den-
roids were attached to the sea floor. They had
ush-like forms with rhabdosomes consisting
f numerous, branching, uniserial stipes some-
mes connected by cross links. Dendroids also
iffer from graptoloids in that the rhabdosome
as thecae of two different types.

Some types of graptoloids and dendroids will
ow be described and illustrated.

hylum Chordata (Subphylum Hemichordata)

lass Graptolithina

iraptoloids (Lower Ordovician-Lower Devonian)

see figure 10.11)

idymograptids (Ordovician)

habdosome consists of 8, 4 or 2 stipes which
sually hang down.

iplograptids (Ordovician–Silurian)

iserial; scandent.

Monograptids (Silurian–Lower Devonian)

Jniserial.

Dendroids (Middle Cambrian–Carboniferous)

Bush-like rhabdosome usually growing up from
he sea floor. Some may have floated attached
o sea weed (figure 10.12).

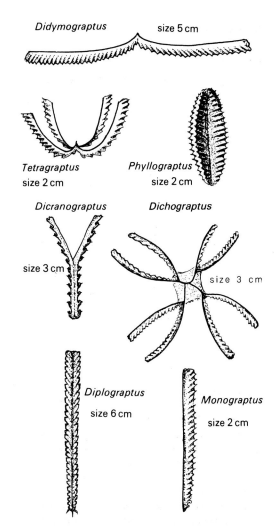

10.11 Graptoloids. The top five are didymograptids

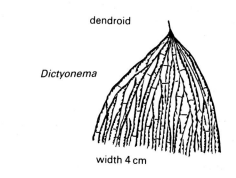

10.12 Dendroid.

Graptolite evolution

The first graptolites were dendroids. They appeared during the Cambrian and became extinct during the Carboniferous. The graptoloids probably evolved from planktonic dendroids such as *Dictyonema*. The earliest graptoloids appeared during the Lower Ordovician. These were didymograptids with two, four or eight stipes. A two-branched didymograptid gave rise to diplograptids during the Middle Ordovician. Most branched forms became extinct before the end of the Ordovician though the diplograptids survived into the Lower Silurian. Monograptids are the characteristic graptoloids of the Silurian. They became extinct during the early Devonian. Evolution within the monograptids resulted in changing thecal shapes. Early forms had straight thecae and from these arose triangulate, lobate and hooked thecae. In some monograptids, thecae became long and isolated. In late Silurian times thecal types had returned to simple forms.

Molluscs

Molluscs are soft-bodied invertebrates which often have calcareous shells. They occupy a wide range of habitats in the sea, in fresh water and on land. The phylum Mollusca is divided into various classes of which the main ones are the **Gastropoda** (slugs, snails, limpets, winkles and whelks), the **Bivalvia** (mussels, cockles, scallops and razor shells) and the **Cephalopoda** (octopuses, squids, cuttle fish and *Nautilus*).

Gastropods

Most gastropods have coiled shells which may have twisted-spire shapes (helical) or flat coils (planispiral) (figure 10.13). The shell opens at the **aperture** which when viewed from the front is usually on the right-hand side. The aperture may be smooth all the way round or it may have a groove called the **siphonal canal** at its bottom end. In the living organism a water-breathing tube called a siphon passes out through the canal. The aperture is sealed by a trapdoor called an **operculum** which the animal pulls in when it withdraws into the shell. The coils or **whorls** of the shell are wound round a central pillar called the **columella**. Externally, the whorls are separated by a line called a **suture** (figure 10.13). In some shells the last whorls

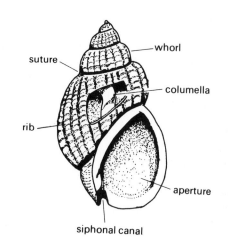

10.13 Morphology of a gastropod.

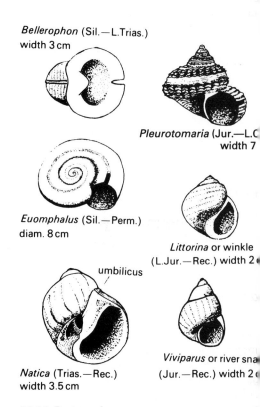

Bellerophon (Sil.—L.Trias.) width 3 cm

Pleurotomaria (Jur.—L.C width 7

Euomphalus (Sil.—Perm.) diam. 8 cm

Littorina or winkle (L.Jur.—Rec.) width 2

Natica (Trias.—Rec.) width 3.5 cm

Viviparus or river sna (Jur.—Rec.) width 2

10.14 Gastropods.

do not meet in the middle of the shell leavi a gap called the **umbilicus**. The shell may ha ribs, spines and knobs running parallel to at a high angle to the sutures. Some exampl of gastropods are shown in figure 10.14.

Bivalves

Bivalves are marine and fresh water organisms whose shells consist of a pair of calcareous valves (figure 10.15). Close to the hinge are the protruding, dorsally situated **umbones**. The umbones are usually asymmetrical and they usually point towards the front or anterior end of the shell. If you hold the shell with the umbones pointing away from you the **left valve** is on your left and the **right valve** is on your right. The valves may be ornamented by ribs radiating from the umbones or by concentric growth lines. The two valves are usually similar or **equivalve**; if dissimilar, they are **inequivalve**.

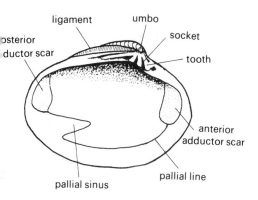

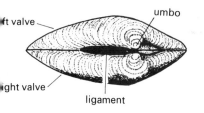

0.15 Morphology of a bivalve.

The valves are joined in the region of the umbones. Each valve has a flattened area called the **hinge plate** which bears an internal or external **ligament** in a **ligament pit**, protruding **teeth** and sunken **sockets**. The ligament consists of a tough, rubbery substance called conchiolin. It acts as a spring which tends to open the valves. The teeth fit into sockets in the opposite hinge plate.

Away from the hinge the valves meet along the **commissure**. In some burrowing bivalves the shell does not close completely and there may be a posterior opening or **gape**. Some forms also gape anteriorly.

The valves are held together by **adductor muscles**. Sometimes, as in the scallop, there may be one central muscle but, more often, there are two muscles one being anterior and the other posterior. Between the muscle scars and close to the margin of the valve is the **pallial line**. The pallial line marks the edge of the inner shell layer secreted by the **mantle**. The mantle is the organ which lines the inside of the valves. In some bivalves the pallial line is bent in at the posterior end of the shell to form the **pallial sinus**. Such a sinus is found in most burrowing forms since it marks the edge of a pocket into which the large siphons or water-breathing tubes can be withdrawn.

Types of bivalve

There is no simple way of classifying fossil bivalves because classification of living forms depends to some extent on the soft parts. Shell shape is not a good guide to classification since it depends largely on the animal's way of life. Because of this, bivalves are described in terms of forms representative of the main types.

Nucula (nut shell) type

Shell small and nearly triangular. Teeth numerous and similar to each other. Burrowers.

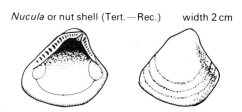

Nucula or nut shell (Tert.—Rec.) width 2 cm

10.16 Nucula *type bivalve.*

Glycymeris (dog cockle) type

Teeth numerous and similar. Muscle scars of equal size.

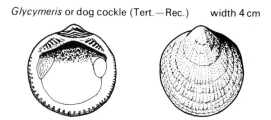

Glycymeris or dog cockle (Tert.—Rec.) width 4 cm

10.17 Glycymeris *type bivalve.*

Mussel type

Teeth small and simple. Muscle scars of unequal size. Attached to sea floor by tough strands (byssus threads).

Mytilus or mussel (Rec.)   length 6 cm

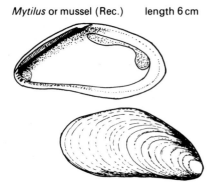

10.18 Mussel type bivalve.

Oyster type

One muscle scar in each valve or two scars of unequal size. The oyster is fixed to the sea floor by its larger left valve.

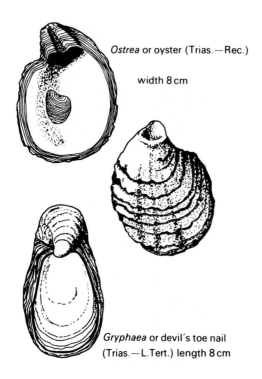

Ostrea or oyster (Trias.—Rec.)

width 8 cm

Gryphaea or devil's toe nail (Trias.—L.Tert.) length 8 cm

10.19 Oyster type bivalves.

Gaper type

Burrowing forms with a wide posterior and narrow anterior gape.

Mya or gaper (Tert.—Rec.)   length 8 cm

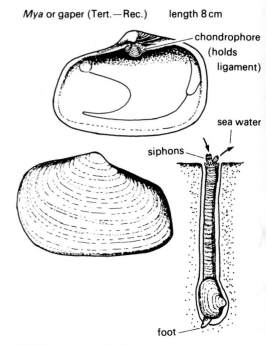

chondrophore (holds ligament)

sea water

siphons

foot

10.20 Gaper type bivalve.

Trigonia type

Teeth very large and thick with grooves running across them.

Laevitrigonia [*Trigonia*] width 6 cm (Trias.—Cret.)

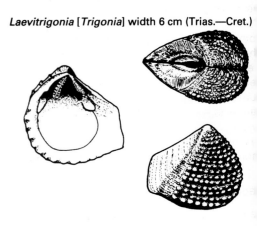

10.21 Trigonia *type bivalve.*

Venus type

few teeth differing from each other in size and shape. Hinge or cardinal teeth lie under the umbo with long lateral teeth on each side.

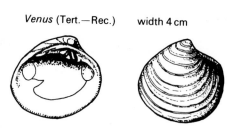

Venus (Tert.—Rec.)   width 4 cm

Cerastoderma [Cardium] or cockle (Tert.—Rec.)

width 5 cm

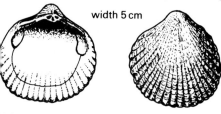

10.22 Venus *type bivalves*.

Bivalve evolution

Bivalves appeared during the Lower Cambrian but they did not become common or diverse until the Lower Ordovician. The sediment-feeding *Nucula* appeared at this time with shallow-burrowing *Venus* type forms and the deep-burrowing *Lucina* types. Byssally-attached mussel types diversified during the late Ordovician. Fresh-water forms appeared during the Devonian and non-marine 'mussels' such as Carbonicola, *Naiadites* and *Anthraconaia* were common during the Upper Carboniferous. These forms were similar to the present-day fresh water mussel, *Unio*. Many bivalves became extinct at the end of the Palaeozoic but during the Mesozoic they became very abundant with the appearance of forms such as the oyster (*Ostrea*), *Trigonia*, *Gryphaea*, and the dustbin-like rudists. Bivalves remained abundant through the Tertiary until the present day.

Cephalopods

Cephalopod molluscs include forms such as the octopus and squid. They are highly evolved marine molluscs with relatively large brains and well-developed eyes. The mouth is surrounded by tentacles which usually have suckers. Shells in present-day forms may be absent, e.g. in the octopus; internal and straight, e.g. in the cuttle-fish and squid; external and coiled, e.g. in *Nautilus*; or internal and coiled, e.g. in *Spirula* Extinct cephalopods include the ammonoids which resembled the *Nautilus* and the belemnites which are the internal shells of cephalopods similar to cuttle-fish.

Cephalopods can be divided into two main groups. **Tetrabranchs** are four-gilled types which include the *Nautilus*, ammonoids and other extinct forms with straight or coiled shells. **Dibranchs** are two-gilled forms which include the octopus, squid, cuttle-fish, *Spirula* and belemnites.

Tetrabranchs

Nautilus (figure 10.23) lives in the near-surface waters of the South-West Pacific. It has a coiled shell divided by **septa** (singular septum) into gas-filled chambers called **camerae**. The septa meet the inside of the shell along lines called

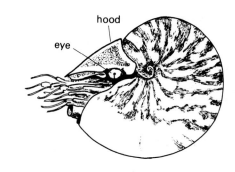

hood

eye

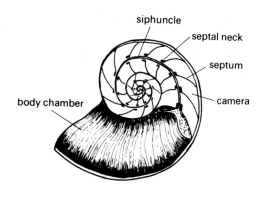

siphuncle

septal neck

septum

camera

body chamber

10.23 *Morphology of* Nautilus.

sutures. The animal lives in the last formed **body chamber**. A tube called the **siphuncle** passes through backward pointing **septal necks** in the centres of the septa and connects the chambers. The shell provides buoyancy. The first-formed chambers contain only gas but the later ones have some liquid which can be added or removed through the siphuncle so allowing the animal to adjust its level in the water.

Nautiloids first appeared in the Upper Cambrian and the Palaeozoic forms had shells which were straight or only partly coiled (figure 10.24). **Connecting rings** are usually present between the septal necks. Straight forms often have calcareous deposits in the first-formed chambers. These deposits probably provided weight which balanced the later gas-filled chambers and so kept the animal horizontal as it swam.

The ammonite Dactylioceras.

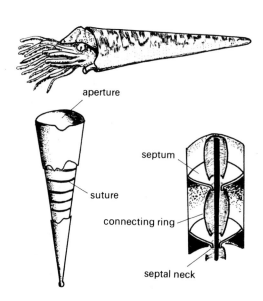

10.24 Morphology of a Palaeozoic nautiloid.

Ammonoids (Devonian–Cretaceous) while essentially similar to *Nautilus* differ in certain respects. Ammonoid shells are sometimes heavily ornamented by radial **ribs** which may be spiny or knobbly. The ribs may come together at **nodes**. A sharp-edged **keel** may run round the outer (ventral) edge of the shell. In an **evolute** shell the last coil runs round the outside of all the earlier coils; in an **involute** shell the last

coil covers and conceals the earlier coils (figure 10.25). In an evolute shell the later coils are thicker than the early coils so the shell is biconcave. The depression inside the last coil is called the **umbilicus**. Ammonoid shell shape is very variable ranging from flat coin shapes to nearly spherical forms. Sometimes, the shell is partly uncoiled.

Most ammonoids have their siphuncles on the outer edge of the shell with the septal necks pointing forward. Ammonoids often have very complex suture lines because the edges of the septa were folded. The folding of the septa made them very strong so they could support the wall of the shell against the pressure of the water. Suture lines are drawn with the ventral end on the left and with an upward pointing arrow indicating the position of the shell aperture. **Saddles** on the suture line project forward (upwards on the diagram) while **lobes** project backwards (downwards on the diagram). The forms of the suture lines allow ammonoids to be divided into three groups. The **goniatites** (Palaeozoic) have angular sutures, the **ceratites** (Triassic) have smooth saddles and toothed lobes and the **ammonites** (Mesozoic) have frilly saddles and lobes. Ammonites had a pair of plates called **aptychi** which sealed the aperture by swinging shut like double doors.

PALAEONTOLOGY

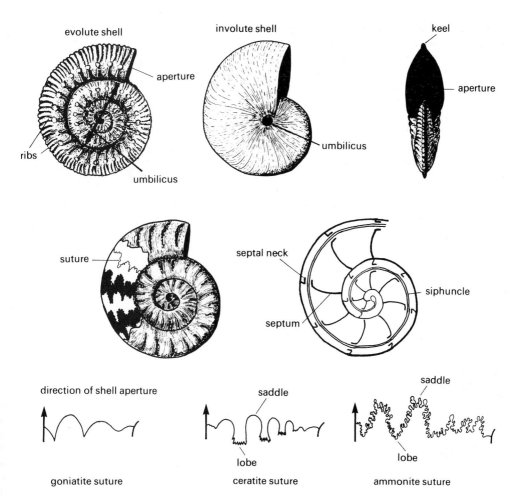

evolute shell

involute shell

keel

aperture

ribs

umbilicus

umbilicus

aperture

umbilicus

suture

septal neck

siphuncle

septum

direction of shell aperture

saddle

saddle

lobe

lobe

goniatite suture

ceratite suture

ammonite suture

0.25 *Ammonoid morphology.*

ibranchs

elemnites are the internal shells of animals
ke cuttle-fish. The shell is in three parts. The
osterior part consists of a solid calcareous
ullet-shaped section called the **guard**. The
lunt anterior end of the guard has a conical
avity called the **alveolus**. The septate **phragmocone**, with a thin siphuncle along its ventral
margin, fits into the alveolus. The pro-ostracum
a dorsal forward projection of the phragmo-
one (figure 10.26).

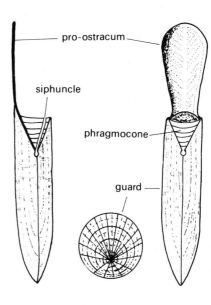

pro-ostracum

siphuncle

phragmocone

guard

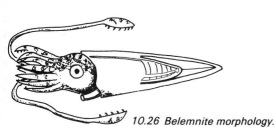

10.26 *Belemnite morphology.*

Classification of cephalopods

Phylum Mollusca

Class Cephalopoda

Tetrabranchs

Nautiloids (Upper Cambrian–Recent)

Orthoceras (Ord.—Trias.)   *Lituites* (Ord.)

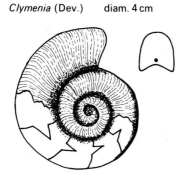

length 10 cm

length 9 cm

10.27 Nautiloids.

Ammonoids (Devonian–Cretaceous)

Clymeniids (Upper Devonian)

Siphuncle on internal (dorsal) margin.

Clymenia (Dev.)   diam. 4 cm

10.28 Clymeniid.

Goniatitids (Upper Devonian–Upper Permian)

Goniatites (Carb.)   diam. 4 cm

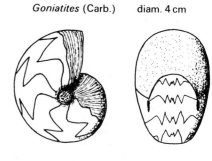

10.29 Goniatitid.

Ceratitids (Triassic)

Phylloceratids (Triassic–Cretaceous)

Phylloceras (Jur.—Cret.)   diam. 12 cm

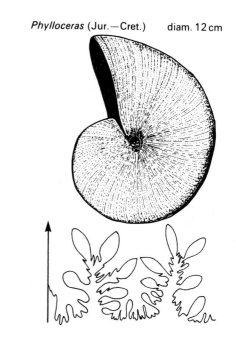

10.30 Phylloceratid.

toceratids (Jurassic-Cretaceous)

Ammonitids (Jurassic-Cretaceous)

Dactylioceras (Jur.)   diam. 7.5 cm

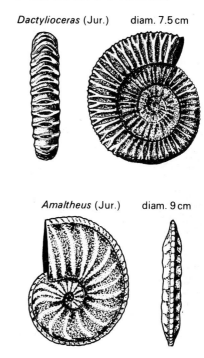

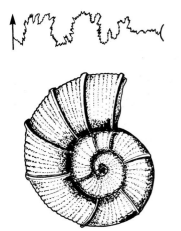

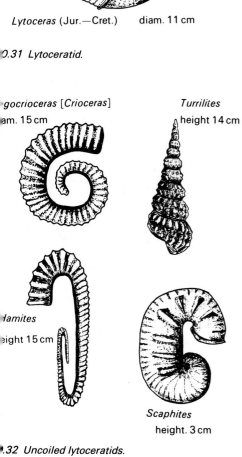

Lytoceras (Jur.—Cret.)   diam. 11 cm

0.31 Lytoceratid.

gocrioceras [Crioceras]
am. 15 cm

Turrilites
height 14 cm

Amaltheus (Jur.)   diam. 9 cm

10.33 Ammonitids.

Dibranchs

Belemnoids (Upper Carboniferous-Lower Tertiary)

Cylindroteuthis (Jur.)   *Actinocamax* (Cret.)

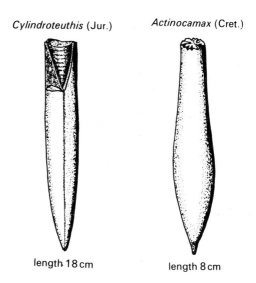

lamites
eight 15 cm

Scaphites
height. 3 cm

.32 Uncoiled lytoceratids.

length 18 cm   length 8 cm

10.34 Belemnoids.

Cephalopod evolution

The earliest cephalopods were the nautiloids. They appeared during the Upper Cambrian and they remained common, mostly as straight or curved forms, through the Palaeozoic. Straight-shelled forms died out during the Triassic leaving flat coiled forms which increased to some extent during the rest of the Mesozoic. During the Tertiary the nautiloids declined so that *Nautilus* is the only surviving genus.

The earliest ammonoids—the Lower Devonian anarcestids—probably evolved from the nautiloids. The anarcestids probably gave rise to the Upper Devonian clymeniids and to the goniatitids which were the dominant Upper Palaeozoic ammonoids. Anarcestids also gave rise to the prolecanitids. (The prolecanitids resemble the goniatitids.) A few prolecanitids survived from the Devonian into the Triassic and these gave rise to the ceratitids. The ceratitids produced the phylloceratids during the Lower Triassic and these survived into the Cretaceous. The phylloceratids gave rise to the lytoceratids during the Lower Jurassic and these became common during the Cretaceous. At various times both the phylloceratids and lytoceratids gave rise to ammonitids. Ammonitids were common during the Jurassic and Cretaceous. All ammonoids became extinct at the end of the Cretaceous.

Belemnoids probably evolved from straight-shelled nautiloids during the Upper Carboniferous. They were abundant during the Jurassic and Cretaceous but became extinct at the beginning of the Tertiary.

Echinoderms

Echinoderms are marine animals such as sea urchins, starfish, brittlestars, sea lilies and sea cucumbers which have spiny, internal, calcareous skeletons (figure 10.35). They usually have five-fold or pentameral symmetry. Echinoderms have a water-vascular circulatory system which allows water to be drawn in and pumped into **tube-feet** which extend from the body to be used in moving, gas exchange and feeding. The main kinds of fossil echinoderms belong to the classes Echinoidea (sea urchins) and Crinoidea (sea lilies).

Echinoids

Non-burrowing sea urchins such as the common sea urchin (*Echinus*) are shaped quite like apples with the mouth on the lower surface and the anus on the upper surface. The animal is covered by spines which fall off after death to show the five-fold symmetry of the skeleton. Sea urchins showing symmetry of this type are described as being **regular**. The skeleton or **test** consists of interlocking plates. The **apical disc** on the upper surface is a double circle of plates enclosing the **periproct**. The periproct is covered by a membrane which holds the anus. The apical disc consists of five large, inner plates called **genital plates** and five small, outer plates called **ocular plates**. Eggs and sperms are released from the genital plates while the ocular plates provide outlets for the **water-vascular** system. Water enters the vascular system through an enlarged porous genital plate called the **madreporite**. From the apical disc run ten rows of double, tubercle-covered plates. The **tubercles** provide attachment for the spines. Opposite the ocular plates are the narrow **ambulacra** (singular ambulacrum) and opposite the genital plates are the wide **interambulacra**. On the ambulacral plates are pore pairs which allow the passage of water into the tube feet. The large interambulacral plates are not porous. The sea urchin feeds by means of five chisel-like teeth which, with their supporting plates, make up a structure called **Aristotle's lantern**. The teeth stick out of an aperture—the **peristome**—on the lower side of the test. The spines have sockets in their bases which fit onto the tops or **mamelons** of the tubercles. Muscles running between the tubercles and the spine bases allow the spines to be moved. Very small spines called **pedicellariae** are also present. The pedicellariae have pincers and they may carry poison. The sea urchin uses them to keep itself clean.

Burrowing sea urchins such as the heart-shaped sea potato (*Echinocardium*) have two-fold or bilateral symmetry (figure 10.36). Such sea urchins are described as being **irregular**. The mouth is forward of centre and it has a projecting lip or **labrum**. (There is no Aristotle's lantern.) The anus lies back off the upper surface of the animal. The mouth has pore-pairs round it which give off food-gathering tube feet. A deep anterior groove contains one ambulacrum. The upper parts of the other ambulacra form sunken petal-shaped grooves. In the petals are distinct pore pairs which give off tube

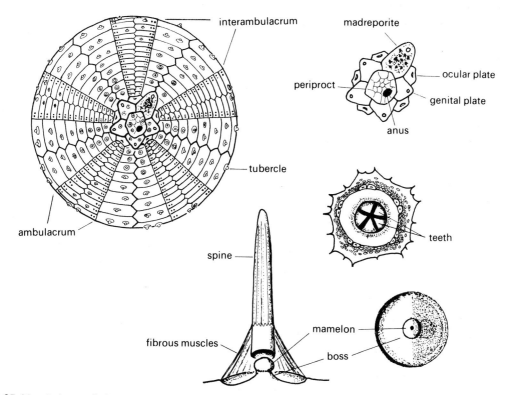

10.35 *Morphology of the common sea urchin* Echinus.

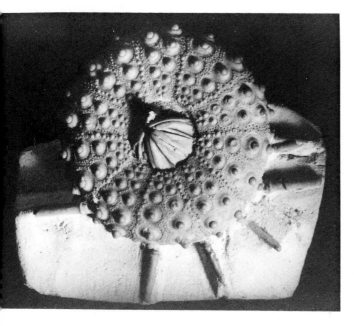

The lower surface of a cidaroid echinoid. Note the large spines and the protruding Aristotle's lantern.

feet used in gas exchange. Behind the mouth is a flat area called the **plastron** which is covered with flattened spines. These spines are used for burrowing. Beneath the anus is an oval strip called the **sub-anal fasciole**. There is also a narrow fasciole forming a strip round the anterior groove. Both fascioles have spines on them which are covered with small beating hairs called cilia. The beating of the cilia produces currents which flow down the chimney- shaped burrow and anterior groove to bring food to the mouth. The cilia on the sub-anal fasciole beat to take waste away from the anus. Some of the water coming down the vertical burrow passes over the petaloid ambulacra where gas exchange takes place.

Some sea urchins live with only their lower surfaces in the sediment. Such forms tend to have higher, less streamlined tests than burrowing forms. They also have less well-developed fascioles and anterior grooves.

Classification of echinoids

Echinoids can be divided into two main sub-classes. **Perischoechinoids** may have many columns of plates making up their ambulacra and interambulacra while **euechinoids** have two columns of plates in their ambulacra and interambulacra.

Perischoechinoids (Ordovician–Recent)

Includes all Palaeozoic echinoids along with cidaroids. They are regular echinoids with one to many columns of plates in their interambulacra and two to twenty columns in their ambulacra (figure 10.37).

Euechinoids (Upper Triasic–Recent)

May be regular or irregular. They have two columns of plates in both their ambulacra and interambulacra (figure 10.38).

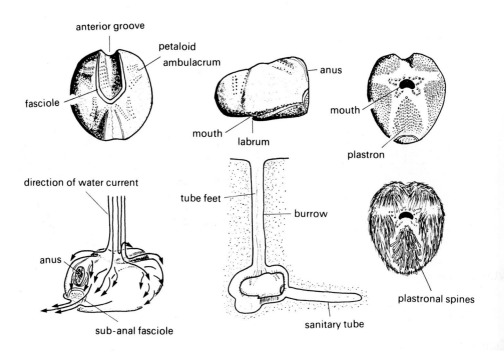

10.36 Morphology and lifestyle of the sea potato Echinocardium.

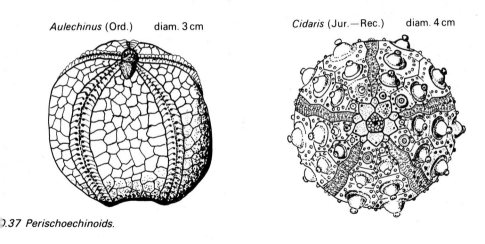

Aulechinus (Ord.)   diam. 3 cm

Cidaris (Jur.—Rec.)   diam. 4 cm

0.37 Perischoechinoids.

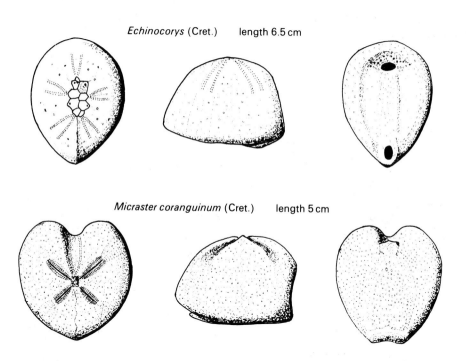

Echinocorys (Cret.)   length 6.5 cm

Micraster coranguinum (Cret.)   length 5 cm

0.38 Euechinoids.

Echinoid evolution

Echinoids appeared during the Ordovician but they did not become common until the Carboniferous. Some of the Palaeozoic forms had flexible tests. The only Palaeozoic echinoid to survive into the Mesozoic was the cidaroid genus *Miocidaris* (Permian–Jurassic) and it was from the cidaroids that the euechinoids evolved during the Triassic.

Irregular echinoids appeared during the Jurassic and the evolution of the Upper Cretaceous form *Micraster* has been studied in great detail (figure 10.39). *Micraster* lived in the relatively unchanging conditions under which the Chalk was deposited. Changes in the form of the test have been interpreted in terms of the animal's degree of adaptation to burrowing. The main changes observed in *Micraster* from older to younger forms are as follows:

1 The test gets broader and the highest and broadest part moves backwards.

2 The anterior groove gets deeper, the mouth moves forward and the labrum or lip becomes more pronounced. These changes probably allowed improved food collection from the incoming current.

3 The petaloid ambulacra get longer indicating that they carried more tube feet for gas exchange. The plates between the pore pairs become rougher suggesting the presence of more cilia to improve water flow.

4 The sub-anal fasciole becomes broader indicating that there were more cilia creating currents to remove waste.

5 The tubercles on the plastron get bigger indicating the presence of larger digging spines.

At any one time the *Micraster* population shows a mixture of these features with some individuals showing more advanced characteristics than others. It is thought that the changes

represent improved adaptation to burrowing. The earliest form *Micraster leskei* was a small, rounded echinoid with a shallow anterior groove and with a labrum-free mouth set back. It probably lived in a shallow burrow. *M. leskei* probably gave rise to two forms—*M. corbovis* which remained a shallow burrower and *M. cortestudinarium*. *M. cortestudinarium* and its descendent *M coranguinum* were deep burrowers. *M. cortestudinarium* also gave rise to a shallow burrowing form, *M. senonensis*, which lost its sub-anal fasciole and developed a tall test.

Crinoids

Crinoids are plant-like echinoderms which are often attached to the sea floor by means of a stalk or stem made up of hollow **columnar plates** or **columnals**. The lower end of the stalk has a root-like **holdfast** to provide anchorage. On top of the stalk is a cup or **calyx** consisting of, from the bottom up, five **infrabasal plates**, five **basal plates** and five **radial plates**. From the radial plates extend five long branched arms or **brachia** made up of brachial plates. The arms give off numerous small branches called **pinnules** which are made up of **pinnular plates**. The animal feeds by spreading its arms to filter sea water. Tube feet extending from the pinnules trap food particles which are then passed by cilia down grooves in the arms to the mouth. The mouth lies in the **tegmen** which forms a lid on top of the calyx. The anus is also on top of the calyx though it may be on the end of an **anal tube** to keep it away from the mouth (figure 10.40).

Classification of crinoids

There is no simple way of classifying crinoids. They may, however, be considered in terms of Palaeozoic and Mesozoic to Recent forms.

Palaeozoic crinoids

All have stalks. Most have a rigid calyx. Anal tube may be present. Some lower brachial plates may be incorporated into the calyx. Pinnules not always present (figure 10.41).

Mesozoic–Recent crinoids

All have very flexible arms with the brachials not part of the calyx. Tegmen flexible. Stalked or unstalked (figure 10.42).

Micraster coranguinum

Micraster senonensis

Micraster cortestudinarium
deep burrower

Micraster corbovis
shallow burrower

Micraster leskei

10.39 Evolution of **Micraster.**

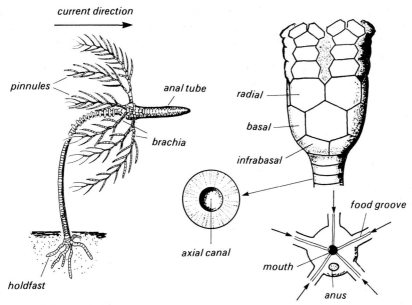

current direction

pinnules

anal tube

brachia

radial

basal

infrabasal

axial canal

food groove

mouth

anus

holdfast

0.40 *Crinoid morphology and lifestyle.*

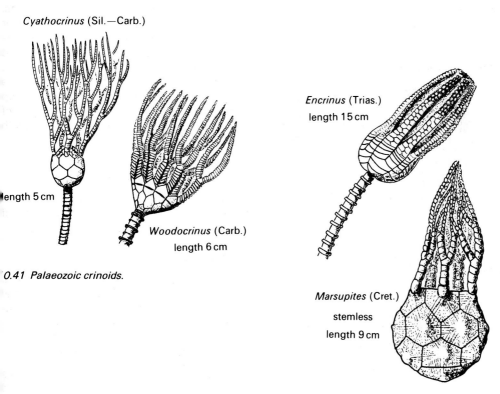

Cyathocrinus (Sil.—Carb.)

length 5 cm

Woodocrinus (Carb.)
length 6 cm

0.41 *Palaeozoic crinoids.*

Encrinus (Trias.)
length 15 cm

Marsupites (Cret.)

stemless

length 9 cm

10.42 *Mesozoic crinoids.*

Evolution of crinoids

Crinoids appeared during the Lower Ordovician and they had become abundant by the Silurian. The Palaeozoic forms became extinct during the Permian apart from one group which survived into the early Triassic. Unstalked forms first became common during the Jurassic and, today, unstalked forms are more common than stalked forms.

Corals

Corals and sea anemones are marine animals which belong to the class Anthozoa of the phylum Cnidaria. They have hollow, bag-like bodies usually showing radial symmetry with a mouth at the top surrounded by tentacles (figure 10.43). The tentacles catch and paralyse small organisms which are then pushed into the mouth. There is no anus so undigested food is removed through the mouth. Sea anemones have no hard parts but in coral the soft part or **polyp** sits on a calcareous skeleton. **Solitary** corals have a single polyp on a cup-like skeleton while **colonial** or **compound** forms have numerous polyps on complex, often branching skeletons. There are three main coral types: **rugose** and **tabulate** corals are Palaeozoic while **scleractinian** corals are Mesozoic to Recent in age.

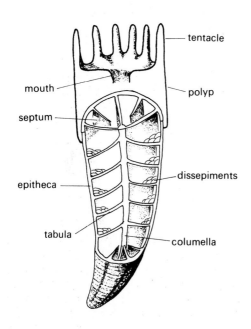

10.43 Coral morphology.

Rugose corals

Rugose (wrinkled) corals are solitary or colonial forms which show bilateral symmetry. They are almost entirely Palaeozoic. The skeleton or **corallum** consists of an outer wall called the **epitheca** within which are vertical, radial partitions called **septa** and horizontal partitions called **tabulae**. Between the septa are small downward-curving plates called **dissepiments**. Up the middle of the corallum, there may be an axial structure which may consist of a zone of tabulae or the joined ends of the septa. A rod-like axial structure is called a **columella**. The top end of the corallum has a cup-shaped hollow called the **calice** which housed the polyp. The calice is floored by tabulae.

The bilateral symmetry of rugose corals derives from the way in which the septa grow in as the animal gets older. The way in which this happens can best be seen by cutting a series of sections through a solitary coral (figure 10.44). Bilateral symmetry tends to be obscured by the addition of new septa as growth continues so that symmetry may become virtually radial.

Rugose corals (figure 10.45) show a wide variety of forms. Solitary forms are usually horn-shaped or cylindrical. Compound forms may be **fasciculate** where the separate branches or **corallites** may resemble a bundle of twigs or **massive** where the corallites are in contact so they form a honeycomb structure.

Tabulate corals

The Palaeozoic tabulate corals are fasciculate or massive colonial forms usually consisting of small corallites. They all have tabulae but other internal structures are either absent or not well-developed. Septa when present often take the form of twelve columns of short spines. The branches of some fasciculate forms are connected at intervals by tubes and some massive forms have pores connecting the corallites (figure 10.46).

Scleractinian corals

Scleractinian corals are Mesozoic and present-day forms with septa in multiples of six. Dissepiments are sometimes present but tabulae are absent. If an axial structure is present it has developed from septa. The skeleton is light and porous and the corals may be solitary or com-

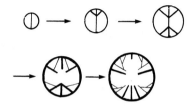

0.44 Sections through a rugose coral showing the insertion of septa from young to old.

ound. Compound scleractinian corals may be similar to compound rugose corals but forms like the present-day brain coral do not occur among rugose corals (figure 10.47).

Classification of corals

Phylum Cnidaria

Class Anthozoa

Rugose corals (Cambrian–Lower Triassic)

Colonial or solitary forms. After formation of first six septa, septa added at four points. Epitheca, dissepiments and tabulae usually present (figure 10.45).

Tabulate corals (Ordovician–Permian)

All colonial. Tabulae distinct. Other internal structures absent or weak. Septa, if present, usually twelve in number (figure 10.46).

Scleractinian corals (Middle Triassic–Recent)

Septa in multiples of six. Dissepiments may be present but tabulae are absent. Axial structure not usually well-developed. Skeleton light and porous. Solitary and colonial (figure 10.47).

Stromatoporoids (Cambrian–Cretaceous)

Stromatoporoids (phylum Stromatoporoidea) are not corals but they do bear some resemblance to tabulate corals (figure 10.48). Stromatoporoids tended to grow in irregular hummocks and sheets. Internally they show vertical pillars separated by horizontal tabulae. Polygonal marks can usually be seen on the upper

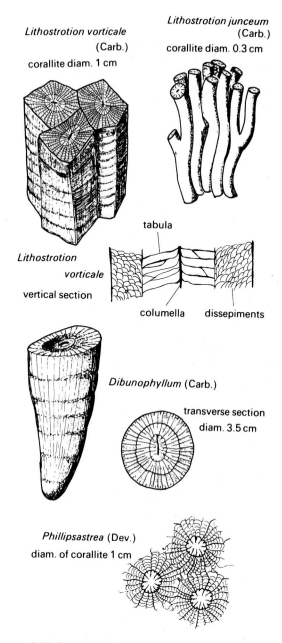

10.45 Rugose corals.

surface. They are an extinct group which from the Ordovician to the Devonian were important reef builders in association with calcareous algae and corals. The classification of stromatoporoids is in doubt. They used to be placed in the same phylum as corals but they are now thought to be related to sponges. It has also been suggested that they were algae.

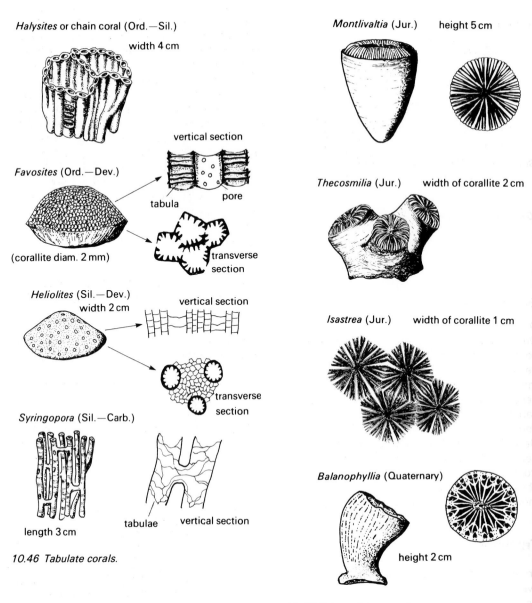

Halysites or chain coral (Ord.—Sil.)
width 4 cm

vertical section

Favosites (Ord.—Dev.)

tabula   pore

(corallite diam. 2 mm)

transverse section

Heliolites (Sil.—Dev.)
width 2 cm

vertical section

transverse section

Syringopora (Sil.—Carb.)

length 3 cm

tabulae   vertical section

10.46 Tabulate corals.

Montlivaltia (Jur.)   height 5 cm

Thecosmilia (Jur.)   width of corallite 2 cm

Isastrea (Jur.)   width of corallite 1 cm

Balanophyllia (Quaternary)

height 2 cm

10.47 Scleractinian corals.

Coral ecology

Present-day corals live in two main ways. Reef-building corals have mutualistic algae in their cells. Corals which have no mutualistic algae are mostly solitary forms. They can live in cold, deep water being most abundant down to depths of about 500 m in areas where the water temperature is between about 5 and 10°C.

Rugose corals were not able to build reefs to the same extent as the scleractinian corals since they did not generally fix themselves to the sea floor. Because of this they tended to live in quiet water off the reefs being built by stromatoporoids and algae. Tabulate corals contributed to stromatoporoid and algal reefs but, since they were not attached, they could not provide the major framework of a reef.

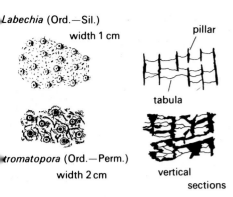

Labechia (Ord.—Sil.)
width 1 cm

pillar

tabula

tromatopora (Ord.—Perm.)
width 2 cm

vertical
sections

0.48 Stromatoporoids.

volution of corals

efinite rugose corals are first found in the rdovician though fossils which may be rugose orals are found in the Middle Cambrian. They ecame common during the Silurian, reached eir peak during the Lower Carboniferous and ecame extinct at the start of the Triassic. abulate corals appeared during the Ordovician nd were abundant during the Silurian and evonian before becoming extinct during the ermian. Scleractinian corals probably evolved om rugose corals during the Lower Triassic. ley became common during the Jurassic and ey remained so until the present day.

rilobites

ilobites are extinct marine arthropods which ed from the Lower Cambrian to the late ermian. Arthropods are invertebrates such as sects, crabs, centipedes and spiders which ave jointed limbs, external skeletons and seg- ented bodies. Trilobites have calcareous exo- eletons. Growth in arthropods takes place tween moulting (ecdysis). Trilobite exoskelet- ns have lines of weakness (**sutures**) which owed easy splitting.

Trilobites get their name from the fact that ey are in three parts from left to right across e body. From front to back they may be divided to the head or **cephalon**, the **thorax** made up hinged segments and the tail or **pygidium** ade up of fused segments (figure 10.49). On upper surface the cephalon consists of a

raised central area called the **glabella** which is separated from flatter **cheeks** by a groove called the **axial furrow**. The outer, posterior corners of the cheeks are the **genal angles** which may be drawn out into **genal spines**. The cheeks are separated into inner **fixed cheeks** and outer **free cheeks** by a wavy **facial suture** which may follow one of three paths. A **proparian** suture leaves the cephalon in front of the genal angle; an **opisthoparian** suture reaches the back edge of the cephalon inside the genal angle; and a **marginal** suture runs along the edge of the cephalon. A marginal suture cannot be seen from the upper surface. The eyes are usually prominent and since they are made up of separate lenses they are described as being **compound**. The eyes are on the inner edge of the free cheek and they sit against a raised part of the fixed cheek called the **palpebral lobe**. The facial suture runs between the eye and the palpebral lobe.

The edge of the cephalon is folded over to form a narrow rim called the **doublure** which is visible on the lower surface. Attached to the central part of the doublure is a plate called the **hypostome** which lies in front of the mouth. An unbranched **antenna** lies on each side of the hypostome.

The thorax consists of a number (2–40) of movable, loosely-jointed segments which in some cases allowed the animal to roll itself into

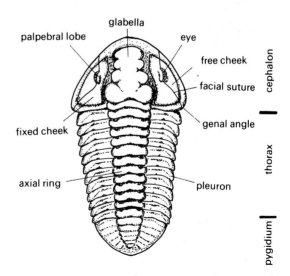

10.49 Trilobite morphology.

a ball. Each segment has a raised central **axial ring** separated by the axial furrow from rib-like **pleura** (singular pleuron) on each side. A **pleural furrow** may run sideways across each pleuron. The lower side of each segment has a pair of projections (**apodemes**) to which limbs were attached. The limbs are two branched consisting of a lower walking leg and an upper gill branch. Appendages of this type also occur on the cephalon behind the mouth. The pygidium is made up of fused plates which also have appendages underneath.

Trilobites probably lived on the bottoms of shallow seas since they have left various types of trace fossils including crawling, ploughing, burrowing and resting marks. Some of them may have been good swimmers since the gill branches of the limbs are sometimes quite like paddles.

Trilobite classification

The trilobites form a very large and diverse group of animals. Since there is no simple way of classifying them we shall describe them in terms of a few typical forms.

***Agnostus* type** (Lower Cambrian–Upper Ordovician)

Small. Only 2 or 3 thoracic segments. Cephalon and pygidium about the same size. Eyes and sutures usually absent (figure 10.50).

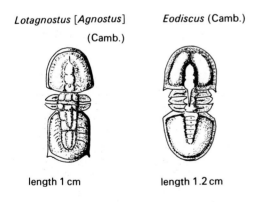

Lotagnostus [*Agnostus*] (Camb.)   *Eodiscus* (Camb.)

length 1 cm   length 1.2 cm

10.50 Agnostus *type trilobites.*

***Paradoxides* type** (Lower Cambrian–Middle Cambrian)

Large round cephalon with long genal spines. Pygidium very small. Numerous thoracic segments usually extended into spines. Eyes large (figure 10.51).

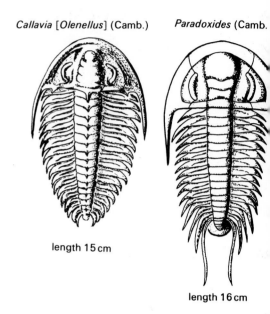

Callavia [*Olenellus*] (Camb.)   *Paradoxides* (Camb.

length 15 cm

length 16 cm

10.51 Paradoxides *type trilobites.*

***Olenus* type** (Lower Cambrian–Upper Ordovician)

Glabella does not extend to front of cephalon. Small pygidium (figure 10.52).

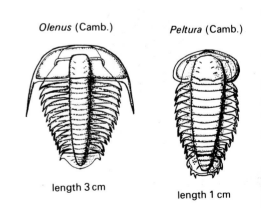

Olenus (Camb.)   *Peltura* (Camb.)

length 3 cm

length 1 cm

10.52 Olenus *type trilobites.*

gygiocaris type (Middle Cambrian–Lower Ordovician)

gidium about the same size as the cephalon. Disthoparian suture. Thorax has 6-9 segments gure 10.53).

Ogygiocaris (Ord.)   Basilicus [Asaphus] (Ord.)

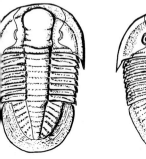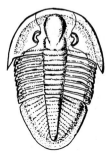

length 6 cm   length 12 cm

0.53 Ogygiocaris *type trilobites.*

Trinucleus type (Lower Ordovician–Middle Silurian)

Large cephalon with suture round the edge. Thorax has 6 segments. Pygidium small and triangular. No eyes (figure 10.55).

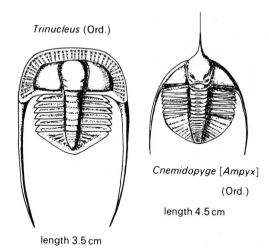

Trinucleus (Ord.)

Cnemidopyge [Ampyx] (Ord.)

length 4.5 cm

length 3.5 cm

10.55 Trinucleus *type trilobites.*

Iaenus type (Lower Ordovician–Upper Devonian)

uite like Ogygiocaris type (figure 10.54).

Illaenus (Ord.)

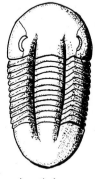

length 4 cm

0.54 Illaenus *type trilobite.*

Proetus type (Ordovician–Permian)

Glabella large. Genal spines usually present. Opisthoparian suture. Thorax has 8-10 segments. Pygidium usually has grooves (figure 10.56).

Proetus (Ord.–Dev.)   Phillipsia (Carb.)

length 2 cm   length 2 cm

10.56 Proetus *type trilobites.*

Calymene type (Lower Ordovician–Middle Devonian)

Glabella large and tapering towards the front. Eyes small. Thorax with 11–13 segments (figure 10.57).

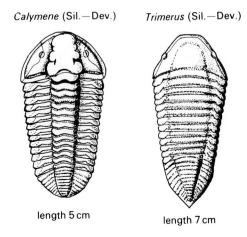

Calymene (Sil.—Dev.)   *Trimerus* (Sil.—Dev.)

length 5 cm   length 7 cm

10.57 Calymene *type trilobites.*

Phacops type (Upper Ordovician–Lower Devonian)

Glabella gets wider towards the front. 11 segments on thorax (figure 10.58).

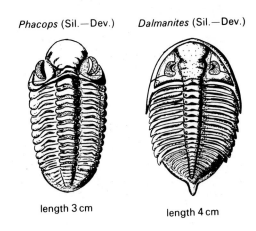

Phacops (Sil.—Dev.)   *Dalmanites* (Sil.—Dev.)

length 3 cm   length 4 cm

10.58 Phacops *type trilobites.*

Evolution of trilobites

Trilobites appeared in large numbers during the Lower Cambrian. They may have evolved from segmented worms (annelids) during the late Precambrian. They reached their maximum development during the Middle Ordovician and gradually declined towards the end of the Devonian. They were rare during the Carboniferous and became extinct during the Permian.

The general evolutionary trends shown by trilobites include changes in the size of the pygidium from being very small to being about the same size as the cephalon; changes in the eyes; development of spines in some forms; and improvements in the articulation of the thoracic segments so the animal could roll itself up.

The earliest trilobites were of *Olenellus* type though *Agnostus* types appeared soon after during the Lower Cambrian. *Olenus* types also appeared during the Lower Cambrian. *Olenellus* types became extinct at the end of the Lower Cambrian and *Olenus* types were the most common Upper Cambrian forms. At the end of the Cambrian many forms became extinct and the main Ordovician forms are types such as *Illaenus*, *Phacops* and *Trinucleus*. *Trinucleus* types became extinct at the end of the Ordovician and Silurian and Devonian forms were mainly types such as *Phacops*, *Dalmanites* and *Calymene*. Most trilobites became extinct during the Devonian though *Proetus* types existed into the Permian.

Bryozoa or Polyzoa

The Bryozoa (moss animals) are mostly marine.

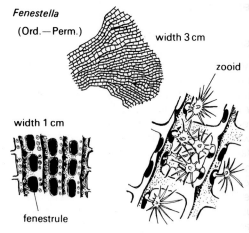

Fenestella (Ord.—Perm.)   width 3 cm

zooid

width 1 cm

fenestrule

10.59 The bryozoan Fenestella *(Ord–Perm).*

they are colonial consisting of small animals (zooids) set in separate chambers of a calcareous or horny exoskeleton. The zooids use tentacles to filter food from the water. The colonies may be branching or encrusting. Some skeletons have a network pattern holding rectangular spaces called fenestrules (small windows). Bryozoa are common living and fossil organisms. Present day forms include sea-mats and sea-mosses. They are common in coral reefs. *Fenestella* (Ordovician–Permian) is a common fossil form (figure 10.59).

Sponges (Phylum **Porifera**)

Sponges (Cambrian–Recent) are aquatic (mostly marine) filter-feeding animals with tough but compressible bodies. Water enters a sponge through numerous small pores (ostia) and leaves through larger oscula. Many sponges have internal skeletons of fine calcareous or siliceous **spicules** (figure 10.60).

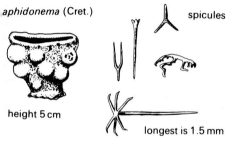

Raphidonema (Cret.)

spicules

height 5 cm

longest is 1.5 mm

10.60 A sponge and sponge spicules.

Vertebrates

Fish

Jawless fish, e.g. lamprey and hagfish, appeared as marine forms at the end of the Ordovician. During the Silurian they developed armoured forms called **ostracoderms** (bony skinned) which lived in fresh and brackish water. The early jawless fish were up to 30 cm long. **Placoderms** (platy skinned) were jawed armour-plated fish which evolved from marine jawless fish during the Upper Silurian. They were common during the Devonian, declined during the Carboniferous and became extinct during the Permian. Placoderms lived in both sea and fresh water. They reached sizes up to about 10 m.

Cartilaginous fish, e.g. sharks, evolved from marine placoderms during the Devonian. Usually only teeth and fin spines occur as fossils because cartilage is not readily preserved. Bony fish, e.g. herring, salmon and pike, evolved from fresh-water placoderms at the end of the Silurian. Lobe-finned bony fish are represented by lung-fish and crossopterygians. Lung-fish presently live in Africa, Australia and South America. They were fairly common during the Upper Palaeozoic but they declined during the Mesozoic. Crossopterygians were common during the Upper Palaeozoic and Mesozoic. They were thought to have become extinct until the coelacanth, *Latimeria*, was caught off Madagascar in 1938 (figure 10.61).

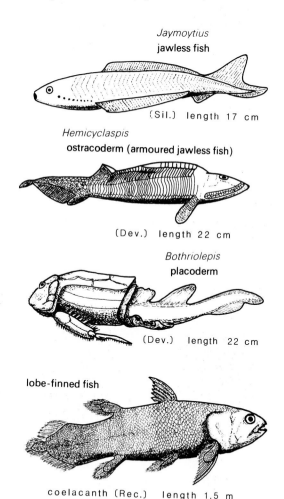

Jaymoytius
jawless fish

(Sil.) length 17 cm

Hemicyclaspis
ostracoderm (armoured jawless fish)

(Dev.) length 22 cm

Bothriolepis
placoderm

(Dev.) length 22 cm

lobe-finned fish

coelacanth (Rec.) length 1.5 m

10.61 Fish.

Amphibians

Amphibians evolved from Upper Devonian crossopterygian fish. The earliest forms were labyrinthodonts (folded teeth) which looked like huge newts. They were common during the Carboniferous but they declined through the Permian and became extinct during the Triassic. Modern amphibians probably evolved from labyrinthodonts during the Triassic (figure 10.62).

Ichthyostega (U.Dev)   length 1 m

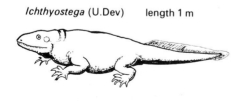

10.62 The amphibian Ichthyostega *(U. Dev.)*

Reptiles

Reptiles evolved from labyrinthodonts during the Carboniferous. The first reptiles, the cotylosaurs or stem reptiles, looked like stubby crocodiles. They were common during the Permian but became extinct during the Triassic. Mammal-like reptiles (theriodonts) evolved from cotylosaurs at the end of the Carboniferous. Theriodonts had teeth, brains, skulls and other skeletal parts like those of mammals. They were common during the Permian but became extinct at the end of the Triassic. Small bipedal reptiles called thecodonts evolved from cotylosaurs during the Triassic. Thecodonts gave

rise to dinosaurs, crocodiles and the flying pterosaurs. Dinosaurs appeared during the Triassic reached their peak during the Jurassic and Cretaceous and became extinct at the end of the Cretaceous. Pterosaurs appeared during the Jurassic and also became extinct at the end of the Cretaceous. Thecodonts may also have given rise to the marine plesiosaurs though plesiosaurs may have evolved from cotylosaurs. The fish-like ichthyosaurs also appeared during the Triassic. Plesiosaurs and ichthyosaurs both became extinct during the Cretaceous. Present-day reptiles such as turtles, lizards and snakes also evolved from cotylosaurs during the Triassic (figures 10.63 and 10.64).

Birds

Birds probably evolved from Triassic thecodonts. The oldest bird, *Archeopteryx* (Upper Jurassic) (figure 10.65) had many features not found in modern birds, e.g. it had teeth, a long bony tail and no projecting keel on its breast bone. It is probable that it could not fly and that its feathers were used to keep it warm. Modern birds such as the cormorant and grebe had appeared by the end of the Cretaceous.

Mammals

Mammals evolved from mammal-like reptiles (theriodonts) during the Triassic. (Theriodonts and dinosaurs may have been warm-blooded.) During most of the Mesozoic mammals were small and not very common. With the extinction of the dinosaurs towards the end of the Cretaceous mammals began to evolve rapidly. Mar-

Skeleton of Tyrannosaurus *(Cret.)*

mammal-like reptile *Cynognathus* (Trias.)

length 2 m

thecodont
Saltoposuchus (Trias.)

length 90 cm

Tyrannosaurus (Cret.)

carnivore

length 14 m

Iguanodon (Cret.)

herbivore

length 8 m

Diplodocus (Jur.)

herbivore

length 27 m

0.63 *Reptiles.*

upials and insectivores appeared during the retaceous and insectivores gave rise to all ther placental mammals. Primitive carnivores creodonts) and primitive hoofed animals (proto-ngulates) evolved from insectivores at the end f the Cretaceous. Creodonts gave rise to dvanced carnivores at the beginning of the ertiary and mammals such as dogs and cats ppeared during the Oligocene. The proto-ngulates gave rise to mammals such as horses,

rhinos, pigs and cattle. The first mammals with trunks appeared about the middle of the Tertiary. Pleistocene mammoths and elephants evolved from late Tertiary mastodons. Cattle appeared about the middle of the Tertiary and camels and deer appeared towards the end of the Tertiary. The ancestors of groups such as rodents appeared early in the Tertiary while the ancestors of whales appeared towards the middle of the Tertiary (figure 10.66).

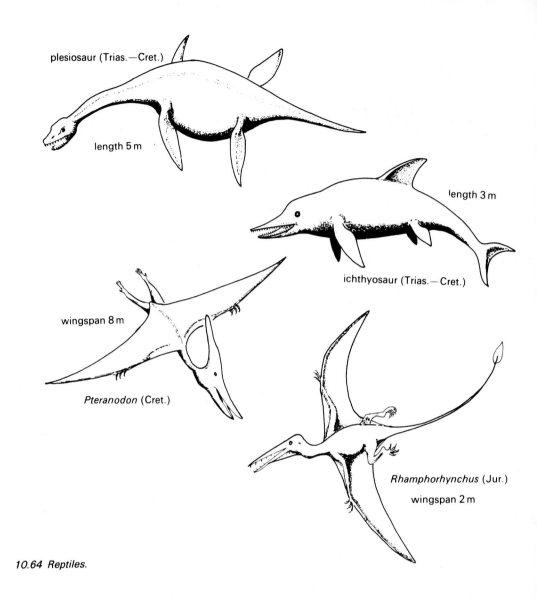

plesiosaur (Trias.—Cret.)

length 5 m

length 3 m

ichthyosaur (Trias.—Cret.)

wingspan 8 m

Pteranodon (Cret.)

Rhamphorhynchus (Jur.)

wingspan 2 m

10.64 Reptiles.

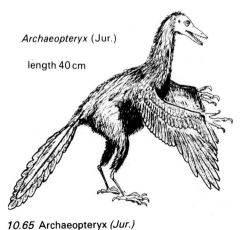

Archaeopteryx (Jur.)

length 40 cm

10.65 Archaeopteryx *(Jur.)*

Horses evolved from *Hyracotherium* of the early Tertiary. *Hyracotherium* was a forest mammal about the size of a fox. Its teeth were not specialized for eating grass and it had four toes on its front legs and three on its hind legs. Increase in size, reduction in the number of toes and the development of teeth suitable for chewing grass saw the appearance of the modern horse at the end of the Tertiary.

Primates can be divided into prosimians, (e.g. lemurs), and anthropoids (monkeys, apes and humans). Prosimians evolved from insectivores early in the Tertiary and anthropoids developed from prosimians towards the middle of the Tertiary.

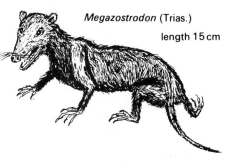

Megazostrodon (Trias.)

length 15 cm

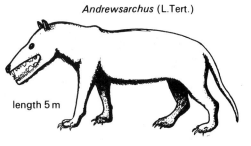

Andrewsarchus (L.Tert.)

length 5 m

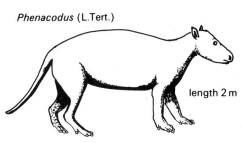

Phenacodus (L.Tert.)

length 2 m

10.66 An early insectivore (Megazostrodon)*, a primitive carnivore* (Andrewsarchus) *and a primitive hoofed mammal* (Phenacodus)*.*

Plants

The plants best represented as fossils are algae, psilopsids (primitive land plants), lycopsids (club mosses), sphenopsids (horsetails), ferns, gymnosperms and angiosperms (figure 10.67).

Algae

Algae are important rock forming plants since they may have skeletons of calcium carbonate or silica. **Stromatolites** are bun-shaped mounds of layered calcium carbonate formed by algal precipitation. They date back to about 3500 Ma ago. Stromatolites are presently being formed by colonial blue-green algae in the very salty conditions of Shark Bay in Western Australia. Since stromatolites may form thick limestones it is probable that blue-green algae were the first reef-building organisms. Other algae which secrete calcium carbonate (collectively called calcareous algae) were also important reef builders often in association with corals and stromatoporoids. Calcareous algae include *Solenopora* (Ordovician–Jurassic) and *Girvanella* (Ordovian–Jurassic). Present-day forms such as *Lithothamnion* (Cretaceous-Recent) can be found on the shore. Microscopic algae such as diatoms and coccoliths are described on p.225.

Psilopsids

Psilopsids are primitive land plants which have forking stems and no true roots. The simplest forms had no leaves. Psilopsids appeared during the Upper Silurian, were common during the Devonian but declined from the start of the Carboniferous. Now, only four species remain.

Lycopsids

Lycopsids or club mosses have roots and small leaves. The spore cases often look like cones. Lycopsids evolved from psilopsids during the Devonian, reached their maximum development during the Carboniferous when they attained the sizes of trees and then steadily declined. Tree-sized forms became extinct during the Permian.

Some of the lycopsid generic names illustrate a problem in naming fossils where the fossils are part of one organism. It is likely, for example, that *Lepidodendron* (stem), *Stigmaria* (roots), *Lepidophylloides* (leaves) and *Lepidostrobus* (spore cases) are different parts of the same plant.

Sphenopsids

Sphenopsids or horsetails have roots and jointed stems. The small leaves are arranged in circles round the stem joints. The spore cases look like cones. Sphenopsids evolved from psilopsids during the Devonian. They were very abundant during the Carboniferous but they declined rapidly from the Triassic.

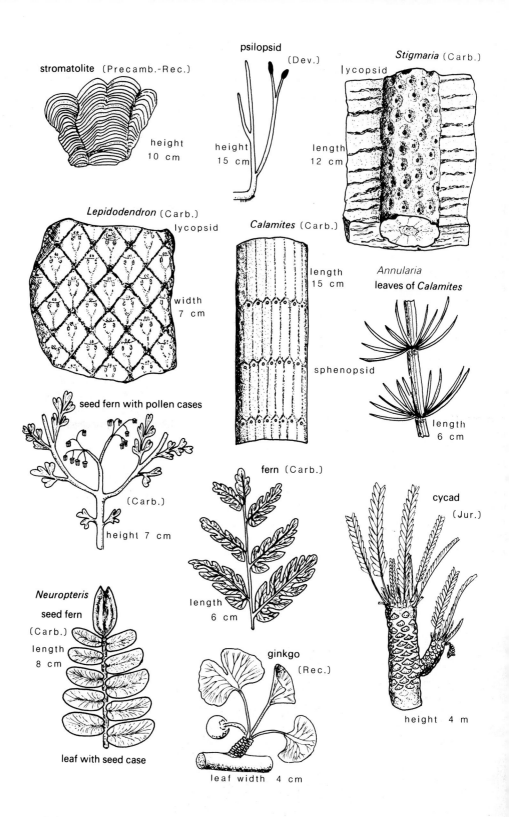

stromatolite (Precamb.-Rec.)

height
10 cm

psilopsid
(Dev.)

height
15 cm

Stigmaria (Carb.)
lycopsid

length
12 cm

Lepidodendron (Carb.)
lycopsid

width
7 cm

Calamites (Carb.)

length
15 cm

sphenopsid

Annularia
leaves of *Calamites*

length
6 cm

seed fern with pollen cases

(Carb.)

height 7 cm

fern (Carb.)

length
6 cm

cycad
(Jur.)

height 4 m

Neuropteris
seed fern
(Carb.)
length
8 cm

leaf with seed case

ginkgo
(Rec.)

leaf width 4 cm

10.67 *Plants.*

erns

erns have large leaves called fronds divided
to small leaflets with spore cases underneath.
hey evolved from psilopsids during the Dev-
nian and became common during the Carbon-
erous when some of them (tree ferns) attained
eights of about 15 m. Ferns are still common
day and tree ferns still grow in tropical
egions.

ymnosperms

ymnosperms are woody plants whose seeds
e not held in fruits. They include seed ferns,
ycads, ginkgos and conifers.

  Seed ferns evolved from ferns at the start of
e Carboniferous. They remained common
rough the Carboniferous but declined and
ecame extinct at the end of the Jurassic. Seed
rns are very similar to true ferns; they differ
having seed-bearing structures on the leaves.
inkgos evolved from seed ferns at the start
f the Permian and cycads evolved from the
ame source at the start of the Triassic. Both
roups were common through most of the
esozoic. They declined during the Cretaceous
nd today they are rare. Cycads have leaves
hich resemble those of palm trees while gink-
os have fan-shaped leaves. Conifers are trees
ith spiny and often evergreen leaves. They
clude common forms such as the pine,
pruce, larch and fir. Conifers appeared during
e Carboniferous and, with cycads and gink-
os, they formed the dominant forest plants of
e Triassic and Jurassic

Angiosperms

Angiosperms or flowering plants are presently
the dominant land plants with about 200 000
species. Besides plants with obvious flowers,
they include grasses and most trees. Angiosperms appeared towards the middle of the
Cretaceous and by the start of the Tertiary, they
had become very common.

The seed fern Neuropteris.

*Fossilized tree trunks, the
Petrified Forest, Arizona.*

Microfossils

Microfossils include a wide variety of organisms such as **protists**; small crustaceans called **ostracods**; tooth-like structures called **conodonts**; algae such as **diatoms** and **coccoliths**; and **pollen grains** and **spores** from land plants (figures 10.68 and 10.69).

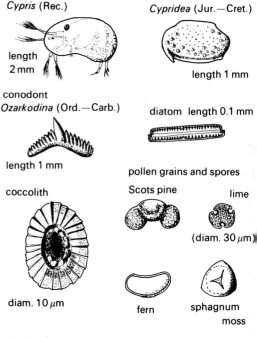

10.69 Microfossils

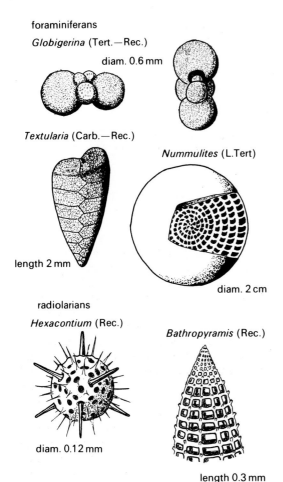

10.68 Microfossils

Protists

Fossil remains of protists most commonly belong to the phylum Sarcodina. Sarcodinians are unicellular and usually microscopic. Many of them have shells or skeletal structures and they move by means of cytoplasmic extensions called pseudopodia (false feet). The main types are the Foraminifera and the Radiolaria.

Foraminifera (Ordovician–Recent) have shells or **tests** which may have apertures from which project the thread-like pseudopodia. The test may be calcareous or it may be made from sand particles or shell fragments stuck together. The test may have one chamber or many interconnected chambers arranged in lines or coils. Most foraminiferans are very small but some forms have a diameter of about 5 cm. They are mostly bottom-living marine organisms but they have also been an important element of marine plankton since the Mesozoic. The remains of planktonic forms contribute to deep sea oozes.

Radiolaria (Precambrian–Recent) are planktonic marine organisms with symmetrical tests which usually consist of silica. Their remains contribute to deep sea oozes mainly at depths below the levels at which the calcareous foraminiferans have dissolved.

Ostracods (late Cambrian—Recent)

Ostracods or mussel shrimps are tiny crustaceans (usually about 1 mm long) with the body inside a double flap. They are both marine and fresh water organisms.

Conodonts (Ordovician—Triassic)

Conodonts are phosphatic, tooth-like structures less than about 2 mm long. They have only been found in place on a fossil of the worm- or eel-like *Clydagnathus* (phylum Conodonta). The conodonts were probably hooks round the mouth which were used for catching prey. *Clydagnathus* resembles the present day bristle-mouthed arrow worms.

Diatoms (Jurassic—Recent)

Diatoms are mostly planktonic unicellular or colonial algae found in the sea and in fresh water. The cell contents are enclosed within an ornate silica skeleton whose two parts fit together like a shoe box.

Coccoliths (Cambrian—Recent)

Coccoliths are the calcareous skeletons of marine planktonic algae. They are very small (diameter 2-25 μm) and they usually have ring or plate structures. The Chalk consists largely of coccoliths.

Pollen grains and spores

Because the pollen grains and spores of land plants are very tough they often survive as fossils. They are most easily obtained from peat.

Trace fossils

Trace fossils are preserved marks left by the activities of organisms. They take a wide variety of forms including tracks, burrows and resting marks. Marks left by present-day organisms can best be studied in shallow ponds and on tidal mud-flats (figure 10.70).

Coprolites

Coprolites are preserved faecal droppings which usually come from fish. They generally consist of calcium phosphate and carbonate and they are often found in black shales. Coprolites may show internal impressions of the animal's intestine and they may contain undigested fragments such as shells, bones and fish scales.

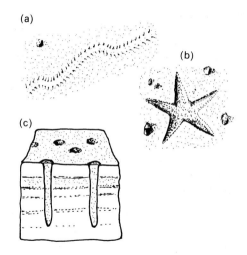

10.70 *Trace fossils:*
(a) *trilobite trail;*
(b) *starfish resting mark;*
(c) *burrows of the worm* Skolithos.

History of life

It is probable that life began about 3800 Ma ago. The oldest fossils (bacteria and blue- green algae) are found in rocks about 3500 Ma old. At this time the Earth's atmosphere had no oxygen so it had reducing rather than oxidizing properties. The early atmosphere is thought to have consisted largely of water vapour and carbon dioxide. In the early Precambrian the energy to produce chemical reactions needed to form complex organic molecules could have come from ultra-violet light which would have penetrated the atmosphere because of the absence of ozone. Some reactions may also have been driven by heat and lightning. Life probably began in shallow water which would be deep enough to absorb lethal ultra-violet light but which would have allowed penetration of wavelengths necessary for photosynthesis.

To begin with, respiration would not have used oxygen. That is, it would have been anaerobic like the process of respiration in yeast. Oxygen produced by photosynthetic blue-green algae would have been poisonous to other early organisms so they probably removed it by joining it to iron to make the insoluble haematite found in early Precambrian banded ironstones. Eventually, as the oxygen content of the atmosphere rose to about one percent of present

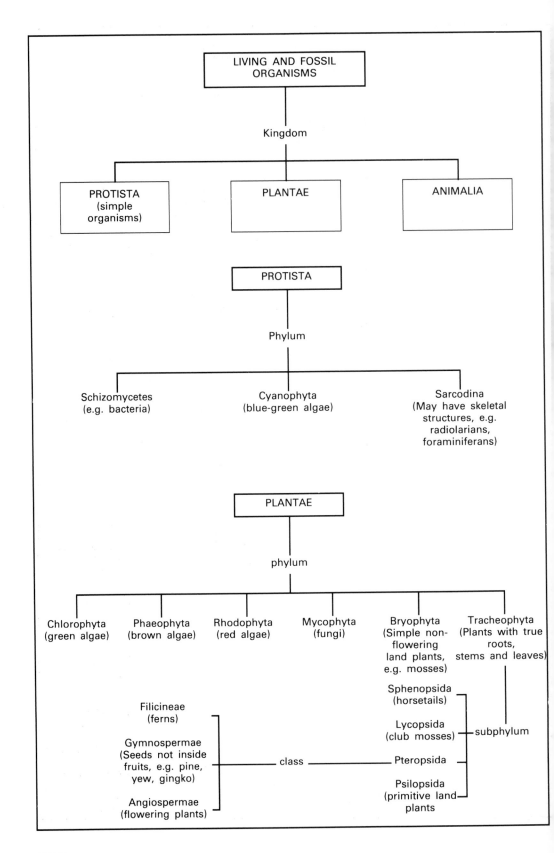

Key 10.1 Classification of Organisms

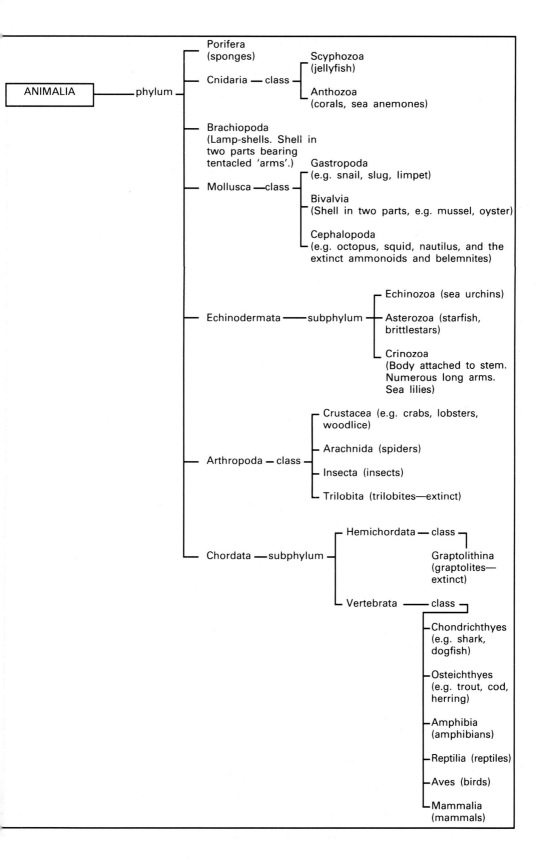

Key 10.1 Classification of organisms

levels it was used in the highly efficient aerobic respiration. This resulted in the disappearance of banded ironstones at about 1800 Ma and in the appearance of red beds indicating the presence of free oxygen in the atmosphere. Multicellular organisms probably evolved when oxygen levels reached about 5 percent of the present atmospheric concentration. When oxygen levels had reached about 10 percent of present levels enough ultra-violet light was being absorbed by ozone to permit organisms to survive on land. The first land plants appeared about 430 Ma ago. They spread rapidly so that by the end of the Carboniferous their photosynthetic activity had produced oxygen levels similar to those of today.

While the oldest trace fossils are probable worm burrows about 1000 Ma old, the oldest fossils of multicellular animals are found in South Australian rocks about 700 Ma old. There are about thirty species of jellyfish, soft corals, worms and doubtful, but possible, echinoderms and arthropods (figure 10.71). From this time, evolution proceeded rapidly because all present-day animal phyla represented by more than a thousand new species, appeared during the Cambrian.

The first land animals were Silurian arthropods similar to scorpions. Wingless insects appeared during the Devonian and they evolved rapidly and developed flight during the Carboniferous. Some Carboniferous insects were like giant dragonflies with wing spans of about one metre.

Because of the similarity between echinoderm larvae and primitive chordates it is thought that vertebrates evolved from echinoderms. Jawless fish appeared during the Ordovician and they gave rise to jawed fish during the Silurian. Cartilaginous and bony fish appeared during the Devonian. Amphibians evolved from lobefin fish during the late Devonian and reptiles evolved from amphibians during the Carboniferous. Mammals evolved from reptiles during the Triassic and birds evolved from reptiles during the Jurassic.

Humans, gorillas and chimpanzees are very similar genetically. It is probable that they diverged from a common ancestor about 5 or 6 Ma ago. *Australopithecus* (southern ape) was a human-like creature which appeared about 4 Ma ago. *Australopithecus* had a brain about the same size as that of the gorilla but its pelvic bones show that it was truly bipedal. Hominids probably evolved from early types of *Australopithecus*. The earliest human was *Homo habilis* (skilful man) who appeared about 2 Ma ago. *Homo habilis* made simple stone tools and he had a bigger brain than that of *Australopithecus*. *Homo erectus* (upright man) appeared about 1 Ma ago. He had a large brain and he hunted large animals and controlled fire. *Homo erectus* became extinct about 0.5 Ma ago. Fossils of modern man (Cro-Magnon man) date from about 50 000 years ago. Cro-Magnon man lived at about the same time as Neanderthal man. Neanderthal man became extinct perhaps because he was killed off by Cro-Magnon man or perhaps the Neanderthal populations were assimilated by interbreeding with the more successful Cro-Magnon populations.

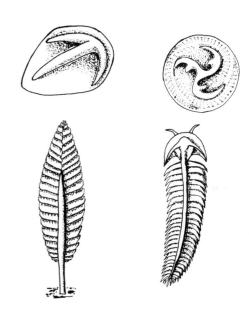

10.71 Multicellular animals from the late Precambrian.

EARTH HISTORY

Stratigraphy or **historical geology** is the study of the Earth through time. Stratigraphy is concerned with studying time relationships among rocks and with interpreting rock features in terms of past environments and geographies. Study of rocks, fossils and present-day geological processes helps us to reconstruct the sequence of changes which have taken place during the long history of the Earth.

Uniformitarianism

To help us reconstruct the changing environments of the Earth in past ages we can use evidence from many sources. In the first place, since it is likely that similar processes have acted through geological time we can study present-day processes and use our interpretation of these as a means of understanding the past. The idea of using the study of present processes as a means of understanding Earth history was first suggested by James Hutton (table 11.1). Charles Lyell later called the idea the **principle of uniformitarianism**. Uniformitarianism does not mean that processes go on at a uniform or steady rate. Instead, it means that the processes acting now are essentially the same as processes which have acted in the past. Uniformitarianism replaced Georges Cuvier's ideas of **catastrophism** which stated that at various times the surface of the Earth was suddenly changed by floods and upheavals during which many organisms became extinct. It should be noted that the principle of uniformitarianism does not exclude sudden changes such as those due to volcanic eruptions, earthquakes, floods and storms. You should realize, too, that the Earth has not always been as it is now. Its geography, climate and biology have seen frequent changes.

Reconstructing past environments

The study of sedimentary rocks may tell us a great deal about the conditions of deposition,

e.g. what can you tell from a study of grain sizes, grain shapes and grain types? The presence of halite and other salts indicates deposition under arid conditions while the presence of glauconite (green mica) indicates deposition in the sea. What would features such as ooliths, cross bedding, ventifacts and mud cracks indicate? How could you tell if a sandstone was deposited in the sea or in a desert?

Geochemical and geophysical evidence may also be useful, e.g. pyrite may be found in sediments deposited under reducing conditions whereas haematite indicates deposition under oxidizing conditions. Also, clay minerals take in elements such as boron. The amount of boron may indicate the salinity of the depositional environment because there is more boron in salt water than in fresh water. The fact that Britain's latitude has changed was shown by palaeomagnetic studies and the verification of sea-floor spreading and continental drift allows us to give an improved interpretation to many aspects of Earth history.

Uses of fossils

Fossils can tell us a great deal about ancient environments. Interpretation of past environments in terms of the fossils which are present means that we are often assuming that the living conditions of the fossilized organisms were the same as the living conditions of their present-day relatives. This assumption is probably valid for organisms which lived in the not too distant past but for very ancient organisms the assumption may not be so good. You should also realize that the Earth's climatic zones may have been wider or narrower than at present.

Indications of the temperature at which organisms lived can sometimes be obtained from fossils. Organisms which build their skeletons or shells from calcium carbonate tend to have high aragonite/calcite ratios in warm water and low aragonite/calcite ratios in cold water. It has also been found that calcareous organisms living in warm water may deposit calcite con-

NAME	DATES	NATIONALITY	MAIN WORK OR IDEA WITH WHICH ASSOCIATED
William Gilbert	1544–1603	English	Showed that the Earth behaves like a bar magnet
Nicolaus Steno (Niels Stensen)	1638–1686	Danish	Suggested that the history of the Earth could be found by studying strata and fossils
Jean-Etienne Guettard	1715–1786	French	Recognised the volcanic origin of the mountains of central France. Made the first geological maps
James Hutton	1726–1797	Scottish	Suggested that processes like those of today have acted through geological time. Recognised significance of unconformities. Showed granite to be of igneous origin
René-Just Hauy	1743–1822	French	Established many of the principles of crystallography
Jean-Baptiste de Lamarck	1744–1829	French	Suggested that evolutionary change in organisms took place by means of the inheritance of acquired characteristics
Abraham Werner	1749–1817	German	Systematized the study of minerals and rocks. Maintained that all rocks including granite, gneiss and basalt were deposited from an ancient ocean. He thought that volcanoes were produced by burning coal seams
Pierre-Simon Laplace	1749–1827	French	Suggested that the solar system was formed from a rotating nebula
James Hall	1761–1832	Scottish	Originated experimental geology. He melted and cooled igneous rocks and he made marble by heating calcium carbonate under pressure
Georges Cuvier	1769–1832	French	Showed how fossils could be used to correlate strata
William Smith	1769–1839	English	Independently of Cuvier and Brongniart, showed how fossils could be used to identify and correlate strata over large areas. Produced the first geological map of England, Wales and part of Scotland
William Nicol	1769–1851	Scottish	Invented the polarizing prism. Showed how rocks could be studied in thin section

Table 11.1   Some well-known names in the history of Earth science

taining high levels of magnesium. Temperature can also be estimated from the $^{18}O/^{16}O$ ratios of fossils because in sea water the level of ^{18}O falls with increasing temperature. In cross-section, belemnite guards may show annual rings like those in a tree. $^{18}O/^{16}O$ ratios in such belemnites give an indication of seasonal changes in sea temperature during the Mesozoic. In the late Mesozoic such studies have shown that warmer climates extended into higher latitudes than at present. During the Lower Cretaceous the sea over Britain had an average temperature of about 15°C while in the Upper Cretaceous the temperature was up to about 20°C.

A study of sea temperatures has also been made using planktonic foraminifera deposited on the ocean floor during the Ice Age which began about 2.5 Ma ago. In addition to changing $^{18}O/^{16}O$ ratios it was found that the species types varied with temperature and that some species changed their direction of coiling with temperature. Examination of the foraminifera in sea-bed cores allowed the sequence of changing water temperature to be established. This was, in turn, related to the advance and retreat of glaciers as the climate changed. On land, recent climatic changes can be found by studying pollen deposited in peat bogs. Pollen grains allow the plants from which they come

EARTH HISTORY

Name	Dates	Nationality	Contribution
Louis Agassiz	1807–1873	Swiss	Showed that glaciers had moved over much of Europe and North America
Charles Darwin	1809–1882	English	Formulated the theory of evolution by natural selection
Alfred Russel Wallace	1823–1913	English	Independently of Darwin, reasoned that evolution took place by natural selection
Lord Kelvin (William Thomson)	1824–1907	Irish	Estimated the age of the Earth from its rate of cooling
Henry Clifton Sorby	1826–1908	English	Developed the study of rocks and minerals using polarizing microscopes
Ferdinand Zirkel	1838–1912	German	Extended and fully developed the work of Sorby
William Davis	1850–1934	American	Suggested that landscapes change through a cycle of erosion
Andrija Mohorovicic	1857–1936	Yugoslavian	Discovered the boundary between the Earth's crust and mantle
William Bragg	1862–1942	English	Did much to develop the study of crystal structures using X-rays
Alfred Wegener	1880–1930	German	Did much to establish the theory of continental drift
Arthur Holmes	1890–1965	English	Did much of the early work on radiometric dating. Suggested that continents could be moved by convection currents in the mantle
Lawrence Bragg	1890–1971	Australian	With his father, William Bragg, contributed a great deal to the study of the atomic structures of crystals
Harry Hess	1906–1969	American	Suggested the process now known as sea-floor spreading
Drummond Matthews	1931–	English	With Vine, confirmed sea-floor spreading by using evidence of magnetic strip anomalies at ocean ridges
Fred Vine	1939–	English	With Matthews, proved the existence of sea-floor spreading

be identified and, since plant types change with climate, this gives us a good idea of changing climate.

The environment may affect the appearance of an organism. In the dog whelk, for example, thin, rough-shelled forms are found in sheltered areas whereas smooth, thick-shelled forms occur on exposed parts of the shore. The diet of dog whelks affects their colour. Dog whelks feeding on barnacles are white whereas those feeding on mussels are dark. Communities of organisms may also be affected by changing conditions, e.g. the diversity of plants and animals decreases away from the tropics while, at the same time, the number of individuals of any one species increases. From the Kattegat east of Denmark to the head of the Baltic there is a decrease in the number of marine species as the salinity declines.

Astronomers have worked out that the Earth's rotation is slowing down because of tidal friction at a rate which would make the day longer by about two seconds in every 100 000 years. Evidence in support of this has come from a study of horn corals which have daily growth rings, e.g. counting daily rings on Devonian corals has shown, as predicted by calculation, that at this time there were about 400 days in a year (figure 11.1).

Fossils may also indicate rates of sedimen-

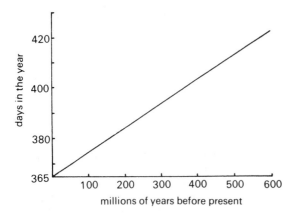

11.1 *Change in the number of days in the year over the last 420 Ma.*

tation, e.g. deep-sea oozes form very slowly. The presence of a large number of trace fossils may also indicate slow deposition since the organisms would possibly have been killed by rapid burial. In addition, trace fossils may indicate the depth of water in which a sediment was deposited because different depths may be marked by different types of feeding and living behaviour. On a sandy or muddy shore, for example, most organisms burrow for protection so a sediment laid down in shallow water tends to be characterized by a predominance of burrows. In deep water, organisms burrow much less so the sediments show mostly grazing and near-surface feeding traces.

Among animals there is a balance between the numbers of predators and their prey. Warm-blooded predators such as mammals require a lot of food so they are few in number relative to their prey. Predatory reptiles are cold-blooded so they do not require much food and, in consequence, they exist in large numbers relative to their prey. The relatively low predator/prey ratios found in fossil dinosaur communities suggest that the dinosaurs may have been warm blooded.

Zones

We can use fossils to divide the geological column into biostratigraphical units called **zones**. A zone is a small part of a sequence containing distinctive fossils which make the zone unique. A zone is named after one fossil called an **index fossil**. A zone may be defined by one species or by a group of species. To

be used to define a zone, a fossil should have a narrow time range so it occurs in a narrow band of sedimentary rocks. It should also be widespread so that the same zone can be recognized in different rock types over a large area. This means that swimming or planktonic organisms such as ammonites and graptolites make the best zone fossils. Sometimes, though, bottom-living organisms such as corals, brachiopods and bivalves can be used as zone fossils but such fossils tend to be restricted to particular rock types.

In Britain, the Cambrian system is zoned largely by means of trilobites while graptolites provide the zone fossils of the Ordovician and Silurian. Graptolites have the disadvantages of having relatively long time-ranges and, because of poor preservation, they are found mostly in deep-water black shales. The stratigraphic positions of near-shore sedimentary rocks is fixed by matching up brachiopod and trilobite faunas with graptolite zones where the deep- and shallow-water sedimentary rocks interdigitate. The Devonian system in Britain consists of marine rocks in the south and continental rocks in the north. The marine sedimentary rocks are zoned by means of ammonoids while the rocks deposited on the continent are zoned by fossils of fresh-water fish. This means that the ages of the marine and continental rocks cannot be matched exactly. Carboniferous rocks were deposited under such a wide range of conditions that goniatites, corals, brachiopods, fresh-water bivalves and plant spores are all used in zoning. British Permian and Triassic rocks were deposited largely under desert conditions. Fossils are few so clearly defined zones cannot be erected. On the other hand, highly refined zones have been established in the succeeding Jurassic system. Here, there are 61 ammonite zones followed by 3 ostracod zones. The Lower Cretaceous is also accurately zoned by means of ammonites while in the Upper Cretaceous (the Chalk) ammonites, echinoids, bivalves, belemnites, crinoids and brachiopods provide zone fossils. The British Tertiary and Quaternary deposits occur in scattered outcrops and zoning is not precise. In marine Tertiary rocks, foraminiferans are the best zone fossils. In the Quaternary, pollen assemblages are most useful on land while foraminiferans allow zoning of deep-sea sediments.

While zones are defined as part of a rock sequence they do have some time significance,

EARTH HISTORY

.g. the zones of the Jurassic have an average ength of about one million years. Also, where he top of a zone is marked by the extinction f the zone fossils and provided they became xtinct worldwide at the same time, the top of he zone represents a time plane.

Changing sedimentary sequences

resent environments of deposition vary conderably. In the deep sea, red clay and oozes re forming and turbidites may be being deposited by turbidity currents. Nearer the shore, ravels, sands and muds are being deposited. warm areas, coral and oolitic limestones may e forming while evaporites may be being eposited in partly enclosed basins. Rivers are uilding deltas and depositing alluvium while kes are being filled in by encroaching plants by sediment brought in by streams. In the eserts, sand is being deposited and dust is eing carried off to be deposited as loess. In old areas, glaciers are depositing boulder clay nd moraines and meltwater is depositing glaofluvial sands and gravels. Under all these ifferent conditions sediments are being deposited whose characteristics reflect the environent of deposition. The word **facies** (general ppearance) is used to describe both the different environments and the different types of diment being deposited, e.g. sediments of the a shore could be described as being of littoral cies while sediments of the continental shelf ight be described as being of shelf facies. On e other hand, sedimentary rocks may be scribed as being of muddy or sandy facies mply to indicate differences in rock types thout precise reference to the site of depotion. Since similar environments have peared again and again through geological ne any facies type may appear repeatedly rough a geological succession.

Facies fossils are those which are restricted certain facies types. They are usually derived om bottom-living organisms which inhabited rticular environments such as coral reefs, kes or sandy beaches. Because of the restricd nature of such environments facies fossils e not widespread so they have only limited e in zoning.

At any one time there are numerous envirments of deposition grading sideways into ch other, e.g. along a shore we might find the ulders and pebbles of rocky shore

grading into the sand of a beach. The sand might then grade into the mud of mudflats. If these sediments were turned to sedimentary rock we would have a rock made up of conglomerate, sandstone and mudstone grading sideways into each other. Such a relationship of sideways facies change is called **lateral variation** (figure 11.2).

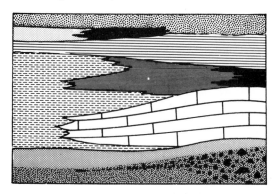

11.2 Lateral variation - sideways change in sedimentary rock type.

When a delta is deposited it builds out into the sea and its inner area is older than its outer edge. Figure 11.3. shows a deltaic sandstone which forms a continuous horizontal layer. Although it looks as if it has all been deposited at the same time different parts of the sandstone have different ages. Rock units like this which look the same but whose age varies from place to place are said to be **diachronous** (across time).

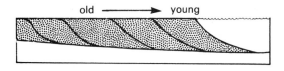

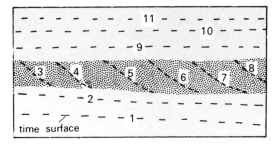

11.3 Formation of a diachronous rock unit. The deltaic sandstone forms a layer whose age decreases from left to right.

Because sedimentary rocks of the same age may be of different facies in different areas it may be difficult to match up or **correlate** the different sequences. We can match up the rocks of different sequences according to type (**rock correlation**) or according to age (**time correlation**). A diachronous rock unit appears as the same rock type in different sequences but its age is not the same in different sequences.

The equivalence of rock types may be established by tracing one sequence into another across the area between exposures or boreholes. The rocks found by drilling may be directly examined as chips or cores, or instruments may be lowered into the borehole to measure properties such as radioactivity or electrical resistance which can be used to correlate rock types in different bores. Time correlation is most often done by means of fossils. Sometimes, a distinctive rock such as a volcanic ash or a lava flow is formed fairly quickly over a very large area. Recognition of such a **marker** or **key bed** in different sequences allows time equivalence to be established. Ancient glacial deposits can also be used in time correlation because they formed over relatively short periods. For more recent times, varves have been used to build a time scale for about the last 17 000 years.

Deep-sea sediments can be time correlated by means of palaeomagnetic reversals. Such reversals are world wide and sudden so ocean floor sediments can be related to the polarity time-scale established from terrestrial lavas.

Relationships within sequences

In any area, deposition is not continuous throughout geological time. Deposition may cease for a time before resuming or the sedimentary rocks may be uplifted and eroded before being covered again at a later date. The relationship between rocks formed before and after a break in deposition is called **unconformity** and the old and young rocks are separated by a **surface** or **plane** of **unconformity** (see p 160). A minor type of unconformity representing a short gap in deposition is called a **non-sequence** or **diastem**. Non-sequences are common but difficult to recognize. They may possibly be detected by the non-appearance of distinctive fossils. Alternatively, the rock below the surface of unconformity may show signs of having been

eroded or it may have been heavily bored by organisms.

The rocks above and below a surface of unconformity may show a number of relationships to each other. In **overstep**, the beds above the surface of unconformity rest successively on different rocks below the unconformity. **Overlap** occurs when beds above the surface of unconformity are progressively deposited over larger areas (figure 11.4(a)). This means that the rocks below the unconformity are overlain by beds which become successively younger. **Offlap** occurs when the beds above the surface of unconformity are progressively deposited over smaller areas (figure 11.4(b)).

(a)

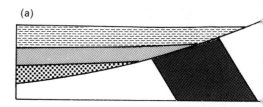

(b)

11.4 (a) Overlap. Younger beds above the unconformity cover a progressively larger area.
(b) Offlap. The younger beds cover a progressively smaller area.

Inverted sequences

In areas such as mountain ranges where the rocks have been strongly folded it sometimes happens that sequences are turned upside down. Such inversions can be recognized by the study of fossils whose age relationships or living orientations are known or by the study of various rock structures and relationships (figure 11.5).

Early history of the Earth

The Precambrian era covers a very long time from the formation of the Earth 4600 Ma ago to the beginning of the Cambrian about 590

(a)   graded bedding

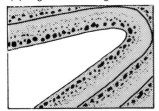

(b)   cross bedding

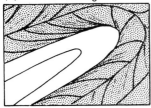

(c)   ripple marks

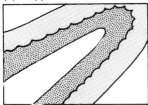

(d)   load casts and flame structures

(e)   mud cracks

(f) fragments of older bed in younger bed

(g)   unconformity

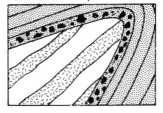

(h) fossils, worm burrows or roots

(i)   part-filled shells or vesicles

(j) relationship between cleavage and bedding

*1.5 Inverted sequences. In the upper limb of each fold the beds are the right way up. In the lower limb the beds are inverted.
(a) graded bedding (b) cross bedding (c) ripple marks (d) flame structures (e) mud cracks (f) included fragments (g) unconformity (h) fossils (i) fossil part-filled with mud (j) cleavage is usually steeper than bedding.*

Ma ago. Since the oldest rocks are about 3900 Ma old we have no direct evidence of the changes which took place for the first 700 Ma of Earth history. Soon after accretion it seems that the Earth was melted by heat from gravitational energy and from short-lived radioactive elements. This melting allowed the density separation of the core and mantle. As the Earth cooled the crust began to form from low-density acid igneous rocks. Initially, the crust may have formed a thin layer over the whole Earth. A

phase of heavy bombardment by infalling asteroids probably cratered the early crust about
4300 Ma ago. Mantle convection currents probably pulled the thin crustal blocks towards each
other and the blocks accumulated over descending currents to form the early continents.
It is probable that the continents reached their
present thicknesses and about half their present
total area by about 2500 Ma ago.

Apart from oxygen, the Earth's atmosphere
has been formed by volcanic outgassing and
by vaporization caused by meteorite impact.
Volcanic gases are largely water vapour and
carbon dioxide and it is likely that the Earth's
atmosphere was originally about 80 percent
water vapour and 20 percent carbon dioxide
with traces of other gases such as nitrogen,
carbon monoxide, hydrogen, sulphur dioxide
and sulphur trioxide. The oceans began to form
about 3800 Ma ago as the Earth cooled and
water vapour began to condense. Life probably
began about 3800 Ma ago. Oxygen was produced by simple photosynthetic organisms but
it was not abundant during the Precambrian.
Its presence in the atmosphere is indicated by
redbeds which first appeared about 2600 Ma
ago. The amount of carbon dioxide in the early
atmosphere declined as organic limestones
became common about 2000 Ma ago. Multicellular organisms probably appeared about
1000 Ma ago.

Precambrian stratigraphy is difficult to
unravel because fossils are very rare and when
found they cannot be used in correlation. Also,
Precambrian rocks may have been altered on
numerous occasions so that relative timescales
are partly based on recognizing periods of
deformation and metamorphism. Elucidation of
Precambrian history has been much helped by
the use of radiometric dating methods.

Geological history of the British area
(*see* table 11.2)

Reconstruction of the changing geography of
any area through geological time depends on
the use of numerous lines of evidence, e.g.
sedimentary rock types with their contained
structures and fossils might indicate deposition
on land or in the sea and interdigitating marine
and non-marine sequences might tell us where
a shore-line was located. The presence of thick
sediments may indicate deposition in a sub-

siding basin while, towards what was once land
marine sediments may thin out and disappear.
Some indication of climate may be given by
fossils, glacial deposits or evaporites.

Ancient plate movements may be indicated
by ocean floor sediments now on land or by
the presence of metamorphic and igneous
rocks possibly formed at destructive boundaries. The closing of oceans may be indicated
by the coming together of originally separated
fossil groups representing organisms which
lived on opposite sides of an ocean.

Britain has suffered a wide variety of changes
brought about by advancing and retreating
seas, by the opening and closing of oceans and
by mountain building, regional metamorphism
and igneous activity. In addition, the latitude
of Britain has changed and climatic changes
have been strongly marked. The present shape
of Britain only began to appear within about
the last 50 Ma. When we show maps of the
British area as it was many millions of years
ago we usually superimpose the outline of
Britain on the maps, not because Britain existed
but simply to provide geographical reference.

Precambrian era (4600—590 Ma ago)
and Cambrian period
(590—515 Ma ago)

British Precambrian rocks are found in two main
areas. A northerly group occurs in the Scottish
Highlands and Hebrides while in the south there
are scattered outcrops in Wales and central
England. In Ireland, the Precambrian lies in
widely separated outcrops in the north-west and
south-east (figure 11.6). It is probable that the
Precambrian of Scotland and north-west Ireland
formed on one continent while the Precambrian
of England, Wales and south-east Ireland
formed on another continent. The two continents were separated by the **Iapetus Ocean**
(figure 11.7). We will begin by looking at the
history of the northern Precambrian continent.

The oldest British rock is the **Lewisian Gneiss**
of north-west Scotland. The Lewisian may be
divided into the Scourian (2900–2200 Ma ago)
and Laxfordian (2200–1300 Ma ago). The
Scourian occupies part of the mainland area
centred roughly on Lochinver in west Suther-
land while other mainland and Hebridean
gneiss is largely Laxfordian.

The Scourian gneisses have been derived
from tuffs, lavas, basic intrusive igneous rock

Distribution of Precambrian rocks.

sedimentary rocks perhaps formed in a
[vol]canic island arc about 3000 Ma ago. About
[29]00-2700 Ma ago these rocks were buried
[to] a depth of about 20 km where they were
[met]amorphosed under granulite facies condi-
[tion]s to become coarsely banded, grey gneiss.
[The] gneisses are mostly acid or intermediate
[in c]omposition. The Scourian has a general
[nor]th-east to south-west structural trend. The
[end] of the Scourian was marked by the intrusion
[of t]he north-west—south-east trending, dolerite
[Sco]urie dykes about 2200 Ma ago.

[T]he Scourian was followed by deposition of
[Lax]fordian sediments. Deep burial about 1850
[Ma] ago altered most of the sediments and parts
[of t]he pre-existing Scourian gneiss. The Lax-
[ford]ian has a north-west—south-east structural
[tren]d. It was metamorphosed under amphib-
[olit]e facies conditions and it includes horn-
[ble]nde and quartz-feldspar gneiss often cut by
[peg]matites.

[T]he Lewisian Gneiss lay on a continent which
[incl]uded the gneisses of Greenland and the
[Can]adian Shield. The Scourian and Laxfordian
[gne]isses may have formed during separate
[peri]ods of mountain building on this early
[con]tinent. In these early times it is not certain
[that] plate movements of the type seen today
[wer]e operating. There may have been no sub-
[duc]tion so metamorphism and deformation

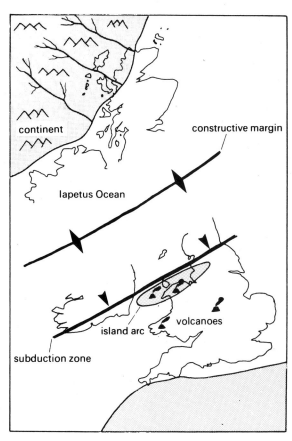

*11.7 Palaeogeographic map of late Precambrian
times.*

may have taken place in shear belts produced
by limited movements between crustal blocks.

The Lewisian Gneiss is succeeded, with
strong unconformity, by **Torridonian** sediments
deposited on the south-east margin of the
northern continent. The Torridonian consists
predominantly of red or brown conglomerates,
arkoses, sandstones and shales. On the mainland north of Skye the lowest Torridonian
belongs to the Stoer Group (1000 Ma old). The
Stoer Group is overlain unconformably by the
Torridon Group (800 Ma old). The Stoer Group
(2 km thick) was deposited mostly by rivers
running on a rugged Lewisian landscape. The
red colour of the beds along with structures
such as mud-cracks indicates deposition under
hot, dry conditions. The latitude was about 15°N.
The Torridon Group (7 km thick) may be divided
into the Diabaig, Applecross and Aultbea Formations. The Diabaig Formation was deposited
in mixed river, lake and marine environments.

ERA	PERIOD OR SYSTEM Age in millions of years (Ma)	MAJOR DIVISIONS		MAIN EVENTS IN THE BRITISH AREA
CAINOZOIC	QUATERNARY —— 2.5 ——	HOLOCENE OR RECENT PLEISTOCENE		Widespread glaciations with intervening warm or temperate periods
CAINOZOIC	TERTIARY —— 65 ——	PLIOCENE MIOCENE OLIGOCENE EOCENE PALAEOCENE		Britain reaches present latitude (50—60°N). Most of Britain above sea level. Climate warm to temperate. Alpine movements produce folds in southern England. Large scale igneous activity in north and west. Deposition of marine, coastal plain and river sediments in southern England. Thick sediments in marine basins round Britain
MESOZOIC	CRETACEOUS —— 135 ——	UPPER	Chalk	Latitude of Britain 35—45°N. Deposition of chalk in clear seas. Most of Britain above sea level during Lower Cretaceous — sediments river and marine mudstones and sandstones. Climate warm
MESOZOIC	CRETACEOUS —— 135 ——	LOWER	Gault and Upper Greensand Lower Greensand Wealden Purbeck	Latitude of Britain 35—45°N. Deposition of chalk in clear seas. Most of Britain above sea level during Lower Cretaceous — sediments river and marine mudstones and sandstones. Climate warm
MESOZOIC	JURASSIC —— 195 ——	UPPER	Portlandian Kimmeridgian Oxfordian	Latitude of Britain 30—40°N. Shallow seas over most of Britain. Upper Jurassic — clays in most areas. Middle Jurassic — shallow water limestones in the south, deltaic in the north. Lower Jurassic — deposited in basins separated by swells
MESOZOIC	JURASSIC —— 195 ——	MIDDLE	Great Oolite Inferior Oolite	Latitude of Britain 30—40°N. Shallow seas over most of Britain. Upper Jurassic — clays in most areas. Middle Jurassic — shallow water limestones in the south, deltaic in the north. Lower Jurassic — deposited in basins separated by swells
MESOZOIC	JURASSIC —— 195 ——	LOWER	Lias	Latitude of Britain 30—40°N. Shallow seas over most of Britain. Upper Jurassic — clays in most areas. Middle Jurassic — shallow water limestones in the south, deltaic in the north. Lower Jurassic — deposited in basins separated by swells
MESOZOIC	TRIASSIC —— 235 ——	KEUPER BUNTER		Marine sedimentation at end of Triassic. Also, marine incursion during middle Triassic. Continental deposition under hot desert conditions. Widespread river, desert and lake deposits. Thick evaporites in places
PALAEOZOIC	PERMIAN —— 280 ——	ZECHSTEIN ROTLIEGENDE		Latitude of Britain 20—30°N. Climate hot. Upper Permian mostly marine dolomitic limestones with evaporites. Lower Permian — river and desert sediments deposited as uplands worn down
PALAEOZOIC	CARBONIFEROUS —— 370 ——	UPPER	Stephanian Westphalian Namurian	Britain crosses the equator. Most igneous activity in Midland Valley of Scotland. Deltas with thickly forested swamps advance into shallow seas
PALAEOZOIC	CARBONIFEROUS —— 370 ——	LOWER	Dinantian	Limestones deposited in warm seas covering much of Britain
PALAEOZOIC	DEVONIAN —— 415 ——	UPPER MIDDLE LOWER		Warm climate. Caledonian Mountains eroded away. Britain on southern edge of continental land mass. Marine deposition in extreme south of Britain. River and lake deposition elsewhere. Widespread igneous activity. Northern and southern Britain welded together
PALAEOZOIC	SILURIAN —— 445 ——	LUDLOW WENLOCK LLANDOVERY		Iapetus Ocean nearly closed. Latitude of Britain about 10—20°S. Mostly greywackes in Midland Valley, Southern Uplands and Lake District. In Wales, greywackes and mudstones pass eastwards into shallow water deposits. Volcanic activity ceases
PALAEOZOIC	ORDOVICIAN —— 515 ——	UPPER	Ashgill Caradoc	Iapetus Ocean starting to close. Both parts of the British area drifting northwards. Northern Britain about 10°S; southern Britain about 40°S. Subduction zone along line of Solway. Lake District on island arc. Granites intruded into Moinian. Moinian and Dalradian metamorphosed. Widespread volcanism. Greywackes and mudstones deposited in most areas with shallow water deposition in northwest Scotland and in the Welsh Borders
PALAEOZOIC	ORDOVICIAN —— 515 ——	LOWER	Llandeilo Llanvirn Arenig Tremadoc	Iapetus Ocean starting to close. Both parts of the British area drifting northwards. Northern Britain about 10°S; southern Britain about 40°S. Subduction zone along line of Solway. Lake District on island arc. Granites intruded into Moinian. Moinian and Dalradian metamorphosed. Widespread volcanism. Greywackes and mudstones deposited in most areas with shallow water deposition in northwest Scotland and in the Welsh Borders
PALAEOZOIC	CAMBRIAN —— 590 ——	UPPER MIDDLE LOWER		Northern Britain about 30°S. Southern Britain about 50°S. In northwest Scotland, quartzites and limestones deposited in shallow shelf seas. In the Highlands, greywackes and mudstones were deposited in deep water. In Wales, turbidites pass eastwards into shelf sediments
PRECAMBRIAN	ORIGIN OF EARTH 4600 Ma	TORRIDONIAN LEWISIAN		Southern and northern Britain on separate continents on each side of Iapetus Ocean. Northern Britain part of N. America, southern Britain part of Europe. In north, Lewisian Gneiss (2900—1300 Ma old) overlain by Torridonian sediments (1000—800 Ma old) deposited on south-east margin of continent. Moine Series largely equivalent to Torridonian. Marine Dalradian rocks deposited from 800 Ma to 500 Ma ago. In southern Britain gneisses are overlain by upper Precambrian sediments and volcanics. There may have been a subduction zone across North Wales and Anglesey

238

Table 11.2 Earth history

MAIN EVENTS AFFECTING THE EARTH	MAIN BRITISH FOSSILS (Those used in zoning are in bold type)	HISTORY OF PLANTS AND ANIMALS
	Bivalves, gastropods, mammals, insects, flowering plants, conifers, **pollen**	Appearance of modern man
Red Sea opens. Iceland begins to form. India collides with Asia — Himalayas form. Australia and Antarctica separate. Greenland and Europe separate. New Zealand separates from Antarctica	**Bivalves, gastropods, foraminiferans,** echinoids, corals, fish, flowering plants, plant spores	Mammals and flowering plants dominant. Belemnites become extinct
Alps start to form. India separates from Antarctica. Gondwanaland and Laurasia breaking up	**Ammonoids, belemnoids, foraminiferans, crinoids, ostracods, bivalves, echinoids, brachiopods, gastropods,** sponges, reptiles, conifers, cycads, ferns, **plant spores**	Dinosaurs and ammonites become extinct. Primates appear. Flowering plants expand rapidly
Atlantic begins to open. Rockies and Andes start to form. Pangaea starts to break up. Gondwanaland and Laurasia separated by Tethys Ocean	**Ammonoids,** echinoids, belemnoids, gastropods, bivalves, corals, brachiopods, echinoids, crinoids, reptiles, conifers, cycads, ginkgos	Seed ferns become extinct. Birds, irregular echinoids and diatoms appear
Continued existence of Pangaea	Bivalves, fish, **plant spores.** Fossils not common	Possible appearance of flowering plants. Dinosaurs, scleractinian corals, mammals, ammonites, belemnites and cycads appear. Rugose corals become extinct
Single continent (Pangaea) formed. Asia collides with Euramerica along Ural Mountains to form Laurasia	Brachiopods, bivalves, **plant spores.** Fossils not common	Ginkgos appear. Trilobites, tabulate corals and goniatites become extinct
Variscan Mountains start to form as Gondwanaland collides with Euramerica	**Corals, brachiopods, ammonoids, non-marine bivalves, crinoids,** gastropods, marine bivalves, bryozoa, amphibians, lycopsids, sphenopsids, ferns, seed ferns, **plant spores**	Probable appearance of belemnoids. Reptiles, conifers and seed ferns appear. Oxygen reaches 20% of atmosphere
Three continents: Gondwanaland, Asia and Euramerica. Caledonian Mountains formed by about 400 Ma	**Ammonoids, fresh-water fish,** brachiopods, gastropods, bivalves, crinoids, nautiloids, corals, trilobites, stromatoporoids, psilopsids	Appearance of ammonoids, mosses, club mosses, horse-tails and ferns. Graptolites become extinct
Iapetus Ocean closed by about 420 Ma ago. Europe collides with North America	**Graptolites,** brachiopods, trilobites, corals, gastropods, bivalves, fish, crinoids, nautiloids, echinoids, stromatoporoids, bryozoa	First land plants (psilopsids). Amphibians and insects appear
	Graptolites, trilobites, brachiopods, bivalves, nautiloids, echinoids, crinoids	Fish, echinoids, crinoids, tabulate corals and foraminiferans appear. Bivalves common
Four continents: Asia, Europe, North America and Gondwanaland (S. America, Africa, India, Australia and Antarctica)	**Trilobites, brachiopods,** sponges, gastropods	First graptolites and nautiloids. Probable appearance of rugose corals. Coccoliths appear. Trilobites dominant. At 550 Ma oxygen forms about 2% of the atmosphere. Nearly all invertebrate phyla present. Brachiopods, bivalves, trilobites appear
Supercontinent breaks up about 700 Ma ago. Separate continents form super continent about 1500 Ma ago. Continents reach half their present area 2500 Ma ago. Oldest rock 3900 Ma. Heavy bombardment by asteroids 4300 Ma ago	Fossils rare	At 670 Ma oxygen forms about 1.5% of atmosphere. At this time soft bodied multicellular animals appear (e.g. worms, jelly fish, echinoderms, arthropods). Radiolaria appear. Oxygen forms about 0.2% of atmosphere about 2000 Ma ago. Red beds appear 2600 Ma ago. Bacteria and blue-green algae in rocks about 3500 Ma old. Oldest sedimentary rock 3800 Ma. Life probably began at about this time. Atmosphere probably consists of carbon dioxide, water vapour, nitrogen, carbon monoxide, hydrogen sulphide and hydrogen.

Table 11.2   Earth History

239

The Applecross and Aultbea Formations were deposited mostly by rivers forming coastal plains and deltas. Distinctive pebbles and the orientation of foreset beds indicate transport from the Greenland area to the north-west.

Strong lateral variation exists within the Torridonian. In the extreme north-west of Scotland the Applecross Formation lies directly on Lewisian Gneiss but in Skye and the adjoining mainland the Diabaig Formation lies conformably on 3.5 km of the deltaic Sleat Group.

The unmetamorphosed Torridonian is separated by the Moine Thrust from metamorphosed Precambrian sedimentary rocks called the **Moine Series** which extend to the Great Glen Fault. Like the Torridonian, the Moinian (about 12 000 m) is unconformable on Lewisian which occurs as thrust slices and fold cores in the Moinian. The Moinian consists mostly of metamorphosed sandstones and mudstones (psammites and pelites) deposited mainly as shelf, shelf-edge and beach sediments under the action of currents which flowed generally north and north-east. The main Moinian metamorphism took place about 1000 Ma ago so some of the Moinian, at least, must have formed before this date. This indicates that the Moinian, while probably largely equivalent to the Torridonian, may be older in part.

Between the Great Glen Fault and the Highland Boundary Fault lie about 24 km of metamorphosed sedimentary and volcanic rocks called the **Dalradian** succession. Dalradian rocks are also found in Shetland and in north and west Ireland. The Dalradian was deposited in the Iapetus Ocean from late Precambrian (beginning about 800 Ma ago) to early Ordovician times (about 500 Ma ago).

The Lower Dalradian consists of sandstones, mudstones and limestones which have been metamorphosed to schists, slates and marbles. Sedimentary structures in these rocks indicate deposition in shallow, shelf seas. The base of the Middle Dalradian is marked by a late Precambrian tillite (about 650 Ma old) which, since it can be traced from north-east Scotland to west Ireland, provides a useful marker bed for correlation. Surprisingly, the existence of the tillite does not necessarily mean that northern Britain was in polar regions. Indeed, palaeomagnetic evidence indicates tropical latitudes so glaciers may have been world-wide at this time. It has been suggested that glaciation at this time could have been caused by the removal of carbon dioxide from the atmosphere by blue-green algae. This would have caused cooling by allowing more of the Sun's heat to be radiated back into space. The presence of stromatolites above and below the tillite is a further indication of deposition at low latitudes. The tillite is followed by dolomite deposited in a coastal area under a hot, dry climate. Then comes about 5 km of quartzite deposited on the continental shelf under the action of currents which flowed towards the north-east. In the upper part of the Middle Dalradian deposition began to take place in deep, fault-bounded basins and on the fault blocks between. Turbidites were deposited in the north-east—south-west trending basins.

Towards the end of the Middle Dalradian the rocks are of Cambrian age. The change from Precambrian to Cambrian is not marked by an unconformity. The top of the Middle Dalradian and the base of the Upper Dalradian contain thick basaltic pillow lavas and tuffs mixed with marine limestones, sandstones and mudstones. The top of the Dalradian consists of thick mudstones, greywackes and conglomerates deposited in deep submarine basins. Dalradian sedimentation continued into early Ordovician times.

In the north-west Highlands of Scotland the Cambro-Ordovician lies with marked unconformity on the Lewisian and Torridonian. The

11.8 Distribution of Cambrian rocks.

EARTH HISTORY

mbro-Ordovician in this area was deposited shallow shelf seas off the edge of the northern ontinent. It consists largely of quartzites (200 thick) at the base followed by about 1300 of limestones and dolomites.

The scattered nature of the Precambrian outops in England, Wales and south-east Ireland akes correlation very difficult both among emselves and with other areas. In south-east eland, upper Precambrian sedimentary rocks e on gneiss which may be older than 1600 la. Gneiss in north Wales and Anglesey may ave been derived by high grade metamorhism from sediments like the overlying upper recambrian greywackes, shales, pillow lavas, ffs and limestones. In Shropshire there are nall outcrops of gneiss and schist overlain by te Precambrian rocks. The late Precambrian onsists of Uriconian lavas, agglomerates and ff overlain by Longmyndian sediments made o of a shaly lower part (Strettonian Series) and a andy upper part (Wentnorian Series). In the lalverns gneiss is overlain by lavas and tuffs, in e Midlands there is a succession of late recambrian tuffs and sediments and in south-vest Wales, schist and gneiss are overlain by te Precambrian tuffs and lavas.

The scanty nature of the evidence provided y the Precambrian in the southern parts of the ritish area means that details of the geological istory are uncertain., It seems likely that Anglesy and north Wales formed mountains above subduction zone while the Longmyndian epresents river deposits derived from the nountains.

On the southern side of Iapetus the igneous nd tectonic activity of the late Precambrian ecreased and, with the onset of the Cambrian, e sea flooded much of the continental margin. he area from Anglesey into south-east Ireland vas a landmass (the Irish Sea Platform) which upplied sediment to the deep Welsh Basin on s south-east side and to the Leinster Basin n its north-west side. In north Wales there are bout 5 km of Cambrian sediments many of vhich are greywackes probably deposited by urbidity currents. In south-west Wales on the outhern side of the Welsh Basin there is a much ninner, more interrupted sequence containing wer turbidites.

On its southern and eastern margins the Velsh Basin gave way to shallow shelf seas xtending at times across into south-east ngland. In the Welsh Borders the widespread

marine incursion is marked by quartzites at the base of the Cambrian. The quartzites pass up into interrupted and condensed sequences of sandstones and thin limestones. In Warwickshire the basal quartzites are followed by mudstones. Overall, the shelf sediments are about 900 m thick.

In the late Precambrian and Cambrian, then, the northern and southern margins of Iapetus had histories which were fairly similar to each other. In the north there was a landmass bordered by shallow seas which gave way southeast to deep basins being filled by turbidites. In the south, the major landmass of the Irish Sea Platform fed turbidites to deep basins on either side and the sea shallowed towards a subdued landmass over southern England (figure 11.9). The width of the Iapetus Ocean is not known though it is thought to have been about 2000 km wide during the Cambrian. The existence of a fairly wide ocean at this time is strongly suggested by the different trilobite faunas found in rocks deposited in the northern and southern shelf areas.

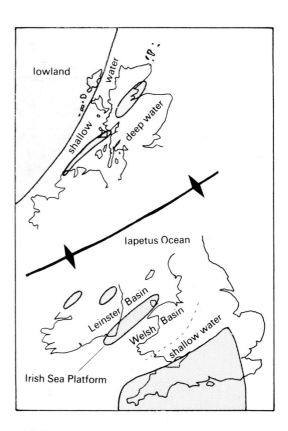

11.9 Palaeogeographic map of Cambrian times.

Ordovician (515–445 Ma ago) and Silurian (445–415 Ma ago) periods

During the Ordovician and Silurian the Iapetus Ocean was slowly closed. Closure is indicated by the fact that the separate, early-Ordovician trilobite and brachiopod faunas of the northern and southern ocean margins had disappeared by the late Ordovician. The Ordovician is also marked by igneous and metamorphic activity indicative of the development of subduction zones during the onset of a phase of mountain building called the **Caledonian Orogeny**.

In northern Iapetus at the beginning of the Ordovician there was little change in the pattern of sedimentation established during the Cambrian. In the north-west Highlands of Scotland limestone and dolomite of the Durness Formation continued to be deposited into Ordovician times. Limestone deposition shows that little sediment was derived from the northern continent perhaps because of its low relief or because the weather was dry and there were no rivers to carry sediment to the sea. In north-east Grampian over 1000 m of turbidites and muds were deposited. These sediments probably came from rugged islands lying off the south-east continental shore. Along the Highland Boundary Fault, Ordovician pillow lavas,

11.10 *Distribution of Ordovician rocks.*

cherts and serpentinites probably represent a slice of ocean floor uplifted at a destructive plate margin. The presence of Cambrian granites in the Moines indicates that ocean-closing movements were initiated during the Cambrian. During the Lower Ordovician the first major phase of the Caledonian Orogeny saw the development of a subduction zone roughly along the line of the Solway Firth. The Dalradian and Moinian above the subduction zone were metamorphosed, deformed and uplifted to form a mountainous landmass which supplied sediment to the sea to the south., At Ballantrae, south Ayrshire, the early Ordovician rocks are ophiolites consisting of mudstones, radiolarian cherts, pillow lavas, tuffs, serpentinites, glaucophane schist and gabbros which probably represent ocean floor material. Strong lateral variations mark the Upper Ordovician in this area. At Girvan, about 20 km north of Ballantrae, ophiolites are covered by thick Upper Ordovician near- shore and deep sea fan sediments about 2600 m thick. The rocks include conglomerates, sandstones, mudstones and limestones. South of Ballantrae, rocks of the same age are mostly greywackes and shales with cherts, tuffs and lavas reaching a total thickness of 4800 m. The rapid changes in thickness are probably the result of fault-controlled deposition on the landward side of an oceanic trench. Another significant change in sediment thickness occurs towards the central area of the Southern Uplands. At Moffat, about 90 km east of Girvan, the Upper Ordovician consists of about 40 m of deep-water graptolitic shales with radiolarian cherts. Correlation between the very different successions at Girvan and Moffat is made possible by means of graptolites. These are very common at Moffat and, while much less common in the Girvan area, there are enough to make correlation possible.

In Scotland, the Silurian is found as inliers in the southern part of the Midland Valley and in an extensive area of the Southern Uplands south of the Ordovician outcrop. In the Midland Valley there are about 2000 m of marine turbidites passing up into shallow marine and fresh water deposits. These rocks indicate a marine regression with a change from a deep-sea through to a non-marine environment. In the Southern Uplands there was a progressive southward spread of greywacke deposition during the Ordovician and this greywacke spread reached Moffat early in the Silurian so that thick

EARTH HISTORY

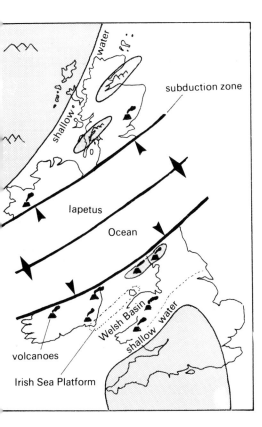

District volcanic island arc. Shallow water deposition close to the continent gave way to deposition in rapidly subsiding basins in north and west Wales. The Welsh Basin was separated by the Irish Sea Platform from other basins to the north. The instability of this area is illustrated by the presence of local unconformities and thick andesites in Wales and in the Lake District. Volcanic activity died out towards the middle of the Silurian as the Iapetus Ocean was progressively consumed.

11.11 Palaeogeography of early Ordovician times.

11.12 Distribution of Silurian rocks.

reywackes overlie about 30 m of early Silurian hales. The Silurian of the Southern Uplands onsists of about 10 000 m of greywackes and udstones probably deposited in an oceanic ench as subduction of the ocean floor conmued towards the north (figure 11.13). The losing of the ocean squeezed up a landmass alled Cockburnland which supplied sediment oth to the trench on the south and to the Midland Valley on the north. At Girvan, the ilurian consists of conglomerates, limestones, andstones and shales quite like those of the pper Ordovician in this area. The sediments re mostly shelf deposits correlated with the hain successions in the central areas of the outhern Uplands by means of the graptolite, *Monograptus*.

In southern Britain, Ordovician and Silurian eposition took place on an unstable sea floor etween the continent to the south and an ceanic trench on the north-west of the Lake

In the Lake District, Lower Ordovician sediments are represented by at least 1000 m of mudstones and greywackes deposited on a sinking sea floor. These early Ordovician sediments are overlain by about 4500 m of Middle Ordovician andesites, rhyolites, tuffs, ignimbrites and agglomerates formed on an island arc above a subduction zone. The volcanic rocks are separated by an unconformity from about 100 m of Upper Ordovician limestones, mudstones and some volcanic rocks. In the Isle of Man there are about 8000 m of early Ordovician greywackes, siltstones and mudstones.

In north Wales the Ordovician is marked by the development of large-scale volcanic activity.

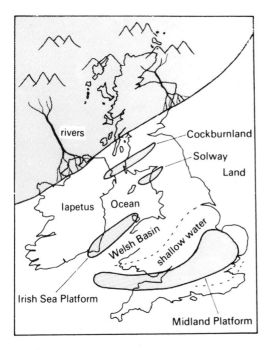

11.13 Palaeogeography of Silurian times.

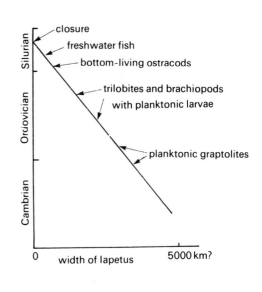

11.15 Closure of Iapetus indicated by faunal migration between the northern and southern provinces. The organisms are found in both provinces after the times shown.

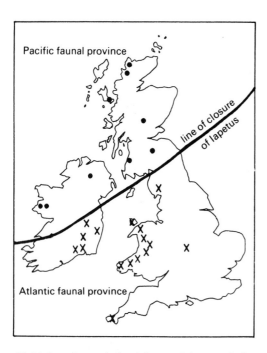

11.14 Locations of Cambrian and Lower Ordovician graptolites, trilobites and brachiopods of the northern (·) and southern (x) provinces. Between them lies the line of closure of the Iapetus Ocean.

The volcanic rocks include andesites, rhyolites, ignimbrites, pillow lavas and tuffs interspersed with greywackes and mudstones to give a total thickness of about 7000 m. The presence of local unconformities, facies change and overlap indicates deposition on an unstable, subsiding sea floor with submarine and island volcanoes providing a source of material for deposition. In south Wales the Ordovician resembles that of north Wales with volcanic and sedimentary rocks such as mudstones, sandstones and impure limestones with an overall thickness of about 3000 m.

In the Welsh Borders deposition took place in shallow seas. In west Shropshire volcanic rocks form part of the Ordovician succession while in east Shropshire there are no volcanic rocks. In west Shropshire the Ordovician is represented by an unbroken sequence (about 3600 m thick) of volcanic rocks, sandstones, siltstones and mudstones with both deep and shallow water faunas. In east Shropshire only part of the Upper Ordovician is found; the succession consists of about 800 m of shallow water sandstones, siltstones and mudstones. East of this, Ordovician rocks do not appear at the surface but they have been found in

EARTH HISTORY

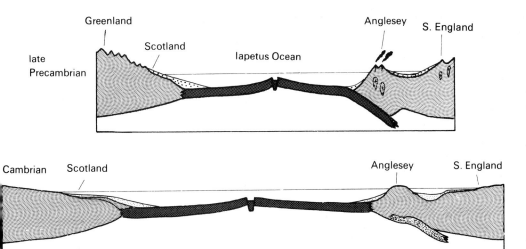

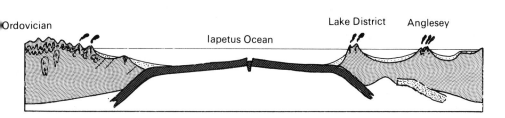

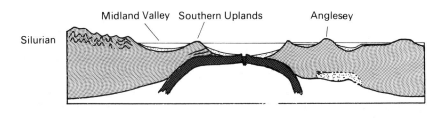

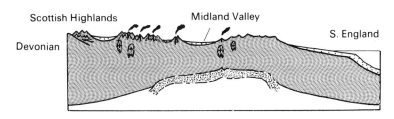

1.16 *Series of north-south sections across the British area from late Precambrian to Devonian times.*

boreholes in Cambridgeshire.

While the Lake District is thought to have been an island arc during part of the Ordovician the status of the Irish Sea Platform is less clear. It has been suggested that it lay above a subduction zone running from Anglesey to south-east Ireland. On the other hand, it has been noted that the Welsh volcanics are of a type which tend to form well back on the landward side of an oceanic trench while the

Lake District volcanics are of the type which tend to occur close to the site of subduction. It may be, therefore, that only one subduction zone existed with the different types of volcanics indicative of different distances from the oceanic trench to the north-west.

In England and Wales the general pattern of sedimentation established during the Ordovician continued into the Silurian. In the Lake District and in north and central Wales deposition took place in subsiding basins while in the Welsh Borders deposition occurred in shallow seas close to land. The major difference between the Ordovician and Silurian is that while the Ordovician is notable for its large quantities of volcanic rocks, there was much less volcanic activity during the Silurian.

In the Lake District the Silurian is represented by about 4600 m of greywackes, sandstones, and graptolitic shales following conformably on the Ordovician. In north and central Wales the Silurian again reaches a thickness of about 4600 m of greywackes, conglomerates, siltstones and graptolitic mudstones and shales deposited in the subsiding Welsh Basin. To the south and east these thick sediments pass into thinner, interrupted sequences toward the Midland Platform landmass. In south-west Wales about 1000 m of lavas at the base of the Silurian are overlain by about 400 m of near-shore sandstones and mudstones belonging mostly to the Middle Silurian. At Llandovery in south-central Wales there is another interrupted sequence of about 2500 m of shallow water sediments. In the Welsh Borders after a well-marked transgression near the beginning of the Silurian about 700 m of near-shore mudstones, fine-grained sandstones and limestones were deposited. Initially, the sea submerged an irregular landscape and the Long Mynd apparently formed a peninsula with an estuary to the southeast and with a shallow sea to the west and north-west. An ancient shoreline is preserved at the south end of the Long Mynd where sea cliffs, stacks and pebble beaches are discernible. To the north-west, littoral shelly sandstone gives way to mudstone deposited further offshore. Following the initial phase of submergence and deposition, the sea spread east into the Midlands. The Middle Silurian of the Welsh Borders and Midlands consists of shallow water shales and limestones. The limestones are rich in fossils such as trilobites, brachiopods, crinoids and molluscs. They are partly reef limestones built by stromatoporoids, corals and bryozoans.

The Upper Silurian of the Welsh Borders consists of shales, mudstones, calcareous siltstones and diachronous limestones deposited under shelf conditions. West of the **Church Stretton Fault** on the western margin of the Midland Platform, the Upper Silurian thickens into shales and siltstones deposited in an offshore basin. To the south of the Welsh Borderland there are preserved submarine canyons which may have been eroded by turbidity currents carrying material north-west from the Midland Platform to the Welsh Basin. Large-scale slump structures in the Upper Silurian are indicative of instability associated with the uplift which eventually led to the end of deposition in the Welsh Basin. Scattered inliers north and south of the Severn Estuary are mostly Middle and Upper Silurian shelf shales, sandstones and limestones with lavas and tuffs.

Caledonian Mountain Building

Lower Palaeozoic plate movements led to the closure of the Iapetus Ocean about 420 Ma ago and to the folding, metamorphism and uplift of the sea-floor sediments to form the Caledonian Mountains about 400 Ma ago. It is thought that plate collision was less violent than that which produced the Himalayas and Alps because the Caledonides show less evidence of huge nappe structures. In Britain the eroded remains of the Caledonian Mountains show a general north-east—south-west trend. The opening of the North Atlantic about 65 Ma ago separated the originally complete Caledonian belt into a zone running from Britain and Ireland into Scandinavia and Spitzbergen and into another zone from east Greenland into Newfoundland and the north Appalachians.

The complex processes which led to mountain building took place over a very long time. While we can say that the Caledonian Mountains had probably formed by about 400 Ma ago it is much more difficult to say precisely when the mountain building movements began. While ocean closing was almost certainly going on at the start of the Ordovician about 500 Ma ago it may be that the process had started much earlier giving phases of orogenic activity such as the Celtic Orogeny (700–600 Ma) which affected the late Precambrian sediments of north Wales, south-east Ireland and the Channel Islands. The main phase of mountain building was the mainly Lower Ordovician Grampian Orogeny (530–465 Ma). This orogeny was

EARTH HISTORY

responsible for the high-grade metamorphism and major deformation of the Moinian and Dalradian. The Grampian Orogeny, itself, was a complex series of events with many phases of metamorphism and deformation forming huge folds and thrusts.

Away from the Scottish Highlands, Caledonian metamorphism and deformation occurred mostly later (Ordovician to Devonian) and with much less severity. The generally upright folding is less complex than that of the Highlands and slates are the dominant metamorphic rocks.

The rate at which Iapetus closed is not known. One estimate puts the width of Iapetus at 2000–3000 towards the end of the Ordovician. If final closure took place at the end of the Silurian this would give a closure rate of 7.5 cm per year. Another estimate puts Iapetus at about 500 km wide during the Ordovician giving a closure rate of about 0.65 cm per year.

Devonian period (415–370 Ma ago)

With the disappearance of Iapetus at the beginning of the Devonian, Britain came to be on the southern margin of a continent which included Scandinavia, Spitzbergen, Greenland and parts of Canada and USA. At this time Britain was in tropical latitudes just south of the equator. Since Britain lay on the southern margin of a continent the sediments in the north of Britain were deposited on land. These continental deposits are known as the **Old Red Sandstone**. In southern Britain there is a change through coastal-plain to truly marine deposition in the extreme south.

The Old Red Sandstone deposits illustrate the changes which occurred at the end of the Caledonian Orogeny. With the ending of plate collision the mountains rose as isostatic equilibrium was restored with the removal of lateral stress. This was accompanied by igneous activity with the intrusion of granites into the rocks of the Highlands, the Southern Uplands and the Lake District and with largely andesitic volcanism in the Cheviots, the Midland Valley and the Firth of Lorne. Sediments from the rising mountains were deposited in subsiding basins or cuvettes within and on the margins of the mountain ranges. Post-orogenic sediments of this type are sometimes described as **molasse**.

In the extreme north, the Orcadian Basin spread from north-east Scotland to the Shet-

11.17 Distribution of Devonian rocks

lands. In this area the rocks are mostly Middle Old Red Sandstone with a thick sequence of river and lake conglomerates, sandstones and mudstones lying unconformably on the Moinian. In Caithness (5000 m thick) the Lower and Middle Old Red Sandstone is unconformably overlain by Upper Old Red Sandstone. In Shetland (10 000 m thick) sedimentation took place continuously from Lower into the beginning of Upper Old Red Sandstone times. The sediments in the Orcadian Basin were deposited in and around a lake which lay in a rapidly subsiding basin. During the wet season, sediment was brought into the basin by rivers from the surrounding mountains while, during the dry season, the lake margin may have retreated to leave extensive areas of dried mud. Parts of the succession consists of varved sediments of carbonate and mud deposited in offshore parts of the lake. The carbonate was precipitated during the dry season while the mud was brought in during the wet season.

The Midland Valley of Scotland has no Middle Old Red Sandstone. Here, nearly 10 000 m of Lower Old Red Sandstone sediments and volcanics are overlain unconformably by nearly 1000 m of Upper Old Red Sandstone. In the

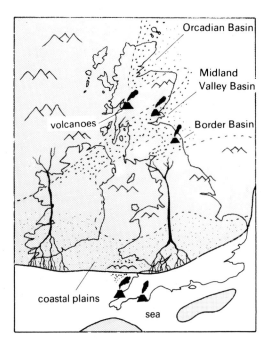

11.18 Palaeogeography of Devonian times.

Borders, the Lower Old Red Sandstone is represented by the volcanics of the Cheviots. Middle Old Red Sandstone is again absent and the Upper Old Red Sandstone is about 250 m thick. During Lower Old Red Sandstone times there was considerable igneous activity with granite being intruded into the Grampians and Southern Uplands and with andesites, rhyolites and basalts being extruded in the Cheviots, the Midland Valley and south of the Firth of Lorne.

The Lower Old Red Sandstone sediments of the Midland Valley consist of conglomerates, sandstones and siltsones brought in by rivers and flood water from the Highlands and Southern Uplands. The basin margins may have been accentuated by the fault-line scarps of the Highland Boundary and perhaps the Southern Uplands Faults. These faults possibly began moving in Silurian times towards the end of the Caledonian Orogeny. Uplift north and south of the Midland Valley caused rapid erosion in these areas and huge quantities of sediment were swept into the Midland Valley often to be deposited in lakes and alluvial fans. Volcanoes, active on the northern and southern margins of the Midland Valley, supplied much of the sediment.

During Lower Old Red Sandstone times the Grampians were probably covered by volcanic rocks. Remnants of these south of the Firth of Lorne are andesites, agglomerates and tuffs with sediments such as conglomerates, sandstones and shales. Sediments are also found on Ben Nevis, in Glencoe and in Aberdeenshire. One of the Aberdeenshire outliers at Rhynie of Middle Old Red Sandstone age is well known for its fossils of psilopsids preserved in their growth positions.

South of the Midland Valley, Lower Old Red Sandstone is found in east Berwickshire in the form of sandstones, conglomerates and siltstones with associated volcanic rocks. Further south, the Cheviots show thick andesites cut by granite.

During Middle Devonian times the Lower Old Red Sandstone suffered folding, faulting and erosion with the result that the Upper Old Red Sandstone is unconformable on the Lower Old Red Sandstone. During Upper Old Red Sandstone times the Midland Valley continued to behave as a depositional basin receiving about 900 m of river and lake deposits. The Upper Old Red Sandstone of the Midland Valley contains sediments called cornstones. Cornstones are beds, usually 1–2 m thick, which consist of carbonate nodules in red, river-lain siltstone or sandstone. Cornstones form as calcareous soil horizons called caliche or calcrete under warm (16–20°C), semi-arid conditions with a seasonal rainfall of 10–50 cm. Such conditions presently exist in some areas between about 35° north and south of the equator.

In the Borders, the Upper Old Red Sandstone was again deposited by rivers. The river deposits are overlain by extensive cornstones as the river systems were interrupted by uplift and lava extrusion at the start of the succeeding Carboniferous period.

The Devonian of southern Britain shows a general transition from continental Old Red Sandstone deposition in Wales and the Welsh Borders through coastal to marine deposition in Devon and Cornwall. The continental successions are much interrupted with the Middle Old Red Sandstone being absent except in west Wales. Here, the Lower Old Red Sandstone (3400 m thick) is unconformably overlain by 400 m of Middle Old Red Sandstone conglomerate which, in turn, is unconformably overlain by 300 m of Upper Old Red Sandstone. Further east, about 2000 m of Lower Old Red

EARTH HISTORY

sandstone is unconformably overlain by about 00 m of an interrupted sequence of Upper Old Red Sandstone. In the Welsh Borders the Lower Old Red Sandstone (1200 m thick) is followed unconformably by up to 150 m of Upper Old Red Sandstone. In Ireland, the Old Red Sandstone successions are complete. In west Wales the Old Red Sandstone is unconformable on the Silurian. In the Welsh Borders there is no distinct unconformity with the underlying Silurian and the early Old Red Sandstone represents a phase of marine regression. The base of the Old Red Sandstone is marked by a distinctive layer called the **Ludlow Bone Bed** (15 cm thick). This bed contains numerous fish and shell fragments along with phosphate pellets. The concentration of these organic remains is due to slow deposition and constant reworking by currents in shallow water as the sea began to retreat to the south. Behind the south-retreating beaches, deposits were of lagoonal and intertidal type and, further inland, deposition took place from rivers running over extensive flood plains and alluvial fans. The base of the Lower Old Red Sandstone (Downtonian) consists predominantly of grey and yellow sandstones and siltstones which upward become red or brown in colour. Cornstones, again indicative of semi-arid conditions, are found in the upper parts of the Lower Old Red Sandstone (Dittonian). Going west away from the Welsh Borders the lower parts of the Old Red Sandstone (Downtonian and Dittonian) consists of a thick sequence of red siltstones called the Red Marl Group.

Uplift took place during Middle Old Red Sandstone times so that Middle Old Red Sandstone is absent from the Welsh Borders and most of Wales. The Upper Old Red Sandstone consists of sandstones, siltstones, mudstones and conglomerates deposited by rivers flowing south from the Caledonian Mountains. In west Wales and south Ireland the late Devonian rocks are marine mudstones and limestones.

In north Devon and Somerset, the Devonian sequence (about 5 km thick) shows marine transgressions interrupted by two periods of continental deposition. The lowest beds (upper Lower Devonian) are mudstones, siltstones and sandstones probably deposited on the continental shelf. The marine beds are followed by about 1 km of continental sandstone (the Hangman Grits) largely deposited by rivers. The Middle Devonian shows a return to marine deposition with mudstones, sandstones and limestones with corals. These shelf conditions continued into the Upper Devonian until they were interrupted by a second thick sequence of river-deposited sandstones and mudstones. The continental deposits are then followed by marine mudstones, siltstones and sandstones of coastal and offshore type.

In south Devon and north Cornwall the earliest Devonian consists of non-marine sandstones, siltstones and mudstones deposited by rivers during the furthest southerly advance of the coastal plains of the Old Red Sandstone continent. From the middle of the Lower Devonian the succession is marine. The sediments which follow the non-marine beds at the base

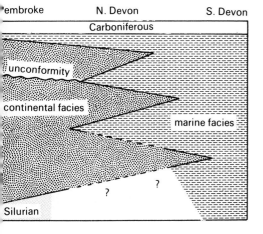

11.19 Transition from Devonian continental deposits in Wales to marine deposits in Devon and Cornwall.

of the sequence are shallow-marine sandstones, mudstones and thin limestones. Above
these come mudstones, pillow lavas and thin
limestones at the start of the Middle Devonian.
Thereafter, the Middle and part of the Upper
Devonian of south Devon consist of thick limestones while in north Cornwall mudstones and
volcanics continue into the Upper Devonian.
The limestones of south Devon are of stromatoporoid and coral types formed as reefs and
from reef debris. In the Upper Devonian of south
Devon deposition took place in deepening seas,
e.g. in the Torquay area limestones of the early
Upper Devonian are overlain by thick goniatitic
mudstones deposited in deep water.

In north Cornwall the Middle and Upper
Devonian consist of thick goniatitic mudstones
again deposited in deep water. Volcanic rocks
including pillow lavas, tuffs and agglomerates
are common along with conglomerates and
crinoidal limestones perhaps formed by the
transport of crinoid fragments by turbidity
currents.

In south Cornwall the Lower Devonian consists of pillow lavas, agglomerates, conglomerates and mudstones which lie unconformably
on the Ordovician. The volcanics are followed
by mudstones and greywackes. In the Middle
Devonian, limestones appear followed once
more by greywackes and mudstones. The sediments in this area were derived from a landmass in the Brittany-English Channel areas.
Because of uplift no Upper Devonian was deposited in this area.

In summary, during the Devonian Britain lay
in south tropical latitudes on the southern
margin of the mountainous Old Red Sandstone
continent (figure 11.18). To the south lay the
Devonian Sea or Rheic Ocean whose shoreline
ran across southern Ireland and southern
England. In northern areas thick river and lake
sediments accumulated in subsiding basins
among the mountains. Granites were intruded
and volcanoes produced thick lava sequences.
From the Caledonian Mountains the land sloped
down across an extensive coastal plain which
stretched from south Wales across into
Somerset and north Devon where coastal and
continental deposits alternated. In Cornwall and
south Devon deposition took place mostly
under marine conditions with turbidites, limestones and pillow lavas being common. By the
end of the Devonian the Caledonian Mountains
had been largely eroded away.

Carboniferous period (370–280 Ma ago)

11.20 Distribution of Lower Carboniferous rocks.

During the Carboniferous, Britain lay on the
equator. In late Devonian and early Carboniferous times a warm, shallow sea interrupted b
islands spread northwards to the edge of th
Scottish Highlands.

In south-west England the marine condition
of the Devonian continued into the Lower Carboniferous (about 750 m thick) with the depo
sition of deep water mudstones with sand
stones, limestones and radiolarian cherts. Tuff
lavas and agglomerates are also present.

In south Wales and in the Bristol area th
Lower Carboniferous was deposited in she
seas lying to the south of a landmass calle
St. George's Land. The earliest Carboniferou
sediments provide evidence of a marine trans
gression across the Old Red Sandstone alluvi
plains. The base of the sequence consists
shales and thin crinoidal and oolitic limestone
deposited near the coastline of the advancin
sea. The early shaley deposits are succeede
by thick limestones which show a gener
upward change from near-shore to offsho
types. The limestones formed under variou
conditions, e.g. the oolitic limestones wer
deposited in shallow, turbulent water whi

limestone deposited in shelf seas is often thickly bedded with fossils such as corals and brachiopods. Dolomitic limestones are thought to have formed in lagoons cut off from the sea by barrier reefs. Six phases of marine transgression and regression have been recognized south of St. George's Land. From thicknesses of over 1000 m in Pembroke, Gower and the Mendips, the Lower Carboniferous thins out completely over St. George's Land.

North of St George's Land basins of deposition are separated from the north Pennine Askrigg and Alston Blocks by faults. The faults are post Carboniferous but they mark the places where the basinal sequences thinned out to cross the stable blocks. In the Craven Basin of Lancashire and west Yorkshire there are at least 2000 m of limestones and goniatitic mudstones. The limestones commonly contain mound-like deposits which probably represent lime mudbanks. The lime mud may have been trapped by dense colonies or organisms such as crinoids and stabilized by algal growth. The mudbanks tend to occur at the basin margins so, as the basin filled up, the mudbanks migrated away from the centre of the basin. The six transgressive and regressive phases found south of St. George's Land are also found in the Craven Basin. Towards the end of Lower Carboniferous times the northern margin of St. George's Land was transgressed and deposition occurred from north Wales to the Midlands. The Askrigg and Alston Blocks were land for about the first half of the Lower Carboniferous though early in the Carboniferous the sea spread round to the north-west of the Askrigg Block to deposit about 1200 m of Lower Carboniferous sediments in the Stainmore Basin.

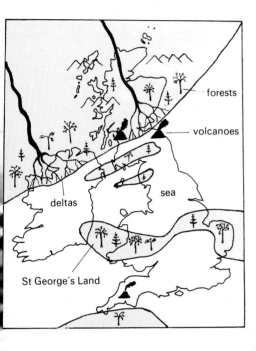

1.21 Palaeogeography of Lower Carboniferous times.

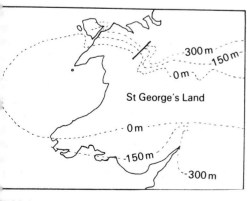

1.22 Isopachytes for the top part of the Lower Carboniferous outline the position of St. George's Land.

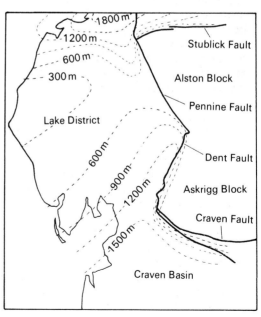

11.23 Isopachytes for the Lower Carboniferous of the Lake District and northern Pennine region.

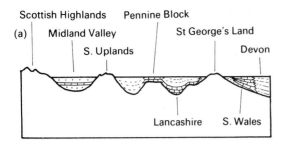

(a) [labels: Scottish Highlands, Pennine Block, Midland Valley, St George's Land, S. Uplands, Devon, Lancashire, S. Wales]

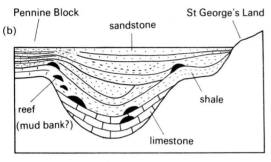

(b) [labels: Pennine Block, sandstone, St George's Land, shale, reef (mud bank?), limestone]

11.24 *(a) North-south section across Britain showing basins of Lower Carboniferous deposition.*
(b) North-south section across the Craven Basin with sediments deposited till the beginning of Coal Measure times.

The Northumberland Basin (2200 m thick) lay between the Alston Block and the Southern Uplands Block. The six marine transgressive and regressive cycles seen further south can also be recognized in this area. Along the north side of the basin the Lower Carboniferous sandstones and conglomerates were brought in by rivers from the Southern Uplands Block to be deposited in coastal plains, deltas and alluvial fans. Deposition in hypersaline, coastal plain lakes subject to periodic desiccation gave a succession of mudstones, siltstones, sandstones and dolomitic limestones (cementstones). At times, deltas spread from the northeast into the Northumberland Basin. During times of delta retreat marine limestones with stromatolites were deposited. The limestones were probably deposited under hypersaline conditions since fossils of normal marine organisms such as corals are not common. The Scremerston Coal Group consisting of shales, sandstones, impure limestones and coals, marks the last delta retreat. Following deposition of the Scremerston Coal Group a marine incursion which also spread over the Pennine

Block brought in sediments of the Limestone Group. The Limestone Group was deposited in cycles of Yoredale type. The rhythms or **cyclothems** (5-80 m thick) consist of marine limestone at the base followed by marine shale, lagoonal shale and siltstone, deltaic sandstone and coal (Figure 11.25). The mechanisms which cause repeated marine to deltaic sequences are not fully understood. It has been suggested that the sedimentary basin subsides at regular intervals. Each subsidence allows the sea to flood in so limestones are deposited. As more sediment is deposited the basin fills up and forests grow on deltas. Sinking then takes place and the cycle begins again. It has also been suggested that the land round the sedimentary basin rises periodically while the basin subsides continuously. Rhythmic sedimentation may also be caused by changes in sea level related to the build up and melting of polar ice sheets. Marine deposition takes place during periods of high sea level and deltaic deposition occurs during periods of low sea level. Finally,

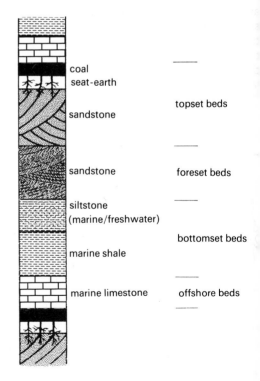

[labels: coal, seat-earth, topset beds, sandstone, sandstone, foreset beds, siltstone (marine/freshwater), bottomset beds, marine shale, marine limestone, offshore beds]

11.25 *A Yoredale cyclothem. Each cycle probably represents the advance of a delta into a subsiding area.*

It may be that each cycle represents the advance of part of a delta into a constantly subsiding area. To begin with, limestone is deposited in the open sea. As the delta advances bottomset shales and silts cover the limestone. The shales and siltstones are then covered by sandy foreset and topset beds as the delta advances further. Plants whose remains form coal grow on the topset beds. The sea returns when the river changes its course and begins building a new delta lobe in another direction. The original delta lobe is carried beneath the sea by the uniform subsidence of the sedimentary basin and limestone deposition begins again. A further change in the river would bring back another cycle of deltaic sediments.

In the Midland Valley the base of the Carboniferous generally consists of mudstones, siltstones, sandstones and cementstones which are conformable with the Upper Old Red Sandstone. The early Carboniferous rocks were deposited in hypersaline lakes which occasionally dried up. During the Lower Carboniferous volcanic activity was widespread. Most notably, about 1000 m of flood basalts formed the Clyde Plateau round Glasgow. Away from the main area of volcanic activity up to 2000 m of oil shales were deposited in a basin west of Edinburgh (Figure 11.26). The oil shales were derived from bituminous muds formed by the decay of plant material on the floors of stagnant lakes. In Fife, the base of the Carboniferous

consists of 1500 m of deltaic sandstones deposited by rivers from the Highlands. The top of the Lower Carboniferous in the Midland Valley consists of marine limestones and deltaic deposits showing Yoredale cyclothems.

During the Upper Carboniferous the Scottish Highlands remained as an upland area which supplied sediment to large deltas spreading south towards St. George's Land. South of St. George's Land coastal plains with deltas lay on the edge of a sea which deepened to the south. Widespread forested swamps which developed towards the end of the Carboniferous gave rise to the Coal Measures.

11.27 Distribution of Upper Carboniferous rocks.

In south-west England, the Upper Carboniferous shows marked lateral variation between deltaic and basinal sequences. The deltaic sequence in the north of the area consists of about 2000 m of sandstones, siltstones and mudstones showing evidence of six sedimentary cycles. Each cycle, which consists of deep water mudstones followed by turbidites passing up to deltaic sediments, is thought to indicate the southerly advance of a delta into a deep sedimentary basin. The basinal sequence is also about 2000 m thick. It consists of mudstones

Highlands

0 m
-300 m
600 m
1200 m
900 m
900 m
600 m
oil shale
300 m
0 m
lava

Southern Uplands

11.26 Isopachyte map for part of the Lower Carboniferous of the Midland Valley of Scotland.

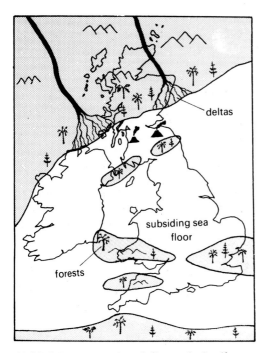

11.28 *Palaeogeography of Upper Carboniferous times.*

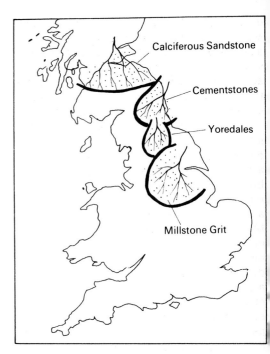

11.29 *Southerly advance of deltas during the Carboniferous.*

and greywackes deposited on a sinking sea floor by turbidity currents from the deltas to the north.

In most other parts of England and Wales the early part of the Upper Carboniferous (the Namurian) is represented by the river-deposited **Millstone Grit**. The rivers north of St. George's Land flowed generally south from the region of the Scottish Highlands depositing sediment in deltas and flood plains which were frequently inundated by the sea. As a delta moved into a marine basin turbidites from the delta front were first to cover the marine sediments. As the advance continued the turbidites were overlain by deltaic and river deposits. The Millstone Grit is most fully developed (2000 m thick) south of the Craven Fault in the Central Pennines Basin. Here, the Namurian consists of coarse arkosic sandstones (grits) and shales. In this area, too, the younger grits reach progressively further south. North of the Craven Fault on the Pennine Block and in Northumberland and Durham the Namurian begins with Yoredale type deposition (limestones, shales and sandstones) which continued from the Lower Carboniferous. The Yoredale type of succession was eventually replaced by a relatively thin Millstone Grit type of sequence.

In south Wales, uplift of St. George's Land preceded deposition of the Millstone Grit which is unconformable on the underlying Lower Carboniferous. Rivers flowed into the south Wales area from St George's Land and from a landmass in the area of the Bristol Channel.

In the Midland Valley of Scotland, the Namurian is initially of Yoredale type with marine limestones and mudstones, deltaic sandstones and coals. In late Namurian times river and deltaic deposition produced sediments (the Passage Group) which resemble the Millstone Grit. Volcanic activity persisted but on a smaller scale to that of the Lower Carboniferous.

The end of the Carboniferous (the Westphalian) saw the deposition of the Coal Measures (3000 m maximum thickness) in widespread swamps between the Scottish Highlands and St. George's Land and south of St. George's Land from south Wales to Kent. Note that, despite the name, the Coal Measures are only about 5 per cent coal. The most common rocks are shales, siltstones and sandstones. The Coal Measures consist largely of cyclothems which are very variable in detail but which ideally would show repeated sequences from marine through lagoonal and deltaic to swamp conditions. Like the Yoredale cycles, the Coal Measure cyclothems probably reflect the advance of changing deltas into continuously subsiding areas. Within the Coal Measures about twenty widespread marine bands show the occurrence of frequent transgressions caused by eustatically changing sea levels.

In general, the Coal Measures may be divided into three parts. The Lower Coal Measures contain numerous marine bands, coal seams are thin and there are few bands of non- marine bivalves. The Middle Coal Measures contain numerous thick coals and non-marine bivalves and plant fossils are common. The Upper Coal Measures show an initial development of marine bands with coal seams becoming less common. Above the top marine band are red-beds deposited on river flood- plains in Scotland and along the north side of St. George's Land. South of St.George's Land, apart from the extreme south-west of England, coal-forming conditions persisted but thick, coarse sandstones of the Pennant Group predominate in south Wales and in the Bristol area. The Pennant sandstones were deposited in the alluvial plains and deltas of rivers flowing from the south. In the concealed Kent Coalfield, the Coal Measures lie unconformably on Lower Carboniferous limestones. Pennant sandstones, in turn, lie unconformably on the upper parts of the Coal Measure sequence.

In conclusion, the Carboniferous period can be divided into the Dinantian, Namurian and Westphalian epochs. The Dinantian saw the advance of warm, shallow seas in which much limestone was deposited, over the southern part of the Old Red Sandstone continent. The Namurian and Westphalian saw the advance of deltas into the seas. On the deltas, thickly forested swamps produced peat which on burial became coal. Volcanoes were active during the Dinantian and some activity persisted into Westphalian times in Scotland.

Variscan or Hercynian mountain building (late Carboniferous–early Permian)

The Variscan fold belt runs from central Europe across into North America (figure 8.55). It impinges on southern Britain and south Ireland producing mainly east–west trending structures. Further north, the weaker effects of the Variscan orogeny produced open folds whose variable trends were dictated by pre-existing

structures in the rocks. The granite batholith of south-west England and the dolerites of northern England and central Scotland are of Variscan origin. At this time, too, veins of economic minerals were formed in places such as south-west England, the Pennines and Ireland. In Britain, the effects of the Variscan orogeny were felt mainly at the end of the Carboniferous and at the beginning of the Permian though the orogeny began during the Devonian. In south-west England folding probably began about 360 Ma ago (Lower Carboniferous) while the granite which cuts the folds is about 270 Ma old (Lower Permian).

The Variscan orogeny may have resulted from the closure of the ocean which lay across Europe during the Devonian and Carboniferous. During these times, Britain may have lain on the continental side of a marginal sea like the Sea of Japan. Like present-day subduction under Japan, Variscan subduction may have taken place some distance away from the continental mainland.

Permian (280–235 Ma ago) and Triassic (235–195 Ma ago) periods

During the Permian and Triassic periods Britain lay in north tropical latitudes on the huge continent of Pangaea. In the hot, dry climate desert sandstones and evaporites were deposited. The continental Permian and Triassic is sometimes called the New Red Sandstone.

During the Variscan orogeny Britain was uplifted and the Lower Permian rocks or Rotliegendes are of molasse type having been formed by the erosion of extensive upland areas (figure 11.31). On the margins of the uplands breccias formed in alluvial fans while out into the lowland areas the breccias pass laterally into dune sandstones and red mudstones. The largest sedimentary basin extended from north-east England into the southern North Sea. The basin was separated from the northern North Sea basin by a raised area running across the middle of the North Sea and on its southern side the basin was bounded by the uplands of the London–Brabant Massif. In this area the Lower Permian consists of dune sandstones (the Basal Yellow Sands) with some conglomerates and fluvial sandstones deposited in wadis. The Yellow Sands reach a maximum thickness of about

11.30 *Distribution of Permian rocks.*

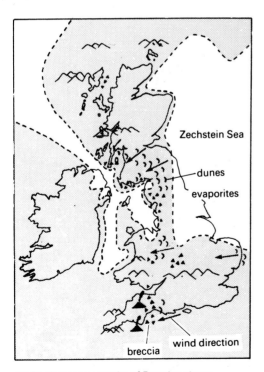

11.31 *Palaeogeography of Permian times.*

60 m in Durham. Southward into Nottingham-shire they pass into breccia formed on the north side of the London–Brabant Massif.

At the end of the Lower Permian the upland areas had been largely worn down and the Upper Permian (Zechstein) is mostly marine. Above the Basal Yellow Sands is the Upper Permian Marl Slate (usually about 1 m thick). Despite its name, the Marl Slate is a silty, dolomitic shale deposited during the initial southward incursion of the Zechstein Sea. This sea spread into north-east England and Germany and an arm of it from the north reached into the area of the Irish Sea. The marine transgression may have been caused by melting of the Gondwanaland ice sheet. Above the Marl Slate is the dolomitic Magnesian Limestone which is about 250 m thick in north-east England. Thin layers of Magnesian Limestone were also deposited in north-west England and in Northern Ireland. Above the Magnesian Limestone are about 130 m of Upper Marls.

The Upper Permian of north-east England and the North Sea shows repeated sequences representing the filling and evaporation of a partly enclosed marine basin. Evaporites make up about 20 percent of the sequence. The Marl Slate represents an oxygen-poor organic-rich deposit of the type presently forming on the floor of the Black Sea. Above the Marl Slate each of the five sedimentary cycles which are present begins with dolomite probably formed by sea-floor dolomitization of calcite. The limestones formed mostly on the margins of the sedimentary basin. Some limestones formed as reefs built by algae and bryozoans while others are oolitic or pisolitic. Towards the centre of the basin the limestone gives way to anhydrite precipitated as the basin shrank. Above the anhydrite come thick layers of halite. In some cycles evaporation was complete so potassium salts are found in the basin centre. The thick evaporites show that the basins were constantly supplied with sea water.

Outside north-east England the Permian was often deposited under desert conditions in fault-controlled basins. In south-west England volcanic rocks at the base of the Permian are followed by red breccias, sandstones and mudstones. In the Midlands, breccias are again followed by sandstones. In Northern Ireland breccias are followed by thin Magnesian Limestone and the overlying Upper Marls contain anhydrite and gypsum. In north-west England

EARTH HISTORY

the Lower Permian is a breccia (Lower Brockram) which is followed by desert sandstone (Penrith Sandstone). The Upper Permian consists of thin Magnesian Limestone overlain by red and grey shales. In Scotland the Permian consists of breccias and sandstones.

The orientation of the cross bedding in the desert sandstones throughout Britain indicates that the Permian winds blew generally from east to west. Since these winds were probably the North-East Trade Winds this adds to palaeomagnetic evidence in indicating a north tropical latitude for Britain during the Permian.

The end of the Permian, which also marks the end of the Palaeozoic Era, saw the extinction of numerous types of organism such as trilobites, goniatites, rugose corals, productid brachiopods and fusilinid foraminifera. It is thought that these and other extinctions were caused by the coming together of the Earth's landmasses to make the single continent of Pangaea which, in turn, led to a drastic reduction in the area of shelf seas. Animals and plants which previously lived in isolated areas were brought into direct competition with each other. The result of this was that less adaptable organisms became extinct.

The Mesozoic Era (235–65 Ma) began with the Triassic period (235–195 Ma). The Triassic saw the appearance of many new life forms, e.g. the ammonites replaced the goniatites, belemnites appeared, the scleractinian corals replaced the rugose corals and bivalves and gastropods diversified. Among vertebrates, the mammals appeared and reptiles such as dinosaurs, pterosaurs, ichthyosaurs and plesiosaurs developed. Towards the end of the Triassic period typical Mesozoic plants such as conifers, cycads and ferns had become widespread.

In Germany, the Triassic is divided into a lower continental division called the Bunter, a middle marine limestone division called the Muschelkalk and an upper, Keuper division also of continental facies. In Britain, the Triassic is largely continental and the Bunter describes lower sandstones and conglomerates while the Keuper is an upper part consisting of fine sandstones, red marls and evaporites. The Triassic is similar to the Permian in that much of it consists of continental red-beds deposited under hot, dry conditions. Uplift at the start of the Triassic raised areas such as Scotland, Wales, north-west France and parts of England such as the London–Brabant Massif, the Pen-

11.32 Distribution of Triassic rocks.

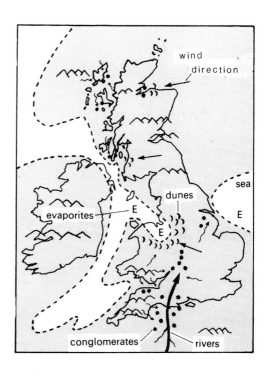

11.33 Palaeogeography of Triassic times.

nines, the Lake District and Cornwall. Between the uplifted areas down-faulted basins received sediment from huge rivers. The direction of river flow can be found by identifying the source areas of transported pebbles. At the start of the Triassic, the main rivers flowed north from the Variscan Highlands depositing Bunter conglomerates and coarse sandstones in alluvial fans and in the beds of braided streams. Away from the upland areas siltstones and mudstones often with mudcracks and calcrete soil horizons were formed in floodplains and playa lakes. Above the pebble beds at the base of the Triassic come sandstones which are mostly river deposited. The finer grain of these sediments indicates a slowing of the rivers as the uplands were worn down. In places, the sandstones are of desert origin.

Above the Bunter conglomerates and sandstones come the fine-grained, Lower Keuper Sandstone which is still of Lower Triassic age. While Lower Keuper Sandstone was being deposited in most parts of England, evaporites (gypsum and halite) were being formed in the southern North Sea and in Yorkshire. In Northern Ireland and south-west Scotland the sediments at this time were mostly coarse desert sandstones.

The Lower Triassic shows marked lateral variation, e.g. in south-west England about 100 m of conglomerates are followed by about 200 m of fine sandstone. In north-west England 400 m of conglomerates and coarse sandstones are followed by nearly 200 m of fine sandstone. In north-east England about 250 m of coarse sandstones are followed by about 150 m of sandstones and marls with gypsum and halite horizons. In south-west Scotland the Lower Triassic consists of about 400 m of desert sandstone.

During the Middle Triassic parts of Britain were covered by a sea spreading from the south. The marine incursion deposited about 60 m of siltstones, marls and shales called the Waterstones over much of England. The Waterstones are followed by Upper Triassic Keuper Marl which overlaps the underlying Triassic. The marl is a red, dolomitic mudstone with frequent evidence of desiccation in the form of mud cracks, rain prints and evaporite deposits which was probably deposited on the mudflats of huge playa lakes. In part, the marls may also have formed as wind-blown dust or loess. Thick Upper Triassic evaporites are found in the

southern North Sea and in a basin which spread from the Midlands north-west through Cheshire. In Cheshire the Keuper Marl (over 1000 m thick) contains about 250 m of halite. Gypsum is common in the Upper Triassic of England and the southern North Sea. In places such as the Midlands, Northern Ireland and south-west Scotland fine-grained sandstones are found in the Upper Triassic.

Towards the end of the Triassic the sea encroached from the south-west on to a generally flat landscape. The topmost Keuper Marls are green and grey dolomitic mudstones probably deposited along the flat coastline of an arid region. Above the green marls come the topmost Triassic or Rhaetic Beds. The Rhaetic Beds (about 30 m thick) are largely marine shales, limestones and sandstones. At or near the base is the Rhaetic Bone Bed which contains the teeth, scales, bones and spines of marine and freshwater animals representing reworked beach deposits as the sea advanced over the Triassic plains.

Jurassic period (195–135 Ma ago)

During the Jurassic period Britain lay between about 30 and 40° north of the equator in an area where the climate was warm and wet. At this time much of Britain was covered by shallow seas. Jurassic rises in sea level are thought to have been caused by the building of oceanic ridges as Pangaea began to split up. The ridges displaced water from the ocean basins which spilled over on to the continents.

The Lower Jurassic or **Lias** consists largely of alternating limestones and shales deposited over a series of basins and swells. Thick sequences dominated by shales were deposited in subsiding basins in places such as Yorkshire (about 400 m thick) and Cardigan Bay (about 1300 m thick). The swells were shoals or low islands raised relative to the basins by faulting. In the North Sea, swells may have developed over rising salt plugs. Over the swells the Lower Jurassic shows thin sequences consisting mainly of limestones and sandstones. The most strongly marked swells (figure 11.37) were located at Market Weighton (30 m thick), Moreton-in-the-Marsh (about 180 m thick), the Mendips (25 m thick) and Portsdown (about 140 m thick).

1.34 Distribution of Jurassic rocks.

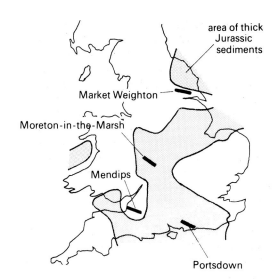

11.36 Areas of thick Lower Jurassic deposition. (In the shaded areas thickness exceeds 100 m.) Sequences thin over the swells.

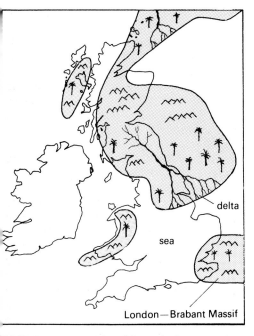

11.35 Palaeogeography of Jurassic times.

The Lower Lias consists of a lower part of alternating bluish shales and grey limestones with an upper part which is predominantly shaley. The alternating strata are thought to have formed by rhythmic sedimentation. A cycle began with the deposition of bituminous shale and calcareous mudstone formed from terrigenous and planktonic material. This was followed by limestone formed from planktonic remains when no sediment came from land areas. The Middle Lias generally has a lower part consisting of shales and sandstones and an upper part consisting of limestones. The Upper Lias is very variable but generally has a lower part of shales and limestones followed by shales and sandstones. In north-west Scotland the Lower Jurassic consists mostly of marine siltstones, sandstones and shales with some limestones. In places, oolitic ironstones of chamosite, siderite and goethite occur in the

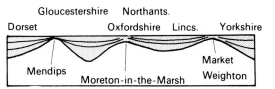

11.37 S.W.-N.E. section across England showing Lower Jurassic deposition in basins and over swells.

Lower Jurassic. Well-known examples are the Lower Liassic Frodingham Ironstone (north Lincolnshire), the Middle Liassic Cleveland Ironstone (Yorkshire) and Marlstone (the Midlands and Lincolnshire) and the Upper Liassic Raasay Ironstone (Hebrides).

The Middle Jurassic shows marked variation in thickness and facies from place to place. At the start of the Middle Jurassic the sea partially retreated to the south and, in places, deltaic and lagoonal environments were established which were occasionally interrupted by marine invasions. In south-west England the Middle Jurassic consists largely of shallow-water marine limestones divided into the **Inferior Oolite**, the **Great Oolite** and the **Cornbrash**. The Inferior Oolite (about 110 m thick) is an interrupted sequence of limestones which are often oolitic, pisolitic, rubbly, marly or shelly. The lower part of the Great Oolite is the Fuller's Earth Formation (300 m maximum thickness in Dorset) which consists mostly of blue-grey clays made up partly of fine volcanic ash in beds up to 1 m thick. The volcanoes were perhaps located in the area of the North Sea (where Middle Jurassic lavas have been found) or in the Western Approaches. The upper part of the Great Oolite resembles the Inferior Oolite in consisting largely of limestones which may be shelly or oolitic or made from calcite sand and mud. The Cornbrash consists of about 10 m of marine limestones which extend over much of Britain and provide evidence of a widespread transgression at this time.

The Middle Jurassic changes northwards as deposition took place under lagoonal and deltaic conditions. In Northamptonshire and Lincolnshire the base of the Middle Jurassic is marked by the oolitic Northampton Sand Ironstone (25 m thick). Above the ironstone is the thin Lower Estuarine Series (6 m thick) which consists largely of dark siltstones and mudstones deposited in lagoons and on coastal flats. Oolitic limestones above these non-marine mudstones indicate a return to shallow marine conditions. The limestones are followed by the grey, non-marine mudstones of the Upper Estuarine Series (10 m thick). This series is followed by oolitic limestone (the Great Oolite Limestone) then by non-marine mudstones which are overlain by the Cornbrash.

In Yorkshire the Middle Jurassic was deposited on the flood-plains and deltas of rivers running from the north. The sediments resemble the Carboniferous Coal Measures in

consisting mainly of sandstones and shales with thin coal seams and seat earths. Marine incursions from the east brought in occasional oolitic ironstones and limestones with ammonites and bivalves. Towards the end of the Middle Jurassic the marine Cornbrash was deposited followed by marine sandstones.

In north-east Scotland the Middle Jurassic is again of fluvio-deltaic origin in its lower part becoming marine towards the top. The rocks are predominantly sandstones and shales with thin limestones and coal seams. In north-west Scotland the Middle Jurassic consists of a lower part of coastal sandstones (400 m thick) followed by lagoonal sandstones and mudstones (200 m thick). The lagoonal deposits are overlain by marine shales.

In England, deposition of the marine **Oxford Clay** began in the Middle Jurassic and continued into Upper Jurassic times. The Oxford Clay is about 150 m thick in the south but it thins to about 15 m in Yorkshire. Following the Oxford Clay are the shallow marine **Corallian Beds** (160 m maximum thickness). The Corallian consists mostly of oolitic and coral limestones, sandstones and clays. In Norfolk, the Corallian is represented by black, deep-water clay while on the north side of the Market Weighton swell the Corallian is calcareous as it is in southern England. A readvance of the sea led to the deposition of the bituminous **Kimmeridge Clay** in restricted marine basins. The Kimmeridge Clay is of variable thickness reaching about 500 m in southern England. It thins to about 50 m in Oxfordshire then thickens to about 120 m in Norfolk. It is absent over the Market Weighton swell then thickens to about 150 m in Yorkshire. Following deposition of the Kimmeridge Clay the sea began to retreat to the south and shallow water sandstones and limestones were deposited. In the south, the Kimmeridge Clay coarsens upwards and gives way to calcareous **Portland** and **Purbeck Beds** which show a general sequence of deposition from open marine through to lagoonal conditions. The lagoons progressively shrank so that gypsum was deposited and dry land conditions existed at times. There were occasional marine incursions which probably came from the north.

North of the London–Brabant Massif in Norfolk the late Jurassic rocks are marine sandstones deposited on the edge of the North Sea Basin. Further north into Yorkshire there is no Jurassic younger than the Kimmeridge Clay. In north-east Scotland the Upper Jurassic is a thick sequence (more than 1000 m) of sandstones, carbonaceous shales and conglomerates deposited in a fault-controlled basin. In north-west Scotland, the largely shaley Upper Jurassic extends up as far as the Kimmeridgian.

In summary, the Jurassic marks a time when shallow seas covered much of Britain. During the Lower Jurassic the Liassic limestones and shales were deposited in a series of basins separated by relatively upraised swells. The Middle Jurassic, though variable, marks a time of marine recession which saw the deposition of shallow-water limestones in the south and deltaic sediments in the north. The Upper Jurassic showed a readvance of the seas with clays deposited in most areas. By the end of the Jurassic the sea had retreated from most areas.

Cretaceous period (135–65 Ma ago)

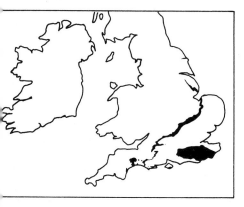

1.38 Distribution of Lower Cretaceous rocks.

Towards the end of the Jurassic period the sea had retreated from much of Britain and the Lower Cretaceous was deposited in restricted areas. In southern England the Lower Cretaceous consists of river and marine mudstones and sandstones while further north in Norfolk and Yorkshire the Lower Cretaceous consists of marine sandstones and mudstones. During the Upper Cretaceous, Britain was covered by shallow seas in which the Chalk was deposited. The sea-floor spreading which opened the South Atlantic during the Jurassic extended northwards and the north Atlantic began to open during the Cretaceous. At this time Britain

lay between about 35 and 45° north of the equator. The Cretaceous brought an end to the Mesozoic era and the close of of the Cretaceous saw the extinction of the dinosaurs and ammonites.

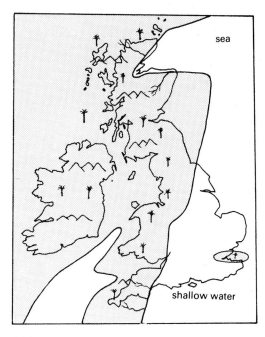

11.39 Palaeogeography of Lower Cretaceous times.

The retreat of the late Jurassic sea left the south of England and the Norfolk–Yorkshire areas as the two partially-separated sites of Lower Cretaceous deposition (figure 11.39). The Cretaceous began with a brief marine incursion which in southern England is marked by the oyster-rich Cinder Bed in the middle of the lagoonal Purbeck Beds. Above the Cinder Bed the remaining Purbeck Beds are limestones and clays deposited in brackish and freshwater conditions. The Purbeck Beds are followed by the **Hastings Beds** (400 m thick). The Hastings Beds consist of sandstones and clays deposited under humid conditions. The sandstones were formed in the floodplains of rivers flowing south from the London–Brabant Massif while the clays were deposited in swamps at times when the supply of river sediment ceased. Rivers from the west carried material into the western part of the southern basin. The Hastings Beds are followed by the **Weald Clay** (450 m thick) which was deposited in swamps as the London–Brabant Massif was eroded down and the transporting power of the south flowing rivers was much reduced. Marine deposition south of the London–Brabant Massif returned towards the end of the Lower Cretaceous and the Weald Clay is followed by the **Lower Greensand** (250 m maximum thickness). The Lower Greensand consists of sandstones and mudstones of variable thickness deposited in shallow near-shore conditions. The presence of glauconite in the sandstones and siltstones confirms its marine origin. Because weathering alters the glauconite, exposures of Lower Greensand usually appear brown or rusty red. The Lower Greensand is followed by the **Gault Clay** (to about 90 m thick) deposited in offshore basinal conditions as the sea transgressed and spread over the London–Brabant Massif. In the south-east the Gault Clay is a richly fossiliferous blue clay. To the west the upper clays pass into the nearshore glauconitic sandstones and siltstones of the **Upper Greensand** (figure 11.40). This westward coarsening indicates that sediment was being derived from Cornwall.

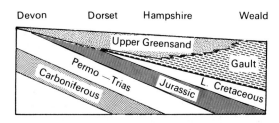

11.40 *Lateral variation in the upper part of the Lower Cretaceous. The Gault Clay passes westward into the Upper Greensand.*

The Lower Cretaceous north of the London–Brabant Massif from Cambridgeshire to Yorkshire was deposited on the southern margin of a sea which extended to the north. In Norfolk the Jurassic Kimmeridge Clay is unconformably overlain by the nearshore glauconitic **Sandringham Sandstone** the upper part of which is Lower Cretaceous. The Sandringham Sandstone (50 m thick) is succeeded by a thin, broken sequence of clays and sandstones. The top of the Lower Cretaceous is marked by the **Red Chalk**. The Red Chalk (1 m thick) is a condensed marly limestone slowly deposited on the Market Weighton swell. The Red Chalk is

equivalent in age to the Gault Clay which thickens south from Norfolk. (At Cambridge the Gault is about 50 m thick while in Bedfordshire it is about 70 m thick.)

In Lincolnshire the base of the Cretaceous lies within the nearshore, glauconitic **Spilsby Sandstone**. This sandstone is followed by clays, limestones, marls and sandstones giving a total thickness of about 100 m for the Lower Cretaceous. The top of the Lower Cretaceous is again marked by the Red Chalk. Further north in Yorkshire most of the Lower Cretaceous consists of about 60 m of marine **Speeton Clay** deposited in offshore conditions on the north side of the Market Weighton swell. Once again, Red Chalk marks the top of the Lower Cretaceous.

At the beginning of the Upper Cretaceous a major transgression left most of Britain covered in clear seas (figure 11.42). The transgression may have been caused by the build up of ocean ridges in the developing Atlantic. The Upper Cretaceous (about 600 m maximum thickness) consists largely of chalk formed from the skeletons (**coccoliths**) of planktonic calcareous algae. Similar algae presently live in clear tropical waters at depths between 50 and 200 m. Calcium carbonate does not accumulate on the sea floor at depths in excess of about 4000 m because it dissolves as it sinks. The coccoliths in the chalk do not appear to have suffered any solution so a depth of deposition not greater than about 600 m is indicated. At the same time the absence of structures caused by strong currents and the presence of sponges whose distribution is controlled by depth indicate a water depth in excess of about 100 m. Flints are common in the chalk. They lie in strings mostly parallel to the bedding. The flints were probably derived from the solution and precipitation of siliceous organic remains such as sponge spicules.

The Lower Chalk generally has a base consisting of condensed, glauconitic sandy marls. Above this, the beds are cyclic with marls alternating with grey chalk (Chalk Marl) indicating repeated influx of muds into the area of deposition. In areas where marls are absent the Lower Chalk contains muddy impurities which give it a grey colour (Grey Chalk). Flints are not common in the Lower Chalk. The Middle Chalk consists mostly of white chalk with flints in the top 10 m or so. The Upper Chalk consists of thick white chalk with flints. The chalk is

EARTH HISTORY

1.41 *Distribution of Upper Cretaceous rocks.*

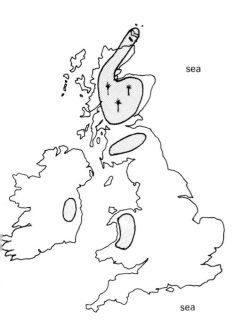

sea

sea

.42 Palaeogeography of Upper Cretaceous times.

relatively soft in southern England but it is hard in Yorkshire. In Northern Ireland and west Scotland the Upper Cretaceous is unconformable on older rocks. It consists of a lower part of glauconitic sandstones and an upper part of hard white chalk.

The end of the Cretaceous, which also marks the end of the Mesozoic, saw the extinction of numerous types of organism. (One estimate is that 75 percent of all species disappeared.) The animals which became extinct include dinosaurs, pterosaurs, ichthyosaurs, plesiosaurs, ammonites and rudists. Belemnites just survived the Cretaceous but became extinct soon after while foraminifera were greatly reduced in number. Earlier in the Cretaceous, flowering plants had become dominant over gymnosperms and placental mammals and modern bony fish had evolved. Extinctions occurred both on land and in the sea and shallow marine communities were strongly affected while fresh water communities were hardly changed. On land, while many small animals died out no type of animal heavier than 25 kg survived. Again, extinctions were very selective. Crocodiles survived while other reptiles in similar habitats died out.

Suggestions to account for the numerous extinctions include climatic changes caused by variation in the Sun's radiation. Blanketing of the Earth by volcanic dust could have excluded light so plants would have died and animals would have been left without food. It has also been suggested that a major regression of the sea at the end of the Cretaceous reduced the area of shelf seas bringing severe competition for available niches so that the least adaptable organisms died out. On land, dinosaurs may have succumbed to disease or they may have been unable to compete with mammals. Perhaps, too, dinosaurs could not adapt to the change of vegetation from gymnosperms and ferns to flowering plants.

A recent explanation of how the major extinctions came about is based on the discovery of a thin but widespread iridium-rich layer separating the Cretaceous and the overlying Tertiary. It has been suggested that this layer resulted from the impact of an asteroid about 10 km in diameter. Such an impact would have produced huge quantities of dust which would have blotted out the Sun. The photosynthesis of land plants and marine phytoplankton would have been much reduced and food webs would have collapsed. Like the other hypotheses this suggestion would appear to account for only part of the evidence, e.g. it would not explain why many species in shelf seas became extinct while freshwater communities remained almost unaffected.

Cainozoic era (65 Ma–present)

The **Cainozoic era** consists of the **Tertiary** (65–2.5 Ma) and **Quaternary** (2.5 Ma–present) **periods**. The Tertiary saw the opening of the north Atlantic with associated igneous activity in west Britain. At the start of the Tertiary, Britain lay between about 40 and 50° north of the equator and it reached its present latitude towards the end of the Tertiary. Much of Britain was uplifted at the end of the Cretaceous and deposition was largely restricted to southern England and the North Sea and other offshore basins. During the Tertiary, mammals and flowering plants evolved and diversified. Early man appeared at the end of the period. During the Quaternary most of Britain was periodically covered by ice spreading from the north. Many large mammals became extinct and modern man evolved.

Tertiary period (65–2.5 Ma ago)

Large-scale igneous activity at the start of the Tertiary heralded the separation of Greenland and Britain and the opening of the north Atlantic. In Britain, the centres of igneous activity lie in a band from Lundy in the Bristol

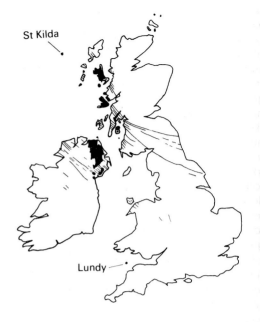

11.44 Distribution of Tertiary igneous rocks.

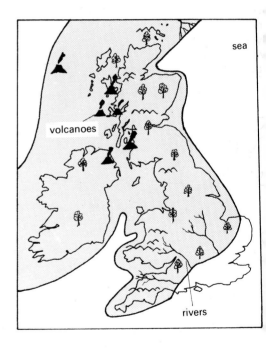

11.45 Palaeogeography of Tertiary times.

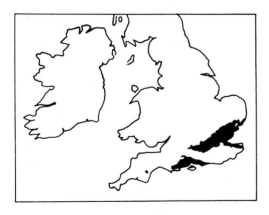

11.43 Distribution of Tertiary sedimentary rocks.

EARTH HISTORY

hannel, north through north-east Ireland into
rest Scotland (figure 11.44). Activity followed
1e general pattern of eruption of flood basalts
ollowed by the intrusion of plutonic rocks
,hich were, in turn, followed by the intrusion
f north-west—south-east dyke swarms.
1neous activity was on a very large scale. In
1e Hebrides lavas are about 2000 m thick. In
kye the volume of basic plutons may be as
1uch as 3500 km³ and the intense heat melted
'recambrian Lewisian Gneiss and Torridonian
'rkose and intruded them as granite. When the
orth Atlantic opened 60 Ma ago Britain lay
lose to the line of separation. The oceanic ridge
'eveloped in a north-east—south-west direc-
on and as Britain moved away from the ridge
1neous activity declined and died out about
5 Ma ago. The question of why the British
'ertiary Igneous Province has a general north–
'outh trend while the Tertiary dykes have a
eneral north-west—south-east trend has not
'een fully answered. Possibly, the igneous
:ctivity in Britain was located above a zone of
'rustal weakness which may have been a failed
'ceanic ridge or a line of fracture at a high
ngle to the ridge. The fractures into which the
ykes were intruded may have resulted from
,visting movements caused by more rapid sea-
oor spreading to the south of the British area.

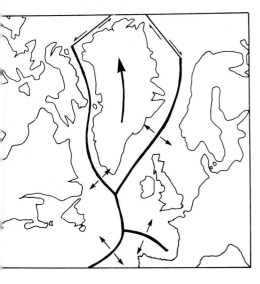

1.46 *Opening of the North Atlantic at the begin-*
ning of the Tertiary.

Most of Britain was uplifted to become land
at the start of the Tertiary and Lower Tertiary
sediments were deposited in basins on the
surrounding sea floor and in parts of southern
England (figure 11.45). In south-east England
deposits in the London–Hampshire Basin show
cycles of coastal plain sediments lying unconformably on the Chalk. In the east of the London
Basin the base of the Tertiary consists of marine,
glauconitic sandstones (the **Thanet Beds**) which
thin and disappear towards the west. The Thanet
Beds are overlapped by the **Woolwich Beds**. The
Woolwich Beds are marine in the east and they
grade through estuarine deposits into the non-
marine **Reading Beds** in the west. The Reading
Beds are yellow and white sands and mottled
clays deposited by rivers from the west. The
Woolwich and Reading Beds are overlain by
the blue-grey, marine **London Clay** deposited
during the most extensive transgression of the
Lower Tertiary. In the west the London Clay
grades up into the sandy **Bagshot Beds** which
were again deposited by rivers from the west.
The London Basin has only the lower part
(**Eocene**) of the Lower Tertiary. In the Hampshire
Basin there is a more complete sequence of
Lower Tertiary sediments (Eocene and early
Oligocene) again showing repeated cycles of
marine and non-marine deposition. The base
of the Tertiary consists of the non-marine Reading Beds overlain by the marine London Clay.
The London Clay is again overlain by the non-
marine Bagshot Beds. Above the Bagshot Beds
are the sands and clays of the **Bracklesham Beds**
which are mostly marine in the east and non-
marine in the west. The Bracklesham Beds are
followed by the glauconitic sands and clays of
the marine **Barton Beds**. Above the Barton Beds
come the freshwater clays, marls and limestones of the lower **Headon Beds**. Yet another
marine transgression deposited the middle
Headon Beds. These marine beds are overlain
by another two sets of non-marine and marine
beds.

Erosion of the Devon and Cornwall areas
supplied a great deal of sediment to the Hampshire Basin and to the Oligocene Bovey Tracey
and Petrockstow Basins of Devon. The Bovey
Tracey and Petrockstow Basins developed
along a major tear fault (the Sticklepath-Lust-
leigh Fault) and they were filled by lake and
river deposits which include lignites and valuable kaolinitic clays.

Indications of climatic conditions during the
Lower Tertiary are derived from the fossil

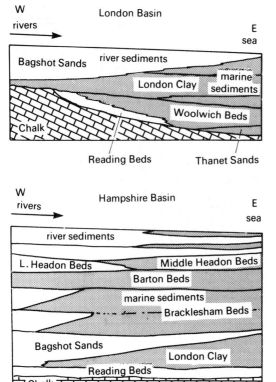

11.47 *Lower Tertiary cycles of sedimentation in the London and Hampshire Basins. Each cycle consists of marine beds in the east and non-marine beds in the west.*

remains of plants and animals of types which survive today. About half of the early Tertiary plant fossils belong to forms presently found only in the tropics while among the rest of the plant fossils about 10 percent are of forms now found only outside the tropics. Such a mixed flora may indicate a Lower Tertiary geography of tropical lowlands backed by cool highlands. Alternatively, the climate may have been of a hot seasonal type with the present tropical forms growing in damp lowlands while the non-tropical forms grew in drier but not necessarily higher areas. A warm climate is also indicated by fossils of animals such as crocodiles and by the presence of lateritic boles (fossil soils) between lava flows in the volcanic regions. The kaolinite of the deposits of Bovey Tracey and Petrockstow in Devon may have been partly derived from the lateritic weathering of granite feldspars.

During the Upper Tertiary (Miocene and Pliocene) Britain drifted about 10° further north to reach its present latitude and the climate was generally colder and drier than during the Lower Tertiary. The Alpine orogeny reached its peak at the end of the Eocene and the beginning of the Oligocene but late Alpine movements in the early Miocene lifted all of Britain above sea level. At this time Britain probably developed a tilt from west to east which saw the establishment of the predominant east-flowing river systems. Miocene movements also produced east-west trending folds in southern England. Miocene deposits are not found on mainland Britain and only a small deposit of marine late Pliocene (30 m thick) is found in East Anglia. The beds (the **Coralline Crag**) consist of sands with bivalves, gastropods and brachiopods deposited by strong currents in warm, shallow coastal waters. Despite its name, the Coralline Crag has no corals. It contains bryozoa which were originally identified as corals.

While Tertiary sedimentation was of restricted extent on mainland Britain, thick deposits formed on parts of the surrounding sea floor. The North Sea has more than 3000 m of Tertiary sandstones and mudstones. Tuffs are found in parts of the Lower Tertiary. Thick deposits are also found in numerous other basins such as those of the Western Approaches and Celtic Sea.

Quaternary period (2.5 Ma–present)

The Quaternary period is divided into the **Pleistocene** (2.5 Ma–10 000 a ago) and **Holocene** (10 000 a–present). The Pleistocene or Ice Age marked the climax of a time of rapid climatic cooling which had begun about 15 Ma ago during the late Tertiary. How temperatures changed can be estimated from study of pollen and other plant remains, from beetles and snails, from foraminifera in deep sea cores and from the ratios of $^{18}O/^{16}O$ in shells and in ice (figures 11.48 and 11.49). At low temperatures organisms have higher $^{18}O/^{16}O$ ratios than at high temperatures. In addition, water containing ^{16}O evaporates more readily than water containing ^{18}O. On precipitation, this water may be stored as glacier ice which develops a high $^{16}O/^{18}O$ ratio while the ocean water develops a high $^{18}O/^{16}O$ ratio. Climatic studies indicate the formation of an ice sheet in Antarctica about 6 Ma ago. In Europe the early part of the Pleistocene (2.5

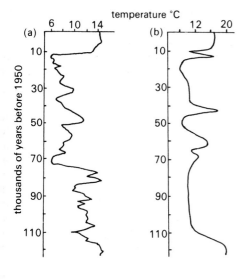

temperature °C

1.48 (a) Temperature of the North Atlantic for the last 125 000 years derived from foraminiferal data.
(b) Average British July temperatures derived from beetle data.

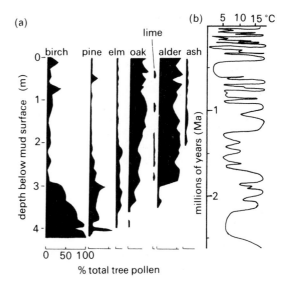

% total tree pollen

11.49 (a) Tree pollen diagram for Blelham Tarn, English Lake District. The amount of pollen from each tree is expressed as a percentage of the total tree pollen. What is the main climatic change indicated by this diagram?
(b) Average summer temperatures of Europe for the last 2.6 Ma derived from pollen data.

0.6 Ma ago) was a time of mainly temperate climate. Major glaciations took place during the latter part (0.6 Ma–10 000 a ago). Between the cold **glacial** periods were temperate **interglacials** similar to our present climate. **Interstadials** are short or cool interglacials. The Pleistocene was also a time when the positions of shore-lines frequently changed. This was due to changing sea levels as ice sheets formed and melted and to isostatic depression and recovery of the land as huge masses of ice were added and removed.

Reconstruction of Pleistocene stratigraphy is difficult because glaciation tends to destroy the marks of earlier events. The most complete sequence is found between the Wash and the Thames where the base of the Pleistocene is marked by the coastal **Red Crag** deposits (2.5 Ma old). These deposits contain pollen and mollusc shells indicative of a climate much colder than the warm temperate climate indicated by the underlying Pliocene Coralline Crag. The Red Crag deposits are followed unconformably by marine and estuarine silts, clays and shelly sands about 2.0–1.6 Ma old deposited under alternating temperate and cold conditions. There was then a gap in deposition till

11.50 Location of marine Pleistocene deposits.

about 600 000 years ago when the temperate **Icenian Crag** deposits were formed during a transgression which left estuarine and shallow marine sands and clays. The Icenian Crag is overlain by beach gravels spreading towards the south-east. Above the beach deposits come sediments indicative of the first of the four glaciations (the **Beestonian**) to affect Britain. In

East Anglia and Essex sands and gravels were deposited under periglacial conditions by a large east-flowing river north of the present Thames. The Beestonian is also represented by till in the Midlands. The climate then became temperate again and **Cromerian** silts, muds and peats were deposited under estuarine and fresh-water conditions. The Cromerian is followed by the glacial **Anglian** stage which consists of periglacial freshwater and estuarine deposits overlain by the **Lowestoft Till**. This till consists mostly of chalk and clay probably derived from the floor of the North Sea. In north-east Norfolk tills of the same age contain boulders derived from Scandinavia. The glacial Anglian deposits are overlain by the temperate **Hoxnian** carbonaceous lake silts and clays. In the Midlands the Hoxnian is overlain by **Wolstonian** till which contains erratics derived from Wales, north England and south Scotland (figure 11.51). The

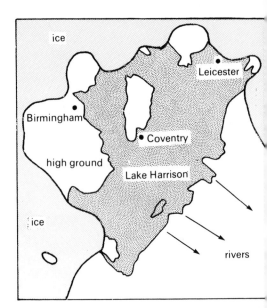

11.52 During part of Wolstonian times Lake Harrison occupied much of the Midlands. The lake existed for nearly 10 000 years.

Wolstonian ice blocked the Severn valley an dammed back a huge lake (Lake Harrison). Th ice touched on Devon and Cornwall and it ma have moved up the English Channel. Erratic on the floor of the English Channel cou possibly have fallen from icebergs. South of th ice front are periglacial features such as ston stripes and polygons and solifluction deposit The major Wolstonian glacial period was fo lowed by river gravels and clays of the temperat **Ipswichian** stage (128 000 years ago).

The history of the last (**Devensian**) glaciatio is well known since its landforms and deposit have changed little since their formation. Th Devensian began about 110 000 years ago bu thick ice sheets did not form until near the en of the stage and the ice reached its maximum thickness (about 2 km) and extent 17 000 year ago (figure 11.53). At this time sea level fe by about 120 m. The climate then began t warm up and by 14 500 years ago the ice wa restricted to highland areas. The ice probab disappeared soon after and sea level rose t a maximum extent about 11 000 years ag during the late-glacial transgression. The se covered isostatically depressed areas which a now raised to form land. The climate coole

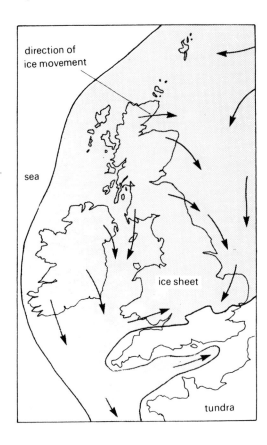

11.51 The extent of the Wolstonian ice sheet about 150 000 years ago.

EARTH HISTORY

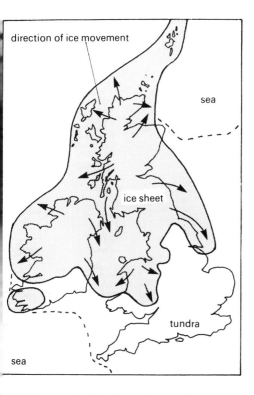

direction of ice movement

sea

ice sheet

tundra

sea

1.53 *The extent of the Devensian ice sheet about 17 000 years ago.*

5000 years ago. However, isostatic changes are still taking place. Most of Scotland is still rising at a rate of about 0.5 mm per year while much of the rest of Britain is sinking at a rate of about 1 mm per year.

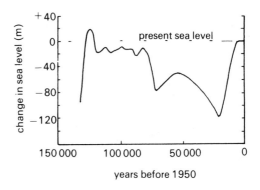

11.54 *Changes in sea level for the last 130 000 years.*

gain and glaciers spread about 10 500 years go during the Loch Lomond Readvance a short istance south of the Scottish Highlands. The ce finally disappeared soon after and Holocene r Recent times began about 10 000 years ago.

When the ice melted sea level rose by 120 ᄀ. Since the isostatic rise of the land was slower han the eustatic rise of sea level large areas vere flooded during the post-glacial **Flandrian ransgression**. The transgression, which eached its greatest extent about 7000 years go, flooded the southern North Sea and separ ted Britain from the continent. Isostatic uplift vas greatest in those areas where the thickest ce sheets had been located and the variable plift led to the formation of raised shorelines vhich slope away from the areas of maximum plift. Rises in sea level are shown by the resence of submerged forests and peat beds vhile rivers which had previously run on to what s now the continental shelf had their valleys rowned to form estuaries and rias. River ter aces such as those along the Thames provide vidence of rivers adjusting to changing sea evels. The sea reached its present level about

Many suggestions have been put forward to account for the cooling which caused the Ice Age. Some theories are based on changes taking place on Earth. Most of the heat at high latitudes is transferred from low latitudes by atmospheric and oceanic circulation. Heat trans fer could, therefore, be affected by the distri bution of land and sea. Ice could exist at the South Pole because there is a landmass which is too big to be warmed from the surrounding sea. At the North Pole ice could exist because the Arctic Ocean is almost land-locked so it is closed to warm ocean currents from the south. It has also been suggested that large-scale volcanism could produce dust which would prevent the Sun's heat from reaching the Earth's surface. The amount of carbon dioxide in the atmosphere can also affect the temperature. After penetrating the atmosphere the Sun's heat is absorbed by the Earth then re-radiated at a longer wavelength. Since this longer wave length can be absorbed by carbon dioxide the more carbon dioxide there is in the atmosphere the more heat is retained. At low carbon dioxide levels the Earth's surface temperature would fall.

Processes occurring outside the Earth include possible variations in the amount of radiation given off by the Sun. The Sun shows cyclic behaviour in sunspot and magnetic activity which in the short term show variation over 11 and 22 years, respectively, but which in the long term seem to have 200 or 400 year cycles. Between 1645 and 1715 there were no sunspots and Britain suffered very cold winters. The Sun's radiation could, then, vary enough to cause Ice Ages but, as yet, there is no proof that this is the case. Changes in the Sun's magnetism cause variations in cosmic ray intensity which, in turn, affect ^{14}C production in the Earth's atmosphere. It has been found that more ^{14}C is formed during times when the climate is cool. This again indicates that changes in the Sun may have caused climatic changes on Earth.

Variation in heating over the Earth could also be caused by variations in the Earth's behaviour as it orbits the Sun. Firstly, the shape of the orbit changes so the distance from the Earth to the Sun varies over a 100 000 year cycle. Secondly, like a non-vertical spinning top, the Earth's axis describes a circle or precesses over a period of about 21 000 years. Thirdly, as it precesses, the Earth's axis wobbles over a period of 40 000 years. A Yugoslavian geophysicist called Milutin Milankovitch analysed these types of cyclic behaviour and showed that their interplay could produce repeated warm and cold periods. The calculated Milankovitch cycles match up very well with variations of [18]O in marine fossils suggesting that cyclic behaviour in the Earth's orbit could cause climatic variations over periods of between 20 000 and 120 000 years. The Milankovitch theory can explain why ice sheets wax and wane but does not explain why the Earth has suffered Ice Ages at other times such as during the Precambrian and Permo- Carboniferous. Possibly, the origins of Ice Ages lie in long term astronomical cycles, e.g. it has been suggested that, during its 225 Ma revolution round the galaxy, the Solar System passes through dusty areas of space which reduce the amount of heat reaching the Earth from the Sun.

It is probable that we are living in an interglacial. Sea level is presently rising at the rate of about 1 mm a year and if our present ice sheets melted completely sea level would rise by about 60 m so flooding many of the world's most populous areas. The rise in temperature necessary to cause the ice to melt could come from our raising the carbon dioxide level of the atmosphere by burning fossil fuels. This could produce a 'greenhouse effect' and allow the atmosphere to retain more of the Sun's heat. Calculations based on future Milankovitch cycles indicate that ice sheets will return to cover Britain in about 50 000 years. The cooling may have already begun. The Earth's climate warmed up from the time of the Little Ice Age of the 16th to the 19th centuries but since the 1940s the climate has been slowly cooling. It remains to be seen if this trend will continue.

EARTH RESOURCES

Earth resources are natural materials or sources of energy which we find useful. Resources such as wood, water and solar energy are described as **renewable** because they replace themselves over fairly short intervals. Resources such as coal and oil are **non-renewable** because they can be extracted and used only once. **Reserves** are a measure of the quantity of a material available for use. **Extractable** or **recoverable** reserves are those which can be economically extracted. **Potential** reserves cannot be economically extracted.

Resources such as building stone, sand and gravel are relatively inexpensive. Because of this they are not generally transported very far and they are described as being of **high place value**. On the other hand, expensive materials such as copper, oil and diamonds are worth transporting over long distances. Because of this they are said to have a **low place value**.

Metals

An **ore** is a rock or material which can be profitably mined for the purpose of metal extraction. Ore consists of worthless **gangue minerals** such as quartz and calcite and useful **ore minerals** which are often sulphides, oxides and carbonates (table 12.1). Compounds such as these can be broken down fairly easily by industrial processes to separate the required metals. The **grade** of an ore is the percentage of metal which it contains. **Cut-off grade** is the lowest grade which can be profitably mined (table 12.2). For any metal the cut-off grade depends on economic factors, e.g. iron is a relatively cheap metal so ores with less than about 25 percent iron are not worth mining. On the other hand, tin can be extracted profitably from ore which contains as little as about 0.5 percent tin. The exhaustion of rich or **high grade** ores leads to a progressive lowering of cut-off grade so large-volume **low grade** ores

METAL	MAIN ORE MINERALS
Aluminium	Gibbsite $Al(OH)_3$; diaspore $AlO(OH)$
Chromium	Chromite $FeCr_2O_4$
Copper	Chalcopyrite $CuFeS_2$; chalcocite Cu_2S; bornite Cu_5FeS_4; malachite $Cu_2CO_3(OH)_2$; azurite $Cu_3(CO_3)_2(OH)_2$; chrysocolla $CuSiO_3.2H_2O$
Gold	Native gold
Iron	Haematite Fe_2O_3; magnetite Fe_3O_4; goethite $FeO.OH$; limonite $FeO.OH.nH_2O$; chamosite $Fe_6Si_4O_{10}(OH)_8$; siderite $FeCO_3$
Lead	Galena PbS
Manganese	Pyrolusite MnO_2
Mercury	Cinnabar HgS
Nickel	Pentlandite $(NiFe)S$; garnierite $Ni_3Si_2O_5(OH)_4$
Silver	Native silver; argentite Ag_2S
Tin	Cassiterite SnO_2
Titanium	Rutile TiO_2; ilmenite $FeTiO_3$
Tungsten	Wolframite $FeWO_4$; scheelite $CaWO_4$
Uranium	Uraninite (pitchblende) UO_2
Zinc	Sphalerite ZnS

Table 12.1   Common ore minerals

become economically extractable. Since the turn of the century the cut-off grade for copper ores has fallen from about 3 percent to about 0.4 percent.

Unit 12

METAL	AVERAGE PERCENTAGE OF METAL IN CRUST	LOWEST ECONOMIC ORE GRADE (CUT-OFF GRADE) % METAL	NUMBER OF TIMES METAL MUST BE CONCENTRATED ABOVE AVERAGE TO REACH CUT-OFF GRADE
Aluminium	8.1	30	3.75
Copper	0.005 5	0.4	73
Gold	0.000 000 4	0.000 01	25
Iron	5.0	25	5
Lead	0.001 3	4	3077
Nickel	0.007 5	0.5	67
Mercury	0.000 008	0.2	25000
Tin	0.00 2	0.5	2500
Uranium	0.000 18	0.1	556
Zinc	0.007	4.0	571

Table 12.2 Concentration of some metals in the Earth's crust

Formation of ores by internal processes (*see* table 12.3)

In ultrabasic and basic magmas, ore minerals such as magnetite, Fe_3O_4, chromite, $FeCr_2O_4$, and ilmenite, $FeTiO_3$, crystallize early. Because they are denser than the magma these minerals may sink to form layers at the bottom of the magma chamber. Such layers are said to have formed by **magmatic segregation**. The chromite- and magnetite-rich layers of the Bushveld gabbro intrusion in South Africa have formed in this way. Another type of magmatic segregation in basic magmas involves the separation and sinking of dense liquids rich in oxides or sulphides of iron, nickel and copper. The liquid may crystallize between the silicate minerals or it may be squeezed into fractures in the rock beside the magma chamber. The Swedish magnetite deposits and the nickel-copper deposits of Norway and Sudbury, Canada, have apparently formed in this way. Another deposit of this type is the Merensky Reef of the Bushveld intrusion. It consists of sulphides of iron, nickel and copper along with chromite, platinum and gold (figure 12.1).

Magmas may give off water rich in chloride and fluoride ions which can react with and replace minerals in the surrounding rocks. This process is called **contact metasomatism** and it tends to be associated with acidic and intermediate igneous rocks since their magmas contain more water than basic magmas. The fluids are acidic so they bring about the most marked changes in limestones. Deposits formed in this way are small but they may be of high grade. Ore minerals present include oxides of iron and sulphides of copper, lead and zinc. The deposit at Iron Springs, Utah, has formed by contact metasomatism. Here, a limestone has been largely replaced by ore rich in magnetite and haematite.

Much of the water present in granitic magma may remain to form a watery, silicate-poor melt after most of the silicate minerals have crystallized. This fluid contains elements which have been unable (because of their ionic radii or charges) to enter the crystal lattices of feldspar, quartz or mica. The watery melt may crystallize as **pegmatite** veins in fissures at the edge of the granite or in the surrounding rock. Sulphides are not common in pegmatites. The ore minerals, which often contain valuable rare elements, are mostly oxides and silicates such as beryl, $Be_3Al_2(SiO_3)_6$, zircon, $ZrSiO_4$, cassiterite, SnO_2, and uraninite, UO_2.

Hydrothermal deposits are formed at temperatures up to about 600°C by hot watery solutions called **brines**. The brines may deposit mineral **veins** as they migrate along joints or fault planes (figure 12.2). The Cornish tin deposits are of this type. In Britain, hydrothermal ores are also found in places such as the Pennines, the Peak District and the Lead Hills of southern Scotland. Sometimes, the ore is **disseminated** or spread in fine fractures through an intrusive igneous rock. The porphyry copper deposits of south-west USA, the western Andes and Papua New Guinea are of this type. Porphyry is porphyritic diorite or granodiorite.

The temperatures of the brine which deposit the ores can be estimated in two ways. Firstly, silver ions substitute to a limited extent for lead

272

ORES FORMED BY INTERNAL PROCESSES

TYPE OF DEPOSIT	METHOD OF FORMATION	EXAMPLES OF DEPOSITS
HYDROTHERMAL	Deposited from hot, watery solutions. The water can come from magma, from sedimentary rocks, from the surface or from rocks being metamorphosed. Ore minerals found in veins or filling fine cracks in the rock	Porphyry copper deposits. Tin—copper—tungsten deposits of Cornwall. Lead—zinc deposits of the Pennines
MAGMATIC SEGREGATION	Sinking of early-formed ore minerals to the floor of a basic magma chamber	Chromite and magnetite layers of the Bushveld Intrusion, South Africa
	Formed by separation and sinking of sulphide and oxide liquids from basic magmas. The liquids crystallize between silicate minerals or they are injected into cracks in the rock around the intrusion	Copper—nickel deposits of Sudbury, Canada
PEGMATITE	Deposited from watery silicate melts left after most of an acidic magma has crystallized. Found in fissures in the edge of the intrusion or in the rock around the intrusion	Uranium deposits of Bancroft, Canada. Lithium deposits of Bikita, Zimbabwe
CONTACT METASOMATIC (PYROMETA-SOMATIC)	Rocks next to an intrusion are replaced by material from the magma	Magnetite deposits of Iron Springs, Utah. Copper deposits of Mackay, Idaho

ORES FORMED BY SURFACE PRESSURES

TYPE OF DEPOSIT	METHOD OF FORMATION	EXAMPLES OF DEPOSITS
SEDIMENTARY	Placer deposits: tough, dense minerals are concentrated during deposition	Tin deposits of Malaysia. Gold deposits of Alaska, Yukon, California, Australia and Siberia
	Precipitates: in some sedimentary environments ore minerals are precipitated chemically or biochemically	Precambrian banded iron formations. Iron deposits of Northamptonshire. Copper—lead—zinc of Kupferschiefer, Germany. Copper deposits of Zambia.
RESIDUAL	Soluble substances are removed by leaching to leave surface concentrations of insoluble material	Bauxite of Jamaica and Guyana. Nickel deposits of New Caledonia
SECONDARY ENRICHMENT	Soluble elements leached from the top part of an ore body are precipitated around the level of the water table	Copper deposit of Miami, Arizona

Table 12.3 Types of ore deposit

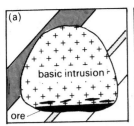

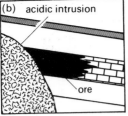

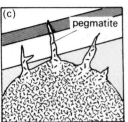

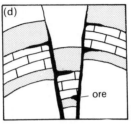

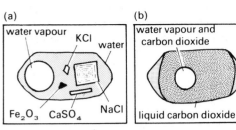

12.3 Fluid inclusions in the minerals of hydrothermal veins contain samples of the brine from which the minerals were deposited.
(a) contains vapour (unshaded), water (shaded) and crystals which are mostly salts.
(b) contains vapour (unshaded) surrounded by liquid carbon dioxide. Water occupies the ends of the inclusion.

12.1 Ore formation by internal processes.
(a) Magmatic segregation. Ore minerals sink to the floor of a magma chamber.
(b) Contact metasomatism. Ore minerals replace rock close to a magma.
(c) Pegmatites. Ore minerals are contained in pegmatites crystallised from the late fluids of a magma.
(d) Hydrothermal deposits. Ores are deposited by brines moving along fault or joint planes.

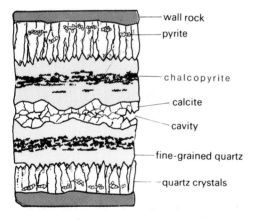

12.2 Section through a hydrothermal vein.

in galena and the degree of substitution increases with increased temperature. Measuring the silver content of galena gives a minimum temperature for ore formation. Secondly, minerals in hydrothermal veins may contain minute **fluid inclusions**. These are drops of the original brine trapped during crystallization. An inclusion may contain salt crystals, water and a gas bubble which have separated from the hydrothermal brine as it cooled (figure 12.3). If the fluid inclusion is heated, the salt and gas go back into solution to form a single liquid which fills the cavity in the crystal. The temperature at which a single phase is formed indicates the temperature of the brine at the time of its inclusion.

Hydrothermal brines can be formed in different ways, e.g. the solutions may come from deeply buried sediments. The hydrothermal deposits of the south Pennines appear to have been formed by such solutions. The ores lie in east–west veins in Carboniferous limestone on the eastern limb of the Pennine anticline. Fluid inclusion studies indicate temperatures of formation increasing towards a maximum of about 150°C in the east. It would appear that the hydrothermal fluids have come from the North Sea sedimentary basin. The average geothermal gradient is 30°C per kilometre so burial of at least 5 km under conditions of average heat flow would be necessary to produce the hydrothermal brines. The brines appear to have been connate water sqeezed out by the pressure of the overlying sediments. The brines then seem to have migrated up-dip from the North Sea area towards the Pennines depositing galena and sphalerite along with the gangue minerals fluorite, baryte, quartz and calcite.

The heat to produce hydrothermal solutions may come from igneous intrusions. The water could come from various sources. Some could be meteoric water which has worked its way down from the surface; some could be connate water expelled from sediments by heating; some could be removed from rocks by metamorphism and some could come from the magma itself. Heat from an intrusion sets up convection currents in the water which then rises through fissures above the intrusion cooling and depositing minerals as it goes (figure 12.4). Hydrothermal deposits associated with intrusions very often contain sulphides whose metals have probably been dissolved from the surrounding rock by the circulating brines. Since sulphides are extremely insoluble it would appear that the metals are not carried as sulphides in solution.

The probable nature of hydrothermal brines has been found by the interception of hot salty solutions during drilling operations. An example of what could be a brine was discovered near the Salton Sea, California, in 1962 during drilling to find a source of geothermal power. This brine deposited minerals containing silver, copper, arsenic, bismuth, lead and antimony in the drill pipes. Table 12.4 shows some of the constituents of Salton Sea brine, ocean water and fluid inclusions. You can see that while the Salton Sea brine has a concentration of dissolved materials about seven times that of sea water, its sulphur content is very low. This indicates that the metals are carried not as sulphides but mostly as chlorides. For sulphides to be deposited the metal chlorides must come into contact with a source of sulphur, e.g. sphalerite could be formed by this reaction:

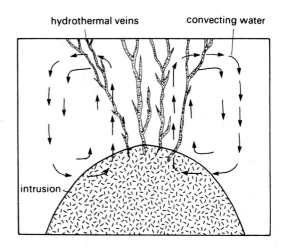

12.4 Convecting water above an intrusion deposits hydrothermal veins.

zinc chloride + hydrogen sulphide → zinc sulphide + hydrochloric acid

(in brine)   (in rock)   (sphalerite)

SUBSTANCE PRESENT	CONCENTRATION — PARTS PER THOUSAND		
	Salton Sea brine	Ocean water	Fluid inclusion
Calcium	28	0.4	18
Copper	0.008	trace	0.15
Potassium	17.5	0.4	2.7
Sodium	50.4	10.6	57.1
Chloride	155	19	124
Hydrogen sulphide	0.016	Trace	Trace
Sulphate	0.005	2.6	3.3
SALINITY	About 25%	About 3.5%	May be over 50%

Table 12.4 Compositions of Salton Sea brine, ocean water and a fluid inclusion

Precipitation is helped by high concentrations of sulphur to react with the chlorides and by the presence of rocks which can react with and remove the hydrochloric acid. For this reason, hydrothermal ores are often found in limestones.

Cooling of the hydrothermal brine tends to cause precipitation of the ore minerals. Since the solubilities of the ions are different they tend to be precipitated at different temperatures. Because of this , hydrothermal ores are precipitated with the least soluble minerals nearest to the heat source and with the most soluble minerals furthest from the heat source, e.g. the Cornish deposits are associated with granite round which are overlapping zones of ore minerals giving an indication of temperature decrease away from the intrusion. Minerals such as cassiterite, SnO_2, and magnetite, Fe_3O_4, are precipitated at high temperatures; chalcopyrite, $CuFeS_2$, galena, PbS, and sphalerite, ZnS, are precipitated at medium temperatures; and pyrite, FeS_2, and cinnabar, HgS, are precipitated at low temperatures.

Formation of ores by surface processes
(*see table 12.3*)

When rocks are weathered some of their constituents may be dissolved and carried away in solution to be precipitated under different chemical conditions in another area. Almost all of the world's supply of iron comes from chemically precipitated ores the most important of which are the **banded iron formations**. These ores contain from 15–40 percent iron in the form of haematite, Fe_2O_3, which lies in thin layers alternating with chert. Banded iron formations were formed during the Precambrian when the atmosphere had a high content of carbon dioxide. The high solubility of CO_2 made the surface waters acidic and this allowed them to carry Fe^{2+} in solution. On reaching the sedimentary basin the Fe^{2+} was altered to Fe^{3+} by oxygen given off by photosynthesizing algae. The insoluble Fe^{3+} was then precipitated as haematite. The ores from banded iron formations are of low grade and they have to be upgraded into the form of pellets containing more than 60 percent iron before being fed

to the blast furnace. Banded iron formations are found on all continents. The best known deposits are those of Lake Superior, Labrador, Brazil and Western Australia.

No banded iron formations have formed since the Precambrian. Instead, the sedimentary iron ores, which may be oolitic like those of the Jurassic system in England, consist of chamosite (iron silicate), siderite, $FeCO_3$, and goethite, $FeO.OH$. These ironstones appear to have been chemically precipitated in shallow water under oxygen-poor or reducing conditions. The fact that ooliths of chamosite and siderite formed recently in places such as off the Niger delta suggests that the reducing conditions necessary for the transport of Fe^{2+} are caused by the presence of decaying organic matter. The iron may have been carried as $Fe^{2+}(OH^-)_2$ contained within very small (colloidal) particles of organic matter.

Sulphides of copper, lead and zinc also occur as sedimentary chemical precipitates. The copper deposits of Zaire, Zambia and the Kupferschiefer of Europe are of this type. The Kupferschiefer is a thin black shale laid down under strongly reducing conditions in the Permian Zechstein Sea. The metals may have been precipitated when their ions came into contact with hydrogen sulphide given off by bacteria living in the bottom muds of the sea. The source of the metals in the Kupferschiefer remains a problem because sea water appears to have a concentration of Cu, Pb and Zn much too low to allow the concentration of such an ore. However, in 1963 it was discovered that metalrich hydrothermal brines sometimes run out on to the floor of the Red Sea. Possibly, the metals in the Kupferschiefer were derived from similar brines on the floor of the Zechstein Sea. It should be noted, however, that the Red Sea sits astride a constructive plate margin which provides heat to make sea water move by convection through the sea-bed igneous rocks. The water dissolves metals from the rocks and the metals are precipitated when the brine from hydrothermal springs meets the cold, oxygenated sea water (figure 12.5). Perhaps a similar heat source was available for the Zechstein Sea.

An effect of chemical weathering is to remove soluble ,materials from a rock leaving behind insoluble **residual deposits** which may be sufficiently enriched in metal to constitute a workable ore. Among common elements, those which form the least soluble compounds are

276   EARTH RESOURCES

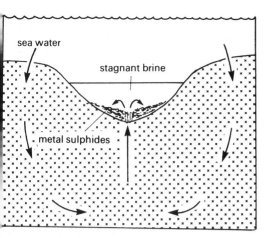

12.5 *Ore minerals are being deposited by hydrothermal brines running onto the floor of the Red Sea. The brines are formed by sea water circulating through the hot sea floor at a constructive margin.*

aluminium, iron and silicon. Under temperate conditions the insoluble end products of chemical weathering are hydrated iron oxides, clays and quartz. Under the hot, humid conditions of the tropics, however, clays are broken down into aluminium oxide and silicon dioxide. Ground water with a pH between 4 and 10 (not too acidic or too alkaline) dissolves SiO_2 much more effectively than it dissolves Al_2O_3. Such ground water can carry away the SiO_2 leaving the deposit enriched in minerals such

as gibbsite, $Al(OH)_3$ and diaspore, $AlO(OH)$. Deep tropical chemical weathering produces soils called laterites which are rich in insoluble hydrated oxides of iron and aluminium. **Bauxite**—a laterite with a high proportion of aluminium oxide—is the main ore of aluminium. Bauxites develop best on rocks such as granite and limestone which are poor in unwanted iron (figure 12.6).

Laterites which form on ultrabasic rocks may produce residual deposits of nickel. The nickel is leached from the laterite and concentrated as garnierite (hydrated nickel silicate) in a zone between the laterite and the unaltered ultrabasic rock (figure 12.7). Deposits of this type are mined in Cuba and New Caledonia.

Hydrothermal veins may develop high metal concentrations by **secondary enrichment** in a zone around the water table. Oxidizing conditions above the water table convert insoluble sulphides to soluble sulphates. The sulphates are carried downwards to be precipitated as sulphides on meeting reducing conditions at the water table (figure 12.8). For a vein with chalcopyrite the sequence of events is roughly as follows:

chalcopyrite + water + oxygen →
    copper sulphate + iron hydroxide

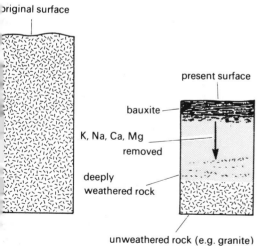

2.6 Residual deposit. Weathering and the removal of soluble materials leaves behind insoluble ores such as bauxite.

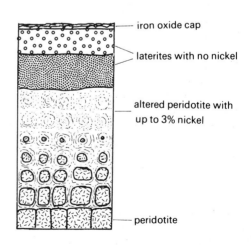

12.7 *Residual nickel deposit. On highly weathered ultrabasic rocks the nickel ore is concentrated between the laterite and the unaltered rock.*

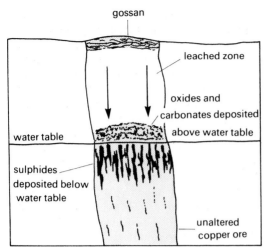

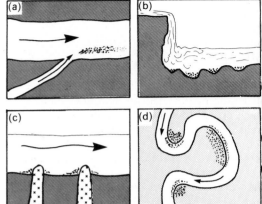

12.8 Formation of an ore deposit by secondary enrichment. Soluble minerals in a hydrothermal vein are carried down to be precipitated and concentrated in the area around the water table.

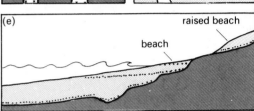

The copper is carried to lower levels in the vein and brightly coloured copper carbonates such as malachite and azurite may be precipitated in the slightly oxidizing conditions just above the water table. Most of the copper ions react with chalcopyrite below the water table to form a new sulphide called chalcocite.

copper ions	+	chalcopyrite	→	chalcocite	+	iron sulphide
Cu^{2+}	+	$CuFeS_2$	→	Cu_2S	+	FeS

The insoluble iron hydroxide remains at the ground surface as a brown residue called a **gossan**. A gossan or 'iron hat' may indicate the presence of underlying ores.

On being weathered from rock, resistant ore minerals may be transported and, by virtue of their high densities, they may be concentrated in the sand and gravel of **placer deposits**. Placers may be of fluvial or marine origin. The ore minerals found in placers include magnetite, ilmenite, chromite and cassiterite (figure 12.9). Placers also provide rich sources of diamonds, gold and platinum. Ancient placer deposits include the rich Precambrian gold-bearing conglomerates of the Witwatersrand, South Africa.

12.9 Conditions under which placer deposits may occur.
(a) Where a rapid tributary enters a slow river.
(b) In potholes in a stream bed.
(c) Against projections in a stream bed.
(d) On the insides of meanders.
(e) On a beach.

Finding ore bodies

In areas which have been well-surveyed most outcropping ore bodies have already been discovered. To find ore bodies which are in unexplored areas or which do not outcrop a combination of **remote sensing, geophysical, geochemical** and **geological** techniques are used.

Remote sensing techniques are those in which information is gathered by instruments mounted in aircraft or in satellites such as *Landsat* and *Seasat*, e.g. a good idea of the general geology of an area can be obtained from satellite and aerial photographs. Geophysical techniques for finding ores are mainly concerned with measuring the magnetic, electrical and radiometric properties of rocks. Aerial magnetic surveys can detect ore bodies containing minerals such as magnetite, ilmenite, pyrrhotite and haematite. These magnetic minerals are often found with other ore minerals. The electrical properties of an area suspected of containing ore can be measured in three ways. In the **line-electrode** method currents are passed into the ground between long electrodes. If an ore body is present it can be detected by the fact that it conducts the electricity better than the surrounding rock. The **self-potential** method depends on the fact that ore bodies may spontaneously generate currents. The **induced potential** method uses artificial currents which set up oxidation–reduction reactions in the ore. When the artificial current is switched off a detectable induced current continues to flow. Since some ore bodies conduct electricity they can be made to behave like radio aerials. Electromagnetic waves transmitted from an aeroplane can be received by the ore body and converted to electricity. This electricity produces its own electromagnetic waves which can then be detected by a receiver called a 'bird' towed behind the aeroplane.

Exploratory drilling for ore in Zimbabwe

Geochemical prospecting seeks unusually high concentrations (positive geochemical anomalies) of metals such as lead, zinc and copper in soils, river sediments, water and vegetation. Even if the metals have been dispersed to some extent by surface processes it may be possible to locate the ore body which is the source of the geochemical anomaly.

When a potentially economic ore body has been found detailed geological studies are undertaken. All possible sources of information are referred to including pre-existing maps and books, plans and other records. The size and shape of the ore body and the quantity and quality of the ore are found by sinking closely spaced boreholes.

Mining ores

At present, most ores are extracted by the **open-pit** or **open-cast** mining of large ore bodies which are often of low grade. For open-pit mining the ore has to be at the surface or covered by only a thin layer of worthless **overburden**. The largest open-pit mines are those working porphyry copper deposits; they may be about 7 km across and about 800 m deep. In such mines the ore is worked from a system of terraces or benches running round the walls of the pit. **Underground** mines are used to extract small, high grade ore bodies. The ore is extracted from excavations called **stopes** which are often driven upwards so the ore can fall to underlying horizontal **levels**. The ore is then collected, crushed and taken to the surface. The deepest underground workings are in South Africa where gold mines may be nearly 4 km deep.

Uses and production of metals

Iron

Iron is used to make industrial and agricultural machinery, motor vehicles, trains, ships, railways, oil-rigs, pipelines and weapons. It is also used in construction and in making cans, nails, wire, springs and many tools and implements. Usage of iron exceeds that of all other metals put together. World production is about 500 000 000 tonnes a year with the largest producers being USSR, Australia, USA, and Brazil. British iron ore production has fallen very

The Mount Tom Price iron ore mine, Western Australia.

The Mount Isa copper mine, Queensland.

rapidly in recent years. In 1972, ore production was about 9 000 000 tonnes while in 1981 it was only 730 000 tonnes (equivalent to about 190 000 tonnes of iron). Production comes almost entirely from the Jurassic ironstones of Lincoln and Humberside. In 1981, British iron consumption was about 20 000 000 tonnes.

Aluminium

Aluminium is used to make aircraft, the super-structures of ships, electric cables and parts of motor vehicles. It is also used for making cooking utensils, frames for windows and doors, foil, bottle tops and cans. World production of aluminium is about 15 000 000 tonnes a year with the largest producers of bauxite being Australia, Guinea and Jamaica. In 1981, British consumption of aluminium was about 450 000 tonnes.

Copper

Copper is used to make electric cables, pipes, coins, brass and bronze. World production is about 8 000 000 tonnes a year with the major producers being USA, USSR, Chile, Canada and Zambia. In 1981, Cornish mines produced about 600 tonnes of copper. British consumption is about 500 000 tonnes a year.

Zinc

Zinc is used as a coating for steel and in brass, die casting, dry batteries and building (roof cladding, flashing and gutters). Zinc oxide is used in ointments, cosmetics, rubber and paint. World zinc production is about 6 000 000 tonnes a year with the major producers being Canada, USSR, Peru and Australia. In 1981, Cornish mines produced 11 000 tonnes of zinc. In the same year British consumption was 240 000 tonnes.

EARTH RESOURCES

Tin

Tin is used to make tinplate for cans and in solder, bronze, type metal and Babbit metal. (Babbit metal is a low friction alloy used for bearings in turbines and pumps.) World production is about 240 000 tonnes a year with the major producers being Malaysia, Thailand, Indonesia and Bolivia. In 1981, Cornish mines produced 3700 tonnes of tin. This gave us about a third of our needs. Off the north Cornish coast, 500 tonnes of tin a year could be recovered by dredging waste from old mining operations.

Lead

Lead is used in batteries, for covering electric cables, for ammunition and for making insecticides. World production is about 3.6 million tonnes a year with the major producers being USSR, USA, Australia and Canada. In 1981, production from Durham and Derbyshire was 7000 tonnes while in the same year our consumption was about 270 000 tonnes.

Nickel

Nickel is alloyed with iron to make steel. It is also used in coins and for electroplating. World production is about 750 000 tonnes a year with the major producers being Canada, USSR, New Caledonia and Australia. In 1981, British consumption was 23 000 tonnes.

Chromium

Chromium is used to make stainless steel and for plating. World production is about 3 000 000 tonnes a year with the major producers being South Africa, USSR and Albania. In 1981, Britain's steel industry used 35 000 tonnes of chromium.

Manganese

Manganese is used to make steel and it is also alloyed with aluminium, copper and nickel. World production is about 9 000 000 tonnes a year with the largest producers being the USSR, South Africa and Brazil. In 1981, the British steel industry used about 260 000 tonnes of manganese ore.

Tungsten

Tungsten is used to make steel, as tungsten carbide for cutting tools and for electric light filaments. World production is about 50 000 tonnes a year with the major producers being China, USSR and USA. At present, Britain does not produce any tungsten to contribute to our needs of about 1000 tonnes a year. However, a large ore deposit on the southern edge of the Dartmoor granite is thought to hold about 40 000 tonnes of tungsten. Possibly, this deposit will soon be mined.

Gold

Gold provides the basis for currency and it is used in jewellery, dentistry, photography and medicine. World production is about 1200 tonnes a year with the major producers being South Africa and USSR.

Silver

Silver is used in photography and jewellery. World production is about 10 000 tonnes a year with the major producers being USSR, Mexico, Peru and Canada.

Mercury

Mercury is used to make amalgam for filling teeth and in making thermometers, electrical goods and pesticides. It is also used in the process of making sodium hydroxide and chlorine. World production is about 6500 tonnes a year with the main producers being USSR, Spain and USA.

Coal

Land plants which decay in the presence of oxygen decompose to give carbon dioxide and water. Under reducing conditions, however, decomposition is incomplete and **peat** is formed. Peat results from the partial decomposition of cellulose and the accumulation of resistant materials such as lignin and bacterial remains. (Lignin forms about 25 percent of wood.) Burial of the peat subjects it to increased pressure and temperature. **Coal** is formed as the peat is compressed and water and other volatiles are removed. It usually takes about 5 m of peat to form 1 m of coal. Because pressure and temperature increase with depth the type of coal which forms depends largely on the depth to which it has been buried. In general, the greater the depth of burial the higher the proportion of carbon and the lower the proportion of hydrogen, oxygen and nitrogen. The **rank** of a coal is the percentage of carbon which it contains and as depth of burial increases the rank of the coal increases (figure 12.10). The sequence of increasing rank is as follows:

$$\text{peat} \rightarrow \begin{array}{c}\text{lignite and}\\\text{brown coal}\end{array} \rightarrow \begin{array}{c}\text{bituminous}\\\text{coal}\end{array} \rightarrow \text{anthracite}$$

Oxygen is lost as carbon dioxide and water while hydrogen is lost as methane (natural gas). Note that oxygen changes much more rapidly than hydrogen with increasing rank because hydrogen is retained in hydrocarbons. Also, the heat producing quality or **calorific value** of a coal increases with rank (figure 12.11).

Lignite and **brown coal** look quite like hard peat but lignite contains recognizable plant fragments while brown coal does not. **Bituminous coal** consists of layers of dull and shiny coal. **Anthracite** is hard and shiny and it may be iridescent. Coal consists of three types of plant material called **macerals**. **Vitrinite** is transparent or translucent in thin section. It has been formed from woody tissue. **Exinite** consists of spore coats and the outer layers of stems and

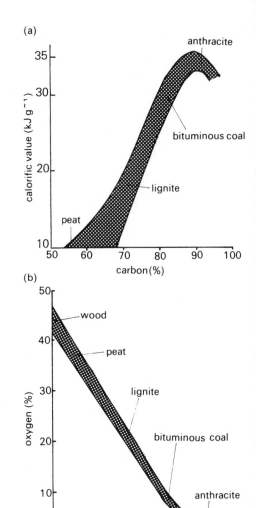

(a)

(b)

12.11 (a) Plot of calorific value of coal against rank.
(b) Plot of oxygen percentage of coal against rank.

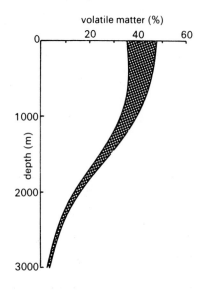

12.10 Increase in rank of coal with depth of burial.

leaves along with resins, waxes and algal frag ments. **Inertinite** is opaque in thin section. has formed from peat mud and from opaqu woody material which is dull and easily pov dered. In hand specimen, mixtures of thes materials give glassy **vitrite** which consist almost entirely of vitrinite; shiny **clarite** whic consists of vitrinite and exinite; and dull **duri** which consists of inertinite and exinite.

Cannel (candle) **coal** is a compact bituminou

coal which consists of peat mud and spores with some algal and fungal material. It may be waxy or resinous and, as its name suggests, it can be lit and burned like a candle. **Boghead coal** consists mainly of algal material and peat mud. Cannel and boghead coal have both formed as oozes or organic muds. They are very rich in volatiles and they were formerly used to produce gas and oil.

The compositions and calorific values of peat and coals are shown in table 12.5. Sometimes, coals are classified as **soft coals** (calorific value less than 24 kJ g⁻¹) and as **hard coals** (calorific values greater than 24 kJ g⁻¹). From the table, which coals would you classify as being hard and soft?

Coal mining

Economic coals are found in rocks from the Devonian to the Tertiary. Mesozoic and Tertiary coals tend to be lignitic because they have generally not been buried deeply enough to allow conversion to higher ranking coal. Palaeozoic coals, on the other hand, are generally of bituminous or higher rank. British coalfields (figure 12.12) lie almost entirely in Carboniferous rocks. The coals are generally bituminous except in South Wales and Kent where high-ranking anthracites are found. Where the coal-bearing rocks come to the surface the coalfield is said to be **exposed**. **Concealed** coalfields are covered by younger rocks (figure 12.13). Most worked seams in Britain are between 1 and 2 m thick. The seams constitute only between about one tenth and one thousandth of the coal-bearing rocks.

Mining is highly mechanized and it takes place by both open-cast and underground means. Open-cast mining can extract coal down to a depth of about 200 m. It is the best method of mining because the mine can be quickly

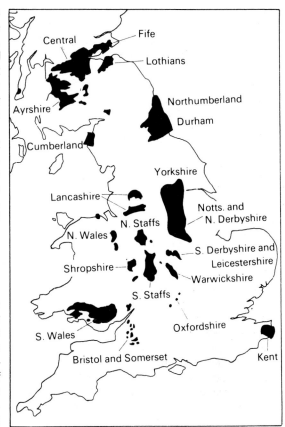

12.12 British coalfields.

brought into production and because 85-95 percent of the coal can be easily extracted by large electric shovels and dragline excavators. For bituminous coal, open-cast mining is profitable with overburden to coal ratios of about 18 : 1. With more valuable anthracites the overburden to coal ratio may be over 20 : 1.

In underground mines chain-hauled power loading machines cut and load coal on to conveyors. The coal faces are about 200 m long and the roof is held up by walking, power-

FUEL	COMPOSITION — WEIGHT %				CALORIFIC VALUE (kJg⁻¹)
	Carbon	Hydrogen	Nitrogen	Oxygen	
Peat	55.44	6.28	1.72	36.56	10
Lignite	72.95	5.24	1.31	20.50	20
Bituminous coal	84.24	5.55	1.52	8.69	30
Anthracite	93.50	2.81	0.97	2.72	34

Table 12.5 Compositions and calorific values of peat and coal

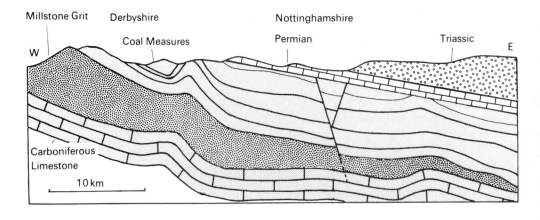

12.13 Section across the Derby-Notts Coalfield. The field is exposed in the west and concealed in the east.

Coal-cutting shearer in operation at Bullcliffe Colliery, Yorkshire.

A core extracted during exploratory drilling for coal.

Opencast coal mining, St Aidan's Mine, Yorkshire. The coal seam is exposed right centre. Mechanical shovels dig the coal while the large dragline excavator removes the overburden. There is a small drilling rig centre foreground.

EARTH RESOURCES

operated steel supports. Underground mining is less efficient than opencast mining because it takes a long time to bring a deep mine into production and because the workings are expensive to maintain and operate. Also, underground mines can only extract between 25 and 75 percent of the available coal.

Parts of coal seams may be lost because of **washouts** and a thick seam may split into a number of thin unworkable seams. A washout (figure 12.14a) is a sediment-filled river channel which has cut through the peat soon after its formation. Seam splitting is caused by different rates of subsidence over the area of peat deposition (figure 12.14b).

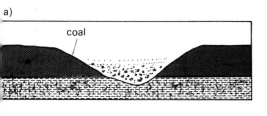

a)

coal

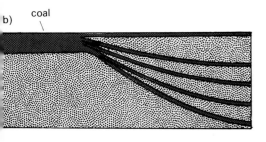

b) coal

12.14 (a) Washout in a coal seam caused by river erosion of peat.
(b) Seam splitting caused by uneven subsidence over the area of deposition

Coal production and reserves

World coal production is presently about 4 billion tonnes a year. (1 billion = 1000 million) Of this, about 3 billion tonnes are hard coal (bituminous to anthracite in rank) while the remainder is soft coal (brown coal and lignite). The major producers of hard coal are USA, USSR, China, Poland and Britain while the main producers of soft coal are East Germany, USSR and West Germany. Total world reserves of coal

are thought to be of the order of 11 500 billion tonnes. Of this, about 750 billion tonnes are thought to be recoverable.

British coal production is usually about 100 million tonnes a year (figure 12.15). About 15 million tonnes of this comes from open-cast workings. More than half of the anthracite produced comes from open-cast mines in south Wales. Total British coal reserves are thought to be about 160 billion tonnes with recoverable reserves being about 45 billion tonnes. How long will this coal last at present production rates?

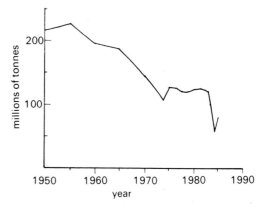

12.15 British coal production since 1950. Production fell rapidly during the miners' strike of 1984-85.

Petroleum

Petroleum may exist as gas (natural gas), liquid (crude oil) or solid (asphalt). Chemically it consists largely of hydrocarbons (compounds of hydrogen and carbon) with small amounts of sulphur, nitrogen and hydrogen (table 12.6).

Crude oils from different areas have different compositions, e.g. Middle East oil has a high sulphur content while North Sea oil is low in sulphur.

Petroleum is formed by the partial decomposition of planktonic marine organisms. The presence of plant pigments called porphyrins indicates that petroleum has formed from algae. Since porphyrins decompose at 200°C their presence also provides evidence that petroleum forms at relatively low temperatures. The planktonic remains accumulate on the floors of low energy marine basins where they are partly

ELEMENT	CRUDE OIL	NATURAL GAS
Carbon	83–87	65–80
Hydrogen	11–14	1–25
Sulphur	to 5.5	to 0.2
Nitrogen	to 1.5	1–15
Oxygen	to 4.5	—

Table 12.6 Compositions (weight %) of crude oil and natural gas

decomposed by anaerobic bacteria to form an organic mud called **sapropel**. Sapropel presently forming on the floor of the Black Sea has 35 percent organic matter. As the sapropel is buried to form a black shale it is compressed and heated and petroleum is produced. Shallow burial produces heavy crude oils while deep burial produces light crudes because the long chain hydrocarbon molecules are broken into smaller molecules by the increased temperatures and pressures. A rock in which petroleum forms is called a **source rock**. Compaction during burial squeezes the petroleum from the source rock and it migrates upslope towards the coarser grained near-shore sediments. The petroleum accumulates in the pore spaces of **reservoir rocks** such as sandstones and limestones. Reservoir rocks require to be both porous and permeable. Generally, the larger the pore spaces the more permeable the rock. Shales often have high porosities but they do not form reservoirs because their small pore spaces make them almost impermeable. Sandstones usually have porosities up to about 25 percent and they are highly permeable. Limestones

generally have porosities up to about 10 pe cent and they are fairly permeable. Howeve their porosities and permeabilities may b increased by the formation of cavities dissolve out by ground water. When petroleum collect in a reservoir rock it has to be sealed in b an overlying impermeable rock called a **cap roc** Cap rocks may be shales or evaporites suc as halite or gypsum.

Petroleum bearing geological structures ar called **traps**. Traps may be of structural o stratigraphic type. **Structural traps** result fro deformation and they include **anticlinal, fau** and **salt dome** traps (figure 12.16). Anticlina traps retain petroleum because the reservo and cap rocks have been bent up so the lo density oil and gas cannot rise any furthe Anticlinal traps hold about 80 percent of th world's known oil reserves. In a fault tra movement has brought a reservoir rock int contact with an impermeable rock across th fault. Fault traps are common but small an they hold only about one percent of the world oil. When salt is deeply buried it behaves plas tically and, being less dense than the overlyin rock, it tends to rise as a **salt plug** . Salt plug are usually about 1 km in diameter and the pierce and deform the overlying rocks to forr salt dome traps. Since the salt is impermeabl it seals in the petroleum of the pierced reservo rocks. Salt plugs may rise 10 000 m creatin a series of traps at various depths.

Lateral variation in sediments may produc lens- or wedge-shaped **stratigraphic traps. Ree traps** are mound-shaped fossilized coral reef which hold about three percent of the world

Microfossils (foraminiferan found during exploratory dr ling for oil.

EARTH RESOURCES

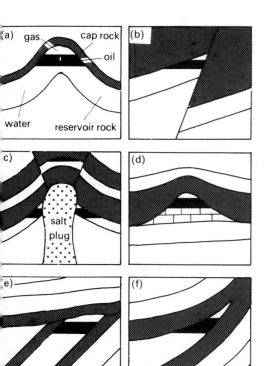

12.16 Petroleum traps:
(a) anticline trap;
(b) fault trap;
(c) salt dome traps;
(d) limestone reef trap;
(e) unconformity trap;
(f) wedge-edge trap.

Finding and producing oil

The first commercial oil well was drilled by Edwin Drake in Pennsylvania, USA in 1859. The well was sunk close to where oil had seeped to the surface. At present we do not have to rely on oil seeps to tell us where oil may be located. Structures capable of holding petroleum may be shown up by aerial photography and geological mapping. Gas seepages may be detected by analysis of air and sea water samples. Geophysical methods used to find potential traps include magnetic, gravity and seismic surveys. Magnetic surveys are carried out by towing a magnetometer behind an aeroplane. They show the thickness of sedimentary rocks because the underlying basement may contain igneous rocks magnetized in different directions. When traversed, the changes in magnetism show up sharply if the basement is near the surface but the changes are blurred if the basement is covered by thick sediments. Gravity surveys use a gravimeter to detect density variations in the underlying rocks. Low-density salt plugs can be located by this method. In a seismic survey sound waves produced by explosions, dropping heavy weights (thumpers)

oil. A stratigraphic trap may also be formed by the deposition of impermeable rock above a surface of unconformity so oil and gas are trapped in the permeable beds below the unconformity. **Unconformity traps** hold about four percent of the world's oil.

Petroleum bearing rocks are not evenly distributed through the geological column. About 85 percent of all crude oil comes from Mesozoic and Cainozoic rocks while the remainder is found in Palaeozoic rocks. There is also a relationship between depth and oil production. Since oil tends to migrate upwards about 90 percent of crude oil comes from rocks shallower than 2500 m.

Marathon Brae A *platform 250 km north-east of Aberdeen.*

Drilling operations on the Marathon Brae A *platform.*

Moving an oil rig through the Siberian forests.

or by detonating gas mixtures in an air gun or sleeve exploder are sent through the rocks. In built-up areas a vibrator truck is used. It carries a heavy weight which is vibrated against the ground. The sound waves are reflected by the underlying rock layers and the reflected waves are picked up by surface geophones. The pattern of wave reflections can be analysed to show the rock structures. Seismic surveys can be carried out very rapidly at sea because the geophones can be towed behind a ship (figure 12.17).

When a potential oil trap has been located drilling is undertaken to find if oil is present in economically viable quantities. The rotating drill bit is cooled and lubricated by drilling fluid (usually artificial mud) pumped down the inside of the drill pipe. As the mud returns to the surface between the drill pipe and the wall of the borehole it brings up broken rock. Instruments can be lowered into the well to measure properties such as radioactivity and resistivity. Sandstones and limestones are not very radioactive while black shales have high levels of

radioactivity. Resistivity or resistance to the flow of electricity rises if a rock is dry or if it contains oil or fresh water. If a rock contains salty water it can conduct electricity better so its resistivity falls. At critical points in a well continuous cores can be cut using a hollow core barrel. All of the information obtained during drilling is recorded as a detailed **well log** (figure 12.18).

When a well strikes oil the oil is pushed to the surface by the expansion of gas above the oil, by gas in the oil coming out of solution and by water pushing up from under the oil. This primary recovery is driven by natural pressure which soon dies away. To obtain more oil secondary recovery methods must be used, e.g. the oil may be pumped to the surface or water or gas may be injected to maintain pressure. Oil flow may also be aided by fracturing the oil-bearing rocks, by treating limestone with acid and by underground heating to reduce the viscosity of the oil. Such primary and secondary recovery methods only extract about one-third of the oil. To improve recovery still further other techniques (enhanced oil recovery) have

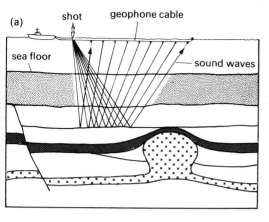

(a)

shot — geophone cable

sea floor

sound waves

(b)

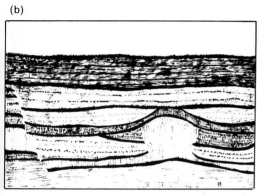

12.17 Seismic exploration at sea. Sound waves reflected from rock layers (a) show up the sites of potential oil traps (b).

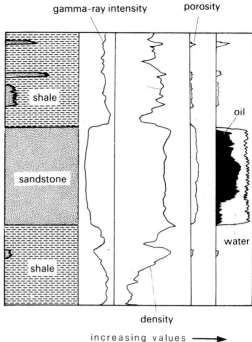

gamma-ray intensity — porosity

shale

sandstone

oil

water

shale

density

increasing values ——→

12.18 A well log shows the properties of rocks found during drilling.

lands. World oil reserves are thought to total about 500 billion tonnes of which about 90 billion tonnes are proven reserves. Total gas reserves are thought to be about 250 trillion cubic metres of which about 85 trillion cubic metres are proven. (A trillion is a million million.)

recently been devoloped. These methods include injecting steam to loosen the oil from the rock or carbon dioxide to make the oil flow more easily. Other chemicals may be injected to thicken the water so it pushes the oil more effectively or to lower the surface tension of the oil so it can pass through the rock more easily. Bacteria may also be used to release oil from the reservoir rock.

Production and reserves of petroleum

In 1982, world oil production was 2750 million tonnes while gas production was 1500 billion cubic metres. The major oil producers were USSR, Saudi Arabia and USA. The major gas producers were USA, USSR and the Nether-

British oil and gas

Natural gas was found by accident at Heathfield, Sussex in 1896. Since then many small oil and gas fields have been found in rocks dating from the Carboniferous to the Jurassic. In 1981, on-shore fields produced 225 000 tonnes of crude oil. The largest field at Wytch Farm in Dorset produced 145 000 tonnes.

Most of Britain's petroleum comes from off-shore fields (figures 12.21 and 12.22). During the Carboniferous most of the British area was relatively stable. The Permian, however, saw the initiation of sea-floor spreading movements which eventually led to the formation of the North Atlantic. The continuation of these move-ments through the Mesozoic produced major faults which broke up the British area into a series of rift troughs with intervening raised areas or 'highs' (figure 12.19). Mesozoic sedimentation was controlled by the movement of fault blocks but with the cessation of major faulting during the Cretaceous, Tertiary and Quaternary sedimentation took place in subsiding basins. The North Sea is separated into northern and southern sedimentary basins by the Mio North Sea—Fyn-Ringkobing High. In the southern North Sea gas from the underlying Coal Measures has risen to be trapped mostly in Basal Permian Sandstone capped by Permian (Zechstein) evaporites. In the northern North Sea most fields produce oil from sites in the Central and Viking Grabens. In these areas sediments of Permian age or younger reach thicknesses up to about 6000 m. Of this about 3500 m are Tertiary. Reservoir rocks are of various ages from Devonian in the Buchan Field to Tertiary in the Forties, Maureen and Montrose fields. The vast majority of fields, e.g. Brent, Ninian and Piper, produce oil from Jurassic sandstones. The main source rock is the Jurassic Kimmeridge Clay though some oil has also come from the Lower Cretaceous Speeton Clay. The Frigg gas field lies in Tertiary sandstones. Deep Mesozoic and Tertiary basins also lie to the south, west and north of Britain. As yet, development of these areas is in an early stage. In 1974 gas was found in the Triassic of the Morecambe Field in the Irish Sea Basin. Oil and gas have also been found in the Lower Cretaceous of the Irish Marathon Field in the north Celtic Sea Basin. Finds have also been made in the English Channel Basin, the Western Approaches Basin, the Porcupine Basin and the West Shetland Basin.

In 1981 oil production from off-shore fields reached 88 million tonnes with the major fields being Forties, Piper, Ninian and Brent. Gas production was about 40 billion cubic metres with the major fields being Leman Bank, Frigg, Indefatigable and Hewett. Oil reserves on the British continental shelf are thought to be between 2100 and 4300 million tonnes while gas reserves are thought to be between 1350 and 2250 billion cubic metres.

Oil shale

Oil shales are brown or black shales which are rich in hydrocarbons. They are flammable and of low density. Thin slices curl up when they are cut off with a knife. Oil shale bitumen is called **kerogen**. The oil is extracted by heating the shale in a retort at temperatures between about 430 and 650°C. Generally, a tonne of oil shale gives about a barrel of oil. Kerogen is derived from algal remains. With increasing kerogen, oil shale grades into boghead coal. Cannel coal resembles boghead coal but it is formed from spore and pollen remains.

Since the world's oil shales hold about 300 billion tonnes of oil they provide a very large potential resource. Unfortunately, the shale has to be heated so producing the oil is very expensive. The largest reserves of oil shale are in USA and Brazil. In Britain, oil shales are found in southern England (Jurassic) and in the Midland Valley of Scotland (Lower Carboniferous). The British oil industry began in 1850 when James Young (1811–83) found he could obtain oil from boghead coals in Lothian. When these were worked out he found he could use the nearby oil shale. The oil shales were worked from 1858–1962.

Tar sands

Tar sands are sandstones impregnated with heavy, viscous crude oil which will not run from wells. Instead, the tar sand is extracted from open-cast mines then it is heated to remove the bitumen. The bitumen is then broken into synthetic crude oil and coke by heating it to about 480°C. Generally, a tonne of tar sand gives 0.5–1.0 barrels of oil. Tar sands hold enormous reserves of petroleum. Huge deposits occur in north-east Alberta where the largest deposit (the Athabaska Tar Sand) contains about 11 percent bitumen. The Alberta reserves are thought to exceed 900 billion barrels. Here, small-scale production of about 50 000 barrels of synthetic crude per day began during the mid-1960s. By 1980, production had reached about 100 000 barrels a day and by the end of the century daily production may have reached 750 000 barrels. Unfortunately, the high processing costs means that the synthetic crude oil is about twice as expensive as crude oil from wells. Very large deposits of tar sand are also found in the Orinoco tar belt of Venezuela and other large deposits exist in USA, Siberia and the Middle East. Smaller deposits are found in Nigeria, Madagascar and the Far East.

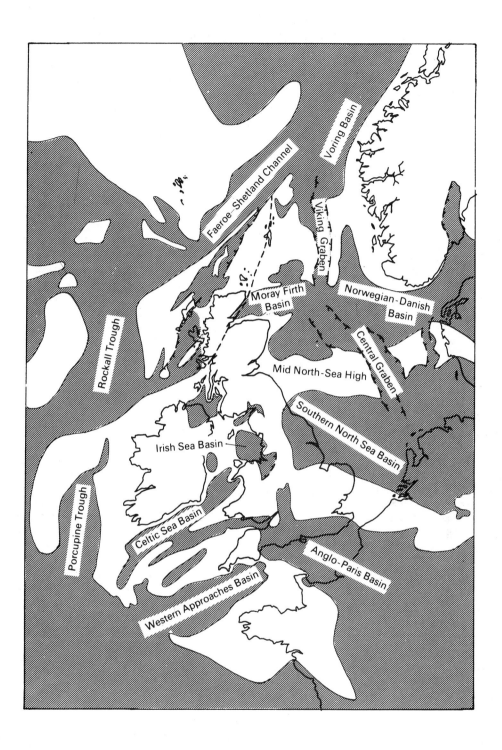

12.19 The geological structure of the British area.

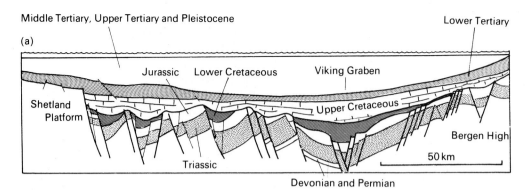

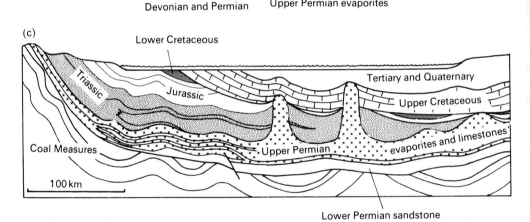

12.20 A series of sections across the North Sea:
  (a) northern North Sea;
  (b) central North Sea;
  (c) southern North Sea.

Nuclear energy

Nuclear power stations generate electricity by using the heat from nuclear reactions to produce steam to drive generators. **Burner reactors** are fuelled by ^{235}U and **fast breeder reactors** are fuelled by plutonium 239(^{239}Pu) and ^{238}U.

Natural uranium consists of 99.3 per cent ^{238}U and 0.7 per cent ^{235}U. Since breeder reactors use the more common isotope they may become increasingly important as reserves of ^{235}U decline. Uranium occurs in the mineral **uraninite** or **pitchblende** in pegmatites and hydrothermal deposits associated with granite.

EARTH RESOURCES

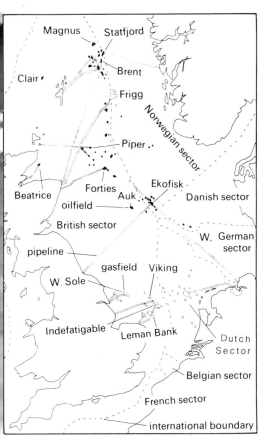

12.21 North Sea oil fields and gas fields.

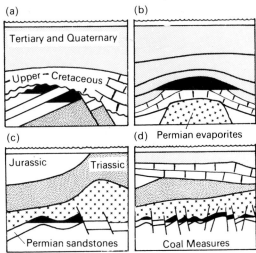

12.22 Geological sections through North Sea fields:
(a) Brent-oil and gas;
(b) Ekofisk-oil;
(c) West Sole-gas;
(d) Indefatigable-gas.

World production of uranium is about 40 000 tonnes a year with the major producers being USA, South Africa and Canada. Recoverable reserves are thought to be about four million tonnes.

Geothermal energy

In some areas it is possible to extract hot ground water and steam through boreholes. The water lies in traps which, like those associated with petroleum, hold the water under pressure and prevent its escaping to the surface. The hot water can be used industrially or to heat build-

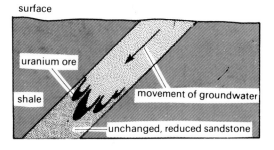

12.23 Roll-type uranium deposit.

Uranium is also found in sedimentary rocks such as black shales, coal and phosphate deposits which were formed under reducing conditions. During weathering, uranium goes into solution as U^{6+} which is precipitated as U^{4+} in reducing environments. Uranium in sediments may be found in uraninite, organic compounds or apatite. Early Precambrian uranium deposits contain grains of detrital uraninite. The absence of oxygen in the atmosphere at this time meant that the uraninite could not dissolve. The high density of the grains caused them to be deposited at the margins of the sedimentary basins. Uranium ore may be concentrated in sedimentary rocks by solution and precipitation from ground water. Near the surface there is enough oxygen in the ground water to dissolve the uraninite. At the boundary between the oxidized and reduced zone roll-type deposits are formed (figure 12.23). Such deposits give high-volume, low-grade ores.

Wairakei geothermal field, New Zealand.

ings and greenhouses while the steam can be used to drive generators to produce electricity. At present, the major developments in electricity generation are taking place in USA, Italy, New Zealand, Mexico, Japan and USSR where high levels of heat flow result form the cooling of recently emplaced magmas. In such areas hot springs and geysers may occur as surface indications of the underlying high temperatures. The ground water may be at temperatures of about 250°C and at pressures of about 30 bars. On drilling, the water turns to steam which may emerge from the borehole with a velocity of about 1000 km h⁻¹. The steam pressure is reduced to four or five bars before entering the generators.

In areas where there has been no recent igneous activity hot water can be extracted from low temperature fields in deep sedimentary basins. In such areas the geothermal gradient is about 30°C km⁻¹ so at depths of 2-3 km the water will be hot enough (over 60°C) to make extraction worthwhile. In Britain potential geothermal areas have been identified with the Hampshire and East Yorkshire–Lincolnshire basins being the most promising (figure 12.24). Near Southampton water at a temperature of 70°C has been found at a depth of 1.6 km. By the early part of next century British geothermal aquifers may give an annual amount of energy equivalent to five million tonnes of coal. It may also be possible to extract hot water from the granites of south-west England where the geothermal gradient is about 40°C km⁻¹. The granite would be fractured with water at very high pressure (hydrofracturing) or by using

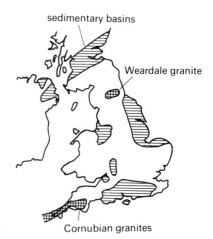

12.24 Potential geothermal areas.

small explosive charges. Water from the surface can then be pumped down and heated as it passes through the fractured granite (figure 12.25).

Building stone

Only certain rocks have properties which make them suitable for building use. The rock may be cut into shape or it may be crushed to make **aggregate**. (The term 'aggregate' also includes sand and gravel.) Rocks used to make roads should be strong and they should be resistant to polish and wear. They should not absorb water because wetting, drying, freezing and thawing produce volume changes which could

EARTH RESOURCES

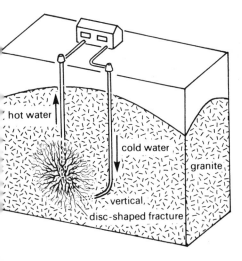

2.25 Water may be heated by passing it through fractured granite.

make the road break up. Also, bitumen should be able to stick to the rock used for the road surface. The best rock for road surfaces is very slightly weathered igneous rock which has no phenocrysts or glass, e.g. dolerite, diorite, felsite. Hard, coarse-grained sedimentary rocks such as greywacke can also be used. Limestone bonds well with bitumen so it can be used just under the road surface. To fill hollows to keep the road level a wide variety of materials can be used, e.g. sandstone, spent oil shale. The best rocks for house building are strong and resistant to weathering. Medium-grained sandstones are good for building because they are tougher than coarse-grained sandstones and because they dry out faster than fine-grained sandstones. At present, rocks such as sandstone, limestone and slate have been largely replaced by bricks, concrete and tiles as building materials.

Britain has very large quantities of hard rocks which are suitable for constructional use. Unfortunately, most of these rocks lie in the west and north of Britain away from the most highly populated areas where demand is greatest. In 1981, 25 million tonnes of igneous rock were quarried in Britain. Production was heaviest in the Leicestershire–Derbyshire area and in Strathclyde. Sandstone production in 1981 was nearly 10 million tonnes. It was used mostly for roadstone. The main producing areas were Shropshire–Warwickshire, Lancashire–Merseyside and North Yorkshire. In 1981, slate pro-

duction was 350 000 tonnes. Slate is used as a roofing material and for making snooker tables. In thick slabs it is used for building dams and sea walls. The main slate producing areas are north Wales and Cumbria.

Sand and gravel

Sand and gravel are widespread through Britain as river, glaciofluvial, beach and offshore deposits. Sand and gravel can also be obtained from ancient unconsolidated deposits such as the Triassic Bunter Pebble Bed and the Permian Basal Sandstone. In 1981, British production of sand and gravel was 97 million tonnes of which 15 million tonnes were dredged from offshore. The most heavily worked deposits are those of the Thames and Trent valleys. In southeast England alone sand and gravel production in 1981 was nearly 40 million tonnes. Most sand and gravel is mixed with cement to make mortar and concrete. In 1981, 4.5 million tonnes of special sands were produced mostly for glass making and for moulding metals.

Carbonate rocks

In Britain the most heavily worked limestones are of Carboniferous age. They occur in scattered outcrops to the north and west of a line running roughly from Somerset to Tyneside. To the south and east of the Carboniferous limestones run bands of Permian Magnesian limestone, Jurassic limestones and chalk. Limestone is the most commonly quarried of all rocks. In 1981, British production was 74 million tonnes with the main producing areas being Derbyshire and Somerset. In the same year dolomite production was 14 million tonnes mostly from Yorkshire and the east Midlands. In 1981, chalk production of 12 million tonnes came mostly from south-east England and Humberside. Limestone has a very large number of uses. Huge quantities are used for roadstone, concrete aggregate and in making cement and steel. It is also used in farming and glass making and as a filler for rubber, paper and asphalt. It can be roasted to give quicklime (calcium oxide) for use in farming, steel making and gas purification. The quicklime can be hydrated to give

Mountainside marble quarries, Carrara, Italy.

Limestone quarry near Buxton, Derbyshire.

calcium hydroxide which has a very wide range of industrial, chemical, building and agricultural uses. Dolomite is used mostly as roadstone, railway ballast and concrete aggregate. It is also used in farming. Chalk is mostly used to make cement.

Cement

The most common type of cement (Portland cement) is made by roasting a mixture of limestone and shale. The limestone provides calcium carbonate while the shale provides silicon dioxide and aluminium oxide. Sometimes, these constituents are found in the correct proportions in a **cement limestone** or **cement rock**. During roasting, water and carbon dioxide are driven off and the remaining calcium oxide, silicon dioxide and aluminium oxide combine to form a variety of calcium silicates and aluminates which rapidly hydrate and set when water is added. About five percent gypsum is added to the cement to prevent over rapid setting. British cement production is currently about 13 million tonnes a year.

Concrete is made by mixing cement with aggregate. Heavy aggregate such as gravel or crushed rock gives strong, impermeable concrete. Light aggregate such as ash or heated clay gives low-density insulating materials such as breeze block. Good aggregates are non-porous and they have rough surfaces to provide a good bond with the cement. Aggregate generally consists of rounded particles with a good mixture of sizes up to a diameter of about 5 cm.

Bricks

Bricks can be made from rocks such as clays, mudstones and shales. Good brick clays must become plastic when damp so they can be easily pressed and they must keep their shape through manufacture. Clay minerals should constitute about 20 percent of the rock. The best clay mineral for building bricks is illite because is plastic and it does not absorb too much water. For refractory bricks, kaolinite is the best clay mineral because it has a very high melting point. The rock should also have about five percent calcium carbonate to prevent shrinkage during firing. It is also useful if the clay rock contains a small amount of organic matter because this burns during firing and so reduces fuel costs.

About 40 percent of British bricks are made from Lower Oxford Clay. It contains about four percent carbon and its carbonate and water contents are such that the clay needs no treatment before processing. About 30 percent of our bricks are made from Carboniferous shales while other sources include Keuper mudstones, boulder clay and Cretaceous and Tertiary clays. In 1973, about 7.2 billion bricks were produced in Britain but by 1982 production had fallen to 3.5 billion. One reason for this decline is that the internal walls of houses are now built from breeze blocks.

Other useful materials

Minerals and rocks have a wide variety of industrial, agricultural and domestic uses in addition to their uses for metal extraction, as energy sources and as constructional materials.

Sodium chloride

Sodium chloride (halite) comes mostly from evaporite deposits. It is used in making chemicals such as hydrochloric acid and sodium hydroxide and in the manufacture of glass, soap, fertilizers, dyes and weed killer. World production is about 170 million tonnes a year with the major producers being USA, USSR and China. British production of about 7 million tonnes in 1981 came mostly from the Triassic of Cheshire. We use about 1.5 million tonnes of rock salt every year to de-ice roads.

Sulphur

Sulphur formed by the action of anaerobic bacteria on calcium sulphate occurs in association with evaporites round salt plugs. It is also found in active volcanoes. Sulphur can be produced industrially from anhydrite, from sulphides such as pyrite and chalcopyrite and as a by-product of petroleum processing. Sulphur is used to make sulphuric acid, fertilizers, pesticides, explosives, rubber and rayon. World production of sulphur is not exactly known. However, the main producers are USA, Poland, USSR, and Mexico. In 1981, Britain produced 75 000 tonnes of sulphur. In the same year we used one million tonnes.

Salt mining, Winsford Rock Salt Mine, Cheshire.

Fluorite

Fluorite (fluorspar) is used as flux in steel making and for making hydrofluoric acid, Freon (the propellant in aerosol cans) and Teflon. Good quality fluorite may be used for making lenses and prisms. Fluorite occurs most commonly as a gangue mineral associated with lead and silver ores. In 1981, British production of about 185 thousand tonnes came mostly from Derbyshire.

Baryte

Baryte (barytes) is used in glass making and as a filler in paint, paper, rubber and linoleum. It can be used to increase the density of drilling mud to prevent oil from rising through a drill pipe. In 1981, British production of 63 000 tonnes came from the area of the Pennines.

Gypsum

Gypsum occurs mostly in evaporite deposits. It is added as a retarder to cement and it is used to treat soils and as a filler in paper. Partial dehydration of gypsum gives plaster of Paris. Plaster of Paris is used in building materials such as plaster-board, in medicine and dentistry and for making industrial moulds. Alabaster is a fine-grained form of gypsum often used to make ornaments. In 1981, about 2.9 million tonnes of gypsum were produced in Britain.

Diamonds

Diamonds occur in kimberlite volcanic pipes and in placer deposits. Since very high pressures are needed to form diamonds it is probable that kimberlite magmas originate at depths of about 400 km. Kimberlite is a porphyritic mica peridotite which is often altered and brecciated. Near-surface weathered kimberlite is called 'yellow ground' by miners because of its high proportion of limonite. Deeper, unweathered kimberlite is called 'blue ground'. Kimberlite pipes are found in shield areas; the kimberlites of southern Africa are of Cretaceous age. Diamonds are the hardest natural substance. Diamond (hardness 10) is actually about forty times harder than corundum (hardness 9). Diamonds of gem quality are usually colourless, blue-white or pale yellow in colour. Low quality diamonds are used as abrasives and for making drill bits. Synthetic diamonds can

The Premier Diamond Mine, South Africa.

An octahedral diamond in Kimberlite.

be made by heating graphite to about 2000°C under pressures of between 65 and 90 kilobars. World diamond production is about 40 000 carats a year with the main producers being Zaire, USSR and South Africa. (A carat is 0.2 g.)

China clay

The granites of south-west England have been partially altered by hydrothermal fluids given off at a late stage in crystallization. In places where the feldspar has a higher sodium than potassium level the feldspar has been altered to china clay (kaolinite) in funnel-shaped zones which narrow downwards to a depth of about 300 m. The altered rock contains up to 15 percent of china clay. The largest deposits occur on St. Austell Moor. The clay is washed from the unaltered quartz and mica by powerful water jets from hoses called monitors in pits up to 130 m deep. The stream of water from the quarry face is then collected and processed to remove particles of quartz and mica. China clay is used to fill and coat paper, in making ceramics and as a filler in paints, rubber and plastics. In 1981 British production of china clay was 2.6 million tonnes. Reserves in south-west England are sufficient to last for at least a hundred years.

During the Tertiary the granites of south-west England were deeply weathered and their feldspars altered to kaolinite which was transported with fine-grained quartz and mica to be deposited in fresh water lagoons as seams of kaolinitic clay. These clays are called ball clays because they were once dug by hand tools which scooped the clay out in lumps or 'balls'. Ball clay is mined by open-pit and underground means in the Bovey and Petrockstow Basins of Devon and around Wareham in Dorset. The quartz in ball clay adds strength to ceramics such as electrical porcelain, sanitary ware and floor tiles. In 1981 British production of ball clay was about 900 000 tonnes.

Geology and engineering

Before engineering work begins in any area the site must be thoroughly inspected. Following a review of earlier information, geological and geophysical surveys can be carried out. These can be augmented by sinking closely spaced boreholes to determine rock types and geological structure. Sometimes, a trench or pit may be dug through the superficial deposits to expose the bedrock. Finally, the engineering properties of the rocks can be determined. Such properties might include strength, stress conditions, moisture content, direction of water flow, permeability and the pressure of water in the rock.

Good foundations for buildings and bridges are formed by igneous and metamorphic rocks along with limestone and sandstone. Clay, shale and boulder clay do not provide good shallow foundations because they shrink when dry and swell when wet. Clays and shales do, however, provide good foundations when the foundations are sunk below the lowest level of the water table. Here, the volume of the rock does not change because it is not affected by seasonal

China clay (kaolinite) workings, St Austell, Cornwall. On the right, clay is being washed out of the altered granite by a high-pressure hose.

Dam foundations of the Dneproges-2 Hydroelectric Station, River Dnieper, U.S.S.R.

variation in rainfall.

Tunnels to carry water, roads or railways may be excavated by drilling and blasting or by rock-boring machines. The major problems associated with tunnelling are rock falls and water influx. Drilling ahead of the tunnel gives warning of approaching difficulties. Rock falls are frequent where the tunnel crosses loosely cemented or well-jointed rocks or where alternating strong and weak rock, e.g. limestone and shale, dip steeply into the tunnel. Flooding may occur if the tunnel strikes a buried river channel, fissured limestones or fault zones. Tunnelling is easiest in uniform rock, e.g. much of the London underground and sewage system have been excavated in the London Clay.

Concrete dams are constructed in mountain valleys while broad shallow valleys can be dammed by earth dams. In Britain there are about 2000 dams which are mostly made of earth with clay cores. The earth provides stability while the impermeable clay prevents the escape of water. The best dam sites are in narrow mountain and moorland valleys on impermeable rock. A deep, narrow reservoir has a relatively small surface area so it loses little water by evaporation. Beds which dip upstream provide the strongest foundations and they are least liable to lose water by leakage along bedding planes. Also, synclinally folded rocks are stronger and less liable to lose water than anticlinally folded rocks. However, synclinally folded rocks have the disadvantage of dipping towards the reservoir from the valley sides. This makes them liable to slip into the reservoir. The rocks of the valley sides should not be liable to slippage because as the reservoir fills, the water table rises to lubricate zones of weakness. Rivers often run along fault zones and these should be avoided. In addition to being weak, fault zones may have associated earthquakes which could cause the dam to fail. Also, dams should not be built on heavily jointed rocks. Sources of potential leakage through permeable soils, aquifers, faults and joints must be investigated before the dam is built. Sometimes leakage zones can be sealed by injecting cement in a process called **grouting**. A dam should not be built on a permeable base because leakage under a dam generates pressure which lifts the dam and may cause it to fail. If possible, dams should not be built on limestone because calcite dissolves especially if the water is peaty and acidic. After a few years the limestone may develop solution cavities. Sandstone with calcite cement may also become permeable as the calcite dissolves away. The rate at which sediment is carried into a reservoir must also be considered, e.g. the Hoover Dam in Colorado has lost half its capacity by silting up since its construction in 1937. One side-effect of filling large reservoirs is the generation of earthquakes which reach magnitudes of about 5 on the Richter scale. The earthquakes seem to be triggered by movement along fault planes in response to the stress produced by the load of water on the crust.

Cuttings and embankments made for roads, railways and canals produce steep, unstable slopes. To improve stability, the slope can be cut in a series of steps or material can be moved from areas where slippage may occur to lower, more stable supporting areas. The slope must also be thoroughly drained to prevent movement of waterlogged soil. Often, stone-filled drains are arranged in a herring- bone pattern on the slope. The slope may be supported by retaining walls or by piles driven into the rock. Retaining walls must have drainage channels at their bases. Grass and trees such as rowan, poplar and ash bind the soil and keep levels of soil moisture constant by taking up water. Rock falls may be prevented by attaching wire mesh to steep slopes. Sometimes strong wire fences are built across slopes to catch falling rocks.

Water

Water is extracted from surface sources such as reservoirs, lakes and rivers and from aquifers. In Britain there are well-marked regional variations in precipitation. In general, the north and west have relatively high levels of rainfall while the south and east have relatively low levels, e.g. Scotland and Wales have average rainfall totals of about 1.4 m a year while England has an average rainfall of about 0.87 m a year. North-west and south-west England both have rainfall totals of about 1.2 m a year while East Anglia has a rainfall of only 0.6 m a year. In addition, water loss by evaporation is greatest in the relatively warm and dry south and east. The difference between rainfall and evaporation is called **residual rainfall**. In Scotland the residual rainfall is about 1 m a year while in East Anglia the residual rainfall is only 0.15 m a year. Regional variations in population, industrial development, precipitation and residual rainfall mean that water sources show regional variation. Also, water must be transferred in a general south-easterly direction towards areas of high water requirement. In the north and west surface sources provide the vast bulk of water requirements. However, south and east of a line which runs roughly from Newcastle to Torquay large quantities of water are extracted from aquifers such as the Chalk and other limestones, Triassic sandstones, Lower Cretaceous sand-

stones and river sands and gravels. The largest groundwater sources lie in the Thames, Severn–Trent, Southern and Anglian Water Authority areas. In future, aquifers may be used to store water pumped into them through injection wells. Storage of this type is widely used in Israel and pilot schemes to inject water have been run in parts of England.

Water is used in the home, in industry and in agriculture. In England and Wales about 13.5 billion cubic metres of water are used every year. Of this about 11.3 billion cubic metres comes from surface sources while about 2.2. billion cubic metres is groundwater. In Scotland the annual requirement of about 2 billion cubic metres comes almost entirely from surface sources. Of the water used about 80 percent is equally divided between the public water supply and the electricity generating boards. Industry takes about 19 percent of the water used while agriculture takes less than 1 percent. Nearly half of the agricultural use is for spray irrigation.

Geological effects of human activities

Our agricultural, building and extractive industries have modified landscapes and surface processes, e.g. clearing natural vegetation, cultivation and overgrazing all increase the rate of soil erosion. Repeated burning changes plant types and soils and increases the rate of run-off. Improved field drainage reduces infiltration and causes rapid run-off and flooding. Dams control run-off and so reduce the risk of flooding. Since dams trap sediment, the rate of erosion may increase below the dam so the river channel becomes deeper and wider. Landslides may occur beside a reservoir because the raised water table may lubricate planes of weakness in the rocks on the valley sides. Large reservoirs may also trigger minor earthquakes. Damming and water extraction may also alter lakes and coasts, e.g. the sizes of the Aral and Caspian Seas have been reduced by the damming of their incoming rivers. In western USA the flow of the Colorado River has been greatly reduced before it enters Mexico and reaches the Gulf of California. Straightening and dredging speeds river flow and increases erosion. Parts of the bed of the Rhine have been eroded down by 2 m since 1900. Sediment may be added to streams by hydraulic mining in which gravel is washed into sluices by powerful water jets. Since 1850, San Francisco Bay has been reduced by 700 hectares because of sediment brought down from placer gold workings in the incoming rivers. The extraction of ground water may also produce visible effect. In Iran, tunnels dug to tap ground water have left aligned crater-like depressions. Extraction of water from a confined aquifer in the area of Mexico City has produced subsidence of about 6 m at rates of up to 15 cm a year. Venice also suffered subsidence because of the extraction of water from beds under the lagoon. Removal of water from the Chalk under London has caused salty estuarine Thames water to flow into the aquifer.

Coastal areas have been affected by the construction of harbours, breakwaters, sea walls, groynes and dykes. In the Netherlands about 740 000 hectares of land have been reclaimed from the sea floor since the 13th century. Round the Wash 16 000 hectares have been reclaimed since the 18th century. Break-waters and groynes may prevent or slow long-shore drift in one area but cause erosion further along the shore. Coastal erosion can be pre-vented by building sea walls, fixing sand dunes and transporting gravel. On the other hand, removing shingle may cause erosion. Because of this, Holderness, Yorkshire, has lost a strip about 4 km wide since Roman times.

The extraction of rocks, minerals and fuels may produce considerable changes. More than 70 percent of rocks and minerals come from open pits which scar the land and produce large waste tips. In Britain, opencast sites may be landscaped when production ends or they may be used as rubbish dumps. If water filled, they may acquire recreational use. The Norfolk Broads are thought partly to represent the remains of prehistoric peat diggings. Under-ground extraction may cause subsidence, e.g. in coal mining areas buildings and roads may be cracked and displaced and drainage may have been affected. In Cheshire, salt extraction has produced surface depressions which now hold round lakes called meres or flashes. The extraction of oil and gas may also cause sub-sidence, e.g. at Wilmington, California, subsi-dence of up to 9 m over an area of 56 km^2 was combated by injecting water into the oil wells to sustain pressure.

Pollutants such as sulphur dioxide kill plants, weaken the vegetation cover and so increase the rate of erosion. Burning fossil fuels has raised the levels of atmospheric carbon dioxide from 290 parts per million (ppm) one hundred years ago to nearly 400 ppm now. Carbon dioxide is used by photosynthesizing plants and it has been suggested that the mass of land plants may have increased by 15 billion tonnes in the last hundred years.

Problems of resource usage

The rate at which a country uses resources depends partly on the size of its population and partly on its level of economic development. In 1980, the world's population was about 4350 million. In 1960 2050 million people lived in the relatively poor developing countries of Africa, the Middle East, Latin America and Asia. In 1980, the population of developing countries had reached 3200 million and by the year 2000 their population will be about 5000 million. In 1960, 950 million people lived in the relatively rich developed countries such as those of Europe, USA, Canada, Japan, Australia and New Zealand. In 1980, the population of the developed countries had reached 1150 million and by the year 2000 their population is expected to be about 1600 million. Despite the fact that three-quarters of the world's population live in developing countries such countries have only about 15 percent of the world's wealth and they consume about the same percentage of annual resource pro-duction. This means that a person living in a developed country is, on average, about fifteen times wealthier than a person living in a devel-oping country. Also, the person in the developed country uses about fifteen times as much of the Earth's resources.

The rate of resource usage generally rises to keep pace with the rates of economic and population growth in a country. This may cause the use of resources to double in a very short time, e.g. if resource usage increases by four percent a year the quantity consumed will double every 18 years. (The approximate time it takes for consumption to double can be found by dividing 70 by the percentage growth rate.) Such percentage growth (**exponential growth**) is shown by savings under compound interest. The human population is also growing expo-nentially. Initial stages of exponential growth do not put much of a strain on resource supply since only small quantities are being doubled. However, when consumption is already large a doubling of use causes problems of supply, (figure 12.26). Also, reserves are depleted at

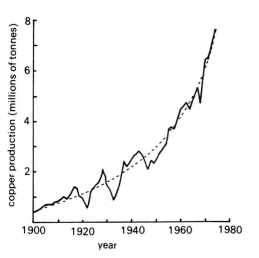

12.26 *Exponential growth of copper production.*

an ever increasing rate and the length of time for which a given resource will last (the **lifetime** of the resource) is drastically shortened. This means that some materials, e.g. mercury, lead, zinc, copper and gold, may soon be worked out. Various factors may operate to increase the lifetime of a resource, for instance, governments and cartels, (e.g. OPEC—the Organisation of Petroleum Exporting Countries and ITC—the International Tin Council) may control production; materials may be recycled or substituted; and economic depression may reduce demand and cause materials to be used more efficiently. Also, figures for reserves are often inaccurate, e.g. during the 1940s estimates of the world's total reserves of crude oil ranged from 50 to 200 billion tonnes. Present day estimates suggest that the Earth may still hold about 500 billion tonnes of oil. Similar uncertainty affects estimates of recoverable reserves. Reserves previously thought unworthy of extraction may be reclassified as recoverable if price rises or technological improvements make extraction profitable, e.g. between the 1930s and the 1970s recoverable copper reserves increased from 100 to 350 million tonnes because ores of progressively lower grades could be extracted.

It seems that we face an uncertain future. Population increase and improved standards of living will continue to cause rapid depletion of Earth resources. Also, huge quantities of resources are consumed for military purposes. We may also face difficulties from increased pollution and use of nuclear energy. It would appear that our problems are self-created—what can we do to solve them?

Index

Certain illustrations have been adapted from already published sources. These are as follows:

Figures 2.1, 6.26, 6.27 and 8.72 — *The Cambridge Encyclopedia of Earth Sciences*, Trewin Copplestone Books Ltd.
Figures 6.6, 6.13, 6.15, 6.23, 6.28, 6.29, 6.33 and 8.65 — The Open University, S101 *Science: A Foundation Course*.
Figures 12.10, 12.11 and 12.13 — The Open University, S238 *The Earth's Physical Resources*.
Figure 7.1 — The Open University, S236 *Geology*.
Figure 11.49(a) — The Open University, S2-3 *Environment*.
Figures 7.1 and 7.3 — C. Gillen, *Metamorphic Geology*, George Allen and Unwin Ltd..
Figures 8.52, 8.53 and 8.54 — E.C. Bullard, J.E. Everett and A.C. Smith (1965) *Philosophical Transactions of the Royal Society*.
Figure 8.47 — G.P.L. Walker.
Figure 8.71 — Understanding The Earth, The Artemis Press.
Figure 8.55 — P.M. Hurley, *The Confirmation of Continental Drift*, © 1968 by Scientific American Inc. All rights reserved
Figure 11.15 — W.S. McKerrow and L.R.M Cocks (1976) *Nature*.
Figures 11.22, 11.23 and 11.26 — after T.N. George (1958) *Proceedings of the Yorkshire Geological Society*.
Figure 11.46 — after W.B. Harland (1969).
Figure 11.48(a) — C. Sancetta, J. Imbrie and N.G. Kipp (1973) *Quaternary Research*.
Figure 11.48(b) — G.R. Coope in *Ice Ages: Ancient and Modern*. Seel House Press.
Figure 11.49(b) — W.H. Zagwijn (1974) *Geologie en Mijnbouw*.
Figure 11.54 — N.J. Shackleton and N.D. Opdyke (1973) *Quaternary Research*.
Figure 12.2 — *Principles of Geology* (3rd edition) J. Gilluly, A.C. Waters and A.O. Woodford, W.H. Freeman and Co. © 1975
Figures 12.3 and 12.9 — A.M. Evans, *An Introduction to Ore Geology*. Blackwell Scientific Publications.
Figure 12.12 — National Coal Board.
Figures 12.17 and 12.20(c) — British Gas.
Figure 12.19 — UK Offshore Operators Association.
Figures 12.20(a) and (b) — after P.A. Ziegler (1977).
Figure 12.22 — *Petroleum and the Continental Shelf of North-west Europe*. Applied Science Publishers.